Traders, Agents, and Weavers

T0269931

For well over a century, traders and weavers worked together to develop a distinctive Two Grey Hills regional pattern. Here, Ed Davies visits the home of one of his best weavers to encourage her efforts. Artwork by Charles Yanito.

Traders, Agents, and Weavers

Developing the Northern Navajo Region

Robert S. McPherson

UNIVERSITY OF OKLAHOMA PRESS : NORMAN

Also by Robert S. McPherson
Both Sides of the Bullpen: Navajo Trade and Posts (2017)
Mapping the Four Corners: Narrating the Hayden Survey of 1875 (with Susan Rhoades Neel, 2016)
Life in a Corner: Cultural Episodes in Southeastern Utah, 1880–1950 (2015)
Viewing the Ancestors: Perceptions of the Anaasází, Mokwič, and Hisatsinom (2014)
Under the Eagle: Samuel Holiday, Navajo Code Talker (2013)
A Navajo Legacy: The Life and Teachings of John Holiday (2005)
Navajo Land, Navajo Culture: The Utah Experience in the Twentieth Century (2001)

Small portions of chapters 6, 7, and 9 were previously published in Robert S. McPherson, *Both Sides of the Bullpen: Navajo Trade and Posts* (Norman: University of Oklahoma Press), 2017.

Library of Congress Cataloging-in-Publication Data

Names: McPherson, Robert S., 1947– author.
Title: Traders, agents, and weavers : developing the northern Navajo region / Robert S. McPherson.
Description: Norman : University of Oklahoma Press, [2020] | Includes bibliographical references and index. | Summary: "Examines the history of Navajo economic and cultural development through the testimonies of traders, government agents, tribal leaders, and accomplished weavers"—Provided by publisher.
Identifiers: LCCN 2019044428 | ISBN 9780806164793 (hardcover) ISBN 9780806190082 (paper)
Subjects: LCSH: Navajo Indians—New Mexico—Economic conditions. | Navajo Indians—New Mexico—Social conditions. | Navajo Indians—NewMexico— History. Classification: LCC E99.N3 M245 2020 | DDC 978.9004/9726—dc23
LC record available at https://lccn.loc.gov/2019044428

The paper in this book meets the guidelines for permanence and durability of the Committee on Production Guidelines for Book Longevity of the Council on Library Resources, Inc. ∞

Contents

Illustrations

Figures

Map

Introduction

Appreciating the View

He was hot and thirsty after riding two days under the October sun. A forbidding landscape lay before his eyes as he searched for signs of life, but all he could see was "the great gray desert, the skyline broken by freakish shapes of earth and rock and the tumbled ruins of ancient pueblo dwellings that bore strange tales of superstition and encounter . . . to the west stretched a pine ridge, an imposing range of jagged mountains, the home of many cold, sparkling brooks, grassy uplands, shady groves of cottonwoods."[1] It was 1904, and the weary traveler, N. C. (Newell Convers) Wyeth (1882–1945) was on one of his first official assignments: to become familiar with the American Southwest. In later years, he secured a reputation for being an outstanding artist, having produced three thousand paintings and illustrated 112 books, but for now, he was just one tired wayfarer getting to his destination, the Two Grey Hills Trading Post.

Wyeth, with an artist's eye, described what he saw, which was not all that inviting. "Two Grey Hills, a remote Navajo [Diné] Indian trading post in New Mexico, looks for all the world like a play-village of tiny squared mud-cakes, built on a vast, undulating playground of sand hills, with a long, low strip of blue-paper mountains slid in behind it. And not until you get within calling distance of the 'post' can you fully determine its identity. In reality it *is* mud, with a few small windows pierced in three of its sides resembling port-holes, and a dirt roof, growing a veritable garden of grass and weeds, out of which peeps the top of a gray stone chimney. To the right of the main building stand two low adobe barns, and to the left a long, flat sheep-shed, fraying off into a spindly corral."² In spite of the warm invitation that trader, Sel Ritchie (more likely Joe Reitz), gave Wyeth to make the store his headquarters while in the area, this was nothing like the East Coast from which the artist hailed. He also did not know at that time that he would later earn money, for a brief moment, delivering mail between Fort Defiance and Two Grey Hills to replace some lost funds.

As Wyeth became more involved in the post and its surrounding community, he grew in appreciation of what he saw. Different experiences broadened his perspective as he observed "blanket weavers seated before ponderous looms, upon which would be stretched blankets of brilliant scarlet and black, or blue and white." He enjoyed watching the children play, observing the goats and sheep with tinkling bells grazing on the steep slopes of the Chuska range, and "absorbing that vision of poetry without intruding on the peacefulness of it all." During his stay, he also became acquainted with a twelve year old Navajo boy, whom he accompanied when single-handedly moving a thousand sheep twenty-five miles to an off-reservation livestock purchaser named "Nip" Arments. The lad, known only as Begay (Son), had done it twice before, each time alone, and one time with twice that number of animals. For two days, the boy herded the livestock, the artist struggled to keep up, and the flock moved ever closer to its destination. "The level horizon of the desert lay before us, toward which we slowly trudged through endless stretches of loose sand, around the bases of towering buttes and down into dry arroyos." Begay, shaking a stick with tin cans dangling on the end, directed the animals so that none were lost, even as they traversed precipitous trails, pushed up steep embankments, and eventually arrived at the distant post. The two corralled the sheep for the night, Wyeth slept in the post, not awakening from exhausted slumber until noon, just in time to catch a glimpse of Begay and his dog heading home over the horizon. The recent arrival to the Southwest had grown in appreciation for the land and its people with an accompanying understanding of its hidden potential.

Wyeth's story captures much of what this book represents. There is no doubt that the Two Grey Hills Trading Post was and is an unimpressive sight, that the Chuska Valley in which it and other posts are situated remains a difficult arid landscape, and that the care and control of livestock requires an intimate knowledge of resources and animals. For travelers passing through, there does not appear to be much happening. But wait. Within the pages of this book, lies a fascinating, unexpected history of different cultures that have not only adapted and adopted but excelled in this environment. Some of that success is dramatic— look at the Ancestral Puebloan architecture in Chaco Canyon or the people who later created artistic products unrivaled in craftsmanship. The effort of these desert people produced a livelihood that allowed them not only to survive, but also to create lasting beauty in form and function. What it took in terms of time, sweat, and muscle was matched by human energy, resourcefulness, and innovation. This was the source of their success.

The theme of this book springs from the land and its people—how those who settled in what is now the northern part of the Navajo Reservation shared and overcame differences through cooperative efforts that developed and complemented each other's existence. More specifically, it explains how Navajo culture and Anglo society gave rise to a way of life that benefited both. Within this story lie four subthemes that illustrate how this happened. The first is "man in the environment"—what it took to live in a harsh high desert terrain, where water was either scarce or at flood stage, where mountain ranges controlled travel and weather, and what was in and on the ground determined economic reality. The second is "man against man." Whether looking at the rise and decline of Ancestral Puebloan culture, the wars fought by the Spanish, Mexicans, and Utes against the Navajos, or the establishment of Anglo control through the reservation system, there was conflict. How this conflict played out had far-ranging consequences and provided a mixed bag of positive and negative results. A third subtheme examines the growth and development of an economic system—the trading post—as a frontier institution that encouraged the livestock industry and developed through government oversight. Within the posts—Two Grey Hills serving as the primary example—two cultures merged their intellectual strength with weaving prowess. As time progressed, the role of these stores shifted, but remained a vibrant force assisting the Navajo people until the 1960s. Finally, there is discussion of weaving as an art and how Navajo women (and some men) excelled in its production. Again, the people living around Two Grey Hills and neighboring stores provide one of the most prominent examples of success.

There is a large body of literature written over the past 130 years about the Navajos. Starting with Washington Matthews's recordings of traditional teachings and ceremonies; to the inclusion of Father Berard Haile's works by the Franciscan Fathers at Saint Michaels; to the epic contributions of Gladys Reichard, Leland Wyman, Clyde Kluckhohn, and other anthropologists during the 1930s through 1960s; to the research of today's New West historians and anthropologists—a steady stream of enthusiasts has interpreted and reinterpreted Navajo culture and its workings. There are now a growing number of Navajo scholars who enrich this field of study with their own understanding. To gain perspective of this growing body of information, a brief review of the current literature surrounding the topics in this book is helpful.

Historians and anthropologists of the past enjoyed ease of access when recording and writing Navajo history and culture. With the intent of preserving information and unearthing past events, these scholars set forth to faithfully record what they learned and to interpret what they saw. Much of their work has withstood academic scrutiny, but the interpretation was filtered through an earlier understanding. Take, for instance, Frank McNitt's *The Indian Traders*, which covers a wide variety of trading post experiences.[3] This author did exhaustive archival research, interviewed dozens of traders and Navajos, walked and drove the land he wrote about, and took an encyclopedic approach that went well beyond just the main topic of trading posts. He produced a classic. Still, this work and others of this time are sometimes accused today of being romanticized and missing the "real" side of the trading post story.[4]

Beginning in the 1960s and 1970s and continuing to the present, the social sciences—history, anthropology, sociology, linguistics, psychology, and so on—have come under the scrutiny of new academic standards that encourage a more interdisciplinary effort to understand what has gone on before. Seeking to provide more balance and greater "insider" knowledge, these disciplines have also taken on current attitudes and topics such as gender studies, women's history, racism, colonialism, and environmental concerns. At times hard-edged and confrontational, this modern literature departs from earlier studies of the western experience as a positive progression for humankind, and now emphasizes much of the stumbling and misdeeds of the past, showing how activism in the present aims to right previous wrongs.

There is no better example of this current approach to writing than Richard White's *"It's Your Misfortune and None of My Own": A New History of the American West.*[5] Greed, abusive power, cultural insensitivity, and exploitation of land and man fostered by a colonial mindset reinterprets what had been cast in a more positive light—the progress and settlement of a region. This is not to suggest that ills of the past had not been previously discussed, but only that much of it did not conclude in the strident activist voice of today's academia. What this framework did to Navajo studies has caused scholars to reevaluate the events of history by casting them in an ultraviolet light that exposes all the bumps and spots—some good, more often bad—that had previously not been apparent. Not all studies wind up as negative diatribes, but most are "issue-oriented" and often foment change.

A few examples from current scholarship on Navajo economy give context for this book. Take, for instance, anthropologist Charlotte Frisbie's *Food Sovereignty the Navajo Way* (2018), in which she advocates for returning to traditional foods, shares recipes old and new, encourages tribal members to adopt a global initiative by marginalized people to reassume diets and practices of the past, and promotes taking control of their culture's food destiny. Or Colleen O'Neill's *Working the Navajo Way* (2005), in which she examines twentieth-century employment of Navajos in everything from railroad construction and coal mining to weaving and government.[6] She concludes that in spite of a heavy adoption of the dominant society's practices, Navajo culture has shown enough resilience to overcome and prosper. For those interested in a current understanding of raising livestock, the weaving industry, and the problems that some Navajo communities face in pursuing this economy, there is *To Run after Them* (1977) by Louise Lamphere.[7]

Trading posts have also had their investigations. Klara Kelley and Harris Francis recently published *Navajoland Trading Post Encyclopedia* (2018), which not only identifies all 259 stores on and off the reservation but also shares a history of each.[8] The authors have paid particular attention to the Navajo names and history of each post as well as discussing the role of Navajo owners and operators, a seldom mentioned topic. These men and women are now due recognition. Trader Juan Lorenzo Hubbell and his empire have been the subject of two books— *Indian Trader: The Life and Times of J. L. Hubbell* (2000) by Martha Blue, and *Hubbell Trading Post* (2015) by Erica Cottam.[9] Both authors look at Hubbell's scars and warts and how he created, then eventually lost, a huge economic empire built off the backs of Navajos through the promotion and sale of their goods. So too, does Teresa Williams in *Patterns of Exchange* (2008), offering discourse on Hubbell but also providing a frank discussion of trader-weaver relations and historic market forces.[10]

Hubbell left a sufficient paper trail, unlike the vast majority of post owners, so that his overly zealous business dealings could later be reconstructed and analyzed quantitatively to evaluate what he did and how he did it. He became the centerpiece of *Swept under the Rug: A Hidden History of Navajo Weaving* (2002) by Kathy M'Closkey.[11] Her wide-ranging book examines past and present unfair practices that took advantage of weavers, ripped off Navajo wealth and placed it deep in the pockets of traders, encouraged the counterfeiting of woven products in a global economy, and tampered with important cultural values. From Hubbell to large corporations and trade organizations today, she argues, there has been an intentional abuse and theft of intellectual and material property in a world where only money matters. The author proves her point by crunching numbers and showing how evil people in the dominant society have been. Her general theme is that traders and related businesses (wool purchasers, weaving industries, market empires) have been unabashed crooks in search of the mighty national and international dollar.

I have taken a different approach. In a recent publication, *Both Sides of the Bullpen* (2017), I examined trading and posts as a cultural setting where two groups came together and mutually benefited, rejecting the notion of massive fraud and theft.[12] Although there was not enough information for me to do an in-depth quantitative analysis, there was sufficient evidence to trace a general outline of cash-and-product flow. Like the vast majority of stores mentioned in Kelley's and Harris's trading post encyclopedia, those I wrote about were small "mom and pop" ventures that often proved ethereal when compared to the Hubbell empire—here one day, gone another, with a string of owners and operators in between. Of course, all were interested in making money through buying and selling, but only a few became rich, and they succeeded because their business dealings were diversified and generally fair. A second reason that I took a less accusatory approach was that

Navajo customers were not nearly as helpless and controlled as some authors assume. They desired the products sold over the counter, knew very well what the market demanded, played one post against another to their benefit, and worked at improving what they had to offer. Some writers might respond that Navajos were pawning goods for credit, which argues for their impoverished condition. In *Both Sides* and in this book, one finds that it was the traders who had to be circumspect in extending credit, not the customer in accepting it. Borrowing against collateral is no more a sign of poverty than it is now, whether buying groceries or a saddle in the past or a car and a house today. In support of this view, every investigative team that the government or agent sent out to uncover malpractice returned having found only peccadillos, not festering malfeasance. For the most part—exceptions here are also noted—the traders were a good group of people who befriended and took care of their customers.

My narrative approach also emphasizes the role of the government, different aspects of the weaving industry, and Navajo animal husbandry. I have allowed the historic record and the people in it to tell their story when possible. Quotes are sprinkled liberally throughout. More than anything, I want the reader to experience, through the eyes of the people who lived it, what they saw and felt. It is their story. As a companion piece to *Both Sides of the Bullpen*, this book examines issues through the eyes of traders, government agents, Navajo leaders, accomplished weavers, and a host of personalities encountering life in a high desert environment. At the same time, there is enough statistical information to mark the ebb and flow in concrete terms of business development over a one-hundred-years-plus period.

A word about the subtitle. *Developing the Northern Navajo Region* offers a number of possible interpretations. Northern Navajo here represents a geographic area that is part of the reservation along the San Juan River and Chuska Mountain range in New Mexico. Even before the arrival of these Indians, the Ancestral Puebloans had established an impressive civilization in the region. The first chapter discusses the impact of their urban development and how the Chuska Valley supported it as they settled the land. There were possibly more people living there than at any other time since, and so looking at the support of Chacoan development and the growth of an expansive material culture to house and feed these people, fits what the title suggests. The settlement of the Navajos into the same area—both before and after reservation boundaries became the law—certainly also ties in. The Shiprock Agency, often referred to as the Northern Navajo Agency, denotes that part of the reservation farthest north, a portion of which now reaches into southeastern Utah. A good part of Navajo expansion took place to the north and west when these lands were opened for settlement at different times, through presidential executive orders. Finally, this region continues to have greater population growth as the Navajo Nation expands its influence as part of an economic and governmental process that started in the early 1900s and continues to this day. Agriculture, mining and oil exploration, demographic development, and a host of new or expanding businesses still depend upon the land with its resources.

A brief summary of each chapter elucidates these points. The most dramatic era of deep history in this region was the establishment of Puebloan urban centers in the Chaco Canyon area from roughly 1000 to 1150 A.D. There is strong evidence that the Chuska Mountains and Valley provided much of the material for the structures and cultural activities necessary to sustain large populations and intense construction efforts. Massive architecture, lengthy road systems, extensive pottery manufacture, extended lumber harvesting, and a wide-ranging religious system were all made possible by resources emanating from the deserts and highlands of the Chuska range. Later, enter the Navajos, who utilized a rich body of lore to personalize the landscape and to teach of the holy people who secured it for them. But that made no difference to the Utes, Spaniards, Mexicans, and Anglos, as they attempted to wrest it from the Navajos and obtain physical resources for themselves. Conflict abounded, culminating in the Fearing Time and Long Walk for many of the Navajos who went to Fort Sumner, and then returned in 1868. This encyclopedic approach of the first chapter establishes the baseline for what follows.

The second chapter visits a new era in this region's history, when the Navajos permanently received the territory as reservation lands and established economic patterns that served them well for the next seventy years. Itinerant traders soon appeared, encouraging the weaving of rugs, sale of wool, and promotion of animal husbandry. The Indians proved adept at meeting requirements of the burgeoning trade. To stabilize conditions and foster growth, the government established the Shiprock Agency to control the northern reservation lands. Attendant "civilization" appeared in the form of strong personalities—Mary Eldridge and Henrietta Cole as women bearing the Christian faith, and William Taylor Shelton as founder of the agency and accompanying school. Irrigation systems, massive construction efforts requiring hewed stone, harvested lumber, baked adobe bricks, and road networks became part of this tale. There were also those who resisted what to them seemed like government encroachment—Ba'álílee, Howard Ray Antes, Little Singer and his father Bizhóshí, Richard Wetherill—even the San Juan River took its turn in frustrating the efforts to bring law, order, and peace to this region. Eventually, however, it happened.

Growing stability ushered in more economic opportunity. The next two chapters center on the development of trading posts, their interaction with government agents, and the ever-closer scrutiny of the business conducted in stores specialized in serving Navajo clientele. Improved weaving, the development of regional styles, more and better wool clips to sell back east, and greater marketing efforts encouraged Navajo production and trader promotion to soar. Using Two Grey Hills as an example of success, the reader is introduced to the role of the agent in working with traders along with a quantitative look at what was occurring in these small, isolated posts. The seventh chapter gets away from store ledgers and government correspondence to examine everyday life at these posts from the perspective of men, women, and children on both sides of the counters.

In spite of the seemingly immutable lifestyle, change was in the air, as chapter 8 makes clear. The establishment of tribal government, drilling for oil, paving roads, and above all, livestock reduction created circumstances that bent, then tore, at the fabric of Navajo life on the reservation. The posts felt the pinch, as did the Navajo people, which sometimes proved painful for both. This began the dissolution of a way of life that had existed for hundreds of years. Before reaching the final stages of this process in the last chapter, there is an interim discussion about wool, weaving, and regional style. Two Grey Hills, renowned for its rugs and blankets,[13] is prominent in this story, taking the reader from start to finish of the weaving process, from the wool on a sheep's back to a finely crafted piece of art, and from design elements to weaver's thoughts. These products, created primarily by women in this region—encompassing the Two Grey Hills, Toadlena, and Newcomb Posts—are examined. Their distinctive style and production, unlike the existence of the trading posts, continues to the present.

The view of this evolving story is based on the perspective of many people. Most obvious are those who lived it and then recorded what happened. Considering that the Navajos did not write much of their history, that the traders were businesspeople trying to wrest a living under difficult circumstances and so were not enamored with recording contemporary events, that government agents were focused on solving problems, and that some people just liked to keep things to themselves—it is amazing that a relatively complete story can be told. This is not to suggest that such a broad region as the Chuska Mountains and Valley, or all of the trading posts within that region or all of the activities of the Shiprock Agency can be covered within the pages of this book. But the general theme of cooperation, in spite of human and environmental challenges, provided a mutually beneficial situation that allowed people to settle in a very challenging area under difficult circumstances and to continue to succeed to this day.

Accounts by those who lived it provide a view from the ground floor. Collecting that view was crucial to making it available in its present form, and it rests upon the shoulders of three people—Frank McNitt, Charlotte Anderson, and Les Wilson. They made the next level of perspective possible. Frank McNitt (1912–1972), born in New York with strong lifetime ties to the East Coast, nevertheless had a fascination with the Southwest and its history. His four books, all of which discuss some aspect of Navajo interaction with members of the white race during the mid-to-late 1800s (including the Navajo Wars, James Simpson's military reconnaissance, trader Richard Wetherill, and trading posts into the early 1900s) highlighted this interest. Most important to the work here is the last one mentioned, *The Indian Traders*.[14] McNitt was an avid researcher, retracing steps upon the land, diving into archival holdings, and conducting interviews of participants in historic events. His book covers primarily the posts in Arizona and New Mexico, with lengthy chapters on many of the big names in trading history but also with many lesser, nondescript operators of posts. During the late 1950s he was particularly active in chasing down the people and stories that added zest and human interest to his topic. As with many researchers, however, he also gathered a lot of information that just could not be used, given the breadth of the topic and publishing considerations. Thankfully, many of his notes and materials are now housed in the New Mexico State Archives in Santa Fe. I have drawn heavily on his interviews and am very thankful for the detail and care he took while conducting them. (Plus his handwriting is very legible—a boon for anyone using his papers.) My endnotes indicate how important these interviews were in getting to know the more personal side of trading. Although he died relatively young (age sixty) with other projects underway, McNitt made a lasting contribution to the history of the Navajo and Anglo people living in the Southwest.

Upon his shoulders stands a woman—Charlotte Ann (Houston) Anderson—who spent countless hours visiting archival resources related to Two Grey Hills and the Northern Navajo region and who copied much of what McNitt had collected. She came at this interest, even passion, in a roundabout way. Like McNitt, she was not from the Southwest, having been born in Missouri and residing during much of her adult life in Ann Arbor, Michigan. Charlotte held a master's degree in special education and fostered a career in working with the hearing impaired. For a pastime, she was an avid weaver, using undyed natural fibers to create products that started with shearing the sheep and ended in a beautifully woven piece of art or craft. She was a perfectionist, and although she used processed wool in some of her projects, she considered herself more of a "naturalist" who thrilled in working with other weavers to make objects that did not use synthetic colors and dyed wool. The thrill, which lasted a lifetime, was to be an originalist in the sense that everything that went into a product, whether carding, spinning, or weaving with wool had to be done in the old-fashioned, handmade way.

Charlotte first came to the Navajo Reservation as a sixteen-year-old in 1954, an experience that sank barbs and "hooked" her into an intense appreciation of Navajo weaving. She became an expert in the craft, and by 1993 she was working with weavers, learning their techniques, and putting on free workshops on "skirting and scouring demonstrations." Described as a "hand spinner, weaver, and 'wool addict' from Ann Arbor, Michigan" she threw herself into what she considered preservation projects that supported traditional Navajo craft.[15] Thus, it is not surprising that she became particularly enamored with Two Grey Hills and its products made from churro sheep's naturally colored wool—a love affair that lasted to the end of her life. Even in her short obituary, it noted that she "especially loved the Two Grey Hills Trading Post" and that any memorial contributions "will be used to encourage and support young spinners and weavers through Two Grey Hills in New Mexico and The Spinners Flock [a local group dedicated to using natural, undyed wool] in southeast Michigan."[16]

Her fascination with the area and its people was not limited to just the craft. At great time and expense, she visited the National Archives in Washington, D.C., records in Santa Fe, and contacted dozens of people who could help in putting a history of the Two Grey Hills together. She amassed boxes of materials, much of which was copied on long sheets of paper, in preparation for a detailed account of this post. Unfortunately, health issues—with both of her parents and her daughter, then herself—prevented accomplishing the goal. Putting others first and realizing that she would not be able to achieve what she had set out to do, Charlotte sent all of her research to the owner of the Two Grey Hills Post, Les Wilson, with the hopes that he could find someone to take on the project of writing the history. Les approached a number of authors and historians who toyed with the possibility. Perhaps it was the large number of boxes of material; perhaps it was the randomness of organization; perhaps it was some of the dust-covered, mouse-nibbled papers; or perhaps they just did not want to tackle writing with materials gathered by others. Whatever the reason, Charlotte's research languished at the Two Grey Hills Trading Post for years.

As karma would have it, a Navajo friend who grew up in the area of the store heard about the project, knew Les was looking for a person to pull the materials together and tell its story, and thought I might be interested. Following a series of contacts and discussions, the deal was sealed, and I agreed to take on the task. As I delved into what all those cardboard boxes contained, there were a number of things that became obvious. First was the richness and breadth of material collected by Charlotte. I have worked in the National Archives before and can estimate the time and money she must have spent during her labor of love. It was not a trifling amount in either case. I am confident that she did a very thorough job in uncovering documents, some of which she annotated as she worked. But it was also obvious that there were gaps in the narrative that needed to be filled. Les was interested in the history of his post, but there was not enough information there—the store's operators were not an authorial breed and so did not record a lot about their activities. Plus, there were far too many different currents rolling through the Chuska Valley to limit the study to a single establishment. Ancestral Puebloan history had its impact, as did missionary efforts, the founding of the agency, William T. Shelton's influence, subsequent agents and government policies, development of weaving skills—and the list continues.

My role was to write a history that made sense. I had materials that had been collected at other times, plus there were places I needed to go to find supplemental information for what was already provided. Given the three focal points of this study—the Chuska Valley, Two Grey Hills with a few associated posts, and the early Shiprock Agency—I have been able to fill in most of the blanks to give a clear picture of what happened and who was involved. The only caveat of slight concern is in the endnotes, where I have tried to identify specific sources for future researchers at the National Archives. No matter how long one stares at a primary source historical document, determining the Record Group and file numbers from which it came, now absent, is difficult. I have done my best to identify provenance for those who wish to pursue the paper trail.

This was the genesis of that project and this book. As readers turn the pages and contemplate the lives and actions of personalities that moved through the past, it is hoped that a clearer understanding and sympathy arises. As with Wyeth as he journeyed to the Two Grey Hills Trading Post, there will be some uncomfortable times and shifting views that may challenge accepted beliefs. Hopefully from those thoughts will grow greater appreciation and empathy for those who struggled through life without the benefits of twenty-first-century conveniences and perspective. This was their time to settle the Northern Navajo for future generations.

Traders, Agents, and Weavers

CHAPTER ONE

Setting the Stage

The Land and Its People to 1870

The history of the Southwest is tied tightly to physical variations found in the land. Few other regions of the continental United States offer such different topographical landscapes and eco-niches as found in the states of the Four Corners region. New Mexico, Arizona, southwestern Colorado, and southeastern Utah share a territory dominated by the Colorado Plateau and present areas of abundant resources juxtaposed to large stretches of what appears to be a wasteland of sand, rock, and sagebrush. Climate, geology, topography, hydrology, flora, and fauna are all intermixed in a salad bowl of different types that foster special adaptation within a specific territory. From this variety come many different cultures and histories uniquely influenced by the area in which they are found.

An excellent example of this is the region of study covered in this book. In a broad sense, the area shared by the boundary between New Mexico and Arizona lies in the midst of the Colorado Plateau, a high country desert filled with sandstone canyons, volcanic necks, laccolithic mountains, and perennial and intermittent streams and rivers, as well as valleys and basins that have become the home and thoroughfare of man through time. Specifically, the two dominant landforms within this area of discussion are the Chuska Mountains, stretching generally from south to northwest along the western border of New Mexico with the San Juan Basin slanting from the eastern slopes of this range to the Chaco River and Wash, the eastern boundary of this study. While this one-hundred-mile streambed is a tributary of the San Juan River and generally parallels the Chuska range, it is ephemeral with a dry sandy

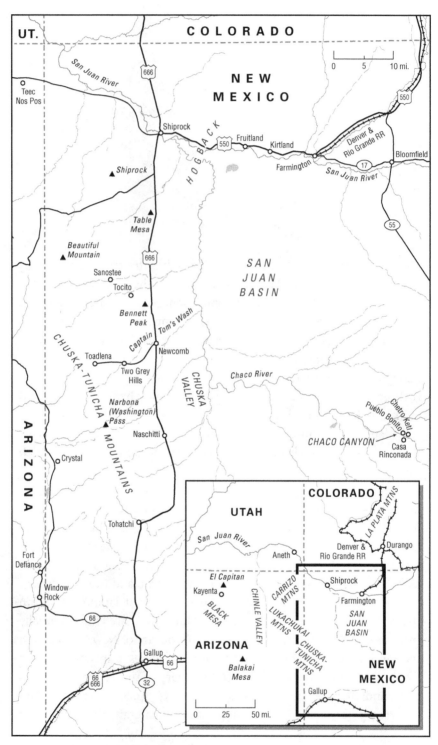

Shiprock and the Northern Navajo Region, circa 1940. Cartography by Erin Greb.

bottom much of the year; yet during the spring and summer months, it is subject to violent flooding from snow melt and rainfall.[1]

Between mountain and stream lies the Chuska Valley, whose breadth varies from ten to forty miles. This valley floor is broken at many points by wide alluvial flats and short stretches of canyon, with its east side filled with a labyrinth of broken mesas, flat-topped ridges, and low hogbacks.[2] Two prominent volcanic dikes and necks protrude from the desert floor—Shiprock and Bennett Peaks—both of which serve as prominent landmarks. There are twenty-two large—and over one hundred smaller—drainages coming from the eastern slope of the Chuska Mountains, over the 5,790 square miles of valley floor.[3] None of these streambeds are a permanent source of water, but at the base of the Chuskas sit a large number of springs, giving rise to communities and agricultural pursuits as well as trading posts.

The western border of this area is the Chuska Mountain range. As recently as the early twentieth century, however, this roughly 8,000-to-9,000-foot-high mass held other names to specify particular portions. Historic maps denote the southern part of the range, south of Narbona Pass (Béésh Łichíí'ii Deeshgizh or Copper Pass) as Sierra de Chuska or Chuska range. The name derived from the Navajo word Ch'óshgai, meaning "White Spruce." North of Narbona Pass was referred to as Sierra Tunicha or "Much Water," while the Lukachukai or "Patches of White Reed" Mountains are located solely in Arizona on the northwestern end of the range. As geographer Herbert E. Gregory noted in 1916, "My Navajo guides informed me that these terms refer to particular spots rather than to areas, a reasonable explanation in view of the fact that on each of the [three] subdivisions of this continuous range spruce and reeds are to be found in several localities and that each is about equally supplied with both lakes and running streams. . . . The use of Chuska for the entire range has been approved by the United States Geographic Board, but the subdivisions Lukachukai, Tunicha, and Chuska are retained for purposes of description as well as for historic reasons."[4]

The eastern flank of the range is a steeply graded slope that is often cut by streams of seasonal water, while the western side of the range is a nearly vertical escarpment with a few passageways for descent, causing this side to be less accessible. To the north of the Lukachukai range lies Red Rock Valley, which separates the Carrizo Mountains, an approximately twelve-mile string of peaks. Attaining the same height as its sandstone-capped neighbors, the Carrizos have a predominantly igneous rock surface. Both ranges share similar vegetation of ponderosa pine, fir, aspen, scrub oak, grassy meadows watered by springs, and slopes covered with piñon and juniper trees.

The Chuska range, in particular, has a powerful influence on the prevailing storm pattern of rain and snow that blows in from a general southsouthwest-west direction. The steep western sides of the range cause the moisture to be released before reaching the eastern slope. While precipitation in the mountains averages 25 inches of water annually, the eastern slope and basin receive a meager 8 to 10 inches. The mountains thus form a rain shadow that increases dependence on springs or wells for agriculture in the Chuska Valley, while runoff from snowmelt and seasonal thunderstorms along the crest of the Chuska massif generates more than half the surface water of today's Navajo Nation. Add to this approximately 150 frost-free days in the basin to grow corn, which requires only 100 days above 32 degrees, and other crops such as beans and squash, which take even less time to mature, and one can see how these plants became important staples for inhabitants in this arid region. The valley floor is also ideal for grazing.[5]

First Inhabitants, 8000 B.C. to 1300 A.D.

Information about the earliest American Indian presence in the Chuska Valley is scant. Paleo Indians are identified primarily through stone spear points such as Clovis, Folsom, and Plano, which have been found in the San Juan Basin and dated to between 9000 and 8500 B.C. These lithic types are associated with big game hunting characteristic of the ending ice age, when mastodons and large buffalo (*Bison antiquus*) roamed the heavily vegetated, well-watered landscape made possible by far cooler temperatures. By 6000 B.C., the Archaic period of American Indian presence was in full swing and more clearly defined. The land and temperatures changed during a drying and warming period at the end of the Ice Age, causing the topography and vegetation to shift dramatically to an environment comparable to what is found in today's Southwest region.

The Indians adapted to different hunting and gathering patterns, known generally as Desert Culture, with its more specialized and larger tool kits for harvesting local resources. The atlatl, with short spears called darts first introduced by the Paleo Indian, continued to be the weapon of choice to take big game like deer, pronghorn antelope, and desert bighorn sheep. Manos and metates assisted in processing seeds, nuts, and plants for food, including a limited amount of corn, while cobblestone-lined pits served as cooking areas outside of brush shelters or in alcoves. Water and seasonal availability of resources determined the size of the hunting-gathering group, its location for encampment, and strategies for food procurement. Travel circuits that would take these hunters and gatherers into the mountains in the spring and summer and into warmer temperatures in the basin during the winter, allowed for variety in diet and for the land to have a seasonal rest.[6]

The literature about the next group of Indians—the Ancestral Puebloans, commonly known as the Anasazi—is immense and growing. Those living in Chaco Canyon during the eleventh and first half of the twelfth centuries have spawned an abundance of books, articles, and research reports.[7] For our purposes, only a brief synopsis of their civilization is offered here. General Ancestral Puebloan presence in the San Juan drainage began roughly 1000 B.C. and ended 1300 A.D. During this time the culture underwent numerous changes, which archaeologists have subdivided with specificity, but here they are referred to simply as Pre-Classic, Classic, and Post-Classic.

The Pre-Classic culture began slowly around 1000 B.C. with the introduction of corn in the Four Corners area, providing a more stable source of food. Slowly, hunting and gathering gave way to an increasingly sedentary lifestyle dependent on crops. Pit houses, circular storage pits, skillfully crafted baskets and sandals, feather and fur robes, and a greatly expanded tool kit developed. By 500 A.D., and with an increasing dependence on maize and squash, new additions joined the ranks—beans now provided a complete diet, dry farming techniques developed, the manufacture of pottery began, more elaborate pit houses evolved, and the bow and arrow replaced the dart and atlatl. Rock art persisted through all phases of this culture, each era having its own unique characteristics. Around 750 A.D. these Indians were building homes above ground in connected, rectangular blocks of rooms, using rocks and jacal (a framework of woven saplings and sticks packed with mud), and some stone and adobe masonry for construction materials. One or more deep pit houses have been found in each of the building clusters and may have served a ceremonial function as a great kiva for religious ceremonies.

The Classic period of Ancestral Puebloan culture started around 1000 A.D. and lasted for the next 150 years. A change in climate provided more dependable precipitation, higher water tables affected springs and seeps, and temperatures were generally conducive to agriculture. The people reacted by moving from a pattern of clustering population in strategic locations to a far-ranging decentralization of large productive communities. Satellite work-and-living sites fanned out from the larger population bases. At no previous time had there been as many people spread over so much of the land, giving rise to increasing social interaction between communities, the construction of public architecture, and an increase of long-range trade. The relatively sudden shift that brought a dramatic decrease in warfare and an increase in prosperity appeared to have come from a strong cultural influence now identified with the development of activities associated with Chaco Canyon. This apparent link that unified different areas gave rise to specialized forms of architecture. An extensive road network converged on "great houses" (multistory room blocks) and great kivas—large, semi-subterranean ceremonial chambers—whose roofs were supported by pillars and spanned by long-beam construction. Unlike the smaller kivas found with many habitation sites, great kivas had a particular ritual function not totally understood by American Indians and researchers today. Homes, at this time built primarily with stone masonry, were above ground, while rock-and-mud storage granaries perched high in cliff recesses or in large granaries within the Puebloan community.

By the Post-Classic era (1150–1300 A.D.), the Chaco phenomenon had ended and Mesa Verde had become a bustling epicenter, spreading its construction and pottery characteristics over a large area of the northern Four Corners region. In the San Juan Basin, it appears that there was an abandonment of many of the smaller communities, a clustering of the population into larger villages, and an infusion of Mesa Verde qualities spreading from the north along with a rapid decline and then absence of Chacoan characteristics. This general pattern suggests the culture was in a state of stress and conflict, encouraging inhabitants to congregate in larger, more defensible sites. Large communal plazas, tower clusters around springs at the head of canyons, evidence of decreased regional trade relations, and the introduction of the kachina cult prevalent during the historic period among the pueblo peoples are all indications the society was undergoing substantial change.

Archaeologists argue about what caused these cultural shifts and the subsequent abandonment of the San Juan drainage area by the Ancestral Puebloans. Some people attribute these changes to environmental factors such as prolonged drought, cooler temperatures, arroyo cutting, and depleted soils. Others, in the past, suggested that nomadic hunters and gatherers, precursors to the historic Ute, Paiute, and Navajo people, invaded the area, although no concrete proof exists to suggest large-scale warfare with outside invaders. Internal turmoil and fractured relations seem a more likely reason for the dissolution.[8] No single explanation satisfactorily answers all the questions, but by 1300 A.D. the Ancestral Puebloans had left the San Juan drainage on a series of migrations that eventually took them to their historic and present homes along the Rio Grande (Eastern Pueblos) and to the areas where the Acoma, Zuni, and Hopi villages (Western Pueblos) now stand.

The Chaco Phenomenon

While each of the phases of Puebloan occupation occurred within the San Juan Basin and our area of concern, the Classic period in which Chaco Canyon played a dominant role is of particular interest. During this era, the major dependence on resources from the Two Grey Hills and neighboring areas, the Chuska Mountains, and the water sources along the eastern slope, suggest a parallel pattern for historic times, although there were dramatic differences in everything from material resources to worldview. This comparison, driven by the land and the cultural situation at the time, will be developed in another chapter, but for now, we turn to this exciting period in Puebloan history, when the environment, new cultural innovation, and a strong religious worldview dictated sophisticated changes and a very different way of life.

A brief description of some of the major structures strung along Chaco Wash as it courses through the canyon sets the stage for understanding the role of the more distant sites in the Chuska Valley. The D-shaped

Pueblo Bonito is one of the most dramatic structures with its eight hundred rooms comprising part of a five-story building. Two great kivas separated by a north-south wall served as part of a strong ritual function that accompanied another thirty smaller kivas and a large courtyard used for community activities. This building, like other major structures in the canyon, gives a visually formidable impression, suggested by archaeologists, to intimidate those who approach the edifice. Chetro Ketl, a neighbor to Pueblo Bonito, is a great house that shares many similarities, with its four hundred rooms within its four-storied construction, dozen small kivas, one great kiva, and large plaza. Casa Rinconada, one of four great kivas that stands alone, has a sixty-four foot diameter and all the characteristic elements of this specialized form of architecture—a masonry firebox, inner bench, four roof-supporting pillars, large seating pits, masonry vaults, and thirty-four niches—divided into two sizes—encircling the kiva. The list goes on, with eighteen major structures in what archaeologists consider "downtown Chaco," and dozens of lesser structures spread throughout the canyon and hundreds beyond.[9]

Many questions concerning why these buildings were made, who controlled their construction, and what their specific use was, continue to be subjects for debate. Explanations as to who built them vary from an elite ruling class that migrated from Mexico and enforced systematic control of activities in the region, to a burgeoning chiefdom derived from the more local Ancestral Puebloan culture, to an evolving priesthood that organized and operated an intense ritual cycle requiring large amounts of goods and services to maintain an elaborate system of worship. The architectural remains such as roads, great houses, great kivas, and masonry styles; exotic materials including macaw feathers, copper bells, cacao, and seashells imported into the area from regions as far south as Mesoamerica; and the lack of conflict during this time compared to the amount of warfare before and after, all point to a strong centralized control that had a dominant influence over the area and its population.

What can be said with more surety is that this flourishing cultural phenomenon depended heavily upon the people and resources of the eastern Chuska Slope area defined previously. While Chaco Canyon proper, due to a relative paucity of agricultural space, water, timber, and other resources, did not have the ability to sustain large numbers of people locally, necessary materials were brought in from elsewhere.

Pueblo Bonito, the most commanding structure in Chaco Canyon, illustrates the tremendous emphasis placed on creating impressive architecture. Whether for political, social, religious, or economic purposes, the buildings, roads, and circular kivas required massive dedicated labor and resources—much of which came from or was supported by Ancestral Puebloan communities located in the Chuska Valley or adjoining mountains. Courtesy of Kay Shumway.

Archaeologists do not agree as to how many residents actually lived in places like Pueblo Bonito or Chetro Ketl—perhaps in all the buildings in the canyon there may have been a high of 5,600 or a low of 2,000.[10] Especially during the most intense period of construction and occupation in the canyon (1050–1115 A.D.), there arose a system of "outliers" along the floor of Chuska Valley where springs and runoff from the slope were available, to support large populations. Previously, much of the building material had come from the Zuni Mountains southwest of the canyon, but now the focus shifted to as many as twenty different communities servicing Chaco proper from the Chuskas to the west, with a total of forty outliers spread throughout the basin.[11]

In the area of what is now called Two Grey Hills, there were a number of sites developed during the rise, florescence, and decline of the Chaco phenomenon. A cursory view of some of these sites (Crumbled House, Newcomb, Skunk Springs, and Tocito) in the Two Grey Hills area along

with a site (Tohatchi) at the far southern end and one at the northern end
(Sanostee) of our study area provides a sense of the size and composition
of these communities serving as outliers to downtown Chaco. Each of
these sites had at least one great kiva and all but one (Tohatchi Basket-
maker Village) had a public facility or great house as part of its composition. It should also be mentioned that in close proximity to every one
of these ruins, Anglo entrepreneurs established trading posts during the
late nineteenth and early twentieth century. Dependence on water and
other resources drew both groups to the same locations.[12]

Moving north twenty-five miles to the general vicinity of Two Grey
Hills, there stands four Puebloan complexes that thrived during the
Chaco era. One that played an extremely important role is Skunk Springs,
known to later Navajo residents as Black House (Kin Łizhin). The central
site, located on a ninety-foot-high prominence that overlooks the valley
floor, has three great kivas, a two-story great house, and a large enclosed
plaza and shrine, and is said by local Navajos to have been the termi-
nus of a clay road that went directly to Pueblo Bonito thirty-five miles
away.[13] Six miles to the east is Newcomb located on Tuntsa or Captain
Tom's Wash, named after Tom Crozier, a cavalry officer who in 1858,
rode up the wash then camped to the north at the site of the future Two
Grey Hills Trading Post. Nine miles north of Newcomb is Tocito where a
comparable ruin is found. Its plaza is set in a depression encompassed by
a wall; the multistory great house, enclosed kivas, and surrounding community follow very closely the patterns found in Newcomb and other
sites inhabited during this era. A final site is located thirteen miles north
of Two Grey Hills, at Sanostee, a name coming from the Navajo words
meaning Crossed Rocks (Tséʼatnáoztʼiʼí). It is located at the confluence of
the Sanostee and Chaco Washes and has two large house mounds that
supported massive structures with enclosed kivas, walled plazas, two
great kivas, and an associated community. As with all of the other sites
discussed, it was located on land suitable for agricultural endeavor.[14]

Chaco Outliers: Resourcing Downtown

What, then, were these outliers providing? Certainly part of that answer
returns to what the function of downtown Chaco was about. As stated
earlier, there is a large literature that argues different theories about why

the monumental architecture was built in an area with such limited resources. Ideas vary, some suggesting a ruling elite that demanded the outlying sites' support. Others believe Chaco served as a trade redistribution center; others see it as a site where intense ceremonialism evolved, supported by pilgrims who descended on Chaco at certain times of the year to worship and hold trade fairs. Regardless of the societal reason, the fact that the Chuska range played a dominant role, especially during this phase, is accepted by most archaeologists. Four products—corn, pottery, timber, and chert—illustrate how dependent Chaco became on them for sustaining the growth and activities of this era.

Archaeologists have studied the molecular structure of corncobs used by the inhabitants of Chaco Canyon and have determined that there was a substantial amount of produce exported from the slopes of the Chuska Mountains to this bustling center of activity. Larry Benson, archaeologist, believes that the amount of winter precipitation, when controlled by irrigation systems, had the ability to sustain 10,000 residents living on the Chuska Slope, including those inhabiting Chaco.[15] For instance, one field at Newcomb that is slightly over four miles long and over a mile-and-a-half wide, located at the western end of the Chacoan "West Road," could date back to 500 A.D. At its height, the water that entered this field might have traveled over four miles in a controlled irrigation system of dams and headgates that diverted the water to sites within bounded plots. This system alone is 150 times larger than the largest previously identified Chacoan agricultural system.[16] Benson estimates that when fully productive, it could have served 1,000 people, and when added to a number of outliers along the Chuska Slope, a much greater population could have been fed. He posits that during peak population just before 1130 A.D. there were between 10,625 and 17,000 inhabitants, compared to the lands within Chaco Canyon with an estimated canyon population of around 2,000.[17]

The next question is how could this large volume of foodstuffs be transported? Once shelled, vegetables like corn and beans can be more easily moved, which fostered a second type of export industry—pottery. Pot sherds, objects loved by archaeologists, can be dated, can give provenance as to where they were made, may indicate the movements of people and their wares, and are relatively indestructible. Pottery manufactured in the Chuska Slope region has a distinct material composition.

A basaltic (igneous) temper called trachyte came from two principle sources—the areas of Narbona Pass and Beautiful Mountain with their accompanying drainages. Beginning around 825 A.D. this distinctive ingredient began to temper the pottery made along the Chuska range so that within a twenty-five-year period, 90 percent of all of the manufactured vessels had switched from sand temper to trachyte temper.[18] The availability of wood for firing, water for production, and good clay deposits were other aspects that encouraged this pottery making.

Current research indicates that the majority of gray ware during the Classic period used in Chaco for cooking, storage, and other mundane duties most likely came from Skunk Springs and may have become a craft specialization produced by a limited number of people. Although durable and functional, this pottery was nothing out of the ordinary in terms of trade appeal for those seeking unique decoration. Approximately 50–60 percent of the vessels used in the canyon came from the Chuskas.[19] An extreme example of the volume of pots coming to Chaco is found at Pueblo Alto, where middens reveal an intense use and destruction of especially Chuskan utility ware. James Judge reports that "based on ceramic frequencies recovered from a sample of the formal trash mound, as many as 150,590 ceramic vessels may have been deposited there. It is estimated that a minimum of 49,270 trachyte-tempered pots were part of this collection, of which 31,360 were gray ware jars . . . which figures to be about 125 vessels per family per year, as opposed to an estimated 17 per family at the village sites in Chaco. [H. Wolcott] Toll (1984) suggests that this may indicate periodic gatherings at Pueblo Alto of nonresidents, with possible ceramic disposal associated with such gatherings."[20]

This utility ware is among the least attractive and yet was carried in large volume between thirty-five and forty miles across a difficult landscape; the shape itself is not that conducive to ease of transportation; the sheer volume concentrated at one site, in particular, raises the question of why; and the sharp decline of this pottery's use at the beginning of the first quarter of the twelfth century also raises questions. Since its dramatic increase and decrease parallels the Classic building phase in Chaco, the expansion of outlier communities with distinctive Chacoan architecture, and other phenomena of this period, all of this appears to have been the result of a unified system that has yet to be understood.

Certainly the road system was another piece of this puzzle. Chaco roads have been examined extensively, even as new portions are discovered each year. Although hundreds of miles of road network have been projected by linking confirmed sections on the ground, there are still many pieces yet to discover, while other parts have been lost through the destruction of the archaeological record. What can be said about this network with surety is that it comprised a complex system for foot travel that emanated from Chaco Canyon in all four cardinal directions, connected many of the outliers within the San Juan Basin, followed a construction pattern that shares similar mathematical measurements, was associated with great houses and great kivas constructed during the Classic period, and had religious as well as more mundane uses.[21] A common theme of "moving to the center" or "finding the center place" is often discussed as a primary goal of historic and contemporary Puebloan peoples, who explain their emergence from worlds beneath during the time of creation, their clan migration histories, and their pursuit of balance in today's world, as part of this very real metaphor.[22] As already noted, the Chuska Slope sites had sections of road as part of their composition.

Another purported function of the roads was to provide ease of transportation for large numbers of ponderosa pine (*Pinus ponderosa*) for the massive construction projects within Chaco Canyon proper. The central complex of buildings is located in an austere desert environment that allows for the use of limited, short trees such as piñon (*Pinus edulis*) and juniper (*Juniperus* spp.), but there were no long substantial timbers for spanning great kiva roofs, building large great houses, and providing the materials to frame doors, windows, and other elements of house construction. Add to this a large population and the necessity of wood for cooking food, firing pots, and heating homes during the winter, and one can see the necessity of having an abundant source. Based on dendrochronology and isotope analysis of existing wooden remains, archaeologists have partially answered the question as to source and number of trees needed to support much of this construction.

As early as 850 A.D., the Ancestral Puebloans were importing large amounts of timber from the Zuni Mountains. Over the years as construction increased, other ranges such as the Jemez Mountains, San Juan, and Mount Taylor also served as sources, but starting in the Classic period around 1020 and eclipsing around 1060 A.D., the Chuska Mountains became the main source for wood. A number of possible explanations for this shift have been offered—the Chuskas are somewhat closer than the Zuni Mountains or may have had more abundant resources and a more extensive outlier system. Archaeologists estimate that during the peak period of construction, when occupants of the Chaco core area expanded existing great houses and built seven new ones as well as great kivas and other buildings, the trees needed for all of the construction arose to an estimated 240,000.[23] Specific spruce and fir analysis from Pueblo Bonito, Chetro Ketl, and four other contemporaneous structures indicate that two-thirds of the wood came from the Chuskas and one-third from the San Mateo Mountains, leading investigators to conclude that "the Chuska Mountains seem to have been the preferred source area for spruce, fir, and ponderosa."[24]

Narbona Pass chert is a primary type of stone used in the northern Chuska Valley to make implements and was yet another product exported from the Chuska Mountains during the Classic period. This pink, translucent stone was initially derived from volcanic activity and is found only in New Mexico at this site. Due to its distinctive color and characteristics, its source of origin is easily identified. Beginning in the tenth century, this stone became a regular import into Chaco Canyon. Remains of this chert are associated more with great houses than with smaller dwellings, and at Pueblo Alto there is "a higher frequency of lithics [made from Narbona Pass chert] than would be expected for the estimated population, mirroring the consumption patterns of trachyte-tempered ceramics."[25] Recognizing that this material dominates the import of stone from outside the canyon, one archaeologist estimates that 27 percent of all that was brought to Pueblo Alto came from Narbona Pass and represents five times more than is found in village sites within the canyon.[26]

Yet all good things must come to an end, and the Chaco florescence was no exception. By 1150 A.D. decline was underway. Since archaeologists deal with physical remains, the frequently cited reasons for the abandonment of the distinctive Chaco lifestyle often hinge on explanations such as drought, soil depletion, and other measurable causes. There is no doubt that starting in 1140 A.D., a fifty-year decrease in summer rains and winter snows threatened the agricultural communities with starvation.[27] One should note, however, that in American Indian thought, a physical manifestation is only the symptom of something spiritually amiss. In other words, a drought, for example, may be an issue, but the root cause of the problem is linked to spiritual and interpersonal relationships so that the rain and snow are withheld until the issue is corrected. Another reason there is no clear explanation for the demise of the Chacoan way of life is that we do not know how the system worked. Some people believe that Chaco was solely a redistribution center that served as a buffer against famine and drought; others explain its key purpose was to host pilgrimage fairs to exchange goods; others suggest a ruling priesthood that controlled the economic system through religious devotion or repressive force; some suggest that the ruling class became too intolerant and lost its power; and others believe that Chaco struggled against rising, competitive powers such as those found at Aztec or Salmon and lost out in the struggle.[28] For whatever reason, Chaco closed, the population moved into a Post-Classic phase of clustering in a more defensive posture, elements of the Mesa Verde–type Ancestral Puebloans entered the San Juan Basin, until by 1300 A.D., the entire population had left the San Juan drainage in the Four Corners region.

Enter the Navajos

The next large group to populate this Southwest landscape was the Navajo (Diné). A basic assumption underlying most of the research associated with their origin is that they came from the north, their language being a long-standing method of proof.[29] Most scholars place the ancestral Athabascans in northwestern Canada and Alaska by the first millennia A.D. Using glottochronology to measure language change between groups over time, linguists have determined that various Athabascan-speaking peoples split off from their ancestors at different times. For instance, the Hupas, now living in California, separated from the Navajos about 1,100 years ago; the Kutchin and the Beaver groups in Canada 890 and 690 years ago respectively; the Jicarilla and San Carlos Apaches 300 years ago; and the Chiricahua Apaches 170 years ago. If these dates are relatively accurate, the Navajos separated from their ancestral stock roughly 1,000 years ago.[30] Since there are many variables that enter into language change, not all scholars agree with these figures, but they do provide an understanding of differences between groups. David Brugge, a well-known anthropologist and ethnohistorian of Navajo history, summarizes his view by saying that "by 1300 the Apacheans must have been close to the northern periphery of the Anasazi region."[31]

Others do not agree that the Navajos were in the Southwest that early, although the times of occupation are being pushed back from the long-accepted date of 1500 A.D. For instance, recent excavations north of Farmington, New Mexico, and just south of the Colorado state line have yielded twelve sites with twenty-three radiocarbon dates that pre-date the 1500s, the earliest going back to the 1300s. Because of this new information "it appears likely that the Navajo were in the Four Corners region by at least 1400 A.D. . . . The period of time between the last Anasazi occupation north of the San Juan River and the earliest Navajo sites is now only about a century, suggesting the possibility that future research may establish contemporaneity between the two cultures."[32] Perhaps this explains why the Navajos have an extensive repertoire of mythological teachings about their interaction with the Pueblos—many of which are tied to specific sites that include Chaco Canyon. In *Viewing the Ancestors: Perceptions of the Anaasází, Mokwič, and Hisatsinom*, a more complete accounting of this period in Navajo history, their use of Anasazi sites and artifacts today, and the powers that are still available through ceremonial performance are outlined.[33] More specific to the present discussion is the mythology of the Great Gambler and his powerful, destructive rein during the time that Chaco reached its height. The trials of his population, his demeaning control over their lives, his inability to pay homage to deity, his uncontrolled hubris, and eventual defeat have become important Navajo stories that teach about the results of correct and incorrect behavior. Chaco is still recognized as a place of intense spiritual power.

A recent book edited by archaeologist Deni J. Seymour looks at the latest research of nineteen scholars examining the entire issue of the Navajos' arrival using everything from archaeology to mythology and from language to DNA.[34] The general conclusion was that most likely the Navajos were here by 1300 A.D. Here they met Utes, Paiutes, and other Numic speakers living as hunters and gatherers. All of these groups left few material remains, generally avoided sites and artifacts used by the Ancestral Puebloans, depended on other traditions, and enjoyed a different lifestyle. In general terms, the Navajos established their terri-tory south of the San Juan River, while the Utes dominated the lands north. Cultural differences between these two groups were pronounced, even though both shared the same type of environment.

One means by which the Navajos laid claim to the area was through their rich body of lore and mythology. The total fabric of their belief sys-tem is welded to a complex, integrated series of stories and teachings that find expression through ceremonies and practices that deal with the physical world in religious terms. Central to these precepts is the land populated by holy people and supernatural forces. Thus, mountains, rivers, rock formations, springs, plants, and animals—most tangible things—are alive, have a spirit, hold a power, can communicate, may harm or help, and are under the control of deity. Indeed, from the Navajo perspective, a person's ability to succeed in this world depends on living in a sustained relationship (*k'é*) and following rules established by the holy people during the time of creation. To do so leads to *hózhó*, often glossed as a peaceful, harmonious relationship created by obedience to these teachings and practices infused throughout nature and society.[35] In this animate universe, everything is either male or female, has a counter-part, responds to both proper and improper practices, can bless or harm, and follows an established pattern of behavior. Nothing is too great or small to fit into this divine plan set in motion by the holy people.

Teachings upon the Land

The region of the Chuska Valley and surrounding environ figures heav-ily in the teachings, songs, and prayers found in the different chantways, serving as a basis for various ceremonies. At times, there may be differ-ences between accounts. Medicine men who perform the same rite may have variations depending on who taught them and the oral tradition. From a Navajo perspective, if this is how a person was taught, there is no need to dispute, but rather one should enjoy the richness of an oral tradition and embrace variation.

One of the most physically prominent parts of the landscape in our area of study is the Chuska-Tunicha Mountains.[36] On a grand scale, this range is part of a male figure that offers a series of important teachings. At the time of creation, when the earth was "soft" and the holy people were shaping the land, they formed Gobernador Knob (Ch'óol'íí—Spruce or Fir Mountain) and then sprinkled dirt from the Carrizo Mountains southward toward today's Gallup, New Mexico. As they created a male figure from the soil, they began to run short of materials and so conserved resources by making passes through this soon-to-be mountain range. They named this figure Bead Mountain (Yo'dí Dził). Richard F. Van Valkenburgh, archaeologist and ethnologist, delineates the form: "The head was Chuska Peak, the neck, Washington [Narbona] Pass, the body the Tunicha Mountains, the right arm the Shiprock trap-dyke, and the left arm, the Crystal New Mexico projection. The Carrizo Mountains, called by the Navajos *Dził Na'ooditii*, The Encircled Mountain, separated at the base making the legs," with his feet at Beautiful Mountain. Van Valkenburgh explains that the gods moved westward again and formed a female companion named Corn Pollen Mountain (Tadidiin Dził). "It also has a human form—a female figure. The head was *Naatsis'áán* [Navajo Mountain—Head of Earth Woman]. One arm is said to be Comb Ridge near Kayenta and the other arm the formation extending west toward Shonto. The body was *Dził Líjiin* (Black Mountain/Mesa); and the lower extremities Balukai Mesa just north of Steamboat Canyon, Arizona."[37]

Talking God and First Man had important roles to play in assigning the qualities, characteristics, and physical nature that each of these individuals would have. They planned for, and through spiritual forces, provided wealth from nature to prepare the land for the Five-Fingered Beings, or humans, who would soon walk the earth. Medicine man Frank Mitchell tells of how these two mountain beings now lie facing each other. Talking God blew on the male to form material possessions (hard goods), put him in charge of game animals and vegetation, and gave him the name Mountain Woman. On the woman he blew amniotic fluid, gave her the name of Water Woman, and put her in control of collected waters and things that live in it. Mountain Woman lay to the south with Whirling Mountain (Carrizo Mountains) given as a footrest, White Spruce (Chuska Peak/Tohatchi Mountain) serving as a headrest, and Rock Gap (Twin Buttes) as his head plume. To the north, Water Woman received Navajo Mountain as a headrest and Much Wool (El Capitan/Aghaałá Peak) as a cane. Now these two could be useful in providing water and vegetation to the Navajo people.[38]

There are yet other divine roles assigned to these mountains. On their peaks, as well as on El Capitan and Shiprock, are Sky Supporters to hold the heavens in place and to assist with spiritual communication between humans and the holy people; Shiprock is said to be a bow or a medicine pouch for the male figure, while El Capitan is sometimes referred to as a wool spindle (*bee'adizí*) for the woman. Ceremonial names delineate the powers held by these and other mountains such as Rain Mountain, Pollen Mountain, Fabrics Mountain, Goods of Value Range, Jewel Mountain, Hard Goods Range, and "Mountain Where One Hears It Raining."[39] These formations work in concert with other sacred mountains to bring blessings to the Navajo people. Medicine men, familiar with the Blessingway ceremony, with its teachings of a peaceful lifestyle, say that Gobernador Knob and Chuska Peak, since they are both dressed with spruce and fir trees, look and speak to each other by using a "rock crystal rainbow."[40] Indeed, the entire Chuska range is associated with wealth and fertility. Thus the mountain name "Goods of Value" is associated with physical wealth like silver, turquoise, livestock, and other tangible property, which are referred to in ceremonial terms as "hard goods," coming from this male formation. Prayers, songs, and less tangible blessings come from the female formation, Water Woman, and are referred to in ceremonial terms as "soft goods."

While the Mountain Woman and Water Woman formations work in harmony together and separately to bless the Navajo people, there are also important places within these bodies that have names and teachings. For instance, Chuska Pass at the southern end of the range is called Wind Blows About within the Rock (Tsé Bii'Naayolí). Within the pass is a spring that serves as a shrine and also a blessing pile, where rocks are left as a testament to prayers and wishes of those who visited there and left an offering.[41] Nearby is Chuska Peak, which plays an important part in the Nightway ceremony (Tł'éé'jí Hatáál), Blessingway (Hózhǫǫjí), Thunderway (Ii'ní), Windway (Níłch'ijí), Lightningway (Na'at'ooyee), and Mountainway (Dziłk'ijí). Descending from the peak's crest is a ridge called Male Mountain's Feather Tie (Dził Bikạ Bits'os Bitłool).[42] Bennett Peak, named after a military officer, Captain Frank T. Bennett, who also served as a Navajo agent (1869–71), is called Black Rock Coming Down (Tsézhin 'Ii'ahí). Narbona, a powerful Navajo leader, stationed watchers on the peak to see if an enemy was approaching. Smoke signals by day and signal fires at night warned the inhabitants. Today, local custom suggests that on the north side of the peak, there is a cave where witches meet to hold ceremonies and perform witchcraft against the unfortunate.[43] Beautiful Mountain (Dziłk'i Hozhónii—"Mountain Beautiful on Top"), also known as Cayetano Mountain, was a well-protected haven for two powerful leaders—Cayetano and later Bizhóshí, who is discussed in chapter 4. Finally, Captain Tom's Wash, which flows from the Chuska Mountains past Two Grey Hills and Newcomb, was called Big Water's Spring (Tó Ntsaa Bitó) and gave rise not only to agricultural efforts of the Ancestral Puebloans and Navajos but also to the establishment of the Two Grey Hills and Newcomb Trading Posts.[44]

Creatures and Places of Power

Navajo mythology—especially in the Mountainway ceremony (Dziłk'ijí)—is replete with teachings about bears living in the Chuska Mountains.[45] Changing Woman, mother of the first Navajo clans, at one time traveled about the landscape during the time of creation. She had five animals she kept as pets to protect her and her fellow travelers. One of those guards was a bear, who viciously attacked any enemies that endangered the group. At the end of the journey, Changing Woman released the bear, saying, "Our pet, you have served us well; but we are now safe among our friends and we need your services no more. If you wish, you may leave us. There are others of your kind in the Chuska Mountains. Go there and play with them."[46] He ambled off in that direction, which explains to the Navajos why bears have been numerous in that area ever since. Perhaps that is why medicine man Frank Mitchell pointed to Beautiful Mountain and declared that Monster Slayer, in an effort to kill monsters that roamed the earth eating Navajo people, killed Tracking Bear Monster (Shash Na'áłkaahii) there. This wily bear disappeared and reappeared through a system of interconnected dens. Monster Slayer studied the creature's action, determined where the bear would surface next, then waited outside until the monster's head protruded enough to be cut off.[47]

Chuska Peak is another site where supernatural bears hold power that can harm people who do not show respect. Two young men, identified only as Elder Brother and Younger Brother, met four women called

"Maiden That Becomes a Bear" and entered their home near the peak. These women's faces were white, but their legs and forearms were covered with shaggy fur. Although their hands were like those of a human, their teeth were long and pointed. These women did not harm the brothers, but showed them how to make and bury prayer sticks as part of a sacrifice.[48] The men continued with their travels. Washington Matthews, who recorded this story in 1887, told of when he was traveling with a group of Navajos who approached within three hundred yards of the base of Chuska Knoll. His companions refused to go any farther because it was the home of these women. Matthews proceeded by himself to ride to the peak by traveling over fallen trees and loose stones. Once he arrived on top, he found a hollow among the rocks with some carved stone images and shell beads left for offerings. He later joined his companions below, mentioning that his horse was getting lame and that it must have gotten injured while traveling over some of the fallen trees. The Navajos felt differently: "'Think not thus, foolish American,' they said. 'It was not the fallen trees that wounded your horse. The *Diyiin* [gods] of the mountain have stricken him because you went where you had no right to go. You are lucky if nothing worse happens to you.'"[49] Apparently, nothing did.

Another story about bears underscores how respect and prayers can lead to a positive outcome, while disrespect and ignorance may end in death. In the 1930s, a bear roaming around Sawmill had "stolen" a five-year-old child who had been missing for days. Family members enlisted the help of a medicine man who knew the chants of the Mountainway ceremony that would urge the bear to release the child. Four days later, following prayers and songs, the searchers found the child unharmed. Around this same time, a second child disappeared, taken by a bear in the Chuska Mountains. This time some white people organized a rescue party, armed themselves with rifles, and went in search. "They didn't do that in the Navajo way. So the bear slammed that baby girl into some rock walls and killed her. She was dead when they found her. They should have prayed to it; the bear knew they were planning to shoot it and so did that."[50] Even in more recent times, children were taught never to say the word "bear" when in the Chuska Mountains, because the animals will be attracted and there may be trouble.[51] Navajos also say that bears from the Chuska and Lukachukai ranges should never cross over to Black Mesa or else they will bring bad luck.

A final example of a land formation that holds significance for the Navajos lies not in the mountains, but in the desert—the 1,800-foot-high volcanic neck called Shiprock (Tsé Bit'a'í—Winged Rock), lying east of the Carrizo Mountains. Due to its prominence, there are a number of different stories with variations embedded within, but there is no doubt that this pinnacle is important to the Navajos. River Junction Curly, Blessingway singer, provides one of the most detailed accounts of these narratives, which is retold here in abbreviated form to give a sense of the richness of the oral tradition that defines so much of Navajo land.[52] Monster Slayer—during his journey to locate, kill, and rid the region of creatures preying on the Navajo people—set out to destroy two Rock Monsters (*tse'ináhálééhlé*—Drops onto Rocks). Armed with lightning arrows, a life feather, flint club, and Holy Wind (tucked in his ear folds to whisper guidance) the warrior chanted, "Supernaturally I came after the monster," as he approached Shiprock. "I am long life; I am one to be feared as supernaturally I came after the monster, *hi yi hi pah!*"[53]

The female Rock Monster descended, snatching Monster Slayer from the ground, then flew to the sharp-edged Shiprock, where she dropped the warrior. Instead of being dashed upon the pinnacle, his life feather allowed him to alight softly, before he crawled into a recess. The monster told its two offspring to eat what she had just left, promising to later return. Monster Slayer emerged from hiding and asked the two young tse'ináhálééhlé when they expected their father back. They answered, "It is usually exactly at noon, when over there along the Mountain-Which-Lies-Elevated [Lukachukai], male rain begins to fall." As for their mother: "When [the sun] is starting down a little, and along Beautiful Mountain, female rain begins, that is the time our mother usually returns." Just as predicted, the rain began at noon, the bird returned, and Monster Slayer shot it from behind a rock wall he had fashioned. The evil creature crashed below, giving rise to a tremendous earthquake. As the sun disappeared, a dark mist with many rainbows surrounded Beautiful Mountain as the mother bird returned with her prey. She, too, was shot down with a lightning arrow and smashed into the ground below.

Now it was time for the children. He called them out from their cave and threatened to kill them. They pleaded for their lives four times before he relented, then seizing the male, he removed its tongue, spoke words over it, and then placed it back in its mouth with the admonition,

Shiprock, a large volcanic neck of igneous stone, with the Carrizo Mountains in the background. This rock formation figures as a prominent site in many Navajo traditional songs, prayers, and stories that teach of power and obtaining safety. Best known is that of Monster Slayer killing two evil birds preying on the people. Courtesy of Kay Shumway.

"From this day on be sure to remember the things you have promised about yourself! In days to come, when earth surface people come into being, they will make use of you." The bird flew off as a golden eagle. He did the same to the younger female bird, providing similar counsel with a pledge that if she failed to live up to her agreement, he would find and kill her. She flew off as an owl to the La Plata range with a charge to provide a warning voice to the Navajos. With the assistance of Bat Woman, Monster Slayer descended the pinnacle.[54] There are still other stories that testify of the power and importance of the Shiprock formation expressed in the form of core survival values, important to the Navajo people as they struggled to make a living and fend off enemies.

Navajos during the Spanish and Mexican Eras

This brings us to a time far more recognizable, as more contemporary history takes over from deep history and religious mythology of the Navajos. What follows is an overview of the interaction of five different cultures—Ute, Spanish, Mexican, Navajo, and Anglo American—during a tumultuous series of events that spanned roughly three centuries (1600–1870). Each of these nations has its own complex history and well-researched literature that will only be dealt with here as it affected events along the Chuska Mountain range and valley area to the east.[55] Broad brushstrokes of generalities give an overview of events, but one should realize that there were always exceptions to the rule—too many to note here. One quick example suffices. Historically, the San Juan River was the tribal boundary separating Ute lands to the north from Navajo lands to the south. To cross the river meant entering enemy territory at a time when warfare was intense. There were, however, small groups of Navajos who, because of trade relations, intermarriage, and formal agreements, were allowed to live in Ute territory, and in some instances, were even protected by their neighbors. Sometimes these friends assisted and even fought for each other against their own tribal members. Cayetano and his family led one such Navajo group that befriended the Utes, but he was very much the exception, as warfare generally raged between the two tribes.

Without doubt, the Chuska Mountains and Slope were important areas of settlement and resources for the Navajos, long before the Spanish entered the region. Initially, the Navajos lived as hunters and gatherers, moving to the mountains in the spring and summer and to lower elevations in canyon country or on the plains during the winter. Unlike the Utes, who lived in mobile tepees made of deer, elk, and buffalo skins, the Navajos built sturdy hogans of logs and dirt for the cold winter months and brush shelters that broke the wind and provided shade when it was warm. Horticulture became increasingly important. As with the Ancestral Puebloans, corn, beans, and squash were agricultural mainstays, as cotton, watermelon, and pumpkins joined their list of cultigens. They dried and stored much of this food in large bell-shaped underground storage pits. There were a few larger irrigation projects along the San Juan River and in the vicinity of today's Chinle and Many Farms, but dry farming techniques with their small check dams or pot irrigation provided limited moisture to many of the small plots distant from perennial sources of water.

The Spanish introduced horses, sheep, goats, and cattle to the Indians of the Southwest, which increased mobility of the Navajos, while they also became more sedentary due to agriculture. The two cultures traded some of these animals, but many were also stolen by Navajo warriors skilled in the art of raids and ambush. Difficult to find, unpredictable in pattern, and highly mobile after obtaining the horse, groups of Navajo men directed by local and regional leaders (*naat'áanii*) raided so successfully, that at times Spanish, Mexican and even Anglo settlements were abandoned. Retaliation followed—not only to punish the culprits, retrieve stolen livestock, and send a message of revenge—but also to kill the men and enslave women and children to serve in the homes and fields of their captors. Each Euro-American group was quick to enlist traditional enemies of the Navajos, often rewarding and sometimes supplying them with the means to take the fight to their opponents. At other times, payment came during the slave fairs held in Santa Fe, Abiquiu, Taos, and other towns in New Mexico.

For the Navajos, who had a history of conflict with their neighbors, this meant that they were often at odds with different pueblo groups spread throughout the territory. The Utes to the north, however, were especially anxious and effective in fighting their traditional enemy; alliances with the Spanish, Mexicans, and Americans soon followed. Times would change, circumstances would shift, agreements would be broken, but generally, the Navajos were most often on the outside and against those allied with Euro-Americans. The clearest explanation of what life was like for the Navajo people living in the Chuska region comes from reports written by people who entered the area on punitive missions or to gather information. With the exception of these forays, there is little written about life in this region until the 1880s, when general warfare had ceased, the Navajos had returned from their exile at Fort Sumner, and they had begun expanding into lands to support a new way of life.

The spread of the Spanish empire from Mexico into New Mexico and beyond, received its first boost toward permanency with the establishment of its capital in Santa Fe in 1610; it took another hundred years to found the town of Albuquerque, and so it is not surprising that until the end of the 1700s and the early 1800s, reports concerning the Navajos living in the Chuska area were vague. The first specific information concerning this hinterland came in 1786, when the governor of Santa Fe learned that there were five regional divisions comprising the Navajo tribe, with one of them located in the Chuska Valley. Collectively, these five groups had one thousand warriors and five hundred horses. In reality, this report referred only to the core groups in relatively close proximity to Spanish territory and not those far-flung elements living across the landscape.[56] Ten years later there was more specificity, identifying ten bands, three of which lived in the Chuska, Tunicha, and Carrizo areas. The report continued that "they sow corn and other vegetables. They raise sheep and manufacture coarse cloth, blankets, and other textiles of wool which they trade in New Mexico. In past times they were enemies of the Spaniards; at present they are their faithful friends and are governed by a general who is appointed by the governor."[57]

The peace did not last long, encouraging Governor Don Fernando Chacon in 1800 to lead an expedition of five hundred men into the Tunicha Mountains to attack Navajo homes. Twenty Navajo chiefs met the advance party, sued for peace, and paid for their crimes with cows, blankets, tanned hides, and one Hopi captive.[58] This is the first recorded account of a punitive expedition into the Chuska range by Euro-Americans, establishing a pattern that grew increasingly common during the next six decades. By 1818, the Spanish faced a general uprising with Utes and Navajos from the Carrizo Mountains, who were upset over their loss of lands and so raided Abiquiu.[59] The conflict droned on, and even with the control of New Mexico passing from the Spanish to the Mexicans in 1821, there was no cessation of hostilities. The Mexicans (Hispanic descendants of the Spanish) proved to be far less organized with weaker military clout than their Spanish progenitors.

Over the next quarter century, the Mexicans and Navajos took their turn punishing each other with the Tunicha Mountains playing a significant role as a place for the Indians to escape. The range with its passes and defensive heights became an important refuge for Navajo protection. In July 1823, Captain Julian Armijo fought a battle in the Tunicha Mountains where fourteen Navajos of both sexes were killed; another expedition of one thousand Mexicans and Jemez Indians was ambushed in Washington Pass in the dead of winter 1835. A year later, again in the winter, a detachment of Mexican soldiers fought against four Navajo rancherias in the Chuskas, killed twenty warriors, and captured a woman, fourteen children, and 5,300 sheep; the same group killed eight warriors near the Carrizo Mountains and captured 2,000 sheep.[60] The Navajos later reported one hundred women and children missing, following the attack.[61] Mexicans and Navajos continued to chip away at each other through raids and a scorched-earth policy until the United States gained control of this territory in 1848 through the Treaty of Guadalupe Hidalgo.

The Early American Era

With a few strokes of a pen, the Navajos faced a new protagonist. At first, this seemed like a wonderful opportunity. After all, hadn't these Americans been fighting their traditional enemies—first the Spanish and then the Mexicans—for centuries? Surely they could link arms with their new ally and render their mutual enemy more stinging defeats. Soon, however, the Indians learned that the United States now assumed the responsibility of protecting all people under its rule, including the Navajos' friends and foes. A new treaty explained these developments. On May 20, 1848, Colonel E. W. B. Newby offered a "Treaty of Peace and Amity" in a meeting held at Beautiful Mountain. The agreement, signed by José Largo, appointed leader of the Navajo Nation with seven other chiefs, committed all to "a firm and lasting peace," safe trade and travel throughout the territory, repatriation of prisoners on both sides, peace among the different factions in New Mexico, and a payment of three hundred sheep and one hundred mules and horses by the Navajos.[62] Although the U.S. Senate never ratified the treaty, the Navajos agreed to live by its terms.

Among the principal leaders in attendance was Narbona (Nahabaahi), a powerful naat'áanii who had lived in the Chuska-Tunicha area most of his life. Fortunately, there is sufficient information preserved through oral history to piece together his life as it spanned all three Euro-American eras. Born in 1766 on the eastern slope of the Chuska Mountains near Sanostee, Narbona was a member of his mother's clan, called the Red-Streaked-Earth (Táchii'nii) people. The two prominent clans in this area were "Middle of the Mountain" (Dziłałnii') and "Holy Being" (Yé'ii Dine'é), the latter being that of his father.[63] Around 1800, Narbona assumed leadership of the Navajos living in the area between the Chuska-Tunicha Mountains and Chaco River, had three wives, a dozen children, and owned over two thousand sheep. As the Spanish and Mexicans colluded with the Utes and other tribes to attack the Navajos, Narbona moved to Beautiful Mountain, enhanced its defensive capability, and prepared to take the fight to his enemies. His raids against a weakened Spanish military and isolated settlements applied sufficient pressure to encourage a treaty between the two warring powers in 1819.[64] In the ensuing years, Narbona continued to defend the Chuska Valley against Utes, Comanches, Apaches, and Mexican settlers, eyeing the land for their own purposes. Conflict followed with two substantial victories won by Narbona in 1835–36, with more raids through 1848.[65]

The Newby Treaty was not enough to halt the conflict. Incessant fighting on both sides continued to fuel the fire, Navajo elders finding it very difficult to control their young men, among whom was Manuelito, Narbona's son-in-law.[66] The old chief had consistently promoted peace with his followers, met in council with military leaders on a number of occasions, and surrendered livestock upon request, but to no avail. During the summer of 1849, Territorial Governor Colonel John M. Washington, in company with New Mexico's first Indian agent, James S. Calhoun, set out with a large force of federal troops, civilian New Mexico Volunteers, and Indian allies in a show of force to encourage the Navajos to adopt peace. The group departed from Santa Fe on August 16 with the goal of pushing into the Indians' heartland of Canyon de Chelly, where an agreement with all the major chiefs was to be signed. By August 12, the force had reached the Tunicha range, having encountered small groups of Navajos along the way.

First Lieutenant James H. Simpson, topographer for this expedition, kept extensive notes on the journey and provided a detailed assessment of the fateful events that occurred. As the force traveled on a general northwest course through the Tunicha Valley, they found large Indian cornfields and a growing number of Navajos coming to greet them and to provide livestock as a sign of their willingness to return things that had been stolen. The pueblo and Navajo auxiliaries accompanying the soldiers rode out to meet the warriors.[67] The formation pushed through the congregating Indians and moved toward their evening encampment on Tunicha Creek, less than a mile south and west of today's Two Grey Hills Trading Post.

The barren lands of the valley that summer gave way to an abundance of lush fields of corn. Simpson commented on the "very extensive and luxuriant cornfields, the plants looking finer than any I have seen in this country . . . owing to the deep planting, which the Navahos practiced more than other Indians. They plant as deep as a foot or a foot-and-a-half. . . ."[68] No doubt the Navajos were using some of the fields created by the Ancestral Puebloans. Washington directed that his men and horses should take full advantage of what was there, regardless of how the Indian caretakers felt; the Navajos were angry as they watched their hard labor devoured by this invading army. A group of Navajo leaders arrived at the camp in the afternoon to meet with Washington and Calhoun. They were told that they were to submit to all demands made in the Newby Treaty or else face a larger, more hostile army. They should also attend the signing of the next treaty at Canyon de Chelly with the rest of the major Navajo leaders. The Indians' response was positive, saying that by noon the next day, all the major chiefs in the area would be present and ready to meet with Washington.

On August 31, at the appointed time, Narbona, José Largo, and Archuleta with an estimated 300 to 400 warriors, listened and then agreed to the stipulations for peace with a promise to have representatives at the future signing. As the meeting ended, one of the New Mexican volunteers spied a horse he believed had been stolen from him a few months previous. Washington ordered the immediate surrender of the animal, but when he was told that the man who possessed it had fled, he ordered that another horse of equal value be seized and that any resistance be met with force. What had been a favorable meeting then went sour, with Navajos mounting their horses and fleeing, the military opening fire—first with rifles followed by three shots from a six pounder (cannon)—succeeded by a cavalry pursuit. Narbona, as an eighty-three-year-old peace chief, was among the last to leave. He was one of seven slain warriors remaining on the battlefield, having been cut down by four or five rounds before being scalped for a trophy.[69] The next day, a small group of Navajos approached Washington, suing for peace and promising to be at the future council. The colonel accepted the offer, and the military moved through the Tunicha Mountains via what was soon named Washington (Narbona) Pass, and continued on to a successful meeting at Canyon de Chelly on September 9.

Better times lay ahead as this intense friction dissipated through efforts of Captain Henry Linn Dodge, the first agent to work directly with the Navajos. Born in Missouri in 1810, a veteran of the Mexican War, and leader of a company of New Mexican volunteers during Colonel Washington's expedition, he understood the benefit of peace. Beginning

Narbona, a powerful leader of the Navajos in the Chuska
Valley, as sketched by Richard H. Kern on August 31,
1849, the day soldiers killed this chief. Colonel John M.
Washington directed the unprovoked attack against the
Navajos, who were attending a peace conference held in the
area of Two Grey Hills. Courtesy of National Archives.

in May 1853, he proved, for the next three years, to be one of the most
successful agents these people would have. Central to his philosophy
was his admiration for those he served. They reciprocated. He placed
their needs above his own, yet was an unflinching realist who pushed the
government to keep its promises, provide supplies, and maintain treaty
agreements. The Navajos respected this and, with a few exceptions, lived

by their obligations. Red Shirt (Bi'ee Lichii), as the Navajos called him, married a young Navajo woman related to the powerful leader Zarcillos Largo, and established an agency near Sheep Springs at the eastern approach to Washington Pass in the Chuska Valley. His stone house became an important symbol of his desire to befriend and permanently live among his charges.[70]

Dodge brought with him George Carter to introduce blacksmithing to the Navajos, an interpreter named Juan Anea, and two Mexican servants to staff his outreach program. More important, he brought a positive attitude. When his neighbors asked how he dare settle in their midst without a large military force, he told them that the president of the United States and the governor of New Mexico had given him the responsibility, that he had "not the least fear of the [Navajos], as [his] intentions were good in every way possible; that he was there to keep peace with all nations; and that they might kill [him] whenever they found that he gave them bad advice or that he was an injury to them or their country."[71] With this introduction, they warmly welcomed him then sought his guidance in controlling the "bad men among them" that had a penchant for war. It was not long before Dodge issued a trading permit to Jervis Nolan to visit Navajos living along the San Juan River and in the Chuska-Tunicha ranges.

Dodge had a huge task before him. He estimated that the Navajo tribe alone comprised eight thousand people, a quarter of whom were warriors.[72] An example of his effectiveness and bond with these Indians began on October 7, 1851, when a Navajo man shot and killed a soldier near Fort Defiance, then fled north. Two weeks later, Major Henry L. Kendrick and Dodge met in council with a group of leaders near the Carrizo Mountains and demanded that the culprit be turned over to authorities. The officer left the meeting thinking nothing would be done; Dodge "was sanguine that the surrender will be affected." In less than three weeks, the agent and officer had their answer. Dodge met a group of returning warriors near Bennett Peak with prisoner in tow. In a letter written two days later, he explained how he had gone to the principal chief Armijo, who lived near Bennett Peak, and explained that the killer should be apprehended and handed over for punishment. The peace chief replied "that the murderer would be brought to this house in seven days, and if he was not I should have his son as a hostage for his delivery at the Fort."⁷³ On the fifth of November, the Navajos turned over a badly wounded prisoner to the soldiers. Armijo's nephew had shot the man in the groin following a dramatic fight in which the man picked up a shield and protected himself against thirty-eight arrows shot at him, many of which struck the shield in the center. Once the military escort and the Navajos reached Fort Defiance, Major Kendrick ordered a summary execution of the prisoner.

A lot of effort and trust on both sides ensured the peace. Dodge continued to listen to Navajo leaders and dispense aid to promote their people's prosperity. He handed out 150 hoes and twelve axes to Navajos in an exceptionally wet spring in 1855 during which they planted five thousand acres of corn, with smaller amounts of wheat, potatoes, and other vegetables. The Indians requested two Mexican-style mills with stone grinders to process wheat to replace their less efficient manos and metates.⁷⁴ He urged the federal government to confirm the treaty specifying reservation boundaries to prevent New Mexicans from encroaching on their neighbors. Nothing bred intense conflict more quickly than feeling the pinch of settlers taking traditional lands needed for survival. In addition to annual budgetary requests for the agency, he looked forward to creating greater economic and educational independence. To this end, Dodge requested four sets of blacksmith tools and one thousand pounds of iron. Eighteen practicing Navajo blacksmiths began making bridle bits, rings, buckles, and other items as the first recorded metal workers and jewelry makers on the reservation.⁷⁵ Little wonder the Navajos trusted and liked their agent.

This relationship, however, was cut short on November 19, 1856. Dodge and Chief Armijo were hunting for deer that day thirty-five miles south of Zuni, when they split up. Armijo returned to the main party of soldiers operating in the area, but Dodge did not, giving rise to a number of searches, none of which bore fruit other than to find a spot where he had been taken captive. Inquiries by friendly Indians among various tribal groups revealed that a group of Coyotero and Mogollon Apaches had been raiding and fighting in the area and had spotted the lone agent, killed him with a carbine, and took his scalp. On February 11, a forty-man detachment returned, having found Dodge's remains in an arroyo near where he had been captured; a week later they were buried at Fort Defiance. Thus ended one of the most revered and successful

Indian agents the Navajos have ever had, while also closing the agency at Sheep Springs.[76]

The Fearing Time and Long Walk Period

Dodge's death saddened the Navajos, who held him in high esteem, opening the door to one of the most destructive periods of their history. Now, the flames of traditional animosity flared into an all-consuming war, when Utes, Pueblo tribes, New Mexicans, and the United States military assumed the task of ending the incessant friction. Each group had their own reasons for wanting to fight the Navajos. For the Utes there were old scores to settle against their traditional enemy, as well as money and encouragement to receive from the federal government. In addition to keeping the Utes away from frontier settlements, it also provided a unique economic and military opportunity that supplemented these Indians' shrinking economy. For pueblo warriors, many were tired of the constant raiding; New Mexicans had similar reasons plus a desire to obtain more land and slaves. As for the United States government, this was an opportunity to end a simmering, low-grade problem that intermittently erupted into large-scale confrontation. The Americans also saw it as a means to unite disparate native tribes and effectively use their knowledge against a common foe, while at the same time conserving military forces that could be sent back east for the approaching Civil War.

For roughly ten years starting in 1858, the Navajos lived through what they now call the "Fearing Time" (Nídahadzid dáá) combined with the "Long Walk" period, resulting in one of the most traumatic eras in their history. Much has been written of this time, when the Navajo people, following what appears to be a fairly short resistance, surrendered in droves to the U.S. military, collected at Fort Defiance and other designated sites, then moved in a series of forced marches to Fort Sumner (Hwéeldi) on the Pecos River in eastern New Mexico.[77] An estimated half of the Navajo tribe, over eight thousand members, remained at Fort Sumner between 1864–68, while the rest scattered to peripheral regions, where they hid from raiding parties anxious to kill and capture people and livestock.

Typical of the thinking of the time, one military commander in July 1858, frustrated in trying to capture a "murderer" in Cayetano's band

who had subsequently fled to the Tunicha Mountains, wrote: "I respect-
fully suggest a large military force take to the field against the Navajos
not later than in September. . . . In the meantime, I hope every encouragement will be given to the Utahs of Abiquiu to repeat their raids. I
have no doubt that a very sufficient force of Mexicans could be had
under the name of guides and spies, under suitable commanders, that
for a promise of booty could be employed at a very low price."[78] Result:
ten Navajos killed and "many wounded," 6,500 sheep and eighty horses
captured, and "all the blankets, buffalo robes and corn destroyed."[79] The
impact of this type of warfare on people living in the Chuska Mountains
and Slope was dramatic. A few examples paint a picture of what life was
like during this reign of terror over the territory, especially by the Utes,
who crossed the traditional boundary of the San Juan River and raided
deep into Navajo lands.

In the early days of the conflict, the Navajos remained in large groups
in order to fight together. Their fields and flocks were well established,
and the young men were confident that they could wage an effective war,
while the older and wealthier Navajos still made overtures for peace. In
mid-October 1858, a group of Navajos stole livestock from Cebolleta. The
citizens of the town pursued the retreating thieves as they made their way
to the Chuska Mountains and caught up with them. Approximately 300
Navajos faced 85 Mexicans and were ready to defend their hundred stolen cattle. They selected a canyon in the mountains and built a number of
small campfires to lure the pursuers into a trap where the Navajos would
have an advantage. Taking the bait, the Mexicans fought for two days
and nights, making a breastwork of logs and dead Indians for protection.
Desperate combat ensued, and "had it not been for the intercession of a
rich Navajo woman, the whole party would doubtless have been mas-
sacred. She, seeing the desperateness of the fight, appealed to her people
to stop after having lost some of their best men. Her entreaties prevailed
and the Indians retreated."[80] Eight Mexicans died outright, and a dozen
others were wounded, some of whom died later. The Navajos returned to
their homes in the Chuskas with their newly acquired livestock.

The Navajo experience during this turbulent time is offered only in
bits and pieces here. Francis Toledo recalls his grandmother telling about
when she was fourteen years old and being led by Manuelito. He collected
the people and moved them to the Chuska Mountains because of enemy

attacks coming from all directions. The exodus was in the winter when the snow was deep, but they reached their destination safely. He then had the people capture eagles for their feathers, make extra bows and spears, and plenty of arrows, counseling, "We will not be killed poorly; we will be considered dangerous."[81] Toledo suggests that the warriors dipped their arrows in snake blood, which caused wounded enemies to swell and die quickly, engendering real fear of Navajo warriors.

Franc Newcomb collected some stories from those who lived during this period, providing a variety of experiences. The Utes captured one boy, at the age of ten, carried him off to Sleeping Ute Mountain, and kept him enslaved for six years until he stabbed his owner and escaped. A woman, when a child, was stolen near Isleta Pueblo, traded to a Jemez man who, in turn, sold her to a Mexican family for some sheep; she eventually married a Mexican. Another ten-year-old girl went with her parents to Fort Defiance, expecting to make the Long Walk under the military's protection. She became separated from the group, was caught by a Mexican, and enslaved for four years. When her father returned to the Navajos' newly promised reservation, he bought his daughter back from her owner, but it cost him everything he had, including two horses. He walked the rest of the way to his homeland. Narbona's granddaughter, Pretty Girl (Zonnie Ahtay or Nishzhóní At'ééd), perhaps summarized best the experience of the women who did not surrender, when she told Newcomb that "many of her childhood memories are of hasty messengers arriving with warnings of raiding parties of soldiers, Mexicans, or Apaches. Then would come the hurried bundling of blankets, pots, and food supplies into long rolls to be carried on their shoulders as they fled back into the mountains to a hidden cave, where they could find shelter until the raiders were gone."[82]

Because the military understood that the Chuska-Tunicha areas were not only the most productive lands for cultivating crops in Navajo territory, but also the best grazing areas for livestock, it concentrated its forces in divesting its opponents of this key terrain. Continuous forays by opposing elements proved effective. Captain J. G. Walker, on a reconnaissance through the area, reported that he found only deserted camps and fields abandoned by the enemy.[83] Just as characteristic was the experience of a military force a few months later executing a search and destroy operation on the eastern crest of the Tunicha Mountains. With the help of a spyglass, a small reconnaissance element, detached from the main force, spied a column of smoke three miles down the mountain. As the soldiers descended toward the camp, they encountered a lone Navajo man who quickly fled to give warning. Pursuit brought the attackers closer to the cluster of hogans and also a well-traveled horse and sheep trail that they believed would lead to the real prize. After charging through the piñon and juniper forest, they entered a glen where six to eight warriors were watching a herd of 62 horses, 120 sheep, and 130 goats. The men fled, leaving the animals in the hands of the soldiers, who next followed the tracks, which took them to a camp of a dozen homes. "Knowing that the alarm was spread throughout Tunicha—as signal smoke and fires were soon made upon the tops of the mountains," the soldiers fired the hogans and returned to Fort Defiance.[84] The report outlining this operation concluded with, "The great mass of the Tunicha Indians have evidently fled from these mountains and probably gone northward to the Valley of the San Juan with their flocks."

There were still those who lingered. In the spring of 1860 the military chased a group of Navajos on the east slope of the Chuska Mountains, beyond Washington Pass, and captured two thousand sheep, fifty horses, and fourteen women and children, but there was no resistance by men. This was all part of a conscious effort to keep the entire range free from Navajos so that they could not return once driven out.[85] Denying this area effectively maintained pressure so that in 1863, Captain Francis McCabe at Fort Canby wrote, "The impression here is that the Navajos have adopted a new policy and have given up on this portion of the country, if not forever, at least until the war is over as there are no Indians in this neighborhood, and with the exception of a band said to be in the Chuskas, who have signified their desire to accept the proposition of the Commanding General, to emigrate to the Bosque Redondo [Fort Sumner], and engage in the cultivation of the soil, they have all gone far southward."[86]

For Navajos who were captured or voluntarily surrendered, they were collected at Fort Defiance and other posts around Navajo land and eventually made the "Long Walk" to Fort Sumner in east central New Mexico. There they spent four years under military control before returning to their homeland; for those who continued to flee, there remained a life of constant vigilance, general privation, and potential hostility until the government signed a treaty recognizing permanent peace in 1868. In the meantime, the Chuska-Tunicha Mountain area rested from decades of turmoil and strife. The days of large-scale conflict, slave raids, and broken agreements leading to war were now over. When the Navajos returned, they entered into a new era of tribal history.

CHAPTER TWO

From Pre-post to Posts

Establishing Economic Patterns on the Land,
1870–1905

A s the Navajos returned from Fort Sumner to a reservation with clearly defined boundaries, they began a new lifestyle. The days of intense warfare were over, their dependence on agriculture and livestock increased dramatically, and their population began to grow. They were a badly chastened tribe, but there were opportunities that lay in the future that allowed for continuation of their own distinctive traditions. While many other American Indian groups during the last quarter of the nineteenth century had reached their nadir, the Navajos were on the climb, beginning to grow and prosper in their desert landscape. It was not a rags-to-riches story that occurred overnight—indeed there were years of drought, famine, and loss that at times seemed overwhelming—but the general trajectory of growth and prosperity was upward. Reason: the Navajos embraced a way to enter the mainstream economy of America by selling livestock, harvesting wool, weaving blankets, and eventually marketing aspects of their culture. The connecting link that made this exchange between two different cultures possible was the trading post, which by the beginning of the twentieth century had become institutionalized. Many other tribes were not as fortunate. With the buffalo gone, the frontier closed, huge cultural gaps between late nineteenth and early twentieth-century Anglo culture and economy, and a reservation system that benefited from not having Indians advance, their chances of prospering were even less than those of the Navajos.

Internal and External Opportunities

Between the return of the Navajos in 1868 and 1900, the people underwent a series of events that prepared them for the florescence of what is
now considered traditional culture during the first third of the twentieth century. The experiences of this nascent period are discussed elsewhere (see endnote) and so will only be touched on here as they relate
to the northern end of the reservation.[1] The government provided
the Navajos 3.5 million acres in the form of a rectangular box that sat
astride the border between what are now the states of New Mexico and
Arizona. Included within these boundaries were the Chuska-Tunicha
range as well as the Chuska and Chinle Valleys and a small portion
of the San Juan Valley, with the tribal agency located in the south at
Fort Defiance. Navajo agents soon realized that the growing population dependent on the livestock industry and agriculture could not
sustain itself on the limited and often barren land that the Navajos had
been given. For instance, in 1879 Agent Galen Eastman argued that his
charges "have as good a right to that belt of country south of the San
Juan, although off their reservation, to herd their flocks as people on
the north side to graze their herds. . . . As there is but little water along
the eastern boundary of the Navajo Reservation, I would recommend
that you urge an additional reservation at once for the Navajos by executive order of ten miles width."[2] Subsequently, in 1880 land additions to
the east and south were made, one to the north and west in 1884, with
three others to the west between 1878 and 1900, reflecting expansion
of the tribe not only in landholdings but also in economic and demographic growth. The returning Navajos, over 7,000 in number, joined
those who had avoided capture, making the estimated number of tribal
members 9,000, a figure that seems far too low; by 1892, the population
had doubled.[3]

The people returned to their accustomed places of habitation to find
their traditional enemies—in the north the Utes—waiting for them.
Although there had been promises of peace, intermittent raiding and
fighting on both sides renewed, encouraging the Navajos to stay well
south of the San Juan River until the inflamed animosity subsided
and more peaceful relations ensued. Slim Woman, granddaughter of

Narbona, tells what these early times were like. After a year's wait at Fort Defiance to receive materials from the government—an iron Dutch oven and skillet, a hoe, ax, shovel and twenty yards of trade cloth—she, with her family and extended family, returned to Narbona's old camp to find everything had been obliterated, with only ghosts inhabiting the site. They moved a few miles away into the Chuska Valley where they built corrals, dikes, and irrigation ditches that soon had water covering the newly planted fields of corn and other vegetables. Fear of the Utes forced the family and others to live in the mountains during the summer, visiting their gardens to turn water coursing down the slope onto them in the spring and to channel the ground flow from summer rains. They built permanent homes in the Tunicha Valley for winter use, and in the spring constructed temporary shelters near their fields on Tunicha Creek (Captain Tom's Wash today) with camouflaged storage pits some distance from the garden. One time the family received word that the Utes were coming their way, and so everyone in the area put their moccasins on backward, stepped in each other's footsteps as they walked single file, and moved north toward the approaching enemy. Once they got close, the Navajos veered to the west and hid in Sanostee Canyon, while the Utes continued on to the Tunicha Valley, where they feasted on corn, melons, and mutton, inadvertently allowing the Navajos to flee deeper into the mountains and safety.[4] As time progressed and the region became more settled, these types of forays ended.

By 1890 the conflict had greatly subsided and there was a general population trend that caused Navajo expansion to the north and a solidifying of their landholdings in the Chuska Valley. Henry C. Adams, a government farmer, wrote to the commissioner of Indian affairs to explain what he saw happening south of the San Juan River and north of Captain Tom's Wash: "During the summer this country is occupied by a large number of Navajos, who raise large crops of corn, wheat, and vegetables. The pasturage being excellent, great herds of horses, cattle, sheep, and goats feed annually on the same. But as winter approaches, the inhabitants move to the foothills to the west or to the San Juan River, where fuel is plenty, where they remain until seed time. . . . Further to the north, along the south bank of the San Juan River, there is a greater density of population than on any other portion of the reservation. . . .

[They have] constructed irrigating ditches by which they are able to raise very good crops of corn, wheat, and vegetables."[5]

Other events beyond the reservation boundaries began to shape what would later be a prosperous economy. Beginning in 1880 the Atlantic and Pacific Railroad started laying track west of Albuquerque; by 1885 this transportation system had become a major boon to opening the Southwest to economic development. It proved to be a prime outlet for transporting Navajo products both east and west. For those living in the Chuska Valley, the founding of Gallup in 1881 was tied directly to the establishment of this line. Farther north in Colorado and Utah, the Denver and Rio Grande Western Railroad, completed in 1883, gave rise to a transportation network for residents living in the more northern part of the reservation.

Towns and industries sprang from the desert, fed by commerce brought in on the rails. In 1875 the government opened northwestern New Mexico above the Navajo Reservation for settlement. A year later, the first settlers established Farmington on the San Juan River, while within the next fifteen years Fruitland (1878), Burnham and Bloomfield (1881), Olio and Jewett (1884), and Aztec (1887) were added to the list of towns that traded with the Navajos. Fifty miles away from Farmington sat Durango, Colorado, a railroad town established in 1880, which shipped freight, not only from New Mexico and surrounding towns like Mancos (1881) and Cortez (1886), but also from posts and towns on the San Juan River in Utah such as Montezuma Creek and Aneth (1878), Bluff (1880), and Monticello (1887). With railroads and towns in place, the Navajo economy was positioned to boom.

This had not always been the case. The families returning from Fort Sumner were totally destitute. Their four long years of imprisonment had consumed everything just to survive with little to spare. Fortunately, their agent, Theodore Dodd, in 1867, a year before their release, pronounced to the government a formula that not only appealed to these Indians but was totally practical for their circumstance: "If the Navajos were furnished liberally with sheep and goats, they would, in a short time, be enabled to furnish themselves with meat for their subsistence, milk for their families, and wool to make a good share of their clothing."[6] And that is what happened. The Treaty of 1868 promised the people 14,000 sheep and 1,000 goats, which were provided a year later, adding to the roughly 4,000 sheep and goats and 500 horses they had in their care when they left Fort Sumner.[7] By 1880 the Navajos owned one million sheep and goats, which by 1892 had grown to an estimated 1,715,984; horse herds expanded from approximately 8,000 in 1870 to 250,000 by 1890.[8]

Farming also became increasingly effective. The government issued corn and wheat seeds, the latter being not nearly as desirable, but the Navajos' previous experience with horticulture stood them in good stead. Especially along the San Juan River, once tension with the Utes subsided, large-scale agricultural projects often employed Anglo government farmers to assist increased production. Agents issued improved technology such as metal hoes, shovels, axes, plows, and wooden wagons, making agriculture more practical and appealing. At the same time, while hunting and gathering continued on an ever-diminishing scale, the use of domesticated plants and animals increased dramatically to the point where some historians believe that the people had become economically self-sufficient by 1880, at least when compared to the pre–Fort Sumner days, with improved standards yet to come.[9]

Enter the trading post. Lehman Spiegelberg obtained the first license to operate a trading post on the Navajo Reservation at Fort Defiance in August 1868. The store was small, its offerings limited, and not much profit resulted, mainly because the Navajos did not have much to barter. Off-reservation trading posts located around the boundaries were just as limited. Even as late as 1880, only one on-reservation and six or seven off-reservation stores existed. Then things started to develop as the railroad took hold, Anglo and Navajo settlement increased, tribal landholdings expanded, numbers of livestock multiplied, and a newfound interest in Navajo crafts evolved. By 1889 there were an estimated thirty off-reservation and nine on-reservation posts, the latter doing about half of the total business.[10] As early as the mid-1870s, wool became of increasing interest to markets in the East. In 1875, Navajo agents recorded 60,000 pounds shipped, by 1882 that number had jumped to 1,000,000, and by 1890 it was 1,370,000. At the same time in the late 1880s, agents reported shipping 300,000 sheep pelts, 100,000 goat skins, and $24,000 worth of woven blankets.[11] The stage was set for a rapid increase of trade with a corresponding number of posts on the reservation.

Meanwhile, stores off the reservation did much of the trading. Agent John H. Bowman, in February 1886, spoke of the business the traders in Albuquerque were doing in wool. Because of lower freight costs, competition, and basic stock items, these men were able to handle high-volume trade with Navajo customers, whom Bowman characterized as "sharp" traders and shoppers willing to go to other stores if they were not satisfied with an existing offer. Most of the wool exchanged hands during June and July following the shearing of the sheep's winter coat. Bowman noted, "Wool is not sold by the pound, but by the 'blanket.' The trader weighs it, and informs the seller, how much he will give for the lot, not how many pounds there are or how much per pound. Custom has made the Indian well acquainted with the value of each lot, and if the trader's offer is not up to his expectations, he bundles up his wool and hunts a more liberal buyer."[12]

Agent Bowman went on to note that there were only three trading posts on the reservation at this time. Besides two stores located at Fort Defiance, there was a small post at Tsaile about fifty miles north, with potential for another one at Chinle, west of Tsaile, where many Navajos had farms with large fields of corn. After identifying Washington Pass as being about thirty-five miles north of Fort Defiance, he mentioned a second possible location for a post, "Manuelitos Camp" in the southeast corner of the reservation. Bowman felt that this was the "best point for trade of any above named [sites] were it not for the fact that the Indians who frequent that locality are of a very lawless disposition and no one has yet been found who was *brave* [his emphasis] to keep a store there any length of time although several have tried it. Still, success in this trade depends as much on inducements and attractions offered, as upon locality."[13] He went on to emphasize the isolation of such a post, the need to speak the Navajo language and understand the people's customs, and that communication with the outside world would be cut off. He concluded by recommending that the commissioner of Indian affairs, "grant every one of good morals who desires to have a license to trade on this reservation. The rules of your department are not difficult to comply with and an extensive competition would be a good thing for the Navajos. If it were not profitable for the trader, he could quit."[14] A little over ten years later, there would be those who took the challenge to permanently settle in the Chuska Valley.

Reserving the Reservation

In spite of the technological and economic progress that the Navajos were making during the last quarter of the nineteenth century, there were both new and old problems that confronted them. Increasing settlement around the borders meant greater animosity over rangelands. What had been initially a fluid movement of livestock owners in search of off-reservation grazing lands became increasingly restricted, especially to the east and north as Anglo towns and ranches grew around the borders and across the San Juan River. Friction, often handled by a series of inept agents and angry citizens, boiled over into lively contests for control of the range. Hispanic and Anglo livestock owners coveted lands on the public domain as well as trespassed on reservation lands, just as the Navajos had usurped their neighbor's ranges. In spite of the land additions made to the reservation by the government, large Navajo herds pushed against the cattle and sheep of the settlers. Another constant source of irritation was the sale of alcohol to the Indians. Small-scale violence erupted, resulting in death and misery on both sides of the sale. Add to this severe droughts and extreme winter weather that characterized 1879 and much of the first half of the 1890s, and one can see how competition over resources became inflamed between these two very different cultures.

There was also resentment over something that the Navajos detested—the loss of their land to miners and companies seeking mineral rights. As early as 1875, Agent William F. M. Arny schemed to separate the Carrizo Mountains and the northern third of the reservation by returning these lands to the public domain in exchange for territory south of the reservation. His goals were to gain access to the mountains, where he believed rich deposits of gold and silver would be discovered, and to free the lands along the San Juan River for Anglo use. The area that the Navajos would receive to the south was partially owned by the Atlantic and Pacific Railroad, which it had obtained in an effort to establish the railroad near the southern bottom of the reservation. Arny's plan soon vaporized, but not before drawing attention to the potential of the range to the north.

Renewed interest in 1889 grew when large groups of miners placed increasing pressure on the northern part of the reservation, so the

Indians pushed back. Navajo Agent C. E. Vandever prevented a band of prospectors and cowboys forming in Gallup from entering Navajo lands. Fired up by the report of rich silver and gold lodes, fifty men prepared to invade the Carrizo Mountains. Both the agent and the military authorities stopped this incursion—or so it was believed.[15]

But by the end of March 1890, eighteen of this group were in the Carrizos, holding out against the Indians. The Navajos, under a leader named Black Horse, offered half of the prospectors' horses to the Utes if they would help rid the area of the miners.[16] Two troops of cavalry and the agent evicted the prospectors, warned them not to return, and escorted them off the reservation. Some, however, persisted and came back in June. Vandever feared that "threats of invasion by other parties have been made and other attempts will surely follow, until such time as the Department investigates the extent of the alleged mineral wealth of that region and determines either to close it against miners or open it for development."[17]

While the agent was reporting his action concerning the prospectors, local newspapers generated increasing interest in the Carrizos. The *Albuquerque Citizen* claimed that "the whole truth has not been told and he [Vandever] believes the district to be much richer in the abundance of precious metals which it contains than the most extravagant accounts have ever represented it to be."[18] The newspaper went on to say that Vandever believed the area should be opened up to miners since the Indians cared nothing about mineral wealth, that it was impossible to stop "enterprising white men," that the Carrizo country was "one of the richest gold districts ever discovered in the United States," and that the mountains were too rich to remain in the possession of "savages." The *Durango Herald* chimed in, confirming the existence of tremendous wealth and stating, "The whole United States Army could not protect these mountains now that it is known to a certainty that gold exists. It will be the Black Hills all over again."[19]

On May 10, 1892, the Navajo Commission met at Fort Wingate and proceeded to the Carrizos to inspect the gold and silver deposits. General A. McCook, chairman of the committee, was to determine if there was a basis for opening land negotiations with the Navajos. After scouting the countryside, geologists, scientists, and prospectors all agreed that the sandstone formations that composed most of the mountain

Through treaty and executive order, the government ceded often barren desert land expecting the Navajos to prosper and embrace the dominant culture's civilizing process. This photo, taken outside a male Navajo hogan, illustrates two of the three major legs of their economy—livestock (distant right) and weaving (foreground). The third, agriculture, is not pictured. Used with permission of Utah State Historical Society.

range were barren of precious metals and that the Indians could keep their land.[20]

The Navajo perspective of these events is instructive. Old Mexican, a young man at this time, told how he was called to a meeting at Red Rock by a very old man with white hair and an eagle (colonel insignia) on his shoulder. This soldier sent out two men each day to prospect for miners, but they always returned having found nothing. The leader then called the Navajos together and explained that the army had come to help and protect the Indians:

> But the fellows who sent the note to Washington are not going to give up the mountain. Therefore, I want you Indians to build houses all around the mountain where there are springs and plenty of water. Those houses will represent a fence around the mountain. . . . The white men who gamble and drink and get into debt, with no way to

pay their debts, they are the ones who come to this reservation looking for gold, scheming for some way to pay their debts. Don't let them get a chance to get the best of you. . . . If you ever see another white fellow around here prospecting for gold, saying that he was sent from Washington, don't believe him. If they ever want any more prospecting done, you will see me back again with my men.[21]

Becoming an Indian Trader

The last half of the 1890s brought more settled conditions as many recent social, economic, and technological aspects came into play. For the Navajos living in the Chuska Valley this would manifest itself in three phenomena—the entrance of trading posts, the establishment of the Northern Navajo Agency at Shiprock (1903), and some last ditch efforts to resist white encroachment. The early years of the trading posts are discussed here, with the other two topics in chapters 4 and 5. While off-reservation stores anxiously exchanged goods with visiting Navajos, on-reservation posts developed more slowly. One reason was the approval process for a license. Each applicant who wanted to become an "Indian trader," as they were known in those days, had to fill out a form that the local agency carefully scrutinized. There were the basic questions such as full name, date of birth, residence, and family status, but also more penetrating ones that asked for education level, any indictment of a crime, defects in physical health, involvement with alcohol, and how many relatives were then in the civil service. Accompanying this application were three form letters filled out by character witnesses who answered questions about the trader's moral and work characteristics. All of this would go to the agent, then through the bureaucracy, and finally the desk of the commissioner of Indian affairs for final approval. Anything that raised doubt along the way could disqualify the applicant.

Another imposition was determining the location of a post. From a practical perspective, the store had to be established where Navajo people were living. Roads and natural lines of drift had to be developed in order to keep the flow of commerce and traffic knocking at the trader's door. There also had to be a source of water for both the trader and his visitors. Usually this meant that there were already Navajos living in the area, using the water, and who possibly had already established a community.

In each settlement there were medicine men or leaders whose personality and wishes had to be considered. Thus, the first hurdle was receiving approval of the people in the area as to whether they wanted to have a post nearby. Any conflict could very quickly stop further development. The agent was the next one to approve or disapprove the request. Being on the wrong side of this powerful individual could also halt any progress, and so there was a certain amount of currying favor.

Once the process had satisfactorily run its course and a location was accepted, the trader had to construct the building and put up a $10,000 bond—not a small task in those days of limited financial resources. Most posts followed a general pattern of starting with a tent, moving to a log building, and once well-established, making a more permanent structure from quarried rock or adobe—all obtained at the trader's expense. Since the reservation land was tribal and federal property, the structure did not belong to the trader, only the inventory on the shelves and his personal belongings and furniture. He and his family could quickly be evicted by the agent, but the trader could also pick up roots any time he chose and move to another post on the reservation or leave entirely. Indeed, there was a great deal of shifting locations as traders chose new sites to ply their trade—selling one's store permit to an approved individual and purchasing the right to use another store. The genealogy of post ownership and those hired to run it from a historical perspective was often convoluted. Using the Two Grey Hills Post as an example, during the first forty years of its existence, there were a dozen individuals who either ran or owned the store.

Early Years at Two Grey Hills—The Noels' Experience

In the remainder of this chapter, the reader is exposed to the establishment of three posts in or near the Chuska Valley—Two Grey Hills, Sanostee, with a brief glance at Teec Nos Pos. Two Grey Hills was the first of the three to be built when brothers Henry R. and Frank L. Noel with Joseph R. Wilkins assumed the task in 1897. Henry Noel, born in 1872 in Baltimore, Maryland, had lived a life of varied occupations—from working with a company in Baltimore to placer mining, farming, and trading with the Navajos. Younger brother Frank had lived a similar life, which encouraged both men to obtain more settled careers. So when Wilkins suggested a partnership, the offer had appeal. Wilkins was older and more experienced, having spent two years running a post at Cottonwood Pass, New Mexico, a couple of years freighting on the reservation, and some time doing placer mining.[22] The three men pooled resources, formed a company called Wilkins and Noel headquartered in Fruitland, and set off for their site, fifty miles to the southwest and seventy-five miles north of Gallup, with two wagons filled with tools and equipment. They set up their tent on a bench above Captain Tom's Wash or Big Water's Spring (Tó Ntsaa Bitó) because of a perennial spring and the surface water that ran for a month from the Chuskas two miles away. The men named the site Two Grey Hills because of two prominent sandstone crags known to the Navajos as "Yellow Clay at an Elevation" (Bis Dah Łitso).[23]

Frank later told of his experiences in a self-published history called *Eighty Years in America*.[24] There were many old posts less fortunate than this one whose histories are now lost. The Wilkins and Noel Company had two wagons each pulled by four horses that hauled lumber, windows, doors, and roofing materials along with trade goods, some of which later came from Gallup. The men fashioned adobes with the assistance of Indian labor and completed their store—one large room for trade with a smaller one as living quarters—just in time to move in before winter. But in less than a year's time, Wilkins sold his share in the post to Frank and Henry, then started on another post at Sanostee.

Two Grey Hills did well, which encouraged Frank, who now felt more financially secure, to marry Mary Eliza Roberts from Fruitland. He took a year to build a sixteen-by-sixteen-foot cabin of pine logs hauled seven miles away from the Chuska Mountains. Other materials he transported from Gallup on a six-day round trip or from Durango, one hundred miles away on a ten-day trip. By 1898 he had finished the cabin, married Mary, and returned to being a trader with the assistance of his new wife. She kept the shelves stocked, especially during those spring days when the wool clip came in. The busiest hours in the store were between 1:00 and 5:00 P.M., when sales inside and the purchase of sheep outside spread the traders' efforts thin. Mary learned rudimentary Navajo and gestures to keep the counters flowing with goods, while Frank handled the heavier chores of bagging wool and working with livestock. Dinner waited until the doors closed on the last customer, occasionally pushing store hours into the evening.

Not much time passed before business developed and the post grew. A series of additions described by Frank testify of the effectiveness of the trade and an expansion of the structure typical of many other prosperous posts:

> The storeroom was about twenty-five feet by fifteen. Also there was a pelt and wool room and a general storage room to unload goods, price and mark them, and then put them on the shelves and in the showcases in the main store. There was a big door in the middle of the big store, which opened into what we called the bull pen, a space ten by twelve feet with a counter four feet high on three sides [of the room] and falling on our end with a gate in it. In this way, the Indians did not go around the shelves with the goods, but everything asked for was placed on the counter, which was about three feet wide, and, if they bought, it was paid for then [an item at a time]. As a rule, the trader dealt with each Indian until he was through, and then some other Indian would start to buy.[25]

One of the most important skills of a trader was his ability to evaluate and fairly price the blankets brought in by customers to exchange for goods. Weavers carried their best products to the post in a protective sack, plunked it down on the counter, where the storekeeper removed it from its cover, then unfolded and spread it out. Evaluation of the blanket included the size, tightness of weave, type of fine or coarse wool, composition of warp—wool (preferred) or cotton—symmetry of edges, and presence of weaving errors. Light, well-woven, and visually beautiful blankets of average size commanded a higher price—perhaps $5 to $25, while saddle blankets went from $2.50 to $4.[26] But it was not just the physical evaluation that took place. The trader needed to show the customer that he had deliberately taken time to appreciate the effort that had gone into the product. Maintaining a relationship with the individual was paramount to the success of the trader and the business of the post. Once the store owner decided a fair amount for the blanket—fair meaning making the customer happy and yet one he could mark up and sell for a profit—he would put the number of dollars he was willing to pay next to the blanket. If the weaver accepted the offer, she would take the money, but if it did not seem enough, she just folded it up and put it back in the sack, ready for a trip to a different post.

Most stores had relatively little cash to work with. This gave rise to two unique practices. The first one was an institutionalized means to help Navajos survive during their feast-or-famine economic cycle tied to the livestock industry. Twice a year, the herds of sheep produced substantial amounts of money so that debts could be paid. The shearing of winter coats in the spring brought sacks of clippings to the post, where they were examined, repacked, and paid for by the pound—the eastern wool markets often determining the price for that year. The fall was the time to sell lambs and other livestock, which like the wool, were shipped east. With a successful wool and lamb crop, past debts were paid.

Pawn, or the loaning of items such as silver bridles, concha belts and bracelets, silver coins sewed on clothing as buttons, finely woven blankets, or some other item that could be sold in a common market, was redeemed when payment was made. Both the trader and the customer received a ticket showing the value of the object and when payment was due. Often a six-month "loan" was extended on this "live" pawn, which became "dead" pawn if the agreed-upon time limit expired without settlement. The trader was technically free to sell the dead pawn, but for good customer relations, often held onto it, sometimes for years at a time, rather than anger the individual or family to whom the treasured object belonged.

Some posts also used tokens—stamped metal discs the size of a coin—with a specific store's design and redeemable value. For instance, if a customer needed a dollar's value of goods, but did not want to purchase something at the time, he might be given a token in place of the actual dollar, with the understanding that he should return to the store that issued it when he was ready to purchase supplies. Tokens ranged in value from a nickel, dime, quarter, and half-dollar to dollar. While some stores honored tokens from competitors, most did not. The federal government, at times, took issue with trading posts creating their own money system just as it did with Navajos taking nickels, dimes, quarters, half-dollars, and dollars, then soldering a loop on the back to serve as buttons or decorations on clothing. Traders were told to refuse the defaced currency when offered in payment, but the system continued to function when not under government scrutiny.

Frank Noel was happy for some time at Two Grey Hills. He and Henry hired Navajos to freight for the store, bought lots of wool and blankets from customers, and joined in on community feasts at harvest time when corn and other crops matured. The two brothers, however, had differing views as to how to run the business, while Mary was having problems with health. Frank decided to return with his wife to Kirtland, so in the spring of 1900, he sold his interest in the store to his newly arrived brother Hambleton Bridger Noel, usually called "H. B." Town life and Frank and Mary's home on a forty-acre plot were appealing, but earning a living was difficult. He dabbled in a variety of occupations including laboring on a railroad construction gang, working as a hired hand on another man's ranch, and logging for a sawmill, but operating a trading post was still in his blood. Frank decided to work for a logging company on the reservation while also hiring out as a part-time clerk in a newly created post at Sanostee, built by his previous companion, Joe Wilkins.

It was a similar story for his brother H. B., who had come to the Southwest for health reasons. His serious case of consumption soon started to ameliorate as the dry exhilarating climate combined with exercise to heal his wracked body. He blossomed in this new environment and was attracted to the life of an Indian trader. In 1900 he purchased half shares from Frank, while Henry taught him the ropes at Two Grey Hills. H. B. described his impression of this post, one of a number he would work at: "We didn't deal in the goods then that the trading posts do today. Trade was mostly in coffee, flour, and calico. The men would come in wearing calico pants with garters around their legs at the knee. There was a can of free tobacco on the counter—we furnished the brown papers too—and they rolled their own cigarettes and the air would get blue with smoke."[27] This store, located on the south side of the wash facing east, was constructed primarily of stone with a back side built of logs. The western portion served as a wool room and living quarters also made of wood.

In spite of the warm memories of daily traffic at the store, there was also a cold reality that H. B. recalled years later when speaking of his experiences. The isolation of the post wore on his nerves, especially in the winter, when the loneliness became unbearable. Historian Frank McNitt captured the feeling of this bleakness during an interview when H. B. "spoke of a winter when it seemed that he and a horse were alone, the only living things in the Chuska Valley. The sky was gray, snow slanting down, as he stared from a window out at the corrals, at the

Early traders of the Chuska Valley. *Standing, left to right:* Frank L. Noel, Henry R. Noel. *Seated:* Edmund Noel, Will Evans, Cyril J. Collyer. The Noels established Two Grey Hills, while Evans built Sanostee, all of them leaving a brief record of the early days of these posts. Frank L. Noel Collection (P-166), L. Tom Perry Special Collections, Harold B. Lee Library, Brigham Young University.

horse penned there, head low and tail to the blowing snow. For perhaps an hour Noel and the horse stood without moving, regarding each other, 'and the thought occurred to me that the horse was as lonely and wretched as I was.'"[28] While it did not require a lot of coaxing for his brother Henry to part with his post and leave trading, H. B. was different and went on to establish a new one at Teec Nos Pos as well as working at Sanostee, Sweetwater, Tocito, Tohatchi, Rock Point, Beclabito, and Fort Defiance.

Win Wetherill and Friction at Two Grey Hills

In 1901, Henry and H. B. sold Two Grey Hills to a man named Winslow "Win" T. Wetherill.[29] Win belonged to a family of traders, including his well-known brothers, Richard and John. He decided to keep H. B. as a clerk for six months after the purchase because of his skills. Win also had a short and troubled career at Two Grey Hills, with problems starting even before he officially assumed ownership. Government farmer Samuel Shoemaker, who worked with the Navajos near Fruitland and other sites along the San Juan River, wrote an acrid letter to Navajo Agent George W. Hayzlett strongly recommending that he not grant a license to Wetherill. While claiming little personal interaction with Win, Shoemaker laid a series of heavy claims—that he felt had been substantiated by people who should know—of exactly what this would-be-trader was like. Charges included providing false information, being unable to obtain the necessary funds for a bond, stealing cattle, and carrying a bad reputation with the people of Mancos, Colorado, where he had lived recently. Most damning was the inference that he and his brothers, through the Hyde Exploring Expedition Company, were trying to consolidate under their control a monopoly of all the prosperous traders on their part of the reservation while destroying the smaller businesses. High prices for goods and low prices for Navajo products would result. As far as Shoemaker was concerned, Win was an "unfit person" and bad character.[30]

Wetherill responded directly to Hayzlett, saying that it was his brother Richard and his father who had been accused of cattle rustling and that the case had been dropped. As for the Hyde Exploring Expedition controlling trade on the reservation, Hayzlett agreed with him that it would be very hard to subjugate a lot of independent traders and that Richard Wetherill's post at Pueblo Bonito was thirty miles east of the reservation and so did not come under his control. New Mexico congressman B. S. Rody got involved, cornering Hayzlett while in D.C. and insisting that Win had no direct contact with the Hyde Company, which to their credit, "is doing a lot of good out near the reservation because it has bought thousands of Navajo blankets from the Indians and paid cash for them so that the price paid to the Indians for their product has gone up almost 300 percent."[31] These traders also purchased much of the produce the Indians sold while giving a much higher price than anyone else. This caused jealousy so that competitors made every effort to keep Wetherill off the reservation. Rody insisted the Hyde Company had no store on the reservation and guaranteed that Win would do more for the Indians than any other trader in their vicinity.

Not everyone agreed. Shoemaker followed with another letter insisting that the Wetherills were intimidating Navajos at their posts, using force to collect debts, sometimes at the point of a gun. Others claimed that Navajos were handcuffed and brought to the Pueblo Bonito store, where their horse and saddle or other livestock were taken away by force and the debtor placed in one of the dark, excavated rooms of the pueblo ruins. The person detailing these crimes—Charles S. Lusk of the Bureau of Catholic Missions in Washington, D.C.—felt that "the company is worse than a lot of Russian Jews, crediting the Indians beyond their means, then intimidating them and obtaining more than is due to them."[32] Hayzlett demanded that Wetherill remove any goods he had bought or brought to Two Grey Hills in anticipation of trade. Win agreed not to trade, but word leaked back to the agent that the trader was open for business anyway. Hayzlett, however, was mindful of Rody's interaction with the commissioner of Indian affairs, and apparently relented, since by March 1902, Wetherill had his license.[33]

Win Wetherill was soon again the topic of discussion in Washington, D.C., as well as on the Navajo Reservation. In a letter to the commissioner of Indian affairs (bypassing Hayzlett), Wetherill told of an Inspector Levi Chubbuck who evaluated a ditch and small dam that the trader and local Navajos built on Captain Tom's Wash. Wetherill's crew had ranged "from 6 to 110" and had spent two-and-a-half months constructing this part of an irrigation system.[34] According to the trader, Chubbuck said that "it was the best piece of work he had seen anywhere." The trader mused, "It was a hard job with the tools we had and the Indians wanted to stop work several times, but I would not stand for it—it is not my way to start a thing and quit half done. There are too many of that kind of people in this country." He went on to suggest that he would have finished the project even if it had cost the whole store! Fortunately for all concerned, he just had to supply the food and the know-how. When the inspector suggested that a large reservoir be constructed by the government to capture the water coming down from the Chuskas, Win corrected him, saying that nothing should be given to the Navajos, insisting they do it for themselves. "Let them make their own [reservoir]. You can if you put the right man with the Indians. All you need to do is to supply the food and with the right leader, they will do anything he asks, but to do it for them is foolish." Apparently Win was the right man, but even though there was an "old Aztec ditch one and a half miles long" above the store that the Navajos wanted him to help get back in service, he was not going to be able to do it, because he had sold the Two Grey Hills Trading Post and would soon be leaving the reservation. The answer to why this "right man" would leave was simple: "Shoemaker does not love me neither does the agent and I do not care to keep fighting for existence here." All he wanted was to be reimbursed for the food he had given the Indians during construction—$419.55 to be exact.

Unfortunately for Wetherill, his circuitous sidestep of the agent did not work. Hayzlett, before agreeing to pay the bill, wanted to inspect the work that had been done. In a lengthy letter sent to the commissioner of Indian affairs, he described what he found: a dam that had washed out with the first spring runoff, a one-and-a-quarter-mile ditch that required an estimated $800 to $1,000 more work to really make it effective by leveling the grade and removing the dirt from caved-in canal walls, and a trader who offered to give him half of the money received if he would sign the request and obtain payment. Hayzlett refused the offer, insisting that he "would not accept one cent from anyone under such a proposition."[35] This was just the warm up. The agent went on "to explain why he [Wetherill] thinks Mr. Shoemaker or myself do not *love* [his emphasis] him. He was granted a license over the protest made by both of us which never should have been done. He opened the store before procuring the license and I had to close it a second time. Then when he did get it over my head, he thought he was in a position to run matters as he pleased." The agent then pointed out that Wetherill had bought a lot of stock from the Navajos and was then grazing the animals on the reservation. Hayzlett directed Shoemaker, before returning to Two Grey Hills, to call on the police located in the vicinity to put this stock off the reservation, intensifying the "lost love." In less than a year after penning these sentiments, Hayzlett left the reservation too, having faithfully fulfilled his five-year political appointment as agent.

Even with Hayzlett and Wetherill gone, the drama surrounding their era at Two Grey Hills continued. Superintendent William T. Shelton, newly appointed agent at the recently founded (1903) Northern Navajo Agency at Shiprock, received directions from Congressman Rody through the commissioner of Indian affairs to continue the ditch work done the previous year—all at Win Wetherill's urging. Shelton was busy with a multitude of tasks associated with running the agency and building a boarding school. Finally in May 1904 he visited Two Grey Hills to assess renewal of the project. His report was anything but favorable. He told of the Indians in the area using an old ditch six miles away from the post with good results. The one that Wetherill had constructed would have brought their fields closer to the store but was an ineffective short-cut that really hampered water getting to the crops. Really, the more successful experience came from a natural arroyo three miles to the north of the post, which dumped water on the lowlands where there were also Navajo fields. For six weeks water from the melting snows in the Chuskas nurtured the Indians' fields during the growing season as compared to five days of water coming from the old Indian ditch and the one that Wetherill connected to it.[36] It should be noted that the lower site watered by the arroyo was used only when there was sufficient snow in the mountains—averaging once every five years. The Navajos used the "old Indian ditch" every year with good success and required relatively little effort. More water, less work, better crops—there was no need to continue efforts on the newly engineered ditch.

Other problems surfaced as Shelton visited with Navajos in the area. In addition to the ditch built by Wetherill being "of no benefit whatever . . . and in fact interfered with the use of the old Indian ditch," it appeared that his bill of over $400 should actually have been for $100 worth of provisions.[37] That was not all. Shelton reported, "These Indians have an entirely different idea as to Mr. Wetherill's interest in them, from what he expresses in his letter. They claim that he imposed upon them in many instances, charging exorbitant prices for goods; such as $40 for Colt revolvers, $18 per bunch for imitation coral beads, selling them for the genuine corals, etc.; and that he depleted their herds, and by bull-dozing and other ways, secured possession of their goods. They also claim that several hundred dollars-worth of jewelry, etc., which he held in pawn, was removed by him from the reservation, and they are now unable to redeem them, though they very much desire to do so."[38]

Case in point: in late 1902 Charlie Bit-cil-li pawned a silver bridle and belt, valued at $51, to Wetherill for $27 and paid off part of the debt, leaving $11.25 still owed. When the Navajo went to Two Grey Hills to redeem his property, he learned that Win had departed and left the objects with his brother Richard at the Pueblo Bonito Post. Richard denied any knowledge of the materials but said he would contact Win about it. As luck would have it, a Navajo woman came into the store wearing Bit-cil-li's belt. When he asked her about it, she said that she had bought it from Richard for twelve sheep but immediately handed the belt over to the Navajo. When the trader saw him with it, he took it away. The chagrined Navajo went to the agent, Reuben Perry at Fort Defiance, who wrote a letter to Richard about the matter, but when the Indian delivered the letter, the trader became abusive, saying it was none of the agent's business and that he would contact Win about the matter—even though he had the belt, bridle, and the $11.25 needed to redeem the objects for the owner. There is no indication as to how this incident ended, but it is a good example of the types of problems agents faced with off-reservation traders.[39]

A Tale of Two Posts—Sanostee and Teec Nos Pos

A quick glimpse at the experiences derived from a second post during this same time is instructive, providing another example of a difficult life in these early years. That store, Sanostee, nestled at the foot of the Chuska Mountains is approximately thirteen miles north of Two Grey Hills and was started by Joe Wilkins a year after he left the Noel brothers. Within the vicinity of the site known to Navajos as "Overlapping Rocks" (Tsé Ałnáozt'i'í) and also "Water Rises in a White Column" (Tó Yaagaii) because of a now inactive artesian well that was once a geyser, there was sufficient Navajo population dependent upon agriculture to warrant the store.[40] Wilkins, after obtaining a license, hired two men—Edwin S. Dustin, an experienced freighter and trader, and twenty-one-year-old Will Evans, who provided a detailed account of this experience and remained in the business for the next forty years.[41] As with the Noel brothers, this trio set off from Fruitland with two wagons of building materials and supplies, passing Shiprock and then heading southwest to their destination. On December 10, 1898, they arrived on the banks of the Sanostee Wash, where a clear stream of water beckoned them to camp. As day turned to night, a heavy snowstorm began, encouraging the two older men to visit a powerful medicine man and community leader named Bizhóshí, who could give approval for establishing a store. Evans received the responsibility of guarding all of the goods and equipment. When he awoke in the morning and shook off twelve inches of snow from his bedding, he could easily see that no one had bothered a thing.

That day the two men returned and construction began, but they reported nothing about their visit. The workers shoveled away the snow, erected a tent, furnished it with a table and chairs, and unloaded the lumber and heavy tar paper for roofing. Within days there stood a building, sixteen by twenty feet, lined with shelves on some walls and a rough counter that framed the bull pen where Navajo customers stood to trade. Supplies were basic—sugar, potatoes, onions, beans, coffee, some cloth, and smaller items that could be sandwiched in between the building supplies. With a rudimentary structure for trade and the tent for a home, the partners decided to have Will remain to tend the store, while Ed and Joe went for more building supplies and trade goods. Little did they know that this would be the winter of the "Big Snow" and that they would not be able to return until spring.

Will watched the two wagons pull out of sight toward Fruitland, masked by a heavy snowstorm. Lonely days turned into lonely weeks, then months as the young man traded all of the goods he had, burned his last log in the cast iron stove, and watched out the window for his returning partners. Snow and bitter cold froze hundreds and then thousands of sheep, forced many Navajos to go afoot, encouraged begging at the trading post's door, and placed even more restrictions on the trader. He broke with Navajo custom and burned wood from a "death hogan" where a person had died, making any use of the structure's materials anathema. Evans described his plight: "Christmas arrived after endless days and nights of utter loneliness. I was not above a tinge of despair, wondering when my friends with their wagons would arrive. I found myself in an interesting situation that Christmas Eve, living in a world rigidly circumscribed by a waist high blanket of white. My domain, if it can be called that, was a few hundred feet of narrow trails through the snow, the longest extending from the store door to the edge of the stream, which was now frozen solid, forcing me to melt snow."[42]

Christmas Day arrived with Navajo neighbors knocking on the post door for some token of a "Melly Ke'eshmish," which came in the form of a cookie for the children and a culled apple for the adults. That was all the trader had, his own stock of supplies continually shrinking before his eyes, with no certain time for replenishment. Indeed, it would not be until March that his companions appeared with two wagons of materials, but for Will, "the spirit of that Christmas Day prevailed, and the thankfulness and good will rested over the little snowbound valley of Sanostee," making the loneliness more tolerable.[43]

With renewed vigor, the three men set about erecting a more permanent trading post, which in turn, drew many Navajos to watch the event. One of them was Bizhóshí, who this time made it clear he did not approve of a store within his territory. Wilkins's permit to build meant nothing to the old man as his clan relatives became increasingly agitated, insisting construction stop immediately. Evans recalls, "Wilkins and I paid no attention to him and kept working. Ed Dustin sat on a nearby fence with a rifle across his knees. The situation became tense. Men on horseback wheeled their horses and wildly shouted to each other, while those on foot gestured and shouted at us and to each other. Bizhóshí came alongside of me and hissed a challenge in his native tongue, which I understood but had difficulty in speaking. I can still visualize that fierce old fellow's bristling gray mustache and his out-thrust jagged teeth as he grated out his words with all of the venom he could muster: 'If you don't stop this work, I will slit your throat like I would a sheep!' He emphasized his threat by jerking the edge of his hand across his throat. To say that I was scared is putting it mildly, but Joe quietly eased my anxiety when he said, 'Let's go ahead; they won't do anything.' We continued working. The shouting persisted for some time; but finally the small mob disappeared, and we had no more opposition."[44]

As the dust settled, the three traders discussed and then agreed that most of the local people really wanted a store in their area, since otherwise their nearest source of supplies was across the Lukachukai Mountains, a long tiresome trip in the best of weather and nearly impossible in winter. The post became a welcomed addition to Navajo life in Sanostee and soon branched into other areas of commerce. Wilkins received a logging contract on the mountain near his store, purchased livestock, became increasingly popular with his neighbors, and although "the people living around Sanostee made rotten rugs—thick and greasy"—they were willing to take traders' suggestions and greatly improved their product for higher sales.[45] Still, there were problems. Wilkins's wife missed the white society of Farmington and wanted to move back to her old friends. Frank Noel, who had been trying his hand at a number of occupations since leaving Two Grey Hills, including logging at Sanostee in the winter and serving at the post in the summer, saw an opportunity and purchased the business in 1905. In his words, "This was the best deal I ever made. I was there for ten years."[46]

The store, supplied by C. H. Algert from Fruitland and operated by Frank and Mary, proved profitable. H. B. joined them for a short time assisting in the blanket trade, while Navajos with wagons received employment freighting for the store. The post became a magnet, drawing people from an increasingly long distance, and so Frank provided a guest hogan where visitors could stay overnight and use firewood, flour, and coffee supplied by the trader who hoped to encourage their business. Corn, piñon nuts, cattle, horses, lambs, sheep pelts, and wool were the staples of the trade that caused the post to prosper. Although there were a multitude of issues to overcome—everything from weather, terrible roads, crossing the San Juan River, fluctuating prices, disease, educating the trader's children—the list goes on—there was real satisfaction and moderate financial success that kept the family happy. Even Bizhóshí settled down, but not before a little dustup. When Bizhóshí's dog got into Noel's chickens, Frank had no choice but to shoot the invader. After recounting how his canine had kept coyotes away from his sheep and goats, how the post was built on his range, and that the store never should have opened and must be closed immediately, the medicine man learned that the trader did not know it was his dog, that Noel was reacting to a bad situation, and that he wanted to pay for the loss. Some flour, coffee, sugar, tobacco, and two silver dollars eased the pain, the men shook hands, and Bizhóshí became a regular customer for years thereafter.[47]

The same time that Frank bought Sanostee, his brother H. B. started a new post at Teec Nos Pos. There are a few instructive points in this venture to consider before closing this chapter. H. B. by this time had robust health, had learned a good deal about the trade—his brother claiming that H. B. was far better than he was at evaluating blankets, thanks to his interaction with Win Wetherill—and had made strong connections with a number of posts on the northern part of the reservation. H. B. was ready to set out on his own. "When I went out to Teec Nos Pos it was wild country. I knew I was up against it, but didn't want trouble."[48] Fifteen hundred Indians greeted H. B. when he arrived at the proposed site and spent all day in deliberation with the trader and a translator. He gave them food for a big meal—flour, some sheep, and coffee, so that by evening, the Navajos agreed that he could build the store and allowed him to sleep in a nearby hogan. To maintain peace in this isolated area, Noel bought an automatic high powered rifle and when not shooting with Navajo friends, hung it in the store behind the counter as a reminder that he was a pretty fair shot.

There was also cooperation with other traders. John Wetherill, who at the same time had started a post at Oljato, Utah, shipped his goods through Teec Nos Pos with Noel's cooperation. Wetherill's loaded wagons would arrive at H. B.'s post with a return order; the trader then transferred the goods to his own wagons and brought the materials to Algert's wholesale company in Fruitland. In 1907, he built the Mexican Water Post, thirty miles west of Teec Nos Pos. This store joined others built by different traders within a ten-year period—Naschitti, Toadlena, Crystal, Captain Tom's Wash (later called Nava, then Newcomb), Red Rock, and Hogback, just to name a few. This proliferation of posts was made possible by a number of different circumstances, which are discussed in the next chapter. Each of these posts, like Two Grey Hills, Sanostee, and Teec Nos Pos, has its own story, yet they share many common elements.

In summarizing those elements, there are a number of points to be made. The physical location of the post needed to support sufficient trade to sustain growth. While there is no magical number and no way to determine what was necessary in those days because of the increasing mobility of the Navajos, fifty to a hundred families can serve as an approximation. In some locales, there might be a concentration of population, such as in Chinle or along the San Juan River or near a railroad where people collected and could sustain themselves. In less favorable conditions, traders occasionally referred to a twenty-five-mile radius when establishing a new post. This distance represented a day's travel between already existing stores. While this figure serves as a talking point, there are too many exceptions. For example, within a thirty-mile straight-line radius from Two Grey Hills, over the years, there arose fifteen different posts, the closest (Newcomb) being six miles, the farthest being Sawmill and Mexican Springs, both at thirty miles. Distance and population figures are only part of understanding why a store developed where it did.

Another factor was approval from the federal government and local people, as personalities like Hayzlett and Bizhóshí make apparent. Other traders, such as John Wetherill and Gladwell Richardson, on a different part of the reservation, faced similar challenges. Indeed, relationships, a fundamental concern in Navajo culture, remained of paramount importance in life at the trading post. Whether buying blankets, bartering over the counter, evaluating pawn, redeeming tokens, or participating in community events—at the base of all that happened, the concept of k'é summarizes the most important principle in successfully navigating Navajo culture. Will Evans with his simple Christmas cookies and apples confirmed in his patron's minds that here was a man who did not have much to offer, but what he had, he was willing to share. The tobacco and cigarette papers on the counter of Two Grey Hills, the careful and deliberate evaluation of a blanket spread out in a "rug room," the sponsoring of a neighborhood feast, the availability of a guest hogan for travelers, the acceptance of a trader's appraisal for that year's wool clip, the price of lambs, and the worth of a stamped token with the trading post's name on it were based in trust and a person's word. A trader who filched from his customers could soon be out of business.

In spite of this need for strong relationships on both sides of the bullpen, it is also obvious that there could be a frequent turnover in either owners or operators of a post. Compare the first five years of Two Grey Hills and its high number of traders with Sanostee, where—after the initial startup—Frank Noel remained for ten years. As mentioned previously, tracing the genealogy of trading post owners can be bewildering. Since Two Grey Hills is our main interest, a complete listing of those involved with the post is given here. To do so with every post mentioned would be a book in itself. The reasons for constant changes were multifaceted. Win Wetherill provided a number of examples; marriage and family life for two of the Noel brothers give another. Some men embraced the loneliness, others could not; gambling that a different post might be more profitable—seeking greener pastures—encouraged many to try a new site; others sought change; still others wished to get out from government regulation and so opened shop off the reservation. Whatever the reason, there was a constant flow of operators in and out of many of the stores serving Navajo people.

The early days of trading posts on the reservation still had a strong tinge of the Old West, where laws were loose, and differences were often settled between individuals rather than through an appointed agent, sheriff, or the military. By the turn of the twentieth century, circumstances were changing. Government control in the form of the Shiprock Agency, Anglo religion and education in the form of missionaries from back east, and a few final military operations were on the horizon, settling much of the turmoil and conflicts differently than in the nineteenth century. We now turn to those "civilizing" influences that had such a large impact on the Navajo people and the trading posts that served them.

CHAPTER THREE

Of Bibles, Books, and Regulations

"Civilization" Comes to the Northern Navajo, 1890–1915

The Four Corners area had always had a bad reputation. Known not only for its isolation, challenging terrain, and inhospitable climate, there were also cowboys, Indians, and itinerant lawbreakers on the lam. It was easy to get lost in what one army surgeon stationed at Fort Lewis, Colorado, in the 1880s called the "Dark Corner," or what a Navajo agent around the same time named "the land of death."[1] Regional literature written by inhabitants of those times recall a litany of bad actors—irrespective of race and culture—who used the canyon country and mountainous areas as escape valves through which to disappear.[2] Each of the four territories or states had its own rogues' gallery evading the law and seeking sanctuary. The last quarter of the nineteenth century witnessed growing pressures to tame this violence and move the region, one of the last to be settled in the continental United States, toward a tamer twentieth century. As previously mentioned, there were a multitude of economic, social, and political forces that pushed people and events in that direction, including trading posts. The role of missionaries in providing education and work skills, coupled with the establishment of the Shiprock Agency under the iron fist of William T. Shelton, had direct impact not only on Two Grey Hills, but on all of the people in the Chuska Valley.

Mary Eldridge—Woman on a Mission

Mary Eldridge was an outsider who quickly adapted. Born in 1849 in South Williamstown, Massachusetts, near the Vermont border, Mary

Louise Deming grew up in a rural environment where hard work and sacrifice were common themes. At the age of twenty, she married William Eldridge and had three children before her husband passed away in 1879. Ten years later she was working in the Haskell Institute in Kansas as dormitory matron and head nurse, but because she opposed the harsh treatment of the students in the attempt to turn them into "white Indians," she was not rehired at the end of her first year because she "was not the proper person to be matron of the girl's building."[3] A year later she was in the Indian Service on the Pine Ridge Reservation when the massacre of Wounded Knee erupted, further dampening her wish for working with American Indians while in government employ. With a newfound friend, teacher Mary Raymond, she signed on to work for the Women's Home Missionary Society of the Methodist Episcopal Church, whose goals centered on providing healthcare and education without coercion. The pair's first assignment: establish a mission among the Navajos along the San Juan River in New Mexico.

From their train stop in Durango, to the stagecoach ride to Farmington, thence by wagon twenty miles west to a lonely site called Hogback near Jewett, the two women gazed at the dry landscape and prepared for their life on a plot of desert ground already purchased by the mission. The only neighbor was Henry Hull, operator of a nearby trading post. Their accommodations—a tent and cook stove—arrived later, were quickly set up, and the last of their lunch purchased in Durango consumed. Navajo people soon arrived without fanfare or enthusiasm, causing Mary Eldridge to write years later, "We were not received with any great degree of cordiality by the Indians, as they had been told that we were coming to steal their children for the eastern schools. As I look back on the experience of our first years here, I sometimes wonder if they had been lifted and we could have seen the trials and bitter antagonism which we were to meet, if our hearts would not have failed us."[4] Regardless of these sentiments, Mary went on to become one of the most effective and beloved of the women missionaries serving throughout the reservation.

Only highlights of her story can be shared here, but there is no missing her hands-on determination to bring healthcare and education to the Navajos, and the lengths she would go to ensure it happened. For instance, the two Marys purchased yarn in Durango as a way of encouraging Navajo women to come to the mission on a daily basis to weave; they later obtained two spinning wheels with the hopes of earning money to pay for expenses through the sale of rugs and blankets just like at a trading post. The ladies' dispensary brought in sometimes thirty to forty sick patients a day, creating need for more space and the building of new structures. Raymond reported that between December 8, 1891, and August 8, 1892, she treated in the small adobe hospital 153 sick and administered medicine to 183 people.[5] This was in addition to the long journeys with Eldridge on horse or mule to visit outlying camps. The women also arbitrated issues between Navajo and white livestock owners, as both sides jockeyed for grazing lands that the opposing side claimed.

Mary Raymond, almost from the outset, was hired by the Indian agent to serve as a government field matron, receiving eighty dollars a month used to supplement the meager flow of cash supporting the mission's efforts. Both women realized that the potential of the San Juan River was immense for feeding many impoverished souls. Their efforts soon became a conduit for the federal government and the Methodist church, as well as individual donors, to donate axes, shovels, plows, wagons, and other equipment for farming and constructing a large irrigation ditch with subsidiary branches. In 1895, Eldridge reported that because of the help she had received from the Cambridge, Massachusetts, branch of the Indian Relief Association, Navajos who had previously had only one ax and a broken-handled shovel to construct a ditch had now sufficient tools to build the "Cambridge Ditch" that watered nearly six hundred acres of land.[6] All of this was done so that "irrigation, allotment of land, and education of all of the children will civilize these people, and the love of God will save them."[7]

God's love, however, was sometimes cast in the shadows. On February 5, 1893, Mary Raymond married Tom Whyte, the operator of a local trading post. He quickly turned into an abusive husband who injured both his wife and their unborn son. Mary fled to the mission, where her brother retrieved her and then sent her to Kansas, but to no avail— both mother and son died shortly after their arrival.[8] Eldridge assumed the task of government matron, requested another female missionary, a third Mary—Mary Tripp—to help with teaching, and received financial assistance from the Indian Rights Association and the National Indian

Association, both headquartered in the East. But summer droughts and extreme cold in the winter killed crops and livestock without mercy, and when this was added to the national financial panics of the 1890s, life along the San Juan became tenuous.

As soon as educator and missionary Mary Tripp arrived, the two women consistently held religious services as well as school. One visitor to a class in 1899 observed, "There were about twenty of the youngsters in a room when the writer visited it. The blackboard exercises were underway, and the little tots developed surprising ability. The copybooks were exhibited, and they too bore evidence of a high degree of efficiency. . . . The young Indians are certainly brighter than the older ones, for the life the older ones lead tends to retard, rather than develop the intellect."[9] The need for a full-time interpreter became apparent, and so a young man named Frank Damon of Scotch-Irish and Navajo descent not only filled the need, but became a shining example of what white enculturation could accomplish. Holding school required another building, and the hospital work intensified, demanding additional space for a growing mission staff that needed living accommodations. New structures arose to meet the demand—a ferry boat assisted visitors, and a well with windmill eventually appeared. Both provided disappointing results, but not before a heavy price in labor and finances made their existence possible.

The Mission at Two Grey Hills

While much more can be said about the mission at Hogback, enough has been shared to provide context for the satellite mission that grew under even more difficult circumstances at Two Grey Hills. Historian John Arrington, born and raised during these times, recalled, "West toward the Beautiful Mountains and the Lukachukai range—to the far western edge of the reservation—the Navajos preserved their racial traditions unaffected by outside influences. They were called Long-Hairs. My neighbors [Navajos in the Farmington area] cut their hair and otherwise imitated fashions and manners of their Anglo companions. They were known as River people."[10]

Into this country rode Mary Eldridge and Mary Whyte on an exploration to determine potential for a satellite mission. These lone women started from Jewett, the new name for the growing community around

Hogback, in the summer heat of mid-July 1893. The first day brought twenty-two miles punctuated with rain showers, a camping spot with no grass and poor water, and little comfort; the end of the second day provided a stopover in an abandoned building without a roof, but bunch grass for the horses and a nicely irrigated field of corn dependent on a dam made of logs, stone, and adobe. The third day brought relief from the heat and greater evidence that the Navajos were living in the Chuska-Tunicha range, herding sheep and tending gardens. Eldridge noted that the camps encountered showed that the Indians inhabiting this area were better off than those living along the river, stating upon her return that "the crops were looking very good . . . and larger than heretofore."[11] Their observation confirmed the potential for missionary work in this area long before traders established the Two Grey Hills Post.

Four years passed, the post became a reality, and a year later, in March 1898, the Two Grey Hills Mission began. Eventually bureaucrats in Washington approved the paperwork, assigning 2.89 acres upon which were a four-room house, barn, and school for use by the Women's National Indian Association.[12] As with the nearby trading post, the land still belonged to the Navajos as part of their reservation property. A wealthy benefactor, J. Lewis Crozier, Esq., provided money for the house, which was named in memory of his beneficence. The mission also assumed the responsibility of postal duties on June 6, 1903, and for the next sixteen years, the building that housed this service was called the Crozier Post Office.

In April, Eldridge, as supervisor for both missions, left Jewett and opened the doors to begin realizing the potential in the area. A month later, Mrs. Henrietta G. Cole, known to the Navajos as Asdzaan Nez-tso (Tall Heavy Woman), walked through those same doors and assumed responsibilities for operating the mission, which included a small kindergarten and clinic. This elderly sixty-year-old woman came from Massachusetts, where she had worked for years in the Williams College Infirmary as head nurse. Eldridge appreciated her skills and noted, "She takes well with the Indians, is full of sympathy and helpfulness, has so much common sense, and adapts herself so well to her surroundings that I am sure she will be a tower of strength to our work."[13]

This initial impression was on solid ground. Amelia S. Quinton, president of the Women's National Indian Association, who was providing different types of support to the main mission and its satellite simultaneously, commented on the tremendous presence and service that Cole provided during an eight-day visit that first year. The missionary had received 320 "calls" for everything from medical assistance, "industrial" help, and a wide variety of other needs that spoke to the "interest and confidence that the Indians had in her. . . . Maladies grave and lighter had been cured, and Mrs. Cole's progress in the Navajo language and in winning the people had been successful beyond expectation."[14] This success was not just at the mission. Quinton continued in her report that six miles northwest of the "station" there was a Navajo community with three hundred individuals who, under the guidance of Eldridge, had created a successful irrigation system, built stockade and log houses, erected fences, and planted a large area with a variety of crops. The Two Grey Hills Mission became increasingly successful.

There were also, however, hard times. Trader Will Evans remembers the effects of the Big Snow during the winter of 1898–99. He was working at Sanostee that April, when Harry C. Baldwin from the Hogback store stopped in. Harry was not familiar with the area but wanted to see how Henrietta Cole was faring, given her isolation and the severity of the winter. Will agreed to show him the way, and the two set off early the next morning to see "Mrs. Cole [who] was mother to us all."[15] They took a trail that skirted the foothills of the Chuska range, but even at this time of the year, the path was dimly marked or covered with melting snow, and was without traffic since many of the Navajos' horses had perished due to severe weather conditions. They passed once-prosperous Navajo camps, many now deserted and littered with large numbers of animals that had perished from snow and cold. Reaching the Two Grey Hills station proved taxing but well worth the effort when Mrs. Cole emerged to greet the travelers.

Fortunately for Henry Noel at the post and Mrs. Cole, there was a Navajo man named Bicheii who lived in the area and who had created a sheltered corral in a cove at the foot of the mountain, where a protective wall prevented the driving wind and snow from killing his sheep and goats. He fed them from the stacks of wild hay he had harvested during the summer, and when those were gone, he cut sagebrush, piñon, and juniper boughs to keep his animals alive. When the traders wanted fresh meat, they would let him know, and he would bring an animal to the post corral for slaughter. Word of the event spread quickly with Navajo neighbors appearing to claim the innards for a meal at home, a welcomed relief from their starving conditions. One old woman particularly stood out in Evans's mind.

> One day a pitifully famished, elderly woman in the ravenous stages of starvation was at hand when the traders had a sheep butchered. The animal was skinned and the hide spread out, fleshy side up. As the entrails spilled onto the skin, she grabbed a section of small intestine then moved aside, fearful that someone might snatch it from her. Holding the gut in one hand, she stripped out what offal she could with the other and began gnawing at the still warm flesh. With her excellent teeth . . . she devoured it all.
>
> I was literally sick and stunned. I had seen people in advanced stages of hunger in the past weeks, but never a human with the ravenous appetite of a wild animal. I had only pity for the poor creature and hoped her meal would do her good.[16]

In a few days, Evans and Baldwin returned, with some difficulty, to their respective posts, but not before each man had indelibly etched in his memory the destitute conditions they had encountered. That spring, as the Navajos picked up the pieces of their lives and livelihood, each trader paid more than usual for the goods brought to their post, understanding that it would take some time for the Indians' economy to recover.

Other visitors, some from the East, gave their own reports of the mission's work at Two Grey Hills. Mary G. Burdette, secretary for the Baptist Home Mission Society, enthusiastically wrote about what she saw. After telling of her group's two-day trip "over a veritable desert," guided by Eldridge, who knew the limited sites where water could be found, she praised the work of Mrs. Cole, situated in her four-room cottage alongside the small schoolhouse and log stable. There the missionary "mothered" her visitors with food, blankets, and rest before they continued on through Washington Pass, then the Hopi Mesas.[17] Some people, however, did not agree as to the amount of progress. That same year, 1901, the fledgling hospital services and small kindergarten changed denominational hands. The Methodists, according to the incoming Baptists, had achieved "only mediocre success," and so turned the mission over to Reverend Robert B. Wright, his wife, and two daughters from Indiana. The couple's salary was well below a thousand dollars a year, and although they represented one of two attempts at "the first and only truly day-school efforts of New Mexico Baptists," their enthusiasm for the project lasted for only five years.[18] Their desire to help the "Red Race" did bear limited fruit. Students attended the school, which expanded its curriculum as communication between the two cultures strengthened. At its height under Baptist supervision, the Two Grey Hills School reportedly had 133 pupils during a single year.[19] Perhaps of equal interest for the Navajos was the more practical side of these white men's religion. Following a long drought, local leaders pledged to more fully accept the Christian God if prayers were said to bring the much-needed moisture. It seems that "God is always an ally where earnest prayers are offered. Rains did come and many snows covered the ground. The Indians' response was noted with better attendance, more conversions, and those interested in bringing others. These children of the desert received social, moral, religious, and welfare care."[20]

Even with divine aid, the Wrights struggled. It was not the two Arbuckle coffee crates that their daughters used for beds, or intense bouts with sickness from food poisoning, or the weeks of loneliness for Mrs. Wright as she waited for her husband's return from the hospital, or her running out of food and wood at the mission—needs thankfully met by Navajo neighbors once they learned of her situation—or the couples' heavy teaching load. Rather it was the daily grind and seeming lack of success in converting their neighbors to Christianity that proved frustrating. There were those who joined the fold and walked the "Jesus Road," but there were far too many who did not. When Mrs. Wright had complications with childbirth while back east, the minister resigned on December 1, 1906, to join her, but not before selecting, under the auspices of the Baptist Home Mission Society, a new location five miles to the west of Two Grey Hills, a spot now known as Toadlena. The apparent reason for the move was the new site's excellent source of water produced by a flowing spring that could irrigate several acres capable of growing crops and fruit trees. There is no indication if Susan McCarty, a "full blooded" Navajo, then acting as assistant missionary at Two Grey Hills, also made the move, but soon the new mission was in operation.[21] Six years later the Christian Reform Church assumed responsibility for education and healthcare in the area and five years after that, also opened a post office. Apparently some of the postal duties previously handled by

Beneath Mary Eldridge's placid exterior there was a woman of grit and determination who thrived in a difficult environment. She worked with individuals with strong personalities and different understandings that would have discouraged most people. Her affinity for bringing Christianity to the Navajos and playing a major role in advancing economic assistance and training won many friendships. Courtesy of Farmington Museum, New Mexico.

the Two Grey Hills Mission had shifted to the local trading post, since in 1916, a storm destroyed the old mission buildings.

Before the mission at Two Grey Hills closed permanently, Lee I. Thayer, a Yale University–trained and Chicago Baptist School graduate, presided over the facility. Lemuel C. Barnes of the Baptist Society visited

Thayer and his wife around 1909, providing an excellent report of the activities and attitudes of these Christian missionaries. Barnes observed Mrs. Thayer teaching English to ten small Indian children, but her husband taught Bible stories in Navajo and was working on his own dictionary and grammar of the language. Following a lunch of coffee and crackers, Mr. Thayer presented a personal gospel message. At night, the children slept in a log addition to the adobe structure. "It has a partition half way to the ceiling. On one side of this partition, in their three beds sleep nine little Indian girls, on the other side of it sleep Mr. and Mrs. Thayer so as to be right at hand in case of need."[22]

There is little doubt what the message through all of this was to these "heathens, pure and simple." Barnes's article drips with it. He painted the missionaries with glowing sainthood when he wrote, "It requires nothing less than the spirit of Christ to faithfully work for these heathen people in such a pagan land. It requires also strength of character and resourcefulness little short of genius to carry a whole Christian civilization into such an aboriginal wilderness."[23] Thus hope sprang eternal, for the Navajos he characterized as "the largest unbroken tribe left." Also, "They have sturdy hearts which make them at the same time harder to reach and better worth reaching than most aborigines. . . . As I write, the mists come back to my eyes at the thought of such heroism as I was beholding in those tender souls who live month after month for Christ's sake and the sake of the stolid barbarians at Two Grey Hills. The two grey hills are hidden behind two bright summits of Christ-like devotion."[24] The storms of life swept much of this hope and characteristic missionary zeal away to another area, when the Two Grey Hills Mission dissolved in 1916.

Genesis of an Agency

While this religious effort to improve Navajo lives continued, there was an even larger, more concerted labor in the form of the Northern Navajo or Shiprock Agency started by the government. The south side of the San Juan River had historically been a gathering place for Navajos planting large gardens dependent on relatively small irrigation efforts. Following the incarceration at Fort Sumner, the people returned slowly, furtively keeping an eye on the Utes to the north, remembering the bitter struggle of the past decade. Until a formal agreement had been made

between the two Indian groups, most Navajos considered it too dangerous to venture too close to the lands of their enemy.

This did not stop Navajo Agent James H. Miller from traveling to the
area with his post trader, John Ayres, Ben Thomas, the agency farmer,
and Jésus Arviso, translator, to determine the feasibility of establishing a
subagency that could encourage agricultural endeavors along the river.
The group camped beside the San Juan and in sight of the Shiprock formation, unaware that two Weeminuche Utes were waiting for an opportunity to steal their horses. Early in the morning of June 11, 1872, a shot
rang out, arrows whizzed over the blanket-wrapped men asleep on the
ground, and all but one of the party's horses were driven away. Miller lay
dead from a bullet wound in the head, the remaining men were unable
to pursue, and there was no way of notifying the military for assistance,
which never materialized. This remained vivid proof of why Navajos
avoided the area.[25]

Thomas V. Keam, the agent in charge during Miller's absence, assumed
control of the agency at Fort Defiance and continued to promote the
idea that the Shiprock area would be an ideal place to establish stronger
control over the region. In September 1872, he retraced Miller's steps
to see for himself, enthusiastically reporting the possibilities of what
he found. He wrote of the future site in glowing terms of its potential:
"In this immediate vicinity, I found some of the best and most fertile
lands in New Mexico, one strip being ten miles long and averaging one
and one-half miles wide, containing 9,600 acres; this and others in the
vicinity have advantages over every other part of the Navajo Reservation in climate and water facilities. Corn enough could be raised here,
and in the immediate vicinity to support the whole Navajo Nation. . . .
This place I selected as the most suitable locality for erecting temporary
agency buildings, store houses, etc."[26] Still, there was one big problem.

Keam bewailed the fact that the Navajos were afraid to use the area.
The Utes continued to raid into the Chuska Valley and along the river,
seizing Navajo crops and intimidating isolated homesteads. In his report
to the commissioner of Indian affairs, Keam wrote, "I would here state
that the few Utes who visit this part of the Reservation, in small numbers (as there are not over three hundred in all who pretend to claim
this country), are a great source of trouble and dread to the Navajos,
and as they have never made an attempt to work, and still persist in this

mode of living, they come to the cornfields of the Navajos in season and make them common property by helping themselves, and the Navajos to avoid trouble bear them patiently."[27] Within months of Keam's report, the superintendent of Indian affairs, Nathaniel Pope, approved the establishment of an agency on the site Miller and Keam designated, with the promise that the military would handle the Ute issue so that the resources of the land could be made available for Navajo use. It took another thirty-one years for this to become a reality. By that time, changes in reservation boundaries for both Navajos and Utes, military interventions, settlement of the frontier by a host of different groups, technological changes, and shifts in Indian policy added to the momentum for having more local control of the burgeoning Navajo population at the northern end of the reservation. The burden of establishing the facility at Shiprock fell on the shoulders of William T. Shelton.

Shelton, a ten-year veteran of the Indian Service when he arrived in New Mexico with the assignment to create a new agency, originally hailed from Waynesville, North Carolina. Having worked with the Cherokee and Havasupai previously, he had already established his reputation as a firm promoter of Christian values with a staunch work ethic that, when combined with a stern sense of law and order, made him an iconic example of turn-of-the-century WASP (white Anglo-Saxon Protestant) values that characterized general American beliefs at the time. His responsibility was to bring peace to the northern borders of the Navajo Reservation, to be an advocate for his charges in settling disputes with neighboring Anglo and Indian elements, to limit habits—alcohol, gambling, polygamy, fighting, and some religious practices—that stood in the way of "civilizing" the Indian, and above all, to promote a work ethic that would lead to economic development and prosperity. With his wife, Hattie Pitts Shelton, by his side, he set out to dramatically change the lifestyle that the Navajos had been living for centuries and to bring them into mainstream America.

The remainder of this chapter looks at the twelve-plus years of Shelton's leadership as the agent at Shiprock. He enjoyed measurable success in promoting Navajo welfare but also some real problems that led to his departure under a cloud of accusations and denial. However, no one can deny that he was a hard worker and an able administrator in the multifaceted undertakings of building an agency, running a boarding school, promoting agricultural and livestock programs, controlling recalcitrant leaders fighting to maintain the status quo, and attempting to change Navajo moral values. His impact was tremendous, as witnessed by his Navajo name of Naat'áani Nééz, "Tall Boss or Leader," the same title by which the town of Shiprock is known today. In fulfillment of what Agents Miller, Keam, and Shelton prophesied, the community is also one of the two largest on the Navajo Reservation, with the 2010 Navajo Census recording a total population of over nine thousand.[28] This is how it all began.

On September 11, 1903, Shelton arrived on site and immediately set to work developing the San Juan School and Agency, later called the Shiprock Agency. Many Navajos already lived in the area and watched carefully as the first log and adobe homes arose, soon to be replaced by larger, more permanent structures built of stone or fired adobe. The first two buildings made of stone were a house for personnel and a day school for education. Other structures followed—a barn, gas house, laundry facility, pump house, and an addition to the cottage. These were made, for the most part, with local materials, the rest being shipped in from Durango. There were problems. Some of the construction contractors wanted to use sandstone, which would soon crumble, or river stones, which were rounded and had to be faced. Shelton would not settle for an inferior product, sending rock samples to Washington, D.C., in response to complaints levied against him by the builders. Members of the Indian Office vindicated the agent's judgment, ensuring there were good foundational and above-ground construction materials.[29]

Fortunately, the agency also had the right kind of clay and sand, which when heated provided a good quality fired brick. As with the rock, Shelton sent samples to Washington, received approval, and had his contractors turn out a huge number—an estimated 531,000—to be used in the school buildings and dormitories for students. The process was not without its problems. Firing brick requires a lot of labor to get the right consistency of water, clay, and sand mixed, mold it by hand, sun dry it, and then heat it in a kiln. The frosts of fall and cold of winter prevented firing, while the floods of spring, rainstorms of summer, and poor results in a kiln all took their toll. An estimated 40 percent of the bricks fashioned for this project were lost to one of these fates.[30] Water to make the bricks came from an irrigation ditch already in operation

nearby, and as long as the Indians and school had priority in using the
water running in the ditch from the river, Shelton approved its use.

The small well that had been sufficient in the early days of the school
needed to be replaced by a far more robust source of water. While Shelton
and government inspectors considered the San Juan River pure enough
at that time, they also realized that circumstances had changed and that
a constant flow of underground water was necessary for all of the functions of a growing boarding school. To that end, builders finished in
June a large twelve-foot-diameter by sixteen-foot-deep well, lined with
rock above the water level to prevent the sides from caving in.[31] The
completed project produced 30,000 gallons of water for ten hours each
day it was pumped, an amount superseding the required 20,000 gallon
goal, encouraging Shelton to write, "The well is in every way a success."[32]

Wood for construction and fuel in this high desert environment presented its own challenges. Firing brick required huge amounts of fuel to
keep an intense heat at a constant temperature for a week. A coal mine
on the south side of the river offered another source of heat but it was
twenty miles distant; the mine at the Hogback was only ten miles away
from the school, but required greater development of infrastructure and
would come later.[33] So initially the firing of brick depended on wood.
The men under contract for this work wanted to take the easiest route
to obtaining it and so started skinning trees that grew along the banks
of the river and trees that served as shade on Indian farms. Shelton soon
put a stop to this, warning them that their activities would cause large-
scale uncontrolled erosion along the river, would anger the Indians
who prized their trees as a protection from the intense summer sun,
and would generally denude the landscape. He pointed out areas farther
away that required hauling timber over longer distances and insisted
that Navajo men receive the employment. Obtaining straight boards
for construction was also an issue. While some were shipped in from
the railroad in Durango, the agent authorized a sawmill, located thirty-
five miles away in the Chuska Mountains near Sanostee, as a more local
source. The contractor, George E. Hopper, built the sawmill in 1905, and
subcontracted with trader Joseph R. Wilkins, who hired Navajos to cut
and haul the trees to the mill and then the lumber to the agency, where a
drying kiln prepared it for the construction projects. Shelton considered
the final product high quality.[34]

Trees from the Chuska range played another role in Navajo economic development when turned into telephone poles. At the turn of the twentieth century, telephones were making their debut in more isolated parts of the West. In towns along the San Juan River and northern New Mexico, the Colorado Telephone Company was stringing lines that not only connected these communities but also sites across the river, the new agency being one of them. Shelton was highly supportive, believing that this service reduced travel time and hardship with electronic ease. By May 1904, the lines had already reached Fruitland and would soon extend ten more miles to Jewett, the agency, and Simpson's trading post fifteen miles to the south on the eastern edge of the reservation. With the agent's permission, Navajos could harvest, ship, and emplace the telephone poles cut on the Chuska Mountains and would receive good prices and wages for their project. Trader Joseph R. Wilkins at Little Water was already interested in purchasing poles for a stretch between Farmington and Largo, New Mexico, and had been involved with previous sales along the San Juan from which some Navajos benefited financially. Shelton supported all these efforts.[35]

One problem that became increasingly prominent was the crossing of the San Juan. With the school and agency on the north side and reservation on the south, there developed a constant stream of traffic that depended on natural fords to get riders and wagons across. During the spring and summer flash floods, it sometimes took days before the waters subsided, tying up men and equipment on both sides. Shelton mentioned that for three or four months in the spring, when a lot of important work like sheep dipping, farming, and hauling lumber was necessary, nothing moved. Acceptable fording sites could quickly deteriorate with a heavy bedload of sand sweeping down the river, miring wagons and teams in what had a day before been a problem-free crossing site. Erratic changes in the flow of water shifted between the banks, which made bridging the stream difficult. Farther upstream, some towns attempted using a cabled ferry system, but the shifting volumes of water tore out the anchor points and swept the boats downstream, sometimes capsizing them and drowning individuals in the river's fifteen-foot-high sand waves.

Shelton, ever the problem solver, set to work. For four years he used Navajo labor to "harden" a site on the river with lumber and riprapping, then tested it for two months of high water. The banks held. The agent went to the Indian Bureau and requested funds for a suspension bridge. A regular steel structure would not work given the span of the river, the length of required beams, and the necessity of using pillars in moving water that did not have good bedrock foundations for necessary footing construction. A suspension bridge would have its entire superstructure above the river and away from water and large floating trees and drift-wood. In 1909 the government allocated $10,000 for a bridge; within two years after completion, it was gone, a fatality of the river.[36]

Tussles over Land, Water, and Personalities

Other issues occurred well before Shelton officially set foot on the school site, some of which were not of his doing. Mary Eldridge's mission had grown significantly. The agent soon hired her and enlisted the aid of her staff in his civilizing of the Indian people in the area. He did not realize that he would soon inherit land issues that had occurred years before and that they would darken his relationship with his newly appointed field matron. The problem arose between two unlikely candidates for turmoil. Enough has been written about Eldridge to know that she aggressively pursued change and sought the welfare of her charges. The other person, Sandoval, was a Navajo man of high standing in the Navajo and Anglo communities. Shelton reported that Sandoval had worked hard to enroll Navajo children in the Fort Lewis boarding school, and that he dressed in "citizen clothes," had a farm that showed exceptional care, was well-respected as a leader in his community, made exquisite silver jewelry, and very closely approached the ideal of a "civilized man." Superintendent Ruben Perry at Fort Defiance appreciated Sandoval's testimony in a murder case that convicted a Navajo person who otherwise would have been freed.[37] Neither agent had a complaint.

Neither did Henry Chee Dodge, Navajo translator and future chairman of the Navajo Tribal Council. He had known Sandoval a long time, in both an official and unofficial capacity, and so provided testimony on his behalf. He swore under oath that Mrs. Eldridge had knowingly settled on part of Sandoval's property even though she was repeatedly told not to; that she had refused to accept his appointment by a previous agent as a regional leader so she could run things according to her own wishes; that since she could not control him, she had disparaged his character, claiming drunkenness and rebelliousness, both of which were disproved; that she had enlisted the aid of Samuel E. Shoemaker, supervisor of constructed ditches along the San Juan, to work with her against anything that Sandoval tried to accomplish; that the previous agent, Hayzlett, had been aware of the problem but had done nothing to fix it; and that she had at times worked at odds with existing agents.[38]

Now the issue sat squarely in Shelton's lap. The more he investigated, the more he sided with Sandoval, turning Eldridge and Shoemaker against him to the point that they preferred charges against him and his entire management of the agency. Both complainants provided sworn testimony, but seemed to be more accommodating when under oath. The list of charges was extensive and was rooted in daily interactions ranging from intimidation to purchasing horses, from boundary lines to incivility, from broken promises to Indian and agent personal qualities, and from misuse of the Navajo police force to improper accounting procedures for government property. One salient point raised in Eldridge's and Shoemaker's statements was that Eldridge, who had been the first in the area and was placed in charge by the superintendent at Fort Defiance, felt displaced when Shoemaker arrived and assumed control, and that Shoemaker, in turn, felt displaced when Shelton arrived. The field matron and the ditch supervisor, who had been at odds with each other, joined in support against the new agent.[39]

Shelton would have none of it, refuting each charge in detail in a twenty-eight page document sent to Indian Bureau investigator Charles H. Dickson. Filled with information about daily operation of the agency, the report, accompanying interviews, and observations convinced Dickson that action needed to be taken, but not against Shelton. He not only supported the agent, but followed much of his advice in concluding the investigation. To bring peace and stability, he recommended and received Shoemaker's and Eldridge's resignations from the Indian Service and departure from the reservation; the buildings constructed on Navajo land with Cambridge Indian Association money were purchased for $700 while Sandoval was paid $50 for the land he had lost; and the unpaid claims of contractors were collected and settled quickly.[40] Dickson's evaluation of the agent left no doubt as to the final outcome of the charges: "Regarding Superintendent

Shelton's management and general businesslike attitude, it is worthy of every possible support from the office."[41]

Shoemaker's departure may have solved one problem, but it created a number of others, among the most prominent being the construction and maintenance of irrigation ditches. The 1890s witnessed the building of formal irrigation ditches along the San Juan and other stream courses that brought increasingly large amounts of agricultural lands under cultivation. Take for instance the Carrizo Ditch that watered lands close to the mountains and that used the same floodplains planted by the Ancestral Puebloans. The three-to-four-foot ditch drained waters from Carrizo Creek and spread the liquid gold over the land through three laterals. This made available three hundred acres for Navajo use.[42] Other "water works" followed. Improving twelve large ditches funneling water from the San Juan, digging laterals to spread the water, excavating a new well for the agency, shoring up the banks of the river and headgates for irrigation, building bridges for ditch crossings, paying for specialists in plotting the lines and overseeing proper slope gradient in the ditches, and purchasing materials for all of this construction required thousands of dollars. Navajo labor was either free or low-wage, but the Indians were eager to put the agency's plows and scrapers to work and to benefit from the finished project. An added bonus from the agent's perspective was that he was able to parcel out sections of land and assign individual family ownership, inculcating an ideal practiced in dominant American society but at odds with traditional leader-controlled economics. Under this system, roughly one hundred acres serviced twenty families.[43]

Still, there were plenty of challenges. Shelton was very aware that with the increasing population along the river, there well could be an appropriation of Indian water by Anglo citizens that would render irrigation impractical. He carefully set about, having surveyed plats and then filing claims on specific ditches and water use, to preempt any misunderstanding of who was there first and what amount of water was necessary to protect Indian rights.[44] The eleven-year-old Cambridge Ditch, four miles in length, still had the most successful irrigation lines in the area, spreading water over 1,200 acres of land. "The Indians living on the farms covered by this ditch are more progressive, generally, than any other Indians on this part of the reservation. They are building substantial homes, planting fruit trees, have sown considerable alfalfa to raise hay for their stock, build good permanent fences to enclose their farms, and altogether they deserve much credit for the progress they have made."[45] The main drawback was that the ditch heading was often not on the fluctuating level of the San Juan River, and so the Indians had to build a riprap wall and dam to divert the water to the right level, while high water consistently wiped out these structures each year. The solution to making a permanent entry way was to "cut a tunnel through a point of rock, some three thousand feet above the present ditch heading, then excavate a ditch, away from the river, for about 3,500 feet below the tunnel to a point where the new ditch will intersect the old one, thus gaining about one foot in grade."[46] With a few modifications, the agent completed the project, but not without herculean effort. Work at improving ditches, riprapping to prevent agency property and agricultural lands from washing away, issues of crop success (corn, wheat, and alfalfa), and the employment of Navajo labor continued to be major concerns for years to come.

Shiprock: Showcase of Progress

Shelton, as a fomenter of progress, took great pride in seeing the agency and school blossom. Just two years after its inception, the *Farmington Enterprise* published a lengthy article about just how successful the attempt to move Navajos down the road of acculturation had been. In it, the author noted that as soon as a person crossed the reservation boundary below Jewett, the roads were new, straight, and in good condition. A mile before the agency, the road merged into a wide, well-graded street, leading to a site where the buildings and grounds were artistically laid out with young shade trees. There were a large number of already finished buildings with others under construction. "The whole institution, when completed as planned, will cover about six blocks, which will be beautifully apportioned with a view both to utility and magnificence. Young trees have been arranged among the larger ones and walks and trivia among fine buildings, beds of flowers and shady nooks. In all, a picture which cannot fail to wean the wary red man from his customs of generations to those of a higher ideal and to habits more satisfactory and effective."[47]

The article continued to extol the virtues of each physical structure, separating them according to their functions as part of the agency or school. The stone home of the superintendent; eight adobe residences alternating as homes for white and Indian employees; a long log warehouse to hold goods to pay for Navajo labor; blacksmith and carpenter shops, a stable, and a camp house completed the agency space. The long spruce log school would soon be replaced by a three-story brick building eighty feet long, which was to be matched by a three-story boy's and a three-story girl's dormitory, with a school warehouse and barn to facilitate agricultural instruction, and a brick hospital soon underway. The main buildings were heated by steam, lighted by acetylene gas lights, and serviced with water from a pump that pushed 35,000 gallons of water a day. Other facilities on the south side of the river included a warehouse, barn, and other buildings to facilitate the government program when the river proved impassable. Satellite farming operations in Aneth, Utah; in the Lukachukai Mountains, Arizona; and at Two Grey Hills, New Mexico, were serviced by greatly improved roads and irrigation ditches. Navajo labor, which sometimes comprised as many as two hundred workers, was at the base of all of these accomplishments, as roads, ditches, sheep dipping plants, the agency coal mine, bridges, farmlands, a sawmill, telephone lines, and 12,000 fruit trees ready for distribution sprang from the desert. Nine white supervisors, including Shelton, served as physician, blacksmith, carpenter, matron, and farmers, alongside twenty full-time Indian employees, including a four-man police force. This did not include approximately fifty people from local communities who also provided services.[48] All of this was in marked contrast to the desert-dwelling Navajo people based in a livestock economy.

As agency and school became increasingly established, Shelton obtained a more accurate account of exactly what he was working with. The Northern Navajo Agency encompassed about 5,000 square miles spread over Arizona, New Mexico, and Utah, with an estimated population of 8,000 Indians, 2,500 of whom were eligible for school, being between the ages of six and eighteen.[49] Small numbers of these children were attending mission schools in Aneth, Farmington, and Liberty (New Mexico), but the vast majority of them were involved in the family livelihood of raising livestock and agriculture.[50] When the government school opened its doors on February 8, 1907, it had 106 pupils, all of whom were boarding, while turning others away due to lack of space.[51] As new buildings opened, more were accommodated, with a short-term goal of raising the number to 150. No Indian children attended off-reservation public schools.

John L. Conway, a local newspaperman, visited the school in April 1908, providing an interesting view, not only of its activities, but also associated values during this Progressive Era in history. After describing the physical facilities in which he observed intense orderliness of the environment with the buildings all aligned, the wide well-kept streets, beautiful lawns, and flower gardens, he remarked:

> The regular routine during the school term is interesting as well as instructive. In the laundry, the children show no signs of sluggishness but hurry to and fro changing the clothes from the wash machine to the rinsing water, guiding them through the wringer and carried to the line to dry. Specimens of the neat work which the Navajo girl is capable of are to be seen in the sewing room. The playroom and dormitories present the same appearance that is noticeable throughout the entire place—cleanliness and order. Numbered books with the Navajo as well as the American name of the pupil neatly typewritten underneath are to be found in the washroom and in the dormitory halls where their school clothes are hung when not in use.
>
> . . . Each pupil spends half of each day in the classroom and the other half on the farm, in the garden or poultry yards, in the industrial shops, in the kitchens, sewing rooms, laundry, or wherever practical instruction can be given that is likely to be of use hereafter. The progress made by the pupils in the San Juan school so far is really remarkable.[52]

Conway goes on to laud the students' ability to carry on a normal conversation in English, their hard work in the beet fields of Colorado, their aptitude in trades, their steady dependability, and their high intelligence compared to other American Indian groups. Still, they were below par when compared to Anglos. "To develop the natural capacities of these desert Bedouins is the object of the San Juan and other Indian schools. It is true of all the Indian tribes, but particularly true of the Navajo, that they are slow with the brain, but quick with the hands. It is, of course, advisable to teach them to speak and write English, and to impart to them at least the rudiments of the common school branches, but beyond this, scholastic training would be of little use or value. If they are to be equipped to hold their own on anything like equal terms with dominant whites, and to work out any other destiny than final extinction, it must be by developing their natural capabilities by a rational system of industrial training."[53] Shelton echoed similar sentiments about the necessity of the education his school was providing and of its practicality, although he was not as outspoken on the racial themes.

On a lighter note, there was time for recreation—but even that was part of acculturation. Shelton wrote that the boys had the run of the farm, chasing jackrabbits and riding in boats, but baseball, football, marbles, and tops were also popular. During inclement weather they played dominoes, checkers, sang school songs, and read books. The girls, on the other hand, sewed, beaded, swung on swings and hammocks, jumped rope, played basketball, and went for walks when accompanied by an employee. Some even wove little Navajo blankets. The two sexes came together for chaperoned Saturday night dances and socials.[54] A headline in a newspaper of the time recognized, "Shiprock, An Object Lesson in Industrial Democracy," with the introductory sentence parroting biblical verse by declaring, "And now abideth these three: Land, Labor, and Organization and the greatest of these is Organization."[55] After commenting on the widespread fields of alfalfa and corn, the 600 melons "placed on the lawn in systematic order" and free for the taking, 600 gallons of canned fruits, dried fruits and vegetables, and 1,000 gallons of sorghum, as well as the Bible study competition in the evening, the author added that one of the biggest contributions was the lack of flies. He attributed it to the cleanliness of the agency and commented, "This shows what could be done at Farmington or elsewhere with proper sanitation and care." He closed his piece by congratulating Shelton on his work of "inestimable value to both the Indian and white man as it will soon bring them together with the same hopes and aspirations."

Health and Welfare—Cultural Interpretation

Shelton's influence also radiated far beyond the classroom. In a cultural, economic, and medicinal sense, the Navajo people invested a great deal of faith in their medicine men. They were (and are) the repositories of religious knowledge, the arbiters in diagnosing and curing illness, the voice of leadership in many communities, and the keeper of traditions. These powerful men often turned vocal at the inroads being made in traditional culture by the agent and his minions. Conflict resulted, some of which is discussed in chapter 4. From a purely medical position, the differences between western healing and that offered by the traditionalists was huge, the former being based in scientific principles, although primitive by today's standards, while the latter was tied to traditional stories that hearkened back to the creation, the use of herbs, religious healing, and faith. The nearest physicians at the start of the Shiprock Agency were located in Farmington, thirty-five miles away. Shelton felt that their services were expensive, undependable, and seldom available, and so importuned the government for assistance. He reasoned: "These Indians appear willing to put aside medicine men, singings and other curative methods when shown the good results of first-class medical attention; and there is not a doubt that many lives would be saved each year, and much unnecessary suffering be prevented by prompt medical attention."[56] To this end, he recommended a physician for the agency.

The necessity for healthcare was underscored by the experiences of Jessie Smith, an eighteen-year-old girl who joined the Methodist mission at Hogback in 1902 as a young inexperienced worker from Colorado. Placed in the dispensary with no other supervision, she treated Navajos coming in for everything from a common cold to diphtheria, pneumonia, syphilis, and appendicitis. One man brought in his seven-year-old son suffering from measles. Jessie scraped off the piñon sap smeared over the festering pustules, provided a pill to reduce the high temperature, and gave comfort. The father, with an angry medicine man who had rendered earlier treatment, came to the clinic and took the boy out, but three days later, the father returned and profusely thanked the nurse-in-training for saving his son's life.[57] Jessie also recalled that when students returned from their summer break in September, the first month was spent removing lice from their hair—especially the girls, since the boys had their heads shaved—as well as treating skin diseases, especially impetigo. Malnutrition was another problem. Little wonder that the establishment of a government hospital at Shiprock relieved much of the pressure felt by this and other mission aid stations.

Five years later Shelton reported a significant increase in the number of sick Navajos seeking help from his lone physician. Many of these patients did not understand how and why the medicine worked, but were pleased with the results; they also expected one dose to create the desired effect, and when it did not, local medicine men argued against its use. "The native medicine man is jealous of the white man, and, as yet, his influence has a tendency to prevent the following out of instructions, both sanitary and medicinal, outlined by the physician."[58] Even the frequency of taking medication in a system based on the movement of the sun created difficulties. Differences in language and understanding the cure of the illness as well as the effect of the medicine created opportunities ripe for misunderstanding. Add to this the Navajos' mobile lifestyle and the proliferation of diseases like tuberculosis, trachoma, and influenza as contact with the dominant culture increased, and one can see how sickness not only spread, but was impossible to wipe out. Shelton continuously requested more physicians and a hospital, but truly effective help for the broader population was years in coming.

Another place that the agency became involved with medicine was in assisting the Navajos in caring for their livestock. Sheep, in particular, were infested with a debilitating disease called scabies, in which mites (*Psoroptes ovis*) burrowed into the hide and caused intense itching, loss of wool, open sores with oozing pus, and even death through diminished health and hypothermia. This scourge was spread through direct contact with infected animals, equipment, or people they had come in contact with, and by grazing sheep on land already infected by other animals.

In the early 1900s, much of the land on the reservation and its surrounding area to the north and east was considered prime sheep country. Navajo and Anglo stockmen were in constant search of range and not afraid to cross boundary lines in the pursuit of grazing areas. The Federal Bureau of Animal Industry, headquartered in Albuquerque, had the responsibility of checking livestock for diseases, assisting owners with advice, and fielding issues affecting grazing and animal welfare. New Mexican and Utah ranchers began registering complaints that Navajo flocks were ranging off reservation and that their herds were infecting those of the Anglos. Shelton soon became embroiled in a series of charges and countercharges.

Complaints, ever since the 1880s, had existed, but with the agency at Shiprock playing an increasingly active role and as lands became more settled, there were increased expectations that something would be done about the spread of disease. In the spring of 1906, Dr. Lewis Metsker, inspector in charge of the Bureau of Animal Industry, accused Navajos of running infected herds on the public domain, suggesting they should return to their own lands and have their sheep treated for scabies. Shelton replied that those Indians off the reservation should be treated as all other livestock owners using the public domain and that many of them were not from the reservation but had lived in surrounding areas, especially to the north, all of their lives. Some who dwelled as far away as Navajo Mountain had large numbers of sheep and were "very wild and uncivilized."[59] Many of these people had never even seen an agent and were not about to come to the reservation to have their sheep dipped to combat scabies. Even some of the Navajos who lived close to dipping vats would not move their animals a short distance, while others complained that the solution through which the sheep swam ruined their wool and the taste of the meat. There was little chance that the other Navajos would travel a long way. Shelton, always shorthanded, hoped to hire some men to supervise the process on the reservation and then to reach out to those farther away. Perhaps dipping stations could be built off Indian lands for those Navajos living at a distance.[60]

The huge geographical area of over 5,000 square miles provided a daunting challenge. Shelton suggested getting materials to construct fifty small on-reservation dipping stations to eradicate scabies. With 50 dipping tanks, 50 water heaters, 2,500 gallons of Black Leaf sheep dip, and 30,000 pounds of sheep dip sulfur, he could handle the flocks on his part of the reservation. One of the problems was that the animals required an initial dipping and then, after ten days, a second follow-up; this procedure had to be performed twice a year. Large flocks quickly denuded the land, and so a series of smaller setups was preferable to having a more centralized system. Shorter distances, less trespass on other people's ranges, easier on the environment—this approach was more user-friendly.

Those off the reservation presented a greater problem. In some areas to the east, white ranchers accepted Navajo use of the land, but to the north, there was not as much accord, especially when some of these herds ranged into the thousands. Shelton gave an example of what happened if flocks congregated as they did at Little Water on the southern end of the reservation. "A large dipping plant was erected and thousands of Indian sheep were brought there for dipping, and while holding them there for one dipping, the grass for many miles around has been destroyed by the sheep and the Indians residing there have been obliged to take their sheep elsewhere to find grass for them to subsist on."[61] Bringing off-reservation Navajos onto the reservation just compounded problems. On the other hand, if Shelton had sites created off reservation he could meet the needs of those Indians; but there was a catch. The government system of accountability for property required the agent to sign for and be responsible for the equipment that was out of his control—which Shelton refused to do.

Moving the equipment frequently had its own problems. As an example, the agent explained about creating a dip over fifty miles away from the agency, traveling on a rough and sandy road, making it necessary to dip the sheep four times a year, twice in the spring, allowing an interval of ten days, then twice in the fall. These dips and tanks were large and made of galvanized iron, not easily handled, and after moving them a few times became torn up and useless. These plants needed to be made permanent so that the Indians could return to use them often.[62] While the Indian Bureau did not grant permission, Shelton proceeded to "loan" an off-reservation Navajo man a large-sized vat to be hauled by his four horse teams. The Indian also received a water heater, 800 feet of lumber, 50 pounds of nails, 2,000 pounds of sulfur dip, and 200 gallons of tobacco dip—enough equipment and a large enough vat to handle 1,500 sheep a day. The agent also sent a government farmer and two other men to assist in the construction of the site. Shelton knew well that this loan was going to be permanent, but took the chastisement on behalf of his charges.[63]

By the end of 1906, the agent had placed half of his fifty vats—mostly on the reservation but some off. Many were located near trading posts including Hogback, Two Grey Hills, Noel's store, Teec Nos Pos, Baldwin's store, and Sanostee as well as at sites that would soon have stores like Beautiful Mountain, Lukachukai, Captain Tom's Wash, and Red Rock, allowing more than 100,000 sheep to be treated that fall.[64] Little wonder that Shelton pointed with pride when he wrote, "The farmer in charge of the sheep industry is continually on the go from one place to another, teaching the Indians how to mix the dip and handle the work, selecting locations for dips, and assisting with the installation of new plants. It will be only a short time until practically every sheep on the reservation will be dipped regularly, and the disease of scabies will be entirely eradicated. . . . I have given the subject much thought and attention, and have pursued the course that I believe will be of most practical benefit to the Indians, that of installing smaller dips and teaching and inducing the Indians to do their own work."[65] In a later correspondence, he noted that of 75,000 sheep dipped recently both on and off the reservation, there was little trace of scabies found on any of them; he then "guaranteed" that white ranchers had a bigger problem with this infectious blight than did his Indians.[66] He even suggested that the past year's furor may have been generated by men who wanted to obtain use of more public domain by evicting Navajo herds. Shelton, ever vigilant, strongly advocated for the Navajos.

The Northern Navajo Shiprock Fair—Instituting an Institution

A final example of the enculturation process of introducing mainstream America to the Navajos is that of the Northern Navajo or Shiprock Fair that Shelton began in 1909, which continues to this day. Inserted into cultural values important to the Navajos—weaving, silversmithing, agriculture, livestock development, wool production, and certain ceremonial aspects—came open competition with neighbors vying against neighbors, trading posts rivaling each other, and region challenging region. Initial results in fostering competition proved gratifying.

On October 20 and 21, people gathered at the agency to participate in the results of two months of planning. The Navajos produced 290 exhibits, each containing from five to sixty articles. Categories included blankets, silver jewelry, buffalo robes, beadwork, horses, cows, sheep, goats, and a wide variety of farm produce. On the top of the agricultural list was corn, then potatoes, pumpkins, squash, beans, watermelons, wheat, oats, alfalfa, apples, and peaches. Judges offered first-to-fourth-place prizes for each category, the rewards ranging from double harnesses, disc harrows, corn drills, and cook stoves to hoes, shovels, and mattocks. There were even awards for the prettiest and cleanest Navajo babies,

The Shiprock Agency and School under Shelton were the flagships of "progress" and "civilization" on the Navajo Reservation. Lawns planted with grass, flowers, and shade trees; orderly and attractive educational facilities; large-scale irrigation projects; and an established police force were examples of how the desert could blossom as a rose—along with these watermelons awaiting the crowds at the Shiprock Fair. Courtesy of Farmington Museum, New Mexico.

the proud mothers receiving a fifty-pound sack of flour.[67] Although the descriptions in the newspapers and some of the fair events were highly paternalistic, they provided an opportunity for the Anglo community to view their neighbors as moving along the path the white man considered "progress." For the Navajos, the event was a chance to socialize and compete for prizes.

The fair drew contestants from more than seventy miles away. There were horse races, footraces, tug-of-wars, dances, relays, and a Nightway ceremony. Trading posts from different areas had booths that competed in all types of industries, especially in that of weaving rugs and blankets. Local and regional styles, as well as the skill of particular weavers, gave a flair of color and meaning that identified people and places associated with specific posts. Specialty rugs declaring the name of the posts, and products from that area fostered regional pride and competition.

Shelton invited tourists to attend, and encouraged Navajos to sell traditional artifacts such as bows and arrows and silverwork, as well as to perform in Indian dances that were part of religious ceremonies but were also purely social events. By 1914 seven hundred blankets graced the traders' booths, five of which were purchased and sent to the Panama-Pacific International Exposition.[68]

Trader Franc Johnson Newcomb gave a particularly detailed account of the 1913 fair and the role Shelton played to showcase the efforts of both school and agency. Each grade had their own exhibit in which classroom art, sewing, embroidery, furniture, leathercraft, silversmith objects, and other skills taught in the school were displayed. There was a school parade led by its own band, followed by sack races, wheelbarrow races, and horse races. One particularly amusing contest involved Navajo females. "The wagon race for women was a spectacular event in which four women stood at the starting line, each holding a team with the harnesses across the horses' backs. At a signal from the starter, these women ran to waiting wagons, fastening straps and buckles as they ran, backed the teams over the wagon tongues and buckled the traces. Then with reins in hand, they climbed into the wagons and drove full gallop around the three-fourths mile race track. It took a strong arm to manage the nervous horses which sometimes bolted when only half hitched, so it was not always the fastest team that won the race."[69]

The festivities continued throughout the day with a huge beef and mutton barbecue, baked beans, and apples served by Shelton's staff and eaten on the agency lawn. In the evening a Yé'ii Bicheii dance began, which lasted all night. The last day of the fair, which had now become a three-to-four day event, was called "Watermelon Day." During the spring and summer, schoolchildren had planted watermelon seeds between each stalk of corn in a vast agricultural project. For instance in 1909, the agency announced that it had produced 30,000 melons, 1,000 bushels of potatoes, 3,000 bunches of celery, 10,000 pounds of onions, 20,000 pounds of tomatoes, 600 gallons of sorghum, and 150 tons of alfalfa. This yield came from 60 acres planted in corn, 20 in alfalfa, 20 in apples, and 15 acres in gardens.[70] Thus Newcomb was not exaggerating when she described four or five wagon loads of melons spread out on the athletic field for a noonday feast. Guards sent word that things were ready and for people to bring their knives, with a single stipulation that everything had to be consumed there and not removed from the grounds. "The place was crowded so that there was barely room to sit. Families of four or five would have three large watermelons—each person claiming half a melon—and the tots would consume almost as much as the grownups. It was quite a sight and I am sure there was never anything like it elsewhere on the Reservation."[71] A truly sweet way to introduce the benefits of education, competition, and "progress."

Yet there is no missing the underlying reason for all of this—the early missionary efforts, establishment of schools, the agency, hospital, livestock programs—the list goes on. Bringing "civilization" to the Navajos fit the agenda of progressive thought, Progressive politics, and cultural worldview of the dawning twentieth century. While much of this was done with good intent, we are able to look back on it a century later and see the gaps in some of the thinking. Perhaps a quote from the *Farmington Enterprise* on October 29, 1909, as it reported on the success of the first Shiprock Fair, provides a precise summary of this worldview. The article explains the purpose of the fair was so that "the ignorance and superstition of a barbarous people might be attacked and the influences which have fettered them might be obliterated, so that freed from its bondage, the Navajo race might take its place among the useful and beneficial elements of the nation, contributing its share toward the industry and enjoying its proportion of the advantages embraced in the common stock."[72] As benevolent as this may seem, there were those who rejected this view and fought against the pressures it created, as seen in chapter 4. What can be agreed upon is that a lot of energy and personal resolve went in to trying to help the Navajos, a very independent people, avoid a fate that seemed, to Anglos at this time, to be inexorably moving them toward extinction. Mission, school, and agency were the triumvirate trying to save the Navajo people.

CHAPTER FOUR

Troublous Times and Temperaments
Shelton Faces Conflicts at Shiprock,
1903–1916

The early years of the Shiprock Agency under William T. Shelton's guidance were a time of innovation, community growth, and economic development, but they were also thirteen years of challenges that came from every direction. In addition to trials the environment presented on an intermittent basis, there were those posed by internal sources such as the Shoemaker and Eldridge friction discussed in chapter 3, headaches with contractors who disputed Shelton's knowledge and authority, and staffing problems with both Anglo and Navajo people serving in difficult positions. One of the most frequent challenges was that of recruiting and maintaining a Navajo police force as the blunt tool for ensuring peace and compliance with agency dictates. Government demands and community politics added their own peculiar wrinkles to daily life.

Yet by far, the greatest challenges to Shelton's authority came from sources within Navajo culture. Even before the start of the Northern Agency, there were local forces that chafed against the bridling effect of Anglo governance with its new requirements. Friction imposed by seemingly arbitrary rules handed down by distant Washington, D.C.; the abolition of old ways that had been part of traditional Navajo culture, some of which had been instituted by the holy people at the time of creation; forceful cultural leaders—especially medicine men—who controlled spiritual power, who were often wealthy, and who maintained a base of poorer Navajos dependent upon their largess to sustain life—all added to potential conflict. In this chapter, another side of the picture painted in chapter 3 looks at less successful events and confrontations faced by Shelton in bringing twentieth-century civilization to a people not always anxious to embrace it. Some examples are dealt with in a cursory manner but are mentioned to give context to more relevant ones that may not be as fully developed elsewhere.

Establishing Law and Order

A decade before Shelton appeared on the scene, there were already rumblings against government coercion emanating from Agent David Shipley in Fort Defiance. He was an unpopular official who lasted less than three years, but he was determined to fulfill his obligation as outlined in the Compulsory Indian Education Act (1887) of filling the local boarding school with Indian children. The Navajos were not necessarily opposed to the idea of white education, but the draconian discipline enforced at the school drove parents to either withdraw or not send their children. Shipley began to cast a net over distant parts of the reservation for new recruits, which brought him to Round Rock and an encounter with the powerful leader Black Horse.[1]

The account that follows is provided by Father Anselm Weber, who received it from Navajo participants ten years after the occurrence.[2] It is particularly good for two reasons. First, the narrator provides specific detail as to how events unfolded from the Navajo perspective, and second, it is framed in Father Weber's own experience in recruiting children for Anglo education, a marked contrast to Shipley's approach. He began by recognizing that the three government schools in the area struggled to obtain enough students, at a time when his own Franciscan brotherhood was nearing the completion of their school in Saint Michaels, Arizona. Weber loaded his wagon with food, blankets, and clothing for the prospective pupils as reinforcement against the cold late-November weather of 1902. His destination was Red Rock to find families willing to send their children to a distant school. Frank Walker, interpreter, accompanied him on a route that took him to J. B. Moore's trading post in Crystal, New Mexico, thence Cottonwood Pass, which separates the Chuska from Tunicha ranges, and then Two Grey Hills. The rough road, snow and ice, and approaching evening made Win Wetherill's offer of food and lodging tempting, but the two decided to push on in the hopes of staying with a particular Navajo family with school-age children. More days of wearisome travel brought them to Bennett Peak, then to Joe Wilkins's post at Sanostee, and eventually to Naakai Dinaee's camp, where they stayed for a number of days visiting with parents and listening to their concerns.

During this time, Weber learned of how not to recruit children based on Shipley's mistakes of ten years ago. The priest had two men—Mister Black and Navajo Killer—who had been there to fill in the details. The agent arrived with a number of Navajo policemen, two interpreters (Frank Walker and Chee Dodge), and a series of demands that indicated to the fifty men from Red Rock and the Carrizo Mountain area that this was going to be a forced issue. Their leader, Black Horse, instructed them to hide their rifles a quarter mile from the store, to act very pleasant, and to engage the Navajo police in a card game with ammunition as stakes so that if a problem arose, the police would be defenseless. Finally a sentence—"I will bet my head against yours"—would be the signal that things were not working out and that physical action to correct it should be taken.

The next day, the meeting went as expected. What had been a peaceful, happy exchange the previous day went sour. The Navajos explained that they had lost a lot of their children to a diphtheria epidemic, that they did not want to send their remaining offspring far away to school, and that they did not want to be forced against their will. Shipley made demands, Black Horse gave the signal, and the room erupted into turmoil. The Indians pummeled Shipley soundly and dragged him outside ready to stone and knife him to death, but some of the Navajo police were able to intervene and get him inside the trading post owned by Charles Hubbell, who stood behind his counter all the time with pistol and Winchester rifle ready to kill anyone who crossed the line. With doors secured, windows barricaded, and a handful of defenders surrounded by a sea of angry Navajos, both groups decided to resume talks. Walker and Hubbell emerged from the post with the agent, while Black Horse negotiated for his people. To his credit, the Navajo took total responsibility for the incident, explained that they would not part with their children, and asked Shipley if he would drop the whole affair, to which the agent agreed. The white men returned to their defensive position, while some Navajos continued to agitate for burning the store and others spoke for peace.

During the fracas, a Navajo policeman slipped onto a horse and rode to Tsaile, where a detachment of twenty soldiers was stationed under Lieutenant W. C. Brown. As soon as news of the incident became known, the officer was on his way, arriving at Round Rock the next day with his men. By then, things had quieted, Black Horse explained what had happened, the "siege" was lifted, and the officer eventually filed a report in support of the Indians' position, even when Shipley, once safe, placed the blame on them. Father Weber noted later that the school at Fort Defiance never saw any children coming from this area, while he was now bringing to Saint Michaels twenty-one of them—some of whom were the sons of Mister Black and Navajo Killer.[3]

The priest related the care he and others took to get the children safely to school. Each of the twenty-one future students received a blanket to shield against the cold; Weber gave up his seat on the wagon and rode a horse; parents and relatives accompanied the children for the entire trip; accommodations for all were made at posts—Sanostee, Two Grey Hills, and Crystal—along the route; everyone helped get the wagon through Cottonwood Pass, while some transported children until it was safe for them to climb back in; and when they arrived at the mission, a warm room and subsequent feast welcomed the half-frozen boys, girls, and travelers. These were points that lay in stark contrast to Shipley's approach and those found in many accounts concerning the boarding school era. They are provided here to illustrate what some did to encourage positive change.

As Shelton established the Shiprock Agency, but long before the school opened its doors, there were two other issues particularly troublesome for him and the Navajo people he supervised—alcohol and rape. Reminiscing about the first problem, he told of a thirty-five mile trip he made to Farmington in 1903, when he met eighteen drunken Indians coming from Durango. There were also those selling liquor to other Navajos and, to make matters worse, gambling was extensively practiced by almost everyone. He noted that "fifteen or twenty, and sometimes more, would congregate at each of the trading posts during the day and waste their time and money gambling. At some of the posts the traders kept a 'tin horn' gambler at their store for the purpose of getting a crowd together and beating them out of their money."[4]

The agent, charged with upholding the law on his part of the reservation, faced a daunting task. Although sales of alcohol could come from

Utah and Arizona, the chief culprits were in New Mexico and Colorado. The Utes sometimes served as intermediaries, but the off-reservation bars, stores, and bootleggers became well known to those traveling afar so that Cortez, Durango, and smaller communities in Colorado competed under the table with entrepreneurs in Largo, Bloomfield, Fruitland, Blanco, Raton Springs, La Posta, Kinbeto, and Ojo Alamo in New Mexico.[5] According to newspapers, Mexicans often served as intermediaries in the sale and purchase of alcohol; there were even some Navajos who had their hair cut to appear as Hispanics in the hopes of buying and selling their own liquor.[6] The government sent a special agent to investigate all the different permutations of the bootlegging business, pursuing wrongdoers and sending them to court.

Shelton had to be ever vigilant. As railroad lines spread across the country, builders saw a ready pool of labor to be tapped on the reservation. The agent became the deciding factor as to whether this would hurt his efforts or spur the Navajos into the wage economy. When approached, he minced no words, stating he could not "recommend too highly [Navajos] for pick and shovel work or any kind of rough work that they are used to. . . . But it must be understood that they must be properly looked after and not permitted to mix with the drinking, gambling, and rough crowds that usually follow railroad camps. These people are practically free from the liquor habit and it is desirable that every precaution be taken to prevent them from being debauched."[7] The system apparently worked, since six months later he reported 140 men laying track between Farmington and Durango, earning $1.60 a day and with no incident of drinking or gambling.

By the end of the second year (1904–5), Shelton claimed to have put a lid on the illicit activity by gaining the "cooperation of the older and more influential Indians, convincing them that gambling was bad business and detrimental to the best interests of the reservation." For battle trophies from the war against gambling, he collected more than three bushels of playing cards. As for the whiskey traffic, he slowed it to a trickle by assigning an apprehended first-time offender ten days of work at the agency, twenty days for a second offense, and ten days added to the sentence for every subsequent infraction. In the next ten years there were only eleven drinkers brought in for punishment, leading Shelton to boast, "I doubt if there is a community in the United States more free from whiskey, drinking, and gambling than this reservation."[8] While this seems idealistic, Shelton's control was a primary factor that had not been possible until he established the agency to help patrol the liquor traffic on the northern boundaries of the reservation.

Another issue confronting the agent was more deeply imbedded in cultural beliefs—that of sexuality. Shelton, as a Christian, followed the belief that monogamy was the correct practice as opposed to polygamy; that marriage should occur when a woman had reached maturity, defined as late teens or early twenties; and that sexual access was controlled by the individual and her family with consummation taking place after marriage—at least that was the ideal. Navajo culture provided a different framework. When a young woman had her first and second menses, sometime in her early teens, she participated in a ceremony, the *kinaaldá*, which notified all that she was capable of having children and being married.[9] She may or may not be offered by her family at that time, but her eligibility was official. A man, as long as he could support more than one wife, might have two or three, and the combination could include a sister or daughter of an already existing wife. Although fidelity in marriage was the goal, men, especially, might take advantage of situations where extramarital relationships occurred, making marriage bonds brittle.

Shelton was dedicated to doing what he could to shift marriage practices into the mold of the dominant society, which many Navajos rejected—especially those who were wealthy or medicine men. He described the situation when he took charge as a "disgrace." He found that many older Navajo men were living with two or three wives and some with four. They would frequently take for a companion a widow who had two or three daughters, and as the daughters became old enough, perhaps twelve or fourteen, would marry them, discarding the old women to shift for themselves or be taken as wives by younger men unable financially to purchase the young girls. These women were never consulted as to who should become their husbands. The trades were made between their parents and the men who wanted to buy them, and the girls very seldom knew when they were to marry or to whom, until they were notified by their fathers that they had been sold. Many of them objected and held out for days against being taken by an old man as his second or third wife, but they were forced to comply with the wishes of their parents and the men who had purchased them.[10] To remedy the situation, the agent let it be known that he would not attempt to break up already existing unions, but if there were any new polygamous marriages, the lawbreaker would face jail time. There were those who challenged his resolve, but he felt that he had, for the most part, slowed the process.

Shelton was not above removing young girls from such a situation and enrolling them in school—either at Shiprock or Fort Lewis. Many proved to be excellent students. As for the men, a lot ended up in hard labor details, improving ditches and working on other agency projects, sometimes for as long as six months. Their punishment put others on notice, and as Shelton pointed out, many of the more sensitive Navajos willingly gave up additional wives when asked to, or selected a suitable husband for their daughters. Agency police kept an ear open in the communities to stop any abuse that might be taking place, but although they opposed this type of behavior, they were also under a great deal of pressure from Navajos that might be relatives.[11]

Another issue was rape. Grazing livestock was a full time pursuit for many families. Older women often stayed around home, involved in weaving or other domestic duties, and so it was left to the children to manage the herds on the range. Sometimes brother and sister would take the sheep out first thing in the morning and remain with them all day as the animals searched for grass. At other times they might go out alone and return the animals to the family corral at night. This left plenty of time for a child or youth to be away from the protective influence of the household and at the mercy of travelers they might encounter. A few examples illustrate what could happen, how traditional society handled rape, and to what level Shelton became involved.

Two Navajo men assaulted Split Lip's twelve-year-old granddaughter while herding sheep. The culprits paid her grandmother a few horses, ending the issue from their perspective. When Shelton heard about it, he removed the girl, "a bright and good child," from the home and put her in school where she did well. The agent also enlisted "the better class of Indians in suppressing such crimes."[12] Lenna Oliver, a Navajo girl who lived near Farmington, had a similar experience. The sheriff arrested the guilty man, Adobe Begay, and placed him in jail, only to have him released soon after. The reason: white taxpayers did not want to foot the bill for his upkeep in prison while he awaited trial, since Navajos

did not pay taxes. Shelton was furious, had Adobe rearrested, and made
sure he stood trial in district court. Other arrests followed such as with
Des-che-ne, a fifty-six year old man who raped his seventeen-year-old
niece, Asdzaan E-yaz-ya, when he caught her herding sheep. He lassoed
her off her horse, threw her down, and attacked her, creating bruises and
cuts on her back and a rope burn around her abdomen. Three days of
singing by medicine men, a trip to the agency doctor, and a complaint
to Shelton, spurred her on to have justice met, but there was always
the question as to whether local officials would let the perpetrator go
before he ever reached district court.[13] Shelton realized that if justice
was thwarted, it would show others that the law could be circumvented,
which could be worse than inaction.

This occurred in February 1905. Three months later, the agent was
dealing once again with the same issue in a different location and person.
Pit-ce-cody, a member of a group of recalcitrant Indians led by a powerful
medicine man named Ba'álílee, encountered his niece away from home,
dragged her off her horse, bound her hands behind her back, and assaulted
her. Sick, bruised, spitting blood, she returned home and remained confined to bed for days. This was the third time for this type of offense by
Pit-ce-cody, but although many in the community were incensed by the
deed, they feared his spiritual power and believed that if he got angry,
the girl would die. Even the four agency police who apprehended him
were concerned with the outcome. Shelton used the incident to obtain
permission for a jail and an increased police force composed of Navajo
men he could depend upon. He received both. He also had a Court of
Indian Offense established at the agency, but found it ineffective because
the three prominent men appointed as judges, were too tied into the culture and family connections and so lenient in their decisions. It was better
to have an impartial off-reservation court system mete out justice.[14]

Rampaging River—The Flood of 1911

Not all the problems on the reservation were in human form. The fall
of 1911 provided an unexpected catastrophe that required over a year
to correct. Starting in mid-July, abnormally strong rains began to cover
the mountains of Colorado and lands of the Four Corners area. Canyons
and rivers that fed into the San Juan River placed heavy streambed loads

and large amounts of water into the flow going past Shiprock. Shelton noted that he had crews, two weeks at a time, shoring up the banks of the river with cottonwood logs, since all of the brush used for riprapping had already been consumed. Still, he was optimistic. In October the precipitation intensified as one two-hour storm dumped 4.8 inches of rain. The weather bureau later reported that between September 1911 and March 1912, twenty-seven inches fell, twice the normal amount for even the wettest areas.[15] Wilhelmina Bero, an eyewitness to events, described the circumstances: "In September 1911, the rains started misty, then showers, and finally a steady rain increasing in volume until it reached the stage of cloudbursts in the mountains, cloudburst after cloudburst. The waters of the San Juan River raised with rapidity until Thursday, October 5th, the river had left its banks."[16]

Each of the communities along the river shared information of the impending disaster—when possible by telephone and when not by men on horseback. Telephone lines went down, roads washed out, buildings disappeared, and people established temporary camps to get out of the weather. Rampaging waters hit the agency particularly hard. Shelton reported that, starting in Shiprock, the entire valley flooded, in many places "from hill to hill." He estimated the depth as twenty times greater than he had ever seen it; he knew that parts of the school lay submerged under six feet of water; that nine adobe structures had melted away; that all the larger buildings held water; and that he had "sent ten to twelve thousand fine melons down to the people living along the Gulf of California."[17]

But it was not the melons that brought the school to its knees. The river washed out the new steel bridge that had been built just two years before. Wilhelmina recalls how she struggled to sleep during the night, deafened by the rush of mounting water. "I told my husband it was impossible to sleep with that roar. He got up, dressed, and started out. He said he wanted to see if the bridge had gone. I told him I had heard an awful crash. He returned about 6 am. The bridge was gone. The east anchorage had pulled out. Tons upon tons of cement concrete had torn loose and been carried across the river. Debris had lodged against the bridge, trees, and buildings, and the ground, already soaked, couldn't hold the pressure."[18] The twisted structure lodged a quarter mile downstream, carried by waters that surged eight feet higher than the bridge.

Although Shelton had a large supply of fired bricks and processed lumber already on hand to start rebuilding the agency immediately, the bridge was the one thing that could not be easily replaced, something he bemoaned in the months following its destruction.[19]

Given the circumstances, loss of life was minimal. Many tourists and traders had come to Shiprock to participate in the annual fair, the school was in session with a full complement of children back from fall break, and the Methodist mission upstream was also in operation with twenty-seven children in attendance. At least one of the traders exhibiting at the fair became disgruntled with Shelton. Frank Noel recalled how all the vendor booths were set up on land too close to the river. As the rains fell and the water rose, he and other traders moved camp to higher ground, and when he went back to the fair ground, his horses were still tied to the trees but were standing in water up to their backs. According to Noel, Shelton insisted that the vendor booths not be moved, but rather than lose thousands of dollars of blankets, silver work, and other items, the traders transferred all their goods to a higher, safer area away from the rising water.[20]

This account is in direct opposition to what Arthur Chapman, a magazine writer from Denver, wrote about Shelton urging the traders to move their booths. Chapman further placed much of the credit for saving life during this disaster on the agent's shoulders. In an article titled "Right Man in Right Place," he praised the agent for insisting that people camped near the river move to higher ground, long before six feet of water swept the campsites clean.[21] He also mentioned how Shelton sent messengers up and down stream to let the unsuspecting know of the deteriorating situation. He dispatched one rider all the way to Aneth and Bluff so that the government station there could assist local residents to move out of danger. Chapman wrote that "the most inspiring sight I ever saw was when the alarm bell rang and the school children formed in line and marched in perfect order to the mesas. This had been planned by Superintendent Shelton and it was carried out to the letter." The agent was also credited with saving many of the people at the Methodist Navajo Mission.

Bero's account, already cited, provides the best description of what happened there. The mission, located approximately four miles west of Farmington, was under the supervision of six adults. The facilities included a two-story adobe house that served as school and dorm rooms for the children, a similar building for staff living quarters, a number of outbuildings for laundry and livestock, and a new structure underway. All were swept downstream. As the flood waters began to encircle the facilities, three of the adults loaded the children in wagons, and with water swishing around the hubs of the wheels, departed for Mary Eldridge's mission two miles upriver. Three men—Western, Simmons, and Tice—remained at the school, not believing they were in imminent danger. At 4:30 in the morning, water lapped around the foundation of the adobe building, eroding the walls and pushing into the interior. Western jumped from the upper story window and was later found by Navajos alive but nearly drowned. Simmons, on horseback, urged Tice to get on a mount and leave, but Tice was no swimmer and did not want to take a chance. Suddenly the house collapsed, throwing Simmons off his horse, into the water and into the current, clinging to various floating objects until he reached a tree branch suspended over the water. Exhausted, he pulled himself up into the tree, climbed to the top, and remained there until the flow subsided. Tice was not as fortunate. When the house collapsed, he apparently was making his way to a nearby tree, but fell into a deep hole where he drowned and was washed downstream for twelve miles where searchers eventually found his body.[22] He was one of the few fatalities in the Shiprock area.

Insight into Navajo reaction to the flood is given in a patronizing newspaper account that belittles their efforts, but captures their view that the river's actions were those of a living entity. As the water peaked, a man named Robb from Taos heard a "great cry" coming from the bank of the river. He went down to investigate and saw: "A big bunch of Indian braves had gathered together . . . and were hard at work weaving a spell to defeat the will of the river devil. Wildly waving their bodies in rhythmic motion while their legs took them through the mazes of their mystic dance to a weird chant, they proceeded to push the river back into its bed. At least they thought they did, for it was about this time that the agent found the flood subsiding."[23] Robb ended his observation by assuring the reader of the sincerity of the Indians and that it was not a show for spectators.

The aftermath of the flood was far less dramatic. Once the water subsided, Shelton and others set to work repairing damages and returning to normal. The railroads in Colorado that fed into New Mexico were particularly hard hit, which slowed the arrival of necessary materials for rebuilding. The Shiprock Agency, on the other hand, went into high gear, processing more lumber and firing bricks—not adobe that "melted"— to replace lost structures. Shelton estimated the cost at $9,800 for the agency with another $1,000 for labor to repair roads, but both figures proved too low.[24] Within a few months' time, with the exception of the bridge, the school was back to normal, focusing on education and replacing the agricultural harvest that had been ripped away by the flood.

Controlling Conflict—Ba'álílee, Antes, and Wetherill

During his stint as agent, Shelton also faced Anglos and Navajos who bristled at being controlled and who resisted—both openly and covertly—the idea of an agent opposing their actions. Often the conflict led to dramatic confrontation, many of which were resolved by the intervention of outside authority. No doubt this was discomfiting to the agent who prided himself on being in control and able to handle issues on his own level. All four of the incidents that are discussed here are covered extensively elsewhere. Three of them are reviewed and summarized to give a sense of some of the problems the agent faced. The last one—the Beautiful Mountain affair—is looked at in greater detail, since it occurred along the Chuska-Tunicha range.

The first example involves a powerful medicine man named Ba'álílee, who lived on the lower San Juan River running through southeastern Utah.[25] Born around 1859, he and some of his family members abandoned Canyon de Chelly due to military pressures and went to Fort Sumner during the Long Walk period. As a young man, he began to carve out his reputation, getting into conflict with Navajo neighbors as well as being involved in a shooting fray at the Aneth trading post in 1884. But it was his name, Ba'álílee, loosely translated as "By His Supernatural/ Magical Power," that indicates an equally real but intangible problem. As a medicine man, he knew six major ceremonies as well as how to divine past and future events through stargazing. His high intellect and broad use of supernatural power allowed him to threaten others through witchcraft and the control of natural elements to harm people. He projected an all-powerful image and gathered around him a following of like-minded men who believed in him, carried out his orders, and reveled in conflict. Confrontation with Shelton proved inevitable.

The new agent, during those early years at Shiprock, had multiple concerns and so tried addressing many of the issues through Navajo police, a tribal and Anglo court system, and an occasional visit to hot spots of discord. Nothing seemed to impede Ba'álílee. He resisted the sheep dipping program; refused to send children to school; intentionally disobeyed agent directives; sheltered miscreants involved in rape, robbery, and bootlegging; and boasted about his resistance. Shelton had had enough. On October 29, 1907, the agent with Captain H. O. Williard and elements of the 5th Cavalry attacked Ba'álílee's settlement four miles east of Aneth. Reportedly the last cavalry charge in the United States against "hostile" Indians, the military swarmed the camp in the breaking light of dawn. The fighting was sporadic as the slumbering Indians learned they were under attack. Two Navajos died, ten captured, with no casualties in the attacking force. The agent and military marched the prisoners to Shiprock, in November to Fort Wingate, and then to Fort Huachuca, where they spent a little over a year before political and legal forces released them to return home. Ba'álílee, a defeated man, gave no further problems.

In that same area and around the same time entered Howard Ray Antes, another problem.[26] Antes, an independent Methodist missionary and his wife, Evelyn, had served as missionaries in various communities in Colorado and New Mexico (including Mary Eldridge's efforts at Jewett) before landing in Aneth in 1895. The couple established on the San Juan River the Navajo Faith Mission, which included the facilities of a small boarding school. The Antes's viewed the Navajos as a group of benighted souls, practicing a culture filled with superstitious beliefs. Salvation came by adopting white civilization, leaving the reservation with all of its government and tribal backwardness, and embracing Christianity. Still, Antes needed to work with the Navajos wherever they were on the evolutionary scale of savagism, barbarism, and civilization, and so he did what he could to improve their condition. This included fund-raising with institutions and individuals in the East, writing frequent letters to the Indian Bureau, and serving as spokesman for the Indians against local white settlers and anyone else who seemed at odds with the Indians' progress.

By 1904, as the Shiprock Agency grew into a reality, Shelton became increasingly involved with the distant Navajo Faith Mission. At first the two entities worked harmoniously with each trying to better the lot of the Navajos, but these relations also held the seeds of conflict. Antes aided some Indians filing on the public domain for allotments, importuned the government for help with more ditches and economic assistance, and often bypassed Shelton's office by writing directly to Washington, D.C., for more and better land for the Navajos and their herds. He believed he had permission to write passes that allowed the Indians to leave the reservation and enter the public domain in competition with white livestock owners and against county ordinances. The final outcome was Antes writing directly to President Theodore Roosevelt, who, through an executive order, carved out on the north side of the river an additional chunk of land that was added to the reservation in 1905. While Shelton essentially supported this move, the settlers using the land were angry—one more encroachment on their ability to make a living, while the Navajos had exclusive use of reservation lands.

Antes also suspected that the government would like him to abandon his property and turn it over to the Navajos. The San Juan River was claiming its own share of land, nibbling away at the mission's outer edges. Shelton at first offered help to stabilize the river's banks but then withdrew it. Angered, Antes started to complain, to the point that when the Ba'álílee incident erupted, he took pen in hand and attacked Shelton, Williard, and the entire handling of the affair. The complaints were enough to bring Colonel Hugh L. Scott, superintendent of the United States Military Academy and special investigator, to Aneth to sit in judgment on allegations spread far and wide. Three days later, Scott exonerated Shelton and Williard of all wrongdoing, chastised Antes for his use of the newspapers and government officials to work against the defendants, and required complete retraction of all claims.

A final conflict between agent and missionary occurred over the school's activities. Shelton claimed to have received complaints that the children were not being fed or clothed appropriately; that Antes had raised substantial donations from people back east, but the money and goods were only profiting the missionary; and that one of the children Antes had taken into his home now needed to be returned to his family, which the missionary refused to do. The boy, Samuel, eventually remained with his foster parents, but not before he wrote a letter to President Woodrow Wilson, the commissioner of Indian affairs, and local authorities asking that he stay with his adopted mother and father. During the investigation into this matter, Shelton received more testimony that Antes was not as good as he appeared to be. By 1909, the reverend had completely fallen out of favor with the agent, had sold his mission to the Shiprock Agency, and had moved to Colorado and subsequently to California. One more problem for Shelton had been eliminated, but not before a lot of fuss and furor and intervention from outside participants occurred.

A third nemesis for the agent came in the form of trader and pseudo-archaeologist Richard Wetherill.[27] Anglo discoverer and promoter of the large Ancestral Puebloan ruins at Mesa Verde, an important figure in the excavation of Pueblo Bonito and other sites in Chaco Canyon, the owner and operator of a trading post in that area, and a cattleman who used off-and-some-on-reservation lands for grazing, Wetherill was intimately involved in economic development in the region and enmeshed in Navajo daily life. Initially, the impressive ruins like Pueblo Bonito and others nearby were beyond the boundaries of the reservation, but through an executive order in November 1907, the lines changed, and Wetherill found his home and post on Indian land. Prior to this there had been some rumblings between him and Shelton over purported cheating and mistreatment of Navajos at the store and use of the range. The agent, however, had no direct control over Wetherill because he was off-reservation. Now, the two came face-to-face on government regulations.

Personality played an important role, with both men having their supporters and advocates and those who disliked them. For example, George Blake, a trader at the Tsaya Post and occasional worker for Wetherill, did not admire the agent, characterizing him as follows in a letter to the commissioner of Indian affairs: "Mr. Shelton has always constituted himself a kind of czar on the reservation, often exceeding the limits of his authority as agent; encroaching on territory not under his jurisdiction; permitting, in the case of other Indian officials, missionaries, traders and others, no rival near the throne. Though the Indians themselves do not like him, he has them thoroughly cowed, and no white man doing business with the Indians can call his soul his own, unless willing to put his neck under Shelton's foot."[28] While Richard Wetherill harbored similar sentiments, he was not confrontational with Shelton, allowing him to stay at his home for visits, generally complying with rules emanating from Shiprock, and sharing friendly relations with his customers.

Shelton, on the other hand, was vocally critical of the trader. In a lengthy report sent to Washington concerning events in the Chaco area, the agent compiled a long list of complaints. A few excerpts show no love lost. Following a ten-day visit to the new executive order lands, some of which were spent with his enemy, Shelton wrote: "There is located at Pueblo Bonito a man named Richard Wetherill who has done more in the past few years to retard the progress of the Indians in this section than all other causes combined. If all reports are true, he has robbed them of thousands of dollars-worth of property. He has not hesitated to assault and abuse them when they displeased him."[29] Specific charges included the trader sharing with Navajos to herd his sheep and then taking much more of the wool than deserved; "jailing" Indians, who did not pay their bills, in a dark room within the Pueblo Bonito ruins; fencing Indian and railroad lands that did not belong to him; controlling other grazing areas and watering holes; taking individuals' property that did not belong to him but that he claimed had been purchased; bullying people for trespassing; purchasing and then selling lumber taken from the reservation for his own private gain; and generally riding roughshod over the Navajos in the area. In fairness to Wetherill, some of these claims were unsubstantiated, many Navajos got along well with him, and Shelton had an ax to grind against a person who had ignored some of his directives.

The discord drew a number of agents who lived near Wetherill to help smooth over issues while reporting any malfeasance on the part of the trader. Their reports did not bear the kind of charges or proof to satisfy Shelton. On June 22, 1910, all of the tension came to an abrupt end. Chischili Begay shot and killed the trader near Pueblo del Arroyo. Some people blamed the deed on an argument over the abuse of a horse, others felt that all of the criticism and investigating by government officials had fueled Navajo discontent, while others saw it as a personal grudge with a Navajo against Wetherill and one of his helpers, Bill Finn. Whatever the reason, Chis-chili Begay rode to the Tsaya Trading Post, obtained a note from trader George Blake, and spurred his horse to Shiprock and Shelton. A day later he was in the Farmington jail awaiting trial.

Initial judicial proceedings began in November 1910, but the actual trial, held in Aztec, New Mexico, took place two years later. Not surprisingly, the entire affair exhibited strong overtones on both sides with Shelton and his allies advocating for Chis-chili Begay and blaming Finn and Wetherill as the source of the trouble, while defenders saw Shelton's heavy hand in developing a story that protected the Indian and worked against anyone who testified otherwise. Once the Navajo finally stood trial in June 1912, claiming self-defense, the court found him guilty, then sentenced him to from five to ten years in the state penitentiary. He was released after serving only three years due to supposed health reasons. Shelton assumed the responsibility for the Indian's behavior once freed; the Navajo died in 1950 at the ripe age of eighty years old. To many observers, the agent had triumphed over Wetherill, an arch enemy, by actively working to protect and then free his killer.

The Beautiful Mountain Brouhaha

The fourth inflammatory episode involving Shelton is the Beautiful Mountain incident. Not only was it a more dramatic confrontation taking place in the Chuska Valley and on an isolated peak of the Lukachukai Range twenty-four miles southwest of Shiprock, but it also involved many of the traders and posts in the area, the United States military, and a number of notable personalities coming together to prevent a fight that could have cost a number of lives. There are two accounts that look at this incident from different perspectives. Trader Will Evans, who helped build the Sanostee Post and spent most of his life running the Shiprock Post, gathered a series of interviews and compiled his understanding of what occurred. This is found in *Along Navajo Trails*.[30] He had the opportunity to discuss with many of the participants—both Anglo and Navajo—some of the circumstances surrounding the incident and was present at the time. Particularly clear is the role of the trading posts in the area, the effect the incident had on the men and women in those posts, and the very specific detail that comes from the oral history of those who lived through the events. Another excellent account is found in Frank McNitt's *The Indian Traders*, which provides a more complete

Bizhóshí, a powerful medicine man and advocate for traditional Navajo practices, worked against Shelton's influence to enforce the dominant society's encroachment. The Beautiful Mountain episode, in support of his son and the practice of polygamy, was just one of his cantankerous ways to resist. Courtesy of Susan E. Woods Family Photo Collection.

rendering based on government documents, correspondence, interviews, and published reports.[31] He offers a strong chronology of events and a broad listing of people involved. Together, the two versions give a wonderful sense of the complexity of circumstances and personalities that made this controversy such a dramatic story. The reader should study both carefully. Here, the primary focus is on Shelton and how he was perceived by those on all sides of this conflict.

Little Singer (Hataałii Yazzie) and his father, Bizhóshí, were not just ordinary Navajos. Both father and son belonged to the old school of those who were unalterably opposed to the white man and inroads of civilization. Their intense devotion to the holy beings, intricate religious ceremonies, and deep spirituality sometimes caused their white neighbors to wonder if these Indians would ever fit in to white society. Bizhóshí was an esteemed rainmaker. Until his death, he painfully and laboriously mounted his gentle pony—scorning help from his younger associates—to ride long distances into the desert or into the hills to help others. His weather-beaten face, drooping mustache, and serrated teeth, some of which were missing, presented a fearful visage when wreathed in anger. In spite of this appearance, he was a born leader.

Little Singer was a replica of his father. Early in life he became Bizhóshí's pupil, adept in the practice of a medicine man, and knowledgeable about the lore of his tribe. He was an unfailing source of those remarkable stories. His knowledge of these things in his early teens supplied the name of Little Singer, a title which remained with him for the rest of his life. While young, his features were smooth, somewhat similar to those of an Inuit (Eskimo), but in old age he favored his father to a remarkable degree.

Despite the rigid observance of Navajo beliefs and ceremonies, Little Singer's objections to the encroachments of Washington and the Indian Bureau caused trouble only once with these authorities. The issue was polygamy, which he believed in and defended as strongly as he did his worship of the holy beings. At the time, Bizhóshí, his sons, and followers lived in Sanostee Valley, near the foot of Beautiful Mountain, thirty-five miles west of the Shiprock Agency and sixty miles below the San Juan River from Farmington. The mountain, well known for its springs, trees, and general vegetation, was also a place with abundant wildlife hunted by the Navajos. It was also a highly defendable spot with steep sides, narrow trails that could easily be sealed off, large rocks and boulders to push on advancing forces, and sufficient water and grazing lands to maintain livestock.

In 1913, government authorities were trying to curb the widespread practice of polygamy among the Navajos. Shelton received word that Little Singer had three wives and was resistant to change and so sent a detachment of Navajo police to Sanostee with orders to bring Little Singer and his three wives to Shiprock for questioning and possible trial in a local Indian court. The police returned in three or four days bringing the women, but not Little Singer, who was away on a trading expedition. When the husband returned and learned of the agent's actions, he reasoned that his wives had been kidnapped, that he would not accept two of them being ejected from his home to fend for themselves just because of some law, and that he did not appreciate the outside meddling.

On September 17, Little Singer and a band of heavily armed Navajos crossed the river at Shiprock and entered the agency grounds. Superintendent Shelton was away on business, there were no armed guards, and only Sophus Jensen, the agency farmer, Mr. Hinds, the clerk, and a policeman called Lame One (Na'nishhod), were there. These men rushed out of the office building to meet the oncoming raiders, but their efforts were futile. Lame One grabbed the bridle reins of Old School Boy's (Ółta'í Sání) horse, but the rider whipped him with his quirt and forced him to turn loose. The rescue party threatened the agency employees with far worse if they did not get out of their way and let them pass. Any other witnesses fled for refuge in the buildings. The three women, one of whom had a baby, were staying at the girl's dormitory. They had been given the peaceful occupation of hoeing in the gardens until Little Singer was captured and brought in. At this time, two of them were in the garden plot hoeing, while the one with the baby, Luce's sister, sat at the front of the jail, which was jokingly called the Department of Justice. During the melee, Luce rode his pony and led a bare-backed horse to his sister, grabbed her and the baby, hastily placed them on the spare pony, and told her to ride home as fast as she could. The other two women mounted horses, and the group crossed the bridge and traveled to a nearby trading post before eventually returning to Sanostee. Jensen, Hinds, and Lame One could not stop them.[32]

Superintendent Shelton returned, as soon as notified, and took control of his forces. He formally charged the troublemakers with various crimes and infractions of rules—ranging from riot and assault with a deadly weapon to horse stealing and flourishing arms in a settlement—then had the district attorney, Somers Burkhart in Santa Fe, give warrants for their arrest to U.S. Marshal A. H. Hudspeth. The agent wanted immediate action, insisting that it was important to set an example while preventing the issue from getting any bigger.[33] He and the marshal realized that they, with the Navajo police force, alone, had little chance of accomplishing the arrest. Prominent Navajo leaders as well as traders urged Bizhóshí and his following to submit to the law, but they refused. The agent requested Chee Dodge, a powerful leader and well-known translator, to assist, but the Navajos felt that the Catholic missionary, Anselm Weber at St. Michaels, would be better to work through because of his influence in Washington.[34]

Dodge believed that Shelton was far too strict when dealing with Indians. He was not alone. In an interview with Peter Paquette, superintendent at Window Rock, Bizhóshí chafed at the treatment he believed the prisoners received under Shelton's rule. He charged the agent with forcing the older woman to provide five schoolchildren and requiring the two younger women to weave baskets and work in the gardens. Other Navajos received twelve month sentences for small infractions. Bizhóshí closed by saying, "Mr. Shelton is a mean man to us. He is there to be mean to us. He stands out ready to jump on us. We are like small birds hiding among the rocks to keep him from picking on us. . . . We do not know where to turn over there. For every little thing he puts us in jail. All the Indians over there know that."[35] Trader Franc Newcomb somewhat agreed, noting that the Shiprock jail was a small affair that was already occupied by some six or seven lawbreakers, and that a short term in jail was Shelton's usual way of enforcing law and order. In fact, these sentences were so frequent that the jail became known as "Shelton's Hotel."[36]

After a failed attempt at talks with the Indians, Father Weber and Paquette arranged for a second meeting at St. Michaels, but this time without Shelton present. Paquette wired the agent that the Navajos had agreed to surrender and go to Shiprock as long as they were pardoned, but if not, they would do "personal violence" to Shelton. Information from traders in the area confirmed that the Indians were getting ready to fight; there were few people at the agency to withstand an attack. Shelton went into high gear, obtaining permission from the commissioner of Indian affairs, Cato Sells, to recruit a sufficient guard to hold the situation until the marshal arrived, but was cautioned to use extreme care in the application of any force. According to the *Farmington Times-Hustler*, Shelton contacted the local judge and asked that "autos be held in readiness and arrangements made for men and munitions of defense so that a ready response might be made. . . . A committee canvassed the town and country by telephone where it could be done for rapid fire rifles and ammunition. The result was that in a short time some twenty men were equipped with good arms and were ready to go on a moment's notice."[37]

Fortunately, there were a number of events to relieve the tension. Hudspeth and two deputies had arrived at Shiprock, while a telegram from Paquette stated that he had been misled by one of his Navajo police and that the threatened violence was a misunderstanding. The commissioner had also ordered James McLaughlin, inspector for the Office of Indian Affairs, to Shiprock, arriving mid-November. Most effective, however, was Father Weber, who had met with the Indians on a number of occasions and had gained their trust. He could not, however, get them to surrender or submit to arrest. McLaughlin and Weber went to trader Frank Noel's store at Sanostee and met with the dissidents, but neither side would budge. From the Indian's perspective, "Mr. Shelton has been bulldozing us and picking on us; in short, he has been doing everything to us except castrating us, and I think he is going to attempt that next."[38] The inspector felt that the only way to change the situation without a huge confrontation was to "overawe" the Indians through the introduction of troops. Noting that the Navajos were well-armed, had purchased large amounts of ammunition, held highly defendable terrain, threatened to attack some trading posts and burn the sawmill, and assumed that the government would not push the issue, the inspector suggested that a battalion of troops would dampen their ardor.[39]

In the meantime, three of the Navajos had surrendered at Shiprock to the marshal, who moved them to Santa Fe for trial; shortly a fourth joined these prisoners. At this point, much of the resolution of the issue fell to two key players—Father Weber and Brigadier General Hugh L. Scott, who traveled from Fort Bliss, Texas, to take charge of the situation while his troops A, B, C, and D, 12th Cavalry, moved by train from Fort Robinson, Nebraska. By November 24, Scott had traveled to Gallup by rail and was approaching Noel's store, while Weber journeyed over the Chuskas toward the same destination. Snow and cold afflicted those in the mountains, while mud and rain not only challenged Scott in his car, but bogged down the cavalry's men and wagons far behind. Fifteen miles from the trading post, the general met Shelton and outlined a plan. The agent insisted that the Indians had been talked to enough, that military action preceded by a forced march to prevent the outlaws from escaping was necessary, and that an assault on Beautiful Mountain led by Navajo police who knew the trails could produce a final solution. Scott would hear none of it. He ordered Shelton and his men to not get any closer to Noel's store and commanded his soldiers to remain at the Two Grey Hills Trading Post.[40] His position was clear: "From what you [Shelton] tell me things cannot get any worse. I shall talk to them first then fight if necessary."[41]

The general proceeded with his son, acting as aide-de-camp, and with trader-interpreter Frank Walker to the store, where he rested, learned more about the situation, and sent out messengers to invite Bizhóshí to come in the next day for talks. According to Noel, Scott told the Navajos shortly after he arrived that he had come a long way, was tired, and knew they were too. He wanted a long rest in order to be fresh in the morning. Mrs. Noel added, "The evening that General Scott and Lieutenant Scott rode into the yard, there were a lot of Indians in the store and both whites and Indians got excited. The General walked in, shook hands with everyone then told Noel to feed the Indians."[42] Father Weber and Chee Dodge arrived in time for the meeting.

The next day one hundred Indians gathered at the store to follow the proceedings. Some offered to bring in Bizhóshí if he refused to surrender, fearing that with soldiers on the reservation expecting trouble, things could get out of hand, and they did not want to get caught up in an affair not of their doing. Once Bizhóshí arrived, Noel provided dinner while Scott showed respect and interest in those Navajos present, putting everyone's mind at ease. Weber, Walker, Dodge, and Noel followed suit, holding side conversations with those present and offering advice as to how to prevent an armed conflict, which Scott repeatedly said he wanted to avoid. In spite of a letter from Shelton saying that rumors were rampant that once the soldiers appeared, Bizhóshí's followers were going to swoop down on the agency and blaze a path of destruction, Scott assured the agent that there was no truth to the rumors and that he should just wait for developments.

The talks proceeded for three days, and at the end everyone who had been charged had either stood trial in Santa Fe and was released or had agreed to go to court. Scott insisted that Bizhóshí stop by Shiprock and offer Shelton an apology, which he did. A few days later, Weber met Scott with his soldiers and prisoners in Gallup and described the feelings of the Indians. "In their presence, he handed me [Weber] a letter he had written on their behalf to the US Attorney. In taking leave of the general, each in turn held his hand and thanked him profusely for saving them. Bizhóshí embraced him. They parted, and General Scott's mission was at an end."[43] His influence in the court proceedings continued. Judge William H. Pope dropped the issue of polygamy and all other charges against the remaining seven defendants except for rioting, to which they all pleaded guilty. Shelton insisted there needed to be some consequence, otherwise he would have no respect or power when other incidents arose.

The trial, brief but to the point, found the seven Navajos guilty of riot and sentenced all but two to ten days in jail. Little Singer and the man who quirted the policeman received thirty days, while Bizhóshí, because of his age, had only ten. Following Scott's suggestion, they served their sentence in Gallup, because if not, "the expiration of their sentence would find them there with no money, unable to speak the language, and without transportation home."[44] The judge lectured the guilty party about the need to obey the law, follow Shelton's directions, and live a harmonious life. The defendants thanked the judge for their mild sentences and served their time without incident.[45] Shelton was not nearly as thankful. In a letter to the commissioner of Indian affairs, he bemoaned the fact that there was no real punishment meted out, making future problems likely. Feeling that the reservation was now in "far worse condition," Shelton wrote, "The Indians who are inclined to commit crimes will be led to believe that the Agent's authority will not be supported by the courts, and one of two things are bound to follow: criminals will go unpunished, or it will be necessary to have troops again to make arrests within a short time."[46] However, he had no choice other than to abide by the ruling and to settle back into administering the agency.

As with everything that Shelton was involved in, there were those who felt he had handled the situation poorly and others who heaped praise upon the man. It is not surprising that Antes took the opportunity to attack Shelton for this and other complaints; Father Weber was no lover of the agent, feeling that he was autocratic in his approach and had no idea how to work with Navajos. Father Fintan Zumbahlen, a Franciscan missionary stationed in Farmington, became the eyes and ears for Weber, reporting on what he saw going on at Shiprock. Shortly after the Beautiful Mountain incident, he wrote to Weber, saying that Major McLaughlin had urged Shelton to resign, but he refused. Next, "The Indians are forcing him to do it. You see, since those Navies got off with such a light sentence, Shelton cannot do a thing with the Indians. He can send his policemen out to bring them in, but nothing doing. They say, bring the soldiers out. They let you off easier than Shelton."[47] Zumbahlen continued, saying that the agent was in Washington, demanding a severe punishment of the troublemakers, and if it did not happen, he would resign. Laced throughout the letter were sentiments such as "he has been playing the hypocrite," "that Shelton is a born bigot," and "if he resigns, all right, but if he stays, I'll get the 'goods on him' yet." Five months later, the priest continued on the same theme, basing his accusations on rumors, but writing that some Navajo police had raped women while imprisoned and that a young boy who supposedly committed suicide had actually been killed by one of the policemen because "he knew too much."[48] Whether true or not, Shelton was in a precarious position, with citizens outside of the agency and employees within attacking his reputation.

On the other hand, there were those who truly appreciated all that he had achieved. The Indian Rights Association, watchdog for dealings that were unfair with Indians, was quick to praise Shelton for his handling of the Beautiful Mountain incident. "Mr. Shelton's success at Shiprock is a matter of pride to all the superintendents in that section of the country . . . for he has the gift of comradeship as well as dauntless courage and great ability."[49] Not shy, the agent, when confronted with criticism, reacted with a barrage of positive accomplishments. On September 19, 1914, the commissioner of Indian affairs wrote to him with a single criticism—the necessity of getting out to visit more of his charges. The agent's answer, outlined in a fifteen-page letter, explained the circumstances and what a good job he was doing. Included in the response was noting Shelton's eleven years of experience with a daily regimen of twelve-to-sixteen-hour work days; the six thousand square miles of his jurisdiction with its rough terrain and limited road network; the dispersed nature of Indian settlements; the fact that few Navajos spoke English; how drinking, gambling, polygamy, and loafing had been curtailed; and that significant steps had been taken to improve the quality of life, including the amount of wool produced, the craftsmanship in weaving and silverwork, agricultural products, and the marketing of goods at the annual Shiprock Fair, not to mention all that the boarding school had accomplished. Indeed, Shelton, in characteristic style, turned any criticism into an opportunity to showcase the positive and enlist help with problems—such as assistance needed to fortify the banks of the river and replace the bridge that had been washed downstream three years before. The response was hardly one you would expect from a man about to resign.[50]

Exeunt under a Cloud

Rumors and supposition turned into black and white accusations when a special edition of the *Farmington Enterprise* ran the amplified headline, "Is Shelton Forced to Resign?" on January 21, 1916. The newspaper alleged that he had "mistreated Indian girls and employees under his jurisdiction" to the point that some had to leave the agency to avoid further overtures.[51] Opening the man to community censure in the court of public opinion, the paper assured "he deserves little sympathy in his downfall," for his "warped morals," committing "grossly immoral indignities" with white and Navajo girls, and using his position of power to take advantage of those who came to him seeking help.

The agent and his following denied everything. Shelton confided in a friend that he, and they, should not be worried about "this blackmailing scheme" and that he had his "ducks all in a row and when the proper time comes [he] will start them swimming."[52] A week later, an article in the *Farmington Times-Hustler* called the claims against Shelton a "grave mistake" and unsubstantiated, but worst of all was the deplorable way they became common knowledge through publication. The Farmington Chamber of Commerce, although slightly guarded, renounced the "underhanded and unfair attack" and praised the agent for past accomplishments, keeping the door open for further judgment as an investigation developed.

Government Inspector H. S. Traylor arrived toward the end of January. In less than a week, he closed the investigation, having secured

Superintendent William T. Shelton with his wife, Hattie, photographed at Shiprock shortly before their departure. Denying to the end any wrongdoing, the agent left behind a strong legacy of law and order and extensive accomplishment in improving the life of his charges in the Northern Navajo Agency. Courtesy of Susan E. Woods Family Photo Collection.

Shelton's resignation. The charges filed by agency employees had been proved enough that Traylor felt no need to continue the probe, commenting that if it did, it would "involve too many homes."[53] An article in the *Farmington Enterprise* that had earlier reported the story and was roundly chastised by many for doing so, commented, "Mr. Shelton, the czar, the autocrat, the boss of Shiprock is no more." But even at that point, they noted his many accomplishments in an editorial that spent as much time extolling his virtues as criticizing his "gross immorality."[54] The agent publicly continued to deny the charges, claimed to have resigned of his own free will, threatened lawsuits against any agency employee who spoke against him, and was in no hurry to depart the area even when his interim replacement, H. F. Coggeshall, assumed control on March 15.[55] He gave as his reason for staying his wife's illness, so he did not depart until early May.

As a side note, shortly before he left, there was a large dinner and reception for him provided by his friends and the people of Farmington, seventy-five in number. He and his wife, Hattie, enjoyed the turkey, ham, lobster salad, cake, and ice cream—hardly the food served to a despised offender. On each side of the toastmaster sat the incoming and outgoing agents and their wives. What followed was "not a word of bitterness spoken. . . . It was a frank testimonial of heartfelt admiration for a work well done by the Sheltons, both for the Navajos and the people of this valley." A series of speakers toasted to specific and general accomplishments with Shelton taking the floor toward the end. He emotionally expressed his gratitude for the many kindnesses shown, declared once again that he had been faithful to his wife and family, that he had planned for many years on returning to his home in Waynesville, North Carolina, and he was now going to do it, but that if things did not work out, he would return to Farmington for his retirement years. He also promised to arrive the next fall in time to visit the annual Shiprock Fair.[56] This close association between agent and town continued. In 1941, a year before Shelton passed away, the *Farmington Times-Hustler* carried an article announcing his fiftieth wedding anniversary with Hattie. He ended the letter that enclosed a clipping from his hometown newspaper, with the admonition to "Please remember us to old friends, Indian and white."[57] To the end, the agent maintained his friendship and apparent innocence.

In summarizing these turbulent yet productive years with Shelton at the helm in Shiprock, one sees a person with immutable values who worked hard to transfer them to a people with a very different worldview. This relationship fostered a certain amount of irony. The San Juan River serves as a good metaphor. It, as with the Navajo people, was the reason that the agency was built. At times placid, at other times a rampaging torrent, a great deal of effort was spent on controlling something that seemed to have a mind of its own. During peaceful times it appeared that things had settled down—a bridge could be built, and there was enough foundation to keep it in operation. But when events near and far created difficult circumstances, all of the riprap, concrete, and steel girders could not withstand the force. Ba'álílee, Antes, Wetherill, and Bizhóshí were part of those floods that tore away at the peaceful fabric of what Shelton tried to accomplish at the school and agency. The control that he so desired to maintain was challenged, and so he often depended on outside sources—Williard, Scott (twice), and a controversial court system—to achieve what he wanted to maintain—but it slipped out of his hands.

There were other ironies. For a man who wanted peace, his personality either cowed his opponents or inflamed them to action. In either case, he was not beloved. While he had a huge effect in ridding the Northern Navajo Agency of gambling, alcohol, and rape, he struggled with stopping polygamy, yet he resigned over charges of immorality. His patronizing "father knows best" attitude toward American Indians did not endear him to those he was assisting; to many white neighbors and employees, he was a bigot and autocrat who did not understand those he was trying to help. Still, in all fairness, he accomplished so much that today, the area that contains the town of Shiprock still carries his Navajo name—Naat'áani Nééz—Tall Leader. The general consensus from the historical record indicates that from the Navajo perspective he was primarily feared and often hated, but grudgingly respected and appreciated for his accomplishments. Shelton was a man for his time, but the time, like the river, was both beneficial and harsh.

CHAPTER FIVE

Earning a Good Reputation

Traders, Weavers, and a Regional Style,
1903–1923

By the turn of the century, Two Grey Hills had proved its viability as one of a number of relatively nondescript posts sitting near the Chuska Mountains. In July 1903 ownership passed to Joseph Reitz (pronounced Ritz), who was no stranger to working with the Navajos. He was born in Milwaukee, Wisconsin, in 1859, and by the 1890s he had joined forces with John B. ("J. B.") Moore in operating the Cottonwood Pass Post, later renamed Crystal, located thirty miles north of Fort Defiance.[1] Moore continued with his wife to build the business, later becoming famous for improving types and qualities of Navajo weaving. In 1897 Reitz sold his interests in the post and apparently spent time driving a brewery wagon in Gallup for a few years. This may have been part of the reason for his going to Two Grey Hills. Based on an interview with trader and local historian John B. Arrington, who knew Reitz well, the man had a heavy drinking habit.[2] What could be a better cure than to have him at an isolated post, thought his wife, where sale and consumption of alcohol were illegal?

Whatever the reason, Joe remained at the post for nine years and never ran afoul of Shelton and his attempts to "dry" the reservation. But once a year, Mrs. Reitz would give him money to go to Gallup to tie one on. Sitting in a bar with a group of friends, he decided to buy drinks all around. Some of the men insisted that he save his money and maybe bring some home to which he replied, "Do you think I'm crazy? If I take any money back, my Old Lady will limit me from now on to just what I spent. Come on, have some drinks on me," and they did.[3] There were times when he needed to be assisted back to the hotel where he was staying and put to bed.

Then again, Mrs. Reitz, apparently, was not the most congenial person to live with. Arrington recalls that during the cold and snowy winter of 1908, just before Christmas, he arrived at the Two Grey Hills Post half frozen. He opened the door and there stood Mrs. Reitz, glaring at this stranger and appearing unfriendly. John asked if Joe was around and received a curt, "Somewhere out back. Is there something I can do for you?"[4] John explained that he was on his way to the Crystal Trading Post, that it was really cold outside, and that he would like to spend the night there. Answer: "I'll send you some food and you can get hay for your horse outside," all delivered with a "real disapproving" gaze. Just then, Joe entered and warmed the talk by welcoming his "good friend," insisting "Take off your coat and get warm—you've got to stay the night with us." Later that evening the Reitzs were reading their mail that had come in from Gallup that day and were enjoying the warmth of the stove. Joe turned to his wife and asked her what time it was, since the clock was behind him but in full view for her. She replied, "See for yourself." Joe and John exchanged glances and continued to read. About ten minutes later, Mrs. Reitz asked Joe if the chickens had been locked up, to which he replied, "Go see for yourself; the chickens are right outside." At that, everyone was laughing and Joe's wife even smiled at John.

Unfortunately, Joe Reitz, like many traders, did not leave much of a paper trail, and so all that is known about him and the post are a few anecdotes. During his stint at the post, however, he entered into a partnership, starting in 1909, with Edward Henry Davies, who later left much more documentation of his activities. He was successful enough there to assume full control of the business in 1912. Davies, born in West Kirby, Cheshire, England, on October 31, 1877, was a veteran of the Boer War, had contracted tuberculosis, came to the United States presumably for health reasons, and received his U.S. citizenship in 1906 in Durango, Colorado. On his application for a shared license with Reitz, he claimed six years' experience as an Indian trader, part of which was at Ilfeld Trading Company, Fort Defiance. The form also noted that he was "industrious, honest and sober," all of which were true.[5] But while working in Fort Defiance, one other characteristic was added—in love.

The following incident gives insight into his personality and determination, qualities he would need at Two Grey Hills. At the ripe old age of thirty-one, Davies, no doubt, was ready to get married. Pearl F.

Harper, working as assistant boys' matron in the boarding school nearby, attracted his eye and courtship soon began. After hours Davies would visit her at the dorm; during her off-time, she would go to the store where he was a clerk. William H. Harrison, superintendent of the school, felt that this "infatuation" was consuming too much time and could lead to something scandalous, although there was no indication of anything inappropriate. Warnings to decrease frequency of visits had little effect except to drive the two lovers deeper into the shadows. One night Harrison decided to catch the couple and obtain proof that they had disobeyed his orders. Going to the boys' dorm, he traveled the candlelit corridors looking for the pair. About to give up and go home, he noticed a clothing room door with an unlatched padlock hanging on the hasp. The superintendent struck a match that illuminated the couple sitting on a bench in what had been the dark. This, added to Harper missing some of her early morning duties, caused Harrison to have Davies fired from his job and to threaten his matron with a transfer.

Correspondence concerning these actions reached the commissioner of Indian affairs, a lawyer who was a relative in Wisconsin, and various officials throughout the government system. While Davies had an otherwise spotless record and was allowed to remain on reservation lands, he was not reinstated to the Ilfeld Trading Company, and Harper was transferred to the boarding school at the Western Navajo Agency in Tuba City. Even better. They both obtained employment at the school, he working as an "additional farmer" and she as a matron. How well this arrangement worked out is unsure, but a year later, Davies was applying for his license at Two Grey Hills with Reitz, and he had his wife with him.[6]

Shaping through External Forces

By the time Davies formed this partnership, the Shiprock Agency had been in operation for six years. The trading system had greatly expanded with a series of posts strung along the base of the Chuska range and scattered over other parts of the reservation. All traders on Indian land had to conform to government regulation or lose their license. If there was any doubt as to what was expected, post operators could turn to their copy of *Laws and Regulations Relating to Trade with Indian Tribes*, theoretically located in each store. The amount and type of stock placed on the shelves, personnel "do's and don'ts," control of measuring devices and prices, Sabbath observance, and a host of other rules restricted employees by a web of guidance. Intermittent inspections by area authorities and written reports ensured compliance. Failure to follow instructions could mean revocation of license and banishment from the reservation.

A few examples given in a letter issued in 1905 illustrate just how restrictive these rules could be and how traders were held accountable under penalty. For instance, if a nonresident were to travel across the reservation with a trader, that individual first had to obtain written permission from the area superintendent, in this case William T. Shelton. "In making application for such a permit, the trader should state who the party or parties are, their business on Indian land, the length of their proposed stay, and must understand that he is personally responsible for the conduct of such person or persons while on the reservation."[7] Traders also had to be strictly moral, and could not participate in Indian ceremonies or dances, charge for lodging or boarding of customers, sell alcohol, or allow gambling. Other rules were on the books such as requiring a permit to hire Indians for employment, including freighting, but these were not as strictly enforced. The superintendent needed to know who was being paid, that the Indians were content with the amount, and that "it must be a cash transaction." Few posts operated with money on a large scale; trade and barter were the general means.

The next rule was totally impossible to live with—for either the trader or the Navajo—and the agents knew it. "Hereafter, traders will not be permitted to receive in pawn or pledge any property whatsoever belonging to Indians, and all traders are required to restore Indian property they now have in pawn to the owners thereof within sixty to ninety days from the date hereof. Any pawned stuff not redeemed by the Indian owners within the period named must be disposed of in accordance with instructions from the superintendent."[8] The entire system of barter depended on pawn, securing a loan transaction that replaced cash for something of equal monetary value and that the borrower wanted to get back. There were two primary times during a year when the Navajos could pay their debts—spring, when the wool clip from the sheep was purchased, and fall, when the lamb crop could be sold. Things like woven rugs and blankets, silver work, hides, and miscellaneous objects might be exchanged throughout the year, but they did not have the salability in eastern markets the way wool and animals for meat did.

This led to a second impossible rule to abide by on the far-flung Navajo Reservation. Traders were prohibited from purchasing livestock unless the Indian had a permit to sell it, there was a specified price that the trader would pay for the animal, and at the beginning of each month, he had to submit a report to the agent specifying how many he purchased. This, as with all other transactions, was to be done in cash. All of this was supplemental to the *Laws and Regulations*. There is little wonder that off-reservation posts flourished long before those on the reservation. Free from detailed control, these stores followed market-demand exchange unburdened by regulation. This was also a reason for the expansion of the reservation, as Navajos moved to the edges in search of more grass, water, and barter at posts eager for business.[9] As trade became increasingly profitable and the golden age of the posts flourished for roughly twenty-five years (1910–35), it became worthwhile to establish more stores on the reservation. Internal and external events such as a growing railroad system, developing tourist industry, purchasing power associated with World War I, availability of cars and trucks with an accompanying road network, demographic growth, and a host of other influences assisted in fomenting this golden era.

Still, this was only half of the equation. Trader Will Evans, a man intimately familiar with the Two Grey Hills area, shared his observations of what was happening to the Navajos during 1907. In his estimation, "The Navajo tribe has never been this prosperous. The Indian has come up from the depths of poverty to conditions of affluence."[10] He attributed this to a number of reasons: the favorable growing conditions of plentiful water and grass as well as abundant harvests, which was the exact opposite of years of drought suffered at the turn of the century; the rapid increase and improved quality of livestock, thanks to the efforts of Shelton; and the use of wagons for shipping goods as well as a road system that was growing in miles and improving in quality. Evans, having just returned from a trip to the Chuska area wrote, "There are a great many instances of wealth in the tribe. Black Sheep [person] living at Two Grey Hills, is reported to be worth $10,000, his wealth being in sheep and cattle. It is easily figured out, as he has upward of 3,000 sheep and a large herd of cattle. He has a grazing ranch in the mountains situated in a very beautiful location. Old 'Ba-chi' is said to have twice the amount of sheep owned by Black Sheep. The former also ranges in the Two Grey Hills country. His sheep are among the largest and finest on the reservation. 'Ya-binny,' living near the H. B. Noel trading post, has a good ranch on the Teec Nos Pos Wash. He raises fruit, alfalfa, and grain and has sheep and cattle galore. He does lots of freighting for the traders, and when on a pleasure trip, rides around with his family in a two-seated rig."[11] Evans also estimated that when he attended a recent Yé'ii Bicheii dance at Teec Nos Pos with over a thousand Navajos present, the value of the silver goods worn by them was around $15,000 dollars, and they also had ready cash. "You could take the same crowd 8 or 10 years ago, and you might say that you could hardly find 20 cents." Prosperity was manifesting itself in many forms.

One of the most important elements was the improvement of weaving products. Evans wrote, "The demand for Navajo blankets and silverware has greatly increased because the American can better afford to purchase them. Twelve or fifteen years ago, I am told, any Navajo rug could be purchased for 25 cents per pound, while today, prices run all the way from 75 cents to $2.50 per pound, while some of the product reaches enormous prices. Five dollars per pound is not a remarkable figure for an extra good article. While market conditions are responsible for this, the article has undoubtedly improved for this reason: better time and increased wealth allows the weaver to spend more time and effort on the product, hence a better production."[12] This was of primary concern in the development of regional style patterns in rugs and blankets, providing the impetus that made Navajo weaving famous and Two Grey Hills the preeminent location for creating quality products.

In 1911 the Office of Indian Affairs, through Shelton, sent a questionnaire to the traders on the New Mexico and Arizona portions of the Navajo Reservation. The government wanted to determine what types of employment were beneficial, which jobs catered to men or to women, and what the post's volume of business was between July 10, 1910, and June 30, 1911. Not all traders responded, and of those that did, some provided short answers, while others went into greater detail. The experiences of a half dozen traders operating in or near the Two Grey Hills region give a clear snapshot of the business in these posts as they entered into the most successful period of Navajo trade.[13] Beginning with Reitz and Davies, they reported purchasing $6,855 in blankets and $125 in silver crafts, trading in no other native crafts. The women did the weaving using all natural wool for the colors and so "no natural dye was now used in this part of the country"; the men produced silverwork, with the traders providing Mexican pesos as the metal. John L. Oliver established Nava, later known as Newcomb, six miles away from Two Grey Hills, around 1904. His mailing address was at Crozier (Two Grey Hills), his neighboring post. He had bought $890 in blankets and $150 in silver; Frank L. Noel at Little Water purchased $6,000 in blankets, $350 in silver work, and $50 in baskets while noting that the "squaws are the grub-getters." A. Arnold at Tohatchi, twenty-six miles to the south of Two Grey Hills, had bought $6,000 worth of blankets, $300 in silver, and $100 in farm produce and odds and ends. He sold artificial dyes during the time that natural dyes were not used, although he went into two pages of detail about natural dyes and how they were obtained in the past.

Olin C. Walker, thirty miles away at Red Rock, reported $10,417 in blankets, $397 in silver, and $150 in baskets and woven belts. He also sent some promotional material for potential customers to give them an idea of how rugs and blankets were woven; there were also pictures of women working at their looms, some brief glimpses into Navajo life, a discussion about the uniqueness of designs, and the cost of a finished product. His prices may be considered representative of the figures cited above, indicating roughly the volume of blankets being sold by all the traders at the time. "A 3x5 blanket is worth from $4 to $10, but averages $5 or $6. A 4x6 from $8 to $20, average price $10 to $14. A 5x7 from $14 to $45, average price from $17 to $25. I make the price right whatever it is."[14] In his accompanying letter, after discussing the preference for wool instead of cotton warp and his problem selling silver work, he touched on a topic important to all traders, which led to a florescence in Navajo weaving. He wrote, "There is room for great improvement in patterns and sizes, making them more saleable and desirable thereby getting better prices and selling more rugs. . . . At present, every trader and jobber of blankets are overstocked with blankets. Yet if they were the right kind, they would sell. The blanket and jewelry industry brings in over half, if not all the money. I pay the Indians for wool, pelts, hay, grain, and stock combined at my post. . . . I am anxious to do a part in anything to increase the product or sale of their product or help in any way to benefit the Indian."[15]

Internal Influences—The Traders

At Crystal, sixteen miles away from Two Grey Hills, sat J. B. Moore, a man credited with taking a giant step in improving the craft. He had bought this store in 1897 from Joe Reitz, who had been in partnership with Joe Wilkins, both of whom had ties with Two Grey Hills. According to Charles Amsden, whose authoritative work *Navaho Weaving* outlines the development of the art form, Moore sent wool back east where it was scoured, carded, and dyed, then sold blankets woven with this specially prepared material by mail order, "having achieved high technical excellence and excessive sophistication in design."[16] He had sixteen highly skilled weavers who received this special wool and created patterns that were often coached or created by Moore as he introduced them into their weaving. This included the Greek fret, a heavy crossform along with diamond patterns, often in conjunction with red as a primary color.[17] Moore has since been credited with fostering a new era in innovative weaving, the development of regional styles, and a much higher quality product. McNitt believed that if he had to choose six traders who influenced Navajo weaving in a positive way, Moore would have to be on that list.[18]

So when Moore filled out his questionnaire, he wrote from experience, clearly outlining what he felt were the solutions and problems in increasing marketing. In his estimates of a year's sale of Navajo crafts, he sold $13,000 in blankets—almost twice the amount provided by any of the other traders in that area—$1,000 in silver, and $500 in other native work. This was a decrease from the previous year's sales because of the slowing of the general American economy. He next went into a discussion about how the craft had changed and what he did to improve the quality. Although he estimated that 75 percent of his blankets were made from wool provided by the Indians, the remaining 25 percent were made from those materials specially prepared in the East. The underlying issue was the cleanliness of the wool so that the dye would adhere properly. The characteristic red wool, as with the other colorings, now came from aniline dyes that he sold, whereas in the past it was obtained by unraveling and spinning bayeta wool flannel, first introduced by the Spanish. Following this explanation, he concluded with, "The real problem confronting the trader is not getting the blankets made, but that of getting them sold. There is at present at least $200,000 to $250,000 of them in the hands of traders, and their wholesalers awaiting purchasers, and this at the cost prices paid the Indians; no trader can absorb indefinitely unless he can sell them."[19]

A short time after completing the survey, Moore was gone from Crystal. Trader John Arrington had firsthand knowledge of why. Mary Anne Cooney Moore, J. B.'s wife, belonged to the Indian Rights Association, an organization designed to further the cause—materially and politically—of American Indians. Described as "tough as a pig's nose," this hefty three-hundred-pound woman, when placed next to her slim husband who was constantly "spitting up his lungs," was a commanding figure. According to Arrington, she had been selling fake turquoise in silver work and passing it off as genuine Navajo craft. There was also the matter of a fifty-gallon drum of kerosene provided by the Indian Rights Association for Navajo use. Mary Anne sold the contents and pocketed the money. An investigation followed, resulting in her and J. B. soon leaving the reservation and the Navajo blanket industry.[20] Their impact in improving the quality of woven goods, however, lingered long after.

There were other watchdogs who monitored activities taking place on and off the reservation. J. S. Lockwood, secretary of the Boston Indian Citizenship Committee, was just such a person. On August 16, 1913, he contacted Cato Sells, commissioner of Indian affairs, asking if trader Frank L. Noel at Little Water and the C. H. Algert Company in Fruitland were operating under the authority of the Indian Bureau. C. H. Algert handled many of the supplies and purchased many of the crafts coming from or going to the posts on the northern part of the reservation, but the organization was not under government control. Sells replied accordingly. Lockwood responded, saying that for the past fifteen years he had been serving as the president of the Indian Industries League, an organization that had been working to take the business of scouring and dyeing Indian wool from the East to the Navajos in the West, thus improving the products of the loom while decreasing prices. As part of this project, he obtained wool from New Mexico, had it cleaned and dyed, readied it for weaving, and shipped it to different missionaries,

Mary Eldridge among them, and traders who gave it to the Indians to work. Months went by and Lockwood became impatient, unsure of the status of his blankets until another missionary, Mrs. H. M. Peabody, who had recently returned from the area, said that she had seen his rugs exhibited at the Shiprock Fair.[21]

By January 1914 Lockwood had received two large and three small rugs, but was now inquiring what had happened to the rest of his yarn, figuring that he was short fifty-five-and-a-half pounds. He appealed to the commissioner to put pressure on Noel, since he came under his supervision, and to make matters right. Shelton became the tip of the spear in the ensuing investigation; he approached J. L. (Joseph Lehi) Foutz, manager of the Algert Company, who took full responsibility for the issue. Foutz, through Shelton, said "that the Indians near Fruitland do not make good blankets and that the yarn was sent to F. L. Noel, whose trading post is forty miles west from that place and is located among some of the best blanket weavers on the reservation."[22] Shelton also contacted Noel, who informed him "that when the yarn was received, he employed some of his best weavers to make the blankets; that he had two large ones made for which he paid the weavers thirty-five dollars each, and three small ones made for which he paid eight dollars each," and that "the remainder of the wool was not suitable for producing good blankets and that the Indian women did not want to work it," and so it was returned to the Algert Company.[23] Shelton, who had known Noel for ten and a half years, considered him "straightforward and honorable in his dealings" and declared that he had done "more than any other trader to advance the interests of the Indians on this reservation." Lockwood and the Algert Company would need to take the complaint about the missing wool to court.

What can be learned from this insignificant episode? First is the realization that businesses and individuals located two thousand miles away took an interest in Navajo weaving and were willing to promote it. Lockwood had invested time and money, enlisted chemists and university (Massachusetts Institute of Technology—M.I.T.) faculty in developing a better product, and was concerned about the low prices Navajo women received for their products. On the other hand, he had little understanding of the motivation and time it took to weave a blanket and what the trader had to go through to have it delivered to his post. Already the

Traders and government employees following a meeting with Agent Shelton during the 1912 Shiprock Fair. *Top row, left to right:* Sheldon Dustin, John Walker, Jesse Foutz, Ike Goldsmith, Bert Dustin, Frank Noel, Alphonso (Fonnie) Nelson, June Foutz, Bruce Bernard, unidentified government employee. *Third row:* Herbert Redshaw, "Al" Foutz, Olin C. Walker, Will Evans, John Hunt, Jim Wade, William Hunter. *Second row:* James M. Holley, Frank Mapel, Edith Mapel, Samuel B. Stacher (Crownpoint agent), George Bloomfield, Mrs. Ed Davies, and Ed Davies with daughter Mary. *Bottom row:* Mr. Treeland, Arthur J. Newcomb, Superintendent William T. Shelton, Joe Tanner, Louisa Wade Wetherill, John Wetherill. Courtesy of Harvey Leake, John and Louisa Wetherill Photo Collection.

Two Grey Hills area was recognized as having some of the best weavers on the reservation, and Noel had given the project to some of the best of the best. Another point to be made is how Shelton knew his traders, and when necessary, protected them from what could have been expulsion from a post. Pearl Davies, years later, commented that she "admired Shelton's treatment of the Indians," although "strict and dictatorial,"— and that is why "it meant something when an Indian was told he would be sent to Shiprock."[24] She quickly added that he would tour the posts, "to see that we were treating the Indians right and that we kept our places clean . . . but he didn't trouble [us] beyond that with special laws and orders." A final point is that between the traders and the Shiprock Fair, their wares were becoming well known.

Just how well known is offered in a report issued by Shelton around the same time that the Lockwood incident came to a close. From his perspective, "the greatest improvements in rugs as well as silverware has been brought about by the means of Industrial Fairs when the best products are exhibited for the inspection of all Indians and visitors and in competing with each other for prizes."[25] He went on to say that the poorest rugs in the last fair were better than the best ones exhibited in the first fair five years before. Recent innovations of having the superintendent certify that a rug was a genuine Navajo artifact, the crossing of breeds of sheep for a better wool product, promotion of native wool instead of store-bought, and discouraging cotton warp and new machines to make the weaving process easier were all part of a plan to ensure that "the average person buying a Navajo rug [will receive a product] made by Indians in their own way from the sheep to the finished article."

When asked about the volume of sales and production, the agent could not be precise, since there was so much off-reservation trading. He knew that the Algert Company handled five thousand blankets a year with an average price of $10. As for jewelry set with turquoise, a lot depended on size and design. "This jewelry brings from fifty cents to five dollars for rings; one dollar to fifteen dollars for bracelets; ten to thirty dollars for necklaces; twenty to fifty dollars for belts; thirty to forty dollars for bridles. Spoons, butter knives and other useful articles sell from a dollar to three dollars each."[26] He estimated that the value of the jewelry owned by his Navajos was about $100,000 and that they sell approximately $10,000 per year. A few years before this, three traders estimated the value of all the goods displayed at the fair—rugs, jewelry, and other products—at $125,000.

With Shelton such a booster, it is surprising that he was not in favor of marketing products in the East. He felt that orders could not be filled promptly—shades of the Lockwood incident—and that a person could obtain a rug more cheaply by working through a trader than by direct purchase from the weaver. Also, Navajos were used to selling their products to the traders in a process that was filled with cultural elements. A normal transaction went something like this. The weaver would bring a rug to a trading post and lay it on the counter where the trader weighed and examined it. He would offer a price, then put the amount of money alongside the blanket and let the woman choose. If she thought she was getting enough for the article, she would take the money; if not, she brought the blanket to the next nearest trader and went through the same procedure until she either received what she wanted or was satisfied that she could not get her price for the blanket, then selling for the best price offered. If the trader or anyone else asked her to price the blanket, she would ask as much again for it as the blanket would bring on the market. The agent feared this is what would happen if the government undertook handling Navajo products. "I am sure these Indians would not be willing to let their blankets go without receiving cash down for them. Unless the government would guarantee them a much larger price than they could get from the traders and then, I doubt very much if they would be willing to wait for returns. In my opinion, the best way to help these Indians with their industries is by some system of advertising which would create a demand for them."[27] For Shelton, the best way to meet everyone's need was at gatherings similar to the Shiprock Fair.

Four months before Shelton relinquished command of Shiprock, he gave a summary report of what a recent census indicated was the state of the Northern Navajo Agency. He had under his jurisdiction approximately 7,000 Navajos, whose primary livelihood came from stock-raising and blanket weaving, with the sale of wool, sheep, and pelts also a part of their mainstay. "It is a poor family which does not own from one hundred to one thousand sheep."[28] In a follow-up report by Special Inspector O. M. McPherson a week later, he added that the Navajos in this jurisdiction owned 283,628 sheep and goats, a quarter of which were goats, 6,500 cattle, and 30,000 horses.[29] McPherson did the math and determined there were far too many horses, given the population size. From his perspective, "They pay no attention to breeding; they simply raise horses . . . [for which] unfortunately, some [Navajos] are poorer because of their ownership of too large a number of unprofitable animals;" still, he had "heard it said that a Navajo 'loves a horse.'" In terms of agriculture, the 5,000 acres under cultivation had flourished, Shelton estimating a 75 percent increase since he had started twelve years ago. In general the economy on the reservation had been one of continuous improvement.

Under Shelton's command there were also projects beyond the agency that boosted the economy. He was credited by one investigator as "the best road-builder in the service" with more than three hundred miles of well-kept, frequently graded and dragged highways suitable for automobiles—a means of travel beginning to enter the area at this time. There was also an additional one hundred miles of unbridged, steep hill, and sandy arroyo roads for wagon travel leading into the hinterland.[30] At Two Grey Hills the department was building a dam and reservoir system, which would add several thousand acres of tillable land. Navajo labor provided much of the work. The government had also determined that the day school at Toadlena was not sufficient and so had expanded facilities into a boarding school. Three new buildings—a boys' dormitory, girls' dormitory, and a dining room with kitchen facility—held the capacity for eighty students, but with the already existing structures and a few small additions, it could be increased to a 120-student capacity.[31]

All of this expansion, activity, and growth was not lost on the traders, who were working hard and benefiting from their labors as markets surged and the economy blossomed during the World War I era. The war in Europe that started in 1914 was an economic boon to the United States, who provided food and war materials to the beleaguered nations embraced in a bloody death grip. The impact of this distant conflict on the Navajo Reservation ensured that the Indians could not produce enough wool or provide enough meat to fill the demand, which at the trading post counters meant brisk sales, fewer woven products, and more raw wool. Business was good, and for those traders who behaved themselves, they had the full support of their new agent in Shiprock, Evan W. Estep.

In 1918 he wrote a report with a series of paragraphs that described thirteen traders within the Northern Navajo Agency. In general, minus some peccadillos, he extolled their virtue and recommended all be reissued licenses when the time came. A few excerpts from some of these citations give a sense of the personality and character of those standing behind the counter. Beginning with Ed Davies, Estep viewed him as a man who could "compete with men in the same line of business in towns or cities," while his store, although off the beaten track, "is noted as the place where the best weave of Navajo rugs is made."[32] He was not alone. H. S. Traylor, two years before this, singled out Davies as "the best, most conscientious, and fairest trader to the Indians. He is absolute in his obedience to the laws of the Department—sanitation and health. He has a very strong influence upon his section, and demands from all a full measure of work, temperance, and right living. He secures the best blankets and pays the Indians twice as much as most traders, with the exception of Mr. Bloomfield. His wife has also a splendid influence among these people and gives a good part of her time and talent to the bettering of their conditions."[33] The inspector went on to suggest that the department write a letter to the couple, commending them on the cleanliness and appearance of their store and their good work in their "neighborhood." "Such a letter in less degree of praise should be written to Mr. and Mrs. Bloomfield of Toadlena."

Estep continued his evaluation, stating that he had visited George R. Bloomfield three or four times during the previous six months and that he was compliant in following all the regulations. The same was true of Arthur Newcomb at Nava on Captain Tom's Wash, where he was a "real for sure store keeper, one who could hold up his end in competition with others in a town off the reservation." W. J. Walker had bought Noel's store at the base of Beautiful Mountain, but had not found as much favor with Estep as some of the other traders. A month before this report came out, Walker was said to have sided with Indians who did not want their sheep dipped. The agent chided him, convincing the trader that Estep was against him and had sent out a circular, targeting him under the guise of addressing all traders. Still, he kept the regulations and Estep claimed no animosity. Olin C. Walker at Red Rock ran a store, "said to be the best money maker on the reservation." The agent concluded by saying that most of the traders knew little about the trading post regulations, but if they could be reduced to the size of a pamphlet, each man could be given a copy with the renewal of his license.

The Dynamic Duo—Davies and Bloomfield

Davies and Bloomfield, like J. B. Moore earlier, were interested in improving the quality of weaving. There has been a long-standing belief that Moore was the one who gave rise to the well-known Two Grey Hills blanket and rug designs. Certainly his promotion of excellence, introduction of certain pattern elements, and marketing practices were not lost on other traders in the area. But the distinctive Two Grey Hills design did not appear while Moore was trading. Frank McNitt, when writing *The Indian Traders*, spent a good deal of time tracking down when Two Grey Hills, Toadlena, and Newcomb developed their unique patterns known as Two Grey Hills. His search in museums, with private collectors, and by trader interview, provided the most complete answer as to when and who encouraged Navajo weavers in the creation of this regional style.

In 1912, when Davies bought full interest in Two Grey Hills and George Bloomfield purchased Toadlena five miles away, the two men decided to collaborate. Both were interested in improving the quality of woven blankets and rugs and so set about in a trial-and-error fashion to introduce designs, clean greaseless wool, and experiment with colors. They learned quickly that the Navajos in that area did not like to use the color red, so prominent in the products woven around Crystal. The natural browns, grays, blacks, and whites that came from the sheep's wool were the preferred colors woven into designs. The traders insisted on cleaner wool, a tighter weave, and that no aniline dyes be used, except perhaps black to frame a rug in a two-inch border with a spirit or pathway line, which is discussed in chapter 8. Higher pay for a product that met increasingly elevated standards encouraged women like Charley Curley's wife, Police Girl, and Mrs. Taugel-clitso, to spend more time and effort in creating master works that would eventually lead to the best woven products on the reservation. Suggestions and corrections were done in private, with George Bloomfield's daughter recalling how he would be "down on his knees, often for as long as two hours, pointing out defects and discussing with the weaver how she could eliminate a 'lazy line,' correct a wobbly design element, or introduce design variation of multiplying complexity."[34]

The process of improvement took time. McNitt and other authorities together concluded that between 1915 and 1925, this distinctive regional style was born and then reached maturity, providing the Two Grey Hills product known today.[35] The weavers had moved from an era in which traders were purchasing weaving at three dollars a pound to now, when rugs are worth many thousands of dollars willingly paid by wealthy tourists. Chapter 8 shares more about what it takes to create and sell such an object, but suffice it to say at this point that these rugs

Yazzie Blackhorse *(left)* and Fannie Charles exhibit a Two Grey Hills rug, typical of the design and craftsmanship that made this regional style world famous. Tight weave, intricate pattern, natural wool, and a variety of geometric shapes are common elements found in this style. Courtesy of Two Grey Hills Trading Post Archive Collection.

and blankets command some of the highest prices in the Navajo world of weaving.

As weaving improved and regional styles developed, there were also questions raised about wool. During and shortly after World War I, market demands for this product reached a height that drove prices ever higher. While Navajo wool was considered a lesser grade when compared with other types that reached markets in Boston and Philadelphia, it was still in demand. Traders purchasing the wool in New Mexico had to spend time cleaning and sorting it, shipping it by wagon to a railhead, and remaining ever vigilant of the shifting market prices back east. They were also responsible to the agent who made sure that fair payment was given to the Navajo customer. Failure to follow agency guidelines when buying the wool could result in the revocation of the trader's license. The following case concerning Ed Davies at Two Grey Hills and Evan Estep at

Shiprock illustrate this type of power exchange, the control of prices, and the impact of events thousands of miles away on Navajo and trader alike.

On May 4, 1919, Estep telegrammed the Indian Office in Washington, inquiring about the current price of wool. He wrote that traders were paying forty cents a pound and "are about to get cold feet."[36] A day later the reply said that there was little wool available, that even the poorer wools from southern Utah and similar areas were commanding at least forty-five cents, while higher grade wools coming from Montana were bringing in fifty-five cents per pound. Estep felt that forty cents was a fair price for the traders to be paying the Navajos, but there were some men, Ed Davies being one of them, who refused to pay such a high cost. Indeed, the traders were "howling to beat the band. . . . Newcomb, Davies, Bloomfield, Foutz, and Walker [are being made] to come through or go out of the game. . . . Mr. Davies has said that he is tired of being brow-beaten by petty government officials and says that he is going to quit the store. . . . [C. C. Manning Company in Gallup] owns half of the Davies store and ordered Davies to quit buying wool at twenty cents and told him to pay forty cents or quit buying, and he has quit."[37] The Manning Company greatly influenced Newcomb and Two Grey Hills, and Davies claimed they had taken a hard line approach for maintaining lower prices. This pushed Estep to look very carefully when it was time to renew trader licenses. He did not stop there, but went on to threaten that the department would build a large warehouse at the agency capable of handling all of the wool produced on that part of the reservation and would purchase it directly from the Navajos. "The 'talk' has had a very good effect on all the traders and incidentally, made all of us very popular with traders and their backers. However, a good many Indians understand and seem to appreciate what we are doing for them and a number of Fort Defiance Indians are coming over the mountain to sell their wool to our traders."[38]

The moment of truth for Davies came on August 2, 1919, when Estep sent his application for license renewal to the commissioner of Indian affairs and recommended that it be denied until the trader got in line with government policy and procedure emanating from Shiprock. Davies was the only trader in that jurisdiction who had not complied and continued to purchase wool at twenty cents per pound. He refused to buckle even after being given a direct order by the government farmer living at Two Grey Hills at the time, who prohibited him from buying any more wool. The trader resented the government interference. Estep characterized him as "an Englishman and pretty high strung. . . . His temper sometimes runs riot with the Indians, and he goes for them pretty hard," but he also was an honest, hardworking man.[39] The agent placed part of the blame on the three wholesale houses in Gallup— C. C. Manning, C. N. Cotton, and the Gallup Mercantile—that supplied goods to the posts and often paid in part or entirely the store's $10,000 bond to the government. They were a "hard lot" who wanted to buy low, sell high, and "make a million." Estep offered to buy the wool Davies had for twenty-five cents, but the trader refused. That was enough—renewal denied. The same happened to Arthur Newcomb, who was also purportedly paying too low a price.

Starting with Davies, his reaction was immediate. Once he received word of the denial, he wrote to Commissioner Cato Sells explaining that he was "astonished" at the refusal, that he had been trading with the Indians for ten years, and that he had "succeeded in building up a strong business with them under strong competition," which never would have happened if he had been unfair.[40] He promised that he was buying the wool at the price he was selling it for in Gallup, plus shipping at two cents a pound, and that he was making little profit. Once advised that he had to raise his rates, he immediately did so. The wool he was accused of buying for only twenty cents per pound had come in as small quantities and did not amount to more than one hundred pounds total. He recognized that it was a privilege to trade on the reservation, that when the Indians prospered he prospered, and that he would cooperate in every respect with the agency's direction. His license was renewed on October 31, 1919.

Arthur Newcomb's dissension adds more to understanding the power of Shiprock's control. There had been a campaign to improve the quality of Navajo wool, which would bring a higher price from the trader and in the market. Newcomb had been purchasing wool at thirty-five cents, claiming that it was just standard "Navajo wool," as the traders called it, with no improved wool to be found.[41] Estep did not take long in challenging the claim. He arrived at Newcomb's store with Special Supervisor Campbell and John H. Holliday, president of the National Wool Warehouse and Storage Company of Chicago, to view the trader's products. Newcomb claimed to have no improved wool, but Holliday pointed out that there was both improved wool and skins from improved sheep. The trader estimated that approximately 20 percent of the wool on hand was of this type. Estep wished to give him the benefit of the doubt by seeing if he would help his customers purchase a better grade of rams in the fall and thus move the work of improving livestock forward. The agent realized that the trader did not speak the Navajo language fluently, and so there was room for misunderstanding. Even though Estep viewed him as an "insurgent" and "talks one way to me and another way to another person," he recommended the issuance of a license with the caveat that he would have more time to observe the trader's actions for future renewals.[42]

Davies was back in the spotlight during the same year for the same issue. On his application for renewal, he did not include a statement as to his cooperation in introducing improved methods of handling wool. The commissioner of Indian affairs returned the paperwork, insisting that Davies declare his intent. The trader responded by saying that he had done his best to cooperate with the Office of Indian Affairs, had graded the wool and paid fair prices—thirty to forty cents per pound—and was still holding his wool since he had received "no offer which would clear me."[43] He then requested that the department give the traders help in identifying the difference between Navajo and improved wool, so that they could all more fully cooperate. Estep concurred, saying that the other traders, like Davies, were having a difficult time in selling their wool because of the poor market. Now they had bought high and would have to sell low, part of which could be blamed on the Indian Office.

George Bloomfield at Toadlena provides a good example of a man who followed directions, gained favor with Estep, and lost money. Remember that the wool clip came in during the spring and the lamb crop in the fall. It was December 1, 1920, when the agent wrote the following: "The Bloomfields have paid good prices the past year for wool and lambs. They have the wool on hand yet and had to hold their lambs at the railroad so long waiting for cars that they lost money on them. They have greatly assisted in putting a number of thoroughbred Rambouillet rams out with the Indians of their district; they bought thirty outright and have helped us in placing some of the one hundred we bought."[44]

Two years later, in 1922, Davies was again under the magnifying glass with the agent. Estep's estimation of Davies is informative, not only for the personalities that were clashing, but also for the conditions of trade in general. After claiming that Davies had never given any help in improving the quality of sheep, Estep said that the trader had paid as much for the Navajo wool as he had for the improved, and that he would not be able to get paid sufficiently for both. Other traders differentiated in their payment, but not Davies. "It is no use to talk to Mr. Davies on any of these matters. He KNOWS (emphasis by agent). He is a clean-cut man, good morals, and could run a business in any community. He is an Englishman and few if any English ever 'fit in' just right in this country. That is his principal difficulty. He has no particular 'love' for an American and none at all for the Red Americans except as customers. Yet he is better than many other traders."[45]

Part of Estep's frustration grew from a misunderstanding that arose during the 1920 Shiprock Fair. While the agent denied allegations by Davies, in the trader's mind he was being coerced into lining the pockets of some of Estep's business associates. One evening, the agent held a dinner in which he invited all the traders as well as two men who sold high quality Rambouillet rams for the livestock improvement program. Davies felt he was being forced to buy ten or more animals at a cost of $35 a head or else his license would not be renewed, and that he would have to turn around and sell the animals to his Navajo customers. He could not afford it, they would not purchase the rams, and the agent seemed to be crowding him out by allowing other traders to come into his area and take away clients. That was why he was attempting to sell his store ownership, but because of the "demoralized condition of the trading business," he could not find anyone willing to invest.[46] He was just as quick to point out that he had by then been at Two Grey Hills for twelve years and was an astute businessman as well as an advocate for the Indians. "When I first came here, their blankets were what we call medium grade, but we kept after them to improve their weave. Today, there are no finer blankets made than in this Two Grey Hills section and the blanket industry is their mainstay for their living." Davies felt more than justified in opposing what he considered government—or at least the agent's—coercion.

Estep was quick to respond. The whole idea of each trader buying at least ten rams was just not true, all the traders thought the idea good except for Newcomb, who spoke out, and Davies, who remained quiet, openly opposed to the idea, and said so to other traders and "his

Indians." Some traders purchased thirty rams, others bought lesser amounts, and no one had to help the agency make a first payment. "None of them will lose a cent on what they have done" and none of the animals were to be given to the Indians.[47] He denied other accusations. There had been no new stores encroaching on Two Grey Hills other than those that had existed for a long time. Estep did everything in his power to protect Davies and Newcomb, even though they had rejected being "hearty co-workers." Davies, when traveling, had employed unlicensed clerks at his store, against government regulations, had not posted prices in the store, and did not share certain aspects of his trans-actions with Shiprock, although technically required. Estep did not think any of these infractions were serious enough to deny the trader a renewal of his license, but the commissioner did. Davies had not "manifested the interest and spirit of cooperation toward our efforts to advance the industrial welfare of the Indians which we rightfully expect of a licensed Indian trader."[48] Sufficient penance and explanation had been given by October 8, 1921, that the commissioner reinstated the license, and Davies continued in business.

Issues—Animals, Pawn, and Wool

Although Estep held the upper hand with on-reservation traders, his influence with those unlicensed off reservation was much more tenuous. Some of these traders would send word to Navajo customers to bring whatever they wanted to sell to stores like the Hogback Trading Post, and there they would get better prices. All the agent could do was to threaten prosecution, but there had not yet been a successful trial to determine if the courts would side with the government or free enterprise. One of the desirable sales included the breeding stock that the agents were using to increase the quality of Navajo wool. Some unlicensed traders tried to form a partnership with one who worked on the reservation, but as soon as word reached the agent, the deal was quashed. The Fruit-land Company Store made overtures but was also stopped, with Estep promising that if it went to court, it would not be a friendly suit and that only a presidential pardon could prevent the convicted party from going to jail. Behind closed doors, the agent was not so sure. He knew that the burden of proof remained with the government—to show that the sheep or cattle had actually come from government coffers. This would be difficult, and so until it became an absolute necessity, bluffing and control of the elements that were under government influence was a better policy than fighting in court.[49]

Another issue, already mentioned, that affected both on- and off-reservation posts and sales was the use of tokens, tickets, store orders, or anything other than money. The reason for this was that agents were supposed to be moving the Navajos away from a barter system, providing them with experiences in handling finances as in the dominant society. Agents, therefore, directed that pawn should be used only in emergencies, that no interest should be charged upon redemption, and that if pawn were to be sold, the Indian would need to receive a thirty-day written notification. While Estep assured the commissioner that "tokens and pawn did not prevail on this reservation," it is difficult to understand how the agent could claim that.[50] Trading posts had entire rooms dedicated to safeguarding pawn; traders recorded these transactions with the person accepting the loan; the lender established the due date for payment, and when missed, let the owner know that the pawn was now "dead" and could be sold. This practice was at the heart of the Navajo trading system.

One might ask if the issues that Estep and the traders faced were limited solely to the Northern Navajo Agency. A quick glance at what was taking place in the neighboring Western Agency, headquartered in Tuba City, Arizona, puts the improvement and sale of wool and the barter system that supported it, into a broader context. In 1919, Superintendent Walter Runke of the Western Agency estimated there were 200,000 sheep and 40,000 goats then on his part of the reservation, following a 15 percent loss from that winter's severe weather.[51] He felt that the sheep of the Western Navajo were very inferior to those of Anglo ranchers, and so over the previous five years he had introduced seventy-five Lincoln rams, which he sold to upgrade the herd. Trader Stewart Hatch in southeast Utah agreed with Runke's observation. Hatch mentioned how traders drew a marked distinction between what they called "American" and Navajo sheep. The former were larger, grain-fed animals that yielded ten to twelve pounds of wool at a shearing, while the latter foraged for their food and became very thin over the winter until spring with increasing access to grass on the summer range. These animals yielded from four to six pounds of wool.[52]

In 1923 on the Western Navajo there was little difference in the sheep's quality or the amount of wool from these experimental breeding practices. Babbitt Brothers in Flagstaff was paying a standard price, which traders willingly accepted. The owners of chain trading posts often determined the price with the independent traders, agreeing to adopt what they decided. Animal products from various agencies went to local buyers—those from southeastern Utah, southwestern Colorado, and New Mexico sent their wool to the Colorado-New Mexico Wool Marketing Association, who, in turn, sold to the National Wool Marketing Association in Boston. Farther south, Navajos sold their wool in Gallup, Albuquerque, and Flagstaff, having it shipped by railroad to the East. All these connections influenced the price and acceptance of the Navajos' product.[53] Arizona trader Tom Kirk told of dealers' surprise when they visited his post from the East. There sat copies of *Kiplinger's Letter*, the *Congressional Record*, and *Boston Wool Market Report*. He explained to the dealers quickly: "They didn't realize that we had to know what was going on in the sheep market in Denver and Kansas City, what the wool market was in Boston, and what the silver market was in Los Angeles and New York. We had to know these things in order to base our prices in buying and trading."[54]

The uphill struggle to improve the quality of wool continued. The government introduced good breeding stock hoping that Indian owners would see the benefit and help pay for the expense, but this proved more easily said than done. Hard to enforce and a point of friction, the concept inflamed both agent and owner. Problems in the corral, fluctuations in market prices, and the sale of wool created situations for a struggling livelihood. Traders reduced payment by two or three cents per pound in order to clean and ship the wool to market, where they still received lower prices than Anglo breeders using superior stock. Agents assisted Navajos in shifting livestock patterns by using new corrals not infected with lice, vermin, and disease that lingered to torment the animals.

Wool at this time (mid-to-late-1920s) sold for between 32 and 45 cents a pound in Boston or Philadelphia markets. The highest prices for Navajo wool in Boston were between 25 and 30 cents, while in Philadelphia, Navajo wool might bring from 30 to 40 cents. There were a number of reasons for this. Navajo wool was coarse in quality, light in quantity, and often poorly prepared to compete with finer grades of Anglo wool.

Agents hoped that by introducing superior animals for breeding, there might be a significant shift in quality and a higher production—perhaps as much as three- or fourfold. As for preparing the wool for sale, that was up to the Navajo stockmen and traders.[55] Fluctuations in the marketplace caused by national events such as World War I and the Great Depression shifted demands for wool, hides, meat, and crafts, affecting what occurred at the trading post counter. As anthropologists Garrick and Roberta Bailey noted, "It is not surprising that when wool prices rose at the outbreak of World War I, the production of rugs declined. In 1918 the Navajos marketed only $316,643 in rugs. After the war the price of wool fell to an average of 17.3 cents per pound, slightly more than its prewar value, while rug production increased rapidly, peaking at about $700,000 in 1920, approximately its prewar level. The market value of wool recovered somewhat by 1923 and remained relatively high through the late 1920s, but never approached wartime capacity. Rug production declined gradually during the mid and late 1920s, and before the depression Navajos were marketing about $400,000 in rugs each year."[56]

Once the buying house purchased the wool, it was cleaned and graded, and a final price paid for it. The estimated loss in weight could be as much as 50 percent by the time the buyers had removed all foreign matter and the wool readied for sale to a manufacturer. Special Advisor F. E. Brandon tells of other problems encountered in the process of selling Navajo wool. "As an example of the reported losses sustained by the traders from time to time, one firm, Richardson and Lowery, purchased their share of the 1920 and 1921 clip from the Indians, paying 35 to 40 cents per pound. On account of the drop in prices they held the wool in storage one-and-a-half years, paid one-and-a-half-cents per pound for freight to market, and other expenses such as storage, insurance, commission, etc., then sold the same wool for 9 cents a pound. Mr. Lowery told me their losses were $38,000 and that they were forced to close one of their stores on account of it."[57] Thus, even during the florescence of the trading post system, there were highs and lows that challenged the best of traders.

By January 1923, changes were afoot on the Northern Navajo. Albert H. Kneale replaced Evan W. Estep as the agent at Shiprock. The political appointment of Herbert J. Hagerman as the man in charge of all five Navajo districts composing the reservation signaled the beginning development of another part of the economy—oil. This revolutionized many of the business practices and governance of the entire reservation, but had a particularly significant impact in the Northern Agency, where initial oilfields were located. The following year Ed Davies left Two Grey Hills after signing the store over to Willis Martin, mayor of Farmington, who also owned the Red Rock Trading Post and an Indian store in downtown Farmington. Roswell Nelson served as post manager at Two Grey Hills starting in 1924. Motorized transportation was quickly replacing horses and wagons as the primary means to ship merchandise on and off the reservation and into the posts. Improved roads followed. Prosperity abounded in the form of more sheep, goats, cattle, and horses than ever before. Yet, embedded in these changes that appeared to be for the betterment of Navajo people, there were also problems and shifts in lifestyle that held problematic consequences for the future. These are discussed in chapter 8.

CHAPTER SIX

Living around a Post

Daily Life in the Chuska Valley, 1910–1950

More than just the purchase of wool, the weaving of rugs and the sale of pelts occurred at Two Grey Hills and other posts during the halcyon days of trade, when Navajos flourished in the livestock industry. Those times, now long gone, were filled with human drama and interesting anecdotes, many of which have now been forgotten. In preserving these experiences, much depended upon those who took pen in hand to record thoughts and events; when people failed to do so, much of it was lost. The history of the Two Grey Hills Trading Post suffers from a paucity of written material during these times. Fortunately, there were three other posts within a thirteen-mile radius—Toadlena, Newcomb, and Naschitti—that fostered skilled writers, often women, who filled in the blanks about daily life amid the traders and Navajos. When combined with government documents, recollections of other participants, and newspapers, a fascinating picture of a life not captured in ledgers emerges. This chapter looks at several elements of social interaction common to the posts in this part of the Northern Navajo Reservation. Many of the people were involved, in one way or another, with the other posts discussed here. This compilation of shared experiences paints a more complete portrait of daily existence in the Chuska Valley.

Roswell Nelson—Facing Friction

Starting with Two Grey Hills, a new trader—Roswell T. Nelson— appeared behind the counters. Previously he had worked as clerk for

George Bloomfield of Toadlena and later Willis Martin in his store at Red Rock (1918–24). On December 1, 1924, Nelson expressed a desire to be independent and so went in search of a post that allowed him freer reign. Two Grey Hills provided that opportunity as Ed Davies relinquished ownership. Nelson rented it from Willis Martin, brought his wife Mildred Krum Nelson, who had served as head teacher in the San Juan Boarding School at Shiprock, and received his official license in July 1925. He was well known for his honesty, industriousness, and thrift, as was his brother Pratt Nelson, who joined as a partner in June 1930.[1]

In an interview Frank McNitt had with Nelson in 1957, the trader spoke about everyday life at the post. He purchased many blankets and rugs that went either to Martin's store in Farmington or to the Fred Harvey Company, which operated a chain of outlets, hotels, and restaurants focusing on the tourist trade in the Southwest. These blankets sold for anywhere between $10 to $50 dollars up to $200 to $300. He estimated that the Two Grey Hills weaving ranked at the top, with Teec Nos Pos and Toadlena coming in second and third. Crossing the counter in the other direction went major commodities desired by the Navajos. For example, a couple of hundred thousand pounds of flour freighted from Gallup by fifteen to twenty horse-drawn wagons in the fall was not unusual. Dry goods and hardware also made the same week-long journey. Nelson knew how to move what he stocked. He told of how he ordered men's hats while working at the Red Rock Post, but they just did not sell. The hair bun in the back got in the way, and so he offered free haircuts with the purchase of each hat. After that he did a "good business." As for his customers, he found the "Navajos honest as far as paying their bills—losses to credit were almost unheard of—much better than the white man."[2]

Unfortunately, not everything surrounding the trade environment was always pleasant. Before Nelson ever reached the Two Grey Hills Post, he had passed through the fires of scrutiny only to be exonerated, after a wide-ranging investigation that questioned his integrity. The events surrounding the incident in question give insight into Navajo character and interaction during times of stress and how appearances combined with supposition can eat away at truth. The problem started when Nelson, working at Red Rock, decided to travel to Farmington for supplies with Selawasane Begay and two other Navajo men. Unknown to the trader, Selawasane Begay made contact with Claude Walker, who owed the Navajo a fair amount of borrowed money. The white man gave the Indian a gallon of whiskey, which he then concealed and transported onto the reservation, without Nelson's knowledge. One bad move led to another as the son offered to share the alcohol with his father, Selawasane, who at first rejected the offer but later gave in. What happened next, as shared in a grieving father's testimony, illustrates with pathos the reason agents took a strong stance against alcohol on the reservation. Selawasane's statement, obtained by a Navajo policeman who made a ninety-mile ride into the Lukachukai Mountains in the middle of a snowstorm, provides a detailed picture of what occurred.

Selawasane, after completing a number of tasks as a Navajo policeman, met his son on the trail not too distant from the Red Rock Trading Post. The young man, after "coming up and placing his arms around his [father's] neck and saying he was kind of lonely for [him]," invited his father to his home west of the post to drink coffee.[3] Soon the jug of whiskey came out and, once offered, Selawasane thought, "I had to take it." The father asked where his son had obtained it and was told, "He went up the river with Nelson and I asked my son if Nelson got it for him and he said 'No' . . . that Nelson did not see the whiskey or know anything about it." The drinks continued and eventually the father "didn't know anything." It was not until his wife was pushing him around and yelling, "Here you are lying here and look at the condition of our son lying outside," that he began to realize that something was wrong. The old man staggered out of the hogan only to find his son lying on the ground, a self-inflicted bullet hole in his head with the blood still oozing out. "He saw the pistol lying by his son and he said, 'I must die sometime anyway and I better go with my son,' so he picked up the pistol and put it to his head and pulled the trigger. It did not go off. He pulled the trigger again and it did not go off but the third time it went off and the bullet struck him in the head and that was all he knew." The bullet hit a glancing blow; Selawasane lived.

Rumors immediately surfaced. Some Navajos in the Red Rock community joined together unconnected observations to explain the suicide and death, claiming that Nelson had purchased and then shared the whiskey with Selawasane Begay. Jim Curley testified that people had seen the young man coming from the trading post with the jug and assumed he had received it from the trader. During the events at the hogan, the son had offered a young niece some of the alcohol, but she refused to drink it and left the area, but not before her uncle said, "he was going to drink quite a bit and was going to the land of the dead people."[4] Although there was only one person, Hastiin Nez, who claimed to have seen Nelson ever sell whiskey to a Navajo in his store, Jim Curley felt it was "doubtful." Nez, at one point, had worked for the trader, but he had gone "crazy in the head" and so was an unreliable source. Curley ended his statement by observing that even though Nelson had moved to Two Grey Hills, Selawasane "makes a visit there once in a while and he does it because he says Roswell Nelson and his son used to be good friends and he goes there to remember his son." Hardly the behavior of a bereaved man toward a trader who had purportedly supplied the alcohol that caused his family tragedy.

The investigating officer, Field Representative H. H. Fiske, agreed. Depending not only on sworn statements, concrete and circumstantial evidence, and character references for all involved, he concluded that Claude Walker was the culprit and that Nelson was totally innocent. The investigator was in complete support of the trader and felt that "Mr. Roswell Nelson, about whom this rumor gained some slight credence, is one of the best types of men on the reservation. Both he and his wife are believed to be most excellent citizens. Personal contact with the man cannot fail to impress one with the belief that he is a clean, upright individual."[5]

This incident illustrates how real investigative skills were necessary to untangle the web of community observation and hearsay. Maintaining the law, in other circumstances, was usually more straightforward. Take, for instance, one of Pearl Davies's experiences in catching a local thief, well before Nelson arrived at Two Grey Hills. Pearl and Ed had noticed how some of their best blankets had mysteriously disappeared. They decided one day to leave the trading post door open during lunch and place a few goods such as coffee, tobacco, and cloth on the counter as if they had been carelessly left there by accident. Soon Guy Shorty, a young Navajo man, entered the store and removed the bait, but not before the owners identified him as the miscreant. Ed notified Shelton, who arrested Shorty and discovered a number of stolen blankets, some of which had been sold to another trading post. The traders purchased the missing goods from the other store, Shelton forced Shorty to work in Shiprock to pay for the stolen property, and he then had the thief work for several weeks more at the agency as a punishment.[6] Justice served.

Once Nelson started at Two Grey Hills, he continued to provide service in the community. As with most traders, his involvement in private and public events was expected. So it was not surprising that on September 25, 1927, he offered to give a tourist having car trouble a ride to Newcomb, about a half hour away. He was joined by owner Willis Martin, who was visiting the store with his wife on a Sunday afternoon. Around 7 P.M. Mildred Nelson answered a knock on the door from an unfamiliar Navajo man asking to buy hay. She wanted to wait until the men returned, but the Indian persisted, and so she relented, took the keys for the doors of both hay barns, and headed out in the gathering twilight. As she moved toward the most distant barn, the man picked up a single tree sitting on a nearby baler and struck her at the nape of the neck, knocking her unconscious. Next, he pulled her body closer to a pet bear the Nelsons kept, hoping the animal would be drawn to the blood, mutilate the body, and erase any signs of foul play. The Indian next returned to the post intending to steal from it, but to his surprise found Mrs. Martin, newborn baby in arms, at the door. He asked where the men were and when he learned they would be returning any minute, he mounted his horse and hastily fled.

For approximately a half hour, Mildred lay in the barnyard, while Mrs. Martin assumed that she was feeding the chickens. But when Roswell's headlights flashed upon the prostrate form of his wife in the dirt, he and the Martins went into action. They sent for the government doctor, J. D. Kennedy, stationed at Toadlena. The physician rendered what aid he could, then rode with the Nelsons to the hospital in Farmington, arriving at 7 A.M. Diagnosed with a fractured skull, Mildred required three weeks of bedrest before she returned to her duties at Two Grey Hills. In the meantime, the Navajos in the community were incensed at the misdeed of the thief, later identified as Juan Cavallero, who hailed from around Crystal, New Mexico. Agent Albert H. Kneale dispatched a Navajo tracker and policeman, Nakai John, who followed the fleeing culprit over the Lukachukai Mountains. The trail was difficult to trace because it went over rocky and mountainous terrain, crossed extensive beds of pine needles, and had been trampled by the hooves of a herd of horses the assailant drove before him to cover the tracks. Still, John was able to not only pursue him, but even determined that he had changed horses along the way without dismounting. The policemen's efforts eventually paid off; he captured the criminal in Gallup and brought him back to Shiprock. The court determined that Cavallero was mentally unstable, and so he received a short sentence in a federal penitentiary and was soon released.[7]

Divining Truth, Obtaining Justice

When the *Farmington Times-Hustler* published the initial story of the attack on Mrs. Nelson, there was a short paragraph at the end of the piece that referenced another side of law enforcement that was very much a part of the trading post experience. In this instance, medicine man Hastiin Klah visited the Newcombs, who were traders at the Nava Post (later renamed Newcomb), and ceremonially diagnosed through divination (type unspecified) what had happened in the attack and what the future outcome would be.[8] Klah predicted, "that Wednesday night Mrs. Nelson would get much better and that Thursday the criminal's 'hands would be tied' meaning that he would be captured. Mrs. Nelson did get much better on Wednesday night, even though all that day her recovery was much in doubt and at this writing (Thursday evening) we do not know if the would-be-murderer has been captured or not."[9] Later, Agent Kneale filled in the details. Klah went to the agent on Wednesday afternoon, and after telling of Mildred's anticipated recovery said, "My medicine also tells me that your policeman will overtake the would-be murderer tonight and tomorrow morning you will have him safely lodged in jail."[10] The next morning, Nakai John sat in the agent's office with prisoner in hand.

Kneale, in reporting this unfolding incident, hedged his bets reporting only that which was already substantiated. The entire role of divination—hand trembling, stargazing, crystal gazing, and wind listening—are basic tenets of Navajo beliefs that allow seeing into the past, present, and future by those who have been given the gift and attained the skills.[11] The practice unites the faith and knowledge of those performing the rite to the powers of the holy beings. Hastiin Klah was a prominent medicine man who held these and many more powers and became a close friend and confidant with the Newcombs when Arthur and Franc assumed ownership of Nava. Even more amazing in using these spiritual gifts was Hosteen (Hastiin) Beaal, to whom Franc devoted an entire chapter in her *Navaho Neighbors*.[12] Not all of those episodes are shared here, but enough to illustrate a common practice performed at trading posts to help the owners, even when, as Anglos, they were initially skeptical and rarely understood the workings of these powers.

Franc and Arthur were skeptics. Although they knew medicine man Hosteen Beaal from the community and counted him as a friend, they were unsure of his ability to obtain answers through hand trembling. When three of their horses went missing, the couple decided to see if he could divine what had happened. He agreed to help and started performing his rite by having clean sand brought to the post, squatting in the middle of it, then blessing himself with corn pollen. His body shook as he chanted, then the trembling ceased and his hand drew lines and trails in the sand. Next he gave a detailed account of the theft—who the culprits were, where they had gone, and what was currently happening to the horses. As it turned out, he was correct—two boys had stolen the horses to race in a ceremony and returned them after the event. Arthur was still not a believer and felt it was more guesswork or logical analysis—that he "should have guessed where they were myself! There was no magic in finding them, just a matter of good common sense."[13] Franc, on the other hand, was not so sure Arthur's assertion was totally correct and considered there may have been more to it.

Two months later, someone stole a valuable saddle and three Pendleton shawls from the store. Beaal, not really interested in payment, agreed to help again. This time, Arthur was stumped and had no logical "guess" as to who could have perpetrated the crime. A minute-by-minute description of how the thief committed the crime, including travels of the individual, the pawning of the materials at another post, and where he went afterward, came from the divining hand of Hosteen Beaal. Following the medicine man's directions, the trader went to the Coyote Canyon Trading Post and retrieved his stolen property. Mr. Grey, the trader, sold the stolen items back for the amount they had been pawned, and Arthur returned home more convinced about the power of hand trembling. Franc asked a Navajo friend how it was done and learned, "Everything that happens leaves its picture in the air. So he goes to sleep and sends his spirit out of his body to find that picture. When it returns, he knows all about what has happened."[14]

News of Beaal's successful crime-busting spread throughout the New-comb–Two Grey Hills region. Thieves became much more wary about Beaal's power, and their fears sometimes led to the sudden reappearance of a stolen item. He also used his powers to find missing people and to solve crimes such as the beating of a trader's wife, the burning of an unoccupied trading post, and determining if an individual would live or die after sustaining injuries. It seemed like nothing was beyond this old man's supernatural power to look into the past, future, or present and answer questions or concerns. And it was done with detailed accuracy that brought results. He even assisted capturing a Navajo man who murdered a trader selling bootleg whiskey, as well as many thefts, but he never demanded much in reimbursement.

He did not limit his assistance to the Newcombs. Marietta Wetherill, wife of Richard, questioned his abilities and so asked him to explain what she was thinking. Beaal said, "To fool me you're thinking of something way off I've never seen. It's some kind of wagon that goes in the air."[15] Marietta admitted that she was concentrating on the elevated trains in New York City. On a more practical note, when the Wetherill post in Chaco had some silver and turquoise stolen, the owners called in the old medicine man for assistance. He sat on the floor of the store, covered his head with a blanket, sang and prayed, then shortly stood up and said he knew who did it and did Richard want the guilty party brought in along with the missing property. After being reassured that there would not be any strict punishment enacted against the guilty party, Beaal set off and returned three days later with a frightened sixteen-year-old boy. The youth was well known at the post and even had a nickname—Five Cents—because he hung around for a long time before spending his meager money amounting to all of five cents. He admitted his wrong-doing and returned the stolen items.[16] Hosteen Beaal eventually became tired and worn from the use of this spiritual power, blind, and incapacitated until he died at the age of one hundred and four. But to the end, he was highly respected by both Anglos and Navajos, serving as a deterrent to crime. Hosteen Beaal was an exceptional individual, parts of whose life, fortunately, were recorded by traders whose experience went from doubt to conviction.

The Bloomfields at Toadlena

There were many other facets to life at trading posts in addition to problems with theft and law enforcement. Toadlena provides a good example of how education and daily activities evolved and flourished due to the existence of the post. Fortunately, the Bloomfield family—George, Lucy, and daughter Grace—were there to record much of what happened. The store first opened its doors in 1909 when brothers Merritt and Robert Smith became attracted to the area with its abundant springs emanating from the Chuska Mountains and the rich agricultural land at its base. For the same reason, the Indian Service determined, two years later, that this was an ideal spot for a school for local Navajo children. George R. Bloomfield, a man who had lived in Ramah and the Mormon colonies in Mexico when he was growing up, went to Toadlena in 1911 to help build and open that school. A year later he bought the trading post from the Smith brothers and remained there with his wife, Lucy, for thirty-four years before selling his interest to his daughter and son-in-law, Grace and Charles Herring, in 1936. They continued the business until 1956, when they sold it to Fred Carson. Thus, the history of Toadlena is intimately connected with and recorded by this family.

George was no neophyte when it came to working with Indians. In addition to having been raised with Navajo and Apache people, he moved to Shiprock to work for Shelton for seven years as an additional farmer. Here he used his agricultural experience, garnered over the years during a somewhat hand-to-mouth existence while also learning how to lay brick and rock, skills that led to his initial assignment at Toadlena. The same year he began there, the disastrous flood of the San Juan River wiped away most of his belongings and forced him and his family to live in the buildings he was creating. He salvaged only two things from the flood: a family organ whose bellows were filled with mud but that was eventually cleaned and returned to service, and a bag of old love letters to Lucy, which Shelton had managed to snag out of the waist-deep water and had hung on a gatepost to dry. Soon George left his agency employment, against the protests and promises of higher pay by Shelton, and moved to his new home and business at the post.[17]

At this point, a few brief notes about the school are in order. By 1914 education was in full swing in a day school accepted by the community.

Shelton assigned A. B. Skelton, temporary farmer, to supervise the facility and run the small farm that provided food and employment for the
students. The permanent supply of running water made irrigation at this
location possible, while "the farmer goes among the Indians and advises
them with farm work and their livestock. He inspects the stock offered
for sale at the four trading posts in that vicinity, one of which is nearby
[Toadlena], one seven miles away [Two Grey Hills], one twelve [Nava/
Newcomb], and the other one twenty [Naschitti]. He helps to settle disputes among the Indians and looks after their interests in every way possible."[18] Shelton was not satisfied to leave it there. He assigned a doctor,
Frederick W. Shaw, to the school and received permission to build an
office, "drug room," and barn for his use in 1915; that same year he built
"three substantial stone buildings" with a capacity of eighty students,
which opened in December. The agent had observed that because of
distance and Navajo lifestyle, a day school did not meet the need, but a
boarding school would.[19]

Jump ahead twenty years to see the growth of these humble beginnings. In 1933–34 there were 240 boarding students with sixty students
in a day school at Nava, started in 1927, the same year that telephones
connected Toadlena, Two Grey Hills, and Nava to the outside world.
The principal presided over seven academic teachers and a home economics instructor who taught grades one through six. Both the boys'
and girls' dormitories had all manner of indoor plumbing, contained
over one hundred beds each and rooms for different activities, and a
consolidated dining facility with hardwood floors. The kitchen had electric appliances including a dishwasher; there was also a laundry facility,
bakery, auditorium, school powerhouse with a thirty-five-kilowatt gen-
erator and two boilers heated with coal, and a ten-acre farm with irrigation. Add to this a twenty-one-bed hospital under the supervision of a
doctor, nurse, ward assistant, and two helpers, and four outlying clinics
at Cottonwood Pass, Sheep Springs, Nava, and Sanostee, and one can see
the influence brought about by an initial trading post established there
just twenty-five years previous.[20]

Amid this change at the Toadlena Trading Post sat George Bloomfield and family immersed in the traditional life of the Navajos. George
wrote, "We all loved the Indian people. They were our friends and neighbors as well as our customers. Their children and ours played together,

went to school together, and were friends."[21] Nowhere does this love and respect show through more clearly than in an article titled "Natana (Navajo Chief) [Naat'áanii]," written by Lucy Bloomfield.[22] The name is a Navajo word for "leader" or "chief" and is what the Bloomfields called this impressive individual, although his name was actually Grey Mustache. Born in 1850 in the area around Fort Defiance, Natana lived near Toadlena and was present most days when the store opened and closed. His influence on the customers was profound, providing a seal of approval or disapproval for much of what went on there. Lucy recalls, "If our prices were right to suit him, they were right for our customers; but if we carried an article that was inferior or too high priced, we just as well throw it under the counter because none of his people would buy it. . . . If the permits to start to buy lambs in the fall came from the Indian Superintendent and Natana said wait, we waited. If the grass was good that year, he would sometimes tell his people to not sell for a couple of weeks longer and their lambs would grow more and weigh heavier and they would get a better price, and wait they did, until their Chief came driving in his lambs for sale."[23] While some traders might have found this type of external control frustrating, the Bloomfields appreciated the sanction of transactions at their post and the trust it created for them in the community.

Trust came in other forms. One year Lucy was sick, George had to run the store, and they needed to obtain money—$2500—in silver dollars to pay for the lambs they were to purchase at $5 a head. They sent Natana with a note and a flour sack to the bank in Gallup to pick up the cash. Three days later he appeared with money in hand—and one day ahead of a man the bank had sent to confirm the money's safe arrival. In the Bloomfields' minds, "We had never worried a minute. Natana would have protected our money with his life." He also abstained from alcohol—fire water, or snake water as he called it—and told of an experience he had that solidified his antipathy toward the beverage. One time when he was in Gallup, he decided to buy a bottle of whiskey, which he took home. He uncorked the bottle, watched a fly land on the stopper, drink some of the liquid, then buzz about the room before returning for another drink. This happened a third time, but the fly did not go anywhere, just sat and cleaned its beak with its front feet until it tore off its head. That did it for Natana; if that is what it did to a fly, he wanted nothing to do with alcohol, and so he poured out the contents of the bottle and never took a drink in his life.

He was a firm advocate of formal education but also did some teaching of his own. George's son, Monte, was just a young boy who had read one too many of his father's *Wild West* magazines. One Saturday, a number of Navajo boys came to the store to buy some candy, but Monte waylaid them behind the corn storage building, then told them to run for their lives as he shot over their heads with a borrowed .22-caliber rifle. Natana heard the commotion, went to see what was going on, and quickly rectified the situation with some corporal punishment. He then went to George and Lucy to explain what he had done and received profuse thanks from the chagrined parents. He also put some of his self-education to work by building the second Anglo-type house in Toadlena and planting an orchard grown from peach pits obtained in Farmington. Those pits yielded bushels of fruit for years. Natana traded some of his first crop with the Smith brothers for a rooster and two hens, which produced a large flock of chickens and many eggs. There was never any question about loaning him money on pawn if he wished to improve his flock of sheep; he was as good as his word.

The Bloomfields were devout Mormons and would later serve for years in their church's Southwest Indian Mission. This did not prevent them from appreciating the counsel Natana gave when marrying young couples, or speeches about proper behavior delivered at ceremonial gatherings, or his recommendations in buying and selling at the post. Private conversations were just as welcomed when about religion. Although the Bloomfields had their own ideas about the afterlife, they agreed with him that there surely was one. As years went by and he became increasingly frail, Natana contemplated his eventual passing. One day he bought a new lantern and some coal oil. When he became ill the traders visited him and found that although there was still daylight, the lamp was lit and hanging at the head of his bed. When asked why, he replied, "Sometime I am going to die and if it is night, I want a light to see which way to go."[24] He kept it lit at night for the rest of his life until he died in 1952. As Lucy noted, "Death and a century caught up with him at the same time, and although his lantern was still there burning away at the head of his bed, yet we are sure that the light of his faith illumined his way to the Happy Hunting Ground of the Indian people."

Shipping seven-foot-long bags of wool from Two Grey Hills. The spring wool clip was one of the primary ways in which the trading post and Navajo economy entered into mainstream America's financial life. Whether by wagon or later by trucks on paved roads, the journey of that wool started from humble beginnings that ended in the financial markets of the East and West Coasts. Courtesy of Two Grey Hills Trading Post Archive Collection.

In addition to saying volumes about Natana, Lucy's attitude also spoke to her values and those of other traders working with the Navajo people. Posts often sponsored Navajo religious ceremonies, not just because it was good for business, but because the men and women working at these stores had true respect for the beliefs of their customers. This is not to suggest that they fully understood or practiced traditional Navajo teachings, but they saw the good that they did in people's lives and how Christianity often fell far short of the integrated Navajo beliefs that held their society together. Supporting those practices helped maintain harmony and peace within the community and gave a common base of values by which disputes could be settled. For outsiders, this was sometimes difficult to understand.

Compare, for instance, the opposing views appearing in different sources around the same time. On October 14, 1927, the *Farmington Times-Hustler* reported "A large Yabicha [Yé'ii Bicheii] dance is in progress near Nava, New Mexico. We would hope for its discontinuance in the interest of good morals and also health, as many lie around on the ground, sowing the seeds of pneumonia and tuberculosis later on."[25]

Lucy Bloomfield described a Mountainway ceremony held at Toadlena just a few years before and shared her very different perspective in her church's periodical, the *Improvement Era*.[26] Considering her own devout qualities, there emanates from her article a deep respect for what she witnessed. At that time, the cost of the ceremony was about $500—a sizable sum—to which she contributed. Her offering pleased the medicine men conducting the nine-day rite, so they quickly extended an invitation for her to attend. The woman, Yanapah Hushclish Eyazzie, for which the ceremony was held, had encountered a big brown bear while traveling a mountain trail. The animal had raised up on its hind legs, pointed its front paw at the Navajo, and pronounced a curse upon her and her unborn child. According to Lucy, bears and coyotes can be a reincarnated Navajo who was being punished for wrongdoing in a previous life, and so the purpose of the Mountainway was to cast out the evil power bestowed on the woman traveler.

While the many intricacies of the lengthy ceremony will not be discussed here, Lucy's attitude will. To get to the dance on the last night, "into a lumber wagon, seventeen strong, we piled, like sardines in a can, only set on end, and away we jolted just at dusk to witness the performance, three grown white people and seven children in all. The balance of our crowd was Navajo neighbors."[27] The comfort she felt personally and for her family members indicates a high degree of respect and friendship when attending the event. She also dressed accordingly, making and wearing an "Indian squaw costume"—velvet shirt, calico skirt, a fringed Pendleton shawl, hair in a traditional Navajo bun, and some borrowed pawned jewelry from the trading post. Her youngest child she strapped into a cradleboard that she wore on her back "which pleased my dusky friends very much. . . . The final verdict was that I was their friend or I would not dress like them." She estimated there were 1,500 in attendance.

Natana took time to address the crowd and encourage them to have the faith necessary that the cursed woman and baby would be healed. "He then gave them a rousing good sermon on the kind of lives they all should lead, telling them to be industrious, build up their herds, take good care of their children, and teach them to be honest and work hard. He exhorted the weavers to make better blankets so they will get more for their products. He told them to set a good example of honesty and truthfulness before their children, so the tribe would grow better and stronger." Once the dance started, Lucy's observations of the different activities and participants seesawed back and forth between seeing them as graceful and beautiful, but also as "weird," "grotesque," and "barbaric." Some men impersonated the holy people, danced around a bonfire in the large brush enclosure, and chanted the songs of healing, while others gathered ashes that were now sacred, and medicine men blessed the patient. The end result of that night for Lucy was that "either through their great faith or Mother Nature's help, the maiden gained strength, and in the course of a few weeks, was well and happy and her baby as fat as only a Navajo papoose can become."

Grace Bloomfield and Charles Herring— Maintaining the Tradition

Lucy, through the eyes of an adult, expressed her love for the people she worked with. Her daughter, Grace, one of eight children, shared similar feelings of her childhood as she grew up at Toadlena and eventually, with her husband, took over the business from her mother and father. The only other white children she had to play with were those of Reverend Paul Brink's family as he served as a Christian Reformed minister for the Navajo children at the school. Each Sunday he stopped by the Bloomfield home and walked with the children to church, singing songs and telling stories along the way. Since the government would not let white children attend the Navajo school at Toadlena, the reverend allowed his study to serve for the Anglo children, who ranged from first to eighth grade. He eventually formed a church in Farmington and was replaced by Reverend Kobes, a nice man, but against the Mormon faith that the Bloomfields practiced.

When not in school, the children had to work. The older boys helped in the store, while the girls and younger ones tended the garden and carried water from a spring a quarter mile from the house. All the females, young and old, followed a regimen with Monday (starting at 4 A.M.) for washing clothes, Tuesday ironing, Wednesday a day off, Thursday cooking, and Saturday bath day. Lucy used a scrub board to wash the clothes, while everything that was white was also boiled. Hauling water had to be a primary occupation for everyone.[28] Still, life was not so hard that the youngsters felt overworked. Grace's autobiography is filled with her love of an almost magical landscape—the springs, streams, canyons, alcoves, and rock formations that surrounded Toadlena. There was even one rock spire that held connections to the supernatural. "On one of these huge sandstone formations, plainly visible, are the footprints of God, followed by the tiny footprints of the baby, going from the base of the huge red rock to the top where they disappear into space. An old legend of the Navajo tells this story of 'Where God Walked with His Baby.' It is told by the old medicine men to the Navajo children, and we learned it along with them. I shall never forget the feeling of wonderment and awe that we always felt when we visited this sacred place."[29]

Another time of wonderment of a different nature was when "drummers," or salesmen, appeared at the post to vend their wares. The Bloomfield family enjoyed having them—George learned of new things to sell, and Lucy fed the guests, often making special baked goods and meals, while also providing comfortable sleeping accommodations. Lucy, ever practical, would take the samples of cloth left by these men for those interested in having a suit made, and sewed them into quilts for the family.[30] The children enjoyed the break in routine. Some of them willingly gave up their beds to sleep in "shiny store-smelling blankets" on the counters in the post. This also meant that the apples, candy, crackers, and cheese on the shelves became more available. The lucky children "filched" some of the spoils of sacrifice, but tried to keep the evidence of crime hidden from an inquiring parent. The drummers—and there were a lot of them—apparently enjoyed their visit too, staying sometimes for a few days. Occasionally, when they returned, they would have some small gift to give as a thank you for the hospitality.

In spite of the wonderment of childhood, Grace also remembers the hard work and conflict that was part of life at Toadlena. Her mother and father were constantly providing service for the community. One time Lucy sat up all night with a sick baby, and when it died, she made a coffin from packing boxes, covered it with white muslin, and performed the funeral for the grieving family. She also ran the post office for twenty-six years, starting in 1920, where she received shipments from Sears and Roebuck and Montgomery Ward that kept the family dressed in clothes and accessories purchased through catalogs. When Lucy and George eventually moved to Mancos, Colorado, to take over another post, she continued to serve as postmistress.

George became an unofficial judge and jury in family squabbles that took place in the community. Archie Hunt and his wife argued about his supposed unfaithfulness with another woman. Late one night the wife came pounding on the trading post door, swearing her husband was going to kill her. Lucy had just hidden the woman in the potato cellar downstairs when another knock on the door brought Archie, drunk with rifle in hand, looking for his wife. After some cups of strong coffee and a lot of talk, he agreed to go to the corn house to get some sleep, where he remained locked in for the night. The next morning, things looked a lot brighter, the couple received counsel from Lucy and George, then continued through life to "raise a large family of beautiful children and are still happy together."[31]

In 1932 Grace married Charles Herring; the couple eventually returned to take over the post at Toadlena and worked for a total of sixteen years there. She and Charles each received their own Navajo names, a common cultural practice, when they began serving across the counters. Other family members also had names bestowed among the Navajos. George had always been "Wiscolie" meaning "No Teeth," Lucy was Wiscolie Basa "Teeth Out's Wife," while Grace used to be "Blonde Hair, Blue Eyes" as a little girl; now she became "Mad Woman" because she scolded customers for not paying their bills; her husband, Charles, was "Little Prairie Dog." These names represented strong bonds of friendship forged with the post's proprietors, until the couple moved to Farmington in 1949.

Charles enjoyed being a trader and fortunately recorded some of his experiences. As with many in this occupation, he lived in a world where the mystical, sacred beliefs of the Navajos intertwined with the everyday activities of life. Louis Bigman, a frequent visitor to Toadlena, used sun gazing to divine events from the past. He would lie down on his back, stare at the sun, and have images form in his eyes while in a trance. A few examples show how specific his answers could be. One person came to him requesting help in locating a lost horse. Louis lay down by the gas pump in the store yard and, in a few minutes, returned with its location, telling the owner that the animal had gone over the mountain and would be found near Crystal. Another time, he helped Franc Newcomb with a lost camera. He directed her to go to her living room and look behind some books on a shelf, and that is where she found it.

Natana's wife also had the gift of divining but her impressions came through hand trembling. One morning when Charles entered the store, he found the front window smashed and some property stolen. He obtained the services of "Grandma Natana" and asked her to determine who had broken in. After handling some of the objects they had touched—a nickel, candy on the floor, and pieces of glass—she "moaned and groaned, and took on" raising her right hand over her shoulder and began shaking.[32] Grandma next went into a trance for a few minutes, then relaxed and said that there were three boys who had entered the post. "They went in, they played store for a while, and then they went back over that way [toward the school]. One of those boys lives down here pretty close. Another one lives over by Sheep Springs, and one lives by Two Grey Hills." Charles found one of the culprits at school, retrieved a stolen pocketknife, and learned the identity of the other two boys—one of whom was Grandma Natana's grandson. Each received severe counseling from the trader.

Deceit and conflict also came in other forms. Charles recalled how many Navajos brought large sacks of potatoes they grew on the mountain in the rich, well-watered soil. The traders told the farmers to bring in only large potatoes, but one man put a stove pipe in the middle of his sacks and pushed a lot of small potatoes into the middle with the larger ones on the outside. When George discovered the ruse, he put the small potatoes in a showcase with the man's name on them. When the Navajo returned to find his deception on display, he begged the trader to remove them. George thought about it for a while then said, "If you promise me never to gyp me on any other deal we have on anything, I will take them out of the case."[33] The humbled man agreed to the terms and the potatoes left the post. A similar incident happened one fall when a different person brought in three sacks of wool, one of which felt particularly heavy. When it was dumped, fifty pounds of sand came out. The Navajo at first did not want to buy back the sand, but after a lengthy discussion, agreed to put the sand on his bill and make things right when he later sold his lambs in the fall.[34] Cheating, however, was not always a one-way street. Charles told of a trader he knew who put a nail through his counter beneath his scale so that when something was being weighed, the loaded scale would go down just so far, giving a false reading.[35] These kinds of traders were generally few and far between and did not last very long at a post.

Charles had a strong respect for Navajo culture and the power it held in events of daily life. He recalled how during an Enemyway ceremony, twenty Navajo men dressed in ceremonial garb rode to the post at a full gallop before dismounting. "Into the post they came without so much as a by-your-leave, dancing, chanting, and proceeding to scatter the sacred pollen all about the post and us. Then they left with great dignity, and without a word, but we understood we had been accorded a great honor, and felt very privileged to be counted as [a friend]." Another time he was helping in a search for a little girl believed to have been stolen by a bear. The searchers found tracks from both shortly before dark. The group decided to get a medicine man, who performed a ceremony and provided all the participants with sacred corn pollen. The search resumed in the morning, and by noon they had found the little girl. Charles wrote, "We never knew if the bear had really been with her because she was not old enough to talk, but her trail and the bear's were intermingled and seemed to be together. The Indians believed that she had been with the bear and that the bear had taken care of her until the searchers came."[36]

Grace believed, just as her husband, that there were mystical powers that Navajo ceremonialism unleashed. During a Mountainway performance, she and Charles sat in the front row of spectators and watched a group of medicine men sing, causing some feathers to stand upright and dance in a basket. After swearing that there were no strings attached to the feathers, she added, "Well, I've always told Charles there were no strings, because I looked really close. Now dad tells of going up on top of the mountain one time, and going to a ceremony, and he said that they planted corn in the ground, and he said they actually saw the corn grow and get ears on it before it quit. I don't know how they did it. I don't know how. They have a knowledge that we don't know of a lot of things. As far as their medicine is concerned, I wish we had all of the knowledge that those old medicine men have, because they help a lot of their people."[37] As noted at the beginning of this chapter, these and other types of experiences do not make their way into the ledgers of trading posts but were still very much a part of the fabric of the life of the owners and their families.

Arthur and Franc Newcomb—Exploring and Preserving

Today, roughly six to seven miles east of the Two Grey Hills Post sits Newcomb, whose long and varied history provides a glimpse into other aspects of the Navajo trade. Located on Captain Tom's Wash and very much in the prehistoric agricultural area of the Ancestral Puebloans, sits Bis Dootł'izh Deez'áhí, or Blue Clay Point. According to Franc Johnson Newcomb, the wife of trader Arthur J. Newcomb and recorder of history and culture in the area, this site was first occupied by some Mormons traveling north to the San Juan River in search of better farmlands. One family saw the springs in the wash, hauled timber from the mountain, and built a two-room log cabin. Two years later, however, what had been public domain shifted to reservation lands, and so the family departed, leaving the cabin vacant until 1904, when John L. Oliver occupied it. The store was only open during the spring and fall when the Navajos had wool and sheep to sell. Five years later he sold his interests in the post to Charles E. Nelson, who also operated it as a seasonal business for four years before selling it to Arthur Newcomb in 1913. Newcomb recognized the potential of it being a year-round operation; he and Franc remained there for thirty-eight years.[38]

The newlywed couple, both with experience in working with Navajos and an interest in the culture, increased the number and size of buildings at the Blue Mesa Trading Post. They changed the name to Nava (using the first four letters of Navajo), but the Postal Service requested a new title because this name was too close to another place—Nara, New Mexico, on the Canadian River. Both communities were receiving the other's mail, and so Nava changed to Newcomb.[39] Since Newcomb was 72 miles southwest of Farmington and 65 miles north of Gallup, it also obtained the unofficial title of "The Half Way Post" for travelers heading to one of those destinations along the sandy, rutted road.[40] On May 9, 1936, the original post burned to the ground due to faulty electrical wiring. The Newcombs rebuilt a new facility in front of the remains of the old establishment and continued to trade until 1951. Arthur had died three years before, and so Franc sold the business to Marshall Drolet and Paul Brink, but never lost her interest in the Navajo people.

While at Newcomb, Franc performed a tremendous work by recording and preserving many aspects of Navajo culture. She copied, with permission, five hundred drawings of sandpaintings and ceremonial designs as well as elements of thirty-two different chantways.[41] Among her publications are two important books that outline the role of the trader in reservation life during the changing times of the first half of the twentieth century. *Navaho Neighbors* and *Hosteen Klah, Navaho Medicine Man and Sand Painter* provide intimate details of ceremonialism and the Newcombs' interaction with the people, especially with Klah, a powerful personality. He is mentioned in a number of places in this book, because of his impact on weaving and events.

One thing that Newcomb and the other posts in the area held in common was that they were in the heart of Ancestral Puebloan country. These ancient people's remains fostered an interest in the culture and provided a pastime of collecting artifacts. At this point in history, protection of cultural sites was just beginning, largely due to the implementation of the Antiquities Act of 1906. But it was not enough to deter many traders on the reservation from taking on the avocation of learning about these earlier people, encouraging Navajos to take them to little-known sites, using the objects they obtained for decoration in their home or selling them to tourists passing through. Franc Newcomb provides some of the best descriptions of how traders approached the task of unearthing the past—something that archaeologists today might find reprehensible and destructive, but was so characteristic of the times. Franc outlines many different ways she amassed a large collection of ancient artifacts, the locations of these sites, and the wide variety of objects obtained from them. Here, only a sampling is given, but even from this, one can see the impact that all the traders and stores would have in uncovering the prehistoric remains of the Chuska Valley.

Starting with more formal investigations, Franc and Arthur alerted professional archaeologists where to search. In 1917–18, Earl Morris from the American Museum of Natural History followed a lead that during nine months of excavation yielded "864 pieces of pottery and 72 skeletons beside barrels and bales of smaller relics such as stone and bone knives, beads, bracelets, shell ornaments, flint axes, arrowheads, and drills."[42] He shipped all of this material to New York City. Morris conducted his last excavation in the area in 1920, but Arthur and Franc returned to some of the sites that had been hurriedly dug to see what they could find. There was a lot. In some instances, bulldozers had dug into the sides of mounds, pits remained open and exposed, and less desirable objects tossed aside. The couple went to work, Franc noting,

> I carried a large sieve and a trowel, while Arthur carried a short shovel and a whisk broom. These ancient people had been buried with quantities of personal ornaments, as well as with their work implements, and with bowls of food. Sometimes I would find hundreds of small white beads, or perhaps beads of black jet with a few pieces of odd-shaped turquoise that had been strung with them. Once I sifted out all of the five-inch bone beads that had formed the breastplate for some ancient medicine man. And once I found ten shell bracelets that had been carved from a conch shell. Large and medium-sized pottery had been taken away, but we found the small pieces just as interesting. There were tiny two inch bowls, jugs with two handles, pitchers, and ladles that had evidently been toys of the children buried here, and there were small mugs and bowls for individual use. I decided to call my collection "Prehistoric Miniatures," and by 1923 I had 900 pieces on display. The Crown Prince of Sweden, who with his party, stopped at our place for lunch on his way from Mesa Verde to Gallup, pronounced it one of the most interesting collections he had ever seen.[43]

Other excursions followed, with a day or two spent here and there. Near Two Grey Hills, she and Arthur dug in a burial pit that yielded three large skeletons. After measuring the leg bones, the couple determined that these men were at least eight feet tall. They visited many of the ruins, fields and irrigation ditches, monuments erected from vertical rocks, roads and pathways through restricted terrain, and burial places on hill and dale, each site yielding its treasures into an ever-expanding collection. But one of the most profitable ways of obtaining artifacts came from Navajo customers looking for trade goods. Franc kept on prominent display some of her ancient wares. Word soon went abroad that she would take good objects in trade, and so as long as the piece of pottery or tool had not been associated with a grave, some Navajos were not afraid to pick it up and bring it to the store. Unique pieces of ceramic in the shape of ducks, turtles, frogs, deer, and other life forms started to come in. Mexican pesos, suitable for silverwork, paid for these objects, later returning to the post in the form of jewelry, which also sold well to tourists.[44]

Franc was extremely interested in a less tangible type of connection between the Navajos and their forebears. Hosteen Klah shared a
great deal of lore with her about the origin of some Navajo ceremonies. Among the most important were the Hailway, Windway, Rainway,
Waterway, and Featherway, all of which were said to have originated
around the same time. Klah explained, "Each one of these ceremonies
was known and given by a different medicine man who seemed to have
been living near one of the prehistoric pueblos now lying in ruins. These
stone houses may have been inhabited when the first Navajo families
arrived here, as the legend calls them 'the homes of the gods,' and the
dwellers were the ceremonial instructors."[45] Klah believed that the
Hailway ceremony that he practiced started at Pueblo Bonito in Chaco
Canyon. The story tells of a young boy from a poor Navajo family who
became involved with the wife of White Thunder. The jealous husband
obliterated the interloper, using thunder, wind, rain, hail, sleet, and
snow, but later the gods reassembled and healed the young man and his
family, bringing him back to life. He became the first practitioner of the
Hailway with its restorative properties.[46]

Life at the Newcomb Trading Post also had its challenges. One of
them came in the form of a competitive store that diluted the customer
base Arthur and Franc depended on. In very remote places on the reservation with small populations, a general rule of thumb among traders
establishing new posts was that no one would build one within a radius
of twenty-five miles or a day's travel. Where resources allowed for more
people to live nearby, stores could be built closer together. In the case of
Two Grey Hills, by 1920 there were four other posts—Newcomb, Sheep
Springs, Sanostee, and Naschitti—within a thirteen-mile radius, but all
were able to share a group of consumers that allowed for prosperity. But
when Roy B. Burnham applied in 1926 to build a store at the mouth of
Captain Tom's Wash, both Arthur at Newcomb and Carl Goodman at
Bisti protested. If the new post were built, it would be between the two at
roughly ten miles straight-line distance from each. To Arthur, this was
an attempt by Agent Albert H. Kneale to wield his power and show the
traders that they needed to be more cooperative in following some of
the programs issuing from Shiprock. Revenge was the motive.

At least in the official documents, Kneale did not see it that way.
In his mind, there had been a post in the same location eight or nine

years previous that was abandoned during the influenza epidemic of 1918. The agent had gone to two of the three headmen in the area and asked them to canvass the population to determine how they felt about another store. Not surprisingly, everyone was supportive—more posts meant more choices and lower prices due to competition. The headmen made sworn statements in favor of the proposal, but soon there were those opposing the move. Apparently Newcomb and Goodman paid their customers to protest, but to no avail. In January 1927, the doors of the competitor opened and remained open until 1962. Arthur's attempt had failed.[47]

Another issue surfaced in the form of cattle. During the dry summer months, the Chuska-Tunicha Mountains with its springs, rain, tall trees, and grass served as a magnet not only for Navajo livestock, but also for Anglo cattlemen living beyond the eastern boundary of the reservation. There were four finger-like ridges that ascended from the desert floor to the top of the range; one of those ridges had a road that went by the Newcomb Post. The Navajos had complained about the Anglo cowboys using this range, and so the Indian Office got involved and demanded the cattlemen remove their livestock and leave these resources for the Indians. This was to be done pronto. One day, as Franc worked in the store, one of her customers came in breathlessly exclaiming that the cattle were coming. This had never happened before, and so the trader stepped outside only to be greeted by an approaching dust cloud punctuated with long horns. Rather than passing by on the north side of the arroyo, the animals were charging in an unruly mass down the road on the south side, leaving no time to react. They swarmed the post.

Franc recalled the terror. Too late to do anything but watch, she saw the herd split around the buildings and stampede beyond. "Here the herd divided and those at the south stormed through the yard, leveling the back and front fences as though they were matchwood, snapping my clotheslines and carrying away towels, diapers, and one of Arthur's best shirts on their horns. The hitch rail was on the north side and two Navajo ponies tied there broke their straps and raced ahead of the cattle. A team of fat, aged horses hitched to a light wagon was engulfed by the stampede and ran in its midst until the wagon overturned and they were halted by its weight."[48] Just behind the herd rode a cowboy who stopped long enough at the post to inquire about where to find water for the cattle and then left. About that same time, a wagon with a Navajo family showed up to trade. As they were unloading some goat pelts, a steer charged up the bank of the arroyo, looking for a target to vent his anger on. A little girl named Jolie drew his attention, but not before her older sister, Ahsonchee (Asdzaan Ch'ii—Red Woman), saw what was happening, told the child to lie flat in a nearby ditch, then ran toward the animal waving a goat pelt. The steer first went for the younger girl but missed, then turned on the older one, butting her through the air for some distance. The attack gave two cowboys pursuing the cattle time enough to rope the horns and back legs of the animal and move him down the trail. The child was fine, but her sister had a shattered arm that required an improvised tourniquet and a trip in Newcomb's car to the hospital. There she remained for four weeks, but once healed had a complete recovery. Franc was happy with the outcome. "Ahsonchee would be called upon to card much wool and to weave many rugs and blankets during the years ahead when she started caring for her own family."[49]

Charles G. Newcomb's Account of Daily Life

Many of the incidents recounted in this chapter are dramatic in nature, and although they were very much a part of the everyday life of a trader, they do not give a feeling for daily existence at a post. For this we turn to an unpublished manuscript written by Charles George Newcomb (Arthur's older brother) and Frank McNitt as he prepared *The Indian Traders*. Twenty-year-old Charles Newcomb came to New Mexico in 1907 to learn the business of a trader in the rough railroad town of Guam. He stayed there learning the rudiments of the Navajo language before moving to the post at Naschitti (Nahashch'idí—Badger), located near Badger Spring in 1911. Eight years later he assumed control of the post at Crystal where he remained for twenty-six years before finishing his fifty-year career near Gallup. As he and McNitt recorded his experiences, there flowed a clear picture and feeling characteristic of many traders and their approach toward the people and the business. Excerpts from Charles's narrative are shared here, offering an intimate, firsthand account.[50] The first part of this story starts with his arrival and impressions of the first day at work after assuming control from George Manning, a partner in the trading firm of C. C. Manning Company.

George's family had run the post since 1901 but now turned it over to this neophyte.

The store was about twenty feet square with high counters on three sides and set out pretty well from the walls, leaving a rather small bull-pen [open space] for the Navajo customers. Out in back were a barn and hay house, a hen house, woodshed, and corral. All of these buildings were made wholly or in part from boards salvaged from Arbuckle coffee boxes and roofed with tin. Next to the Colt .44 revolver and the tin can, I can think of nothing that has had a more civilizing influence on the Southwest than the wooden boxes of Arbuckle coffee. In a Navajo's mind, Arbuckle and coffee—which he is inordinately fond of—were synonymous; other brands there were but for twenty years or more they made no dent on our market. Every trading post carried a large supply of Arbuckles and every trader, in a country where lumber was scarce, used the boxes for any of a thousand useful purposes.

Closely associated in my mind with the Arbuckle name is an image of a pretty lady fitted with diaphanous wings and garments. Her name was Ariosa. She was the Arbuckle trademark and her lovely portrait appeared on every box. A young Navajo couple, friends of mine who were expecting their first baby, once searched my wareroom for unblemished Arbuckle boards with which to make a carrier cradle. When the baby arrived—it was a girl—my friends proudly named her Aliosa, as close as they could come, since to Navajos the letter 'r' does not exist, to our regional goddess and sweetheart, the gal on the Arbuckle box. . . .

At sunup on the third day the Mannings [George and wife] said goodbye. I watched them from the door until their spring wagon disappeared over the arroyo rim. When I closed the door and started through the living room to the store, my footsteps sounded as loud in my ears as a horse crossing a plank bridge. And all of this, the logs and adobe and sheet iron, it occurred to me, was now my domain. And I was very much alone in it.

I opened the store, swept it out, and started filling the shelves. Before long an old lady came in. She asked where the trader was. I told her that Manning had left and I was the trader now, and she could buy from me. Obviously not pleased, she started to leave and then turned

Interior of the Two Grey Hills Trading Post with Ed Davies sitting behind the counter. Trading posts, like this and Toadlena, were gathering places for the community, islands of refuge for those needing help, and an economic starter for those wishing to improve their financial circumstances. In spite of the seemingly simple, slow-paced atmosphere, these stores became the hubs of community development, starting points for schools and government programs, and places for workforce development. Courtesy of Two Grey Hills Trading Post Archive Collection.

back, fetching from somewhere in her garments a string of rather poor Zuni shell and turquoise beads and holding them up for me to see. Perhaps they were worth five dollars—she said she wanted to pawn them for twenty. Rather than lose my first customer with a flat no, I said I would take them in pawn for three-fifty. With an outraged yelp she told me I didn't know anything about beads, and then started calling me the worst of the Navajo names, beginning with "Coyote," "Bear," "Snake," and "Dog." Suddenly she paused in her tirade, smiled, and said as I clearly didn't understand the value of good beads she would agree to pawn them for fifteen dollars. Again I declined. Her stream of abuse resumed, shriller than before. If there had been an audience to laugh at me, I probably would have weakened, but we were alone. I was mean, I was stingy, and she would tell all of the people of her clan and all of the friends of her people not to trade with me. Figuring her age, this could take in a lot of people but I still said no. Finally she left with three dollars and a half worth of groceries. I tagged her bauble, writing in her name, the date, and the amount, and put it away in the safe. A fine beginning—but the day was young!

Lazy Luke (named and introduced to me previously by George Manning), wandered in about ten and spent the rest of the day lying on the floor. Other customers on entering had to step over him, which I think I minded more than they did. When I told him to get up out of there, or at least roll over into a corner, he just grunted. Then at noon, Crazy came in. That was a nickname for Mrs. Manygoats, and while she wasn't really crazy, her thoughts were sometimes erratic, and she was almost deaf. Crazy handed me a sheepskin, worth a standard price of two bits as every Navajo on the reservation knew, and she wanted a bag of coffee, sugar, baking powder, and salt. Coffee alone was worth twenty-five cents, but rather than have her go on for the rest of the day itemizing her wants and my failings, I gave them to her.

So far I wasn't doing so well, but the real test came late in the afternoon. Before leaving, Manning had told me I would need a clerk—I sure would, he said. In his case, his wife had helped him, so that when he had to go out to get hay for an Indian, or go to the warehouse to weigh wool, she would watch the store. Of course I wouldn't be buying wool in March, but I would be selling hay. He warned me not to leave the store untended, but to chase the Navajos out and lock the door. Easy enough to say, I thought now, as the big fellow stood there saying he wanted some hay. A half dozen loafers were in the store, of course, including my horizontal friend, Lazy Luke. I told my customers to clear out—vamoose—while I went to the hay barn. No one moved a muscle or even looked at me, so I told them again. Same result. "All right," I said, "if that is the way it is, this fellow's horse can go hungry." My hay customer did not see the humor in this. He was as big as John L. Sullivan, a lot younger, and probably in much better condition.

"Give me some hay," he growled. "Hurry up—I want to go home."

One of the loafers suggested that I give the barn key to the man and let him get his own hay. This was a great help.

"Sure—but I can't do it," I said. "It's not that I don't trust you. I'm just afraid you wouldn't take enough and cheat yourself."

The thought of the big fellow cheating himself made them all burst out laughing, and I was glad to join in. They said they would all go out to the barn with us to see how much hay the new trader would give for fifteen cents. When I locked up the store that evening, there was no illusion that my first day had been a success. As darkness settled, the slightest sound I made was intensified by the surrounding silence. Never before or since, have I felt so alone.

It would be another month before Charles would get a clerk—Ed Lewis, "a little fellow but rollicky and husky as a half grown bear"— but by then he was feeling more comfortable in his job and getting to know the people. A more relaxed environment and a brisk business continued to make Naschitti a profitable post. One of the mainstays, in addition to wool, woven products, and lambs, were horses.

Horse buyers came on the reservation each year, making a round of the trading posts. We were glad to have them come as they usually left five or ten thousand dollars in gold and silver among the Navajos at the major posts, and of these, Naschitti was one. . . . Ponies bought at our place usually were shipped to Louisiana and there sold to Negro sharecroppers. They [horses] were tough, strong, and cheap, selling for ten to twelve dollars a head. Thousands of them left the reservation this way and I often wondered how and what they felt, leaning into the traces of a plow on a bayou plantation. It was a long time, though, between buyers. Months would pass without our seeing another white person, and when we did have visitors, they generally spent the night. A daybed in the living room took care of two, and we also had a cot on the porch. If these were not enough, we made beds on the floor with sheepskins, Navajo rugs, and blankets. After traveling the wagon roads all day, people were willing to sleep anywhere if there was a roof over their heads. The "Tight Pants"—government people—came oftener than others and pestered us the most. They wanted service besides hospitality and expected it right now and free of charge. In a way this was alright since we seldom charged anyone for meals or a bed anyway, but usually they asked me to sign a voucher to show they had been there. Maybe this was alright too, but somehow I suspected the chit found its way to Washington clipped to an expense account.

There is little in this world that remains the same, as events in 1912 around Naschitti proved. It was the start of a twentieth-century lifestyle that within the next thirty years catapulted the Navajos through a pandemic (1918), into a national depression (1930s), and two world wars. But at this point, one spring day offered nothing but amazement and excitement. Charles recalled:

I happened to glance out a window, one afternoon, and saw Roan Horse approaching at a gallop. He tied his lathered pony at the rail and then sauntered in as leisurely as though he had just concluded a long siesta outside the door. That is the way with Navajos when they come bearing big news. I restrained my curiosity as Roan Horse slowly drank a bottle of soda pop and waited for more of his kinsmen to gather in the store to provide a more suitable audience. When he thought the time was right, Roan Horse turned his elbows on the counter so that he faced the bullpen, took his cigarette between his thumb and second forefinger, and started to speak. "A very funny wagon, without horses, is caught in the sand near [Two Grey Hills]," he began. "It cannot get out, but with its wheels digs itself deeper into the sand. All the while it makes much smoke and much noise."

"What sort of wagon is this that smokes?" asked one of his listeners, an old Navajo.

"Such as you have never seen, Grandfather. With it are two [white men] who with shovels try to dig it out, but only dig it in deeper. I watched this from my horse as I was passing by. They asked me to help them. I said if they would stop the noise of their wagon, I would try, and so one of the men stopped the noise. I tied an end of my rope to the saddle horn and the other end to their wagon. But just then, the white man standing in front of the wagon made the noise again. My pony jumped away in fright, breaking the rope and throwing me from the saddle."

Roan Horse dropped his cigarette on the floor and, with expert aim, spat on it.

"I ran a long way before I could catch my pony," he continued. "But I caught him and came here to tell you this. And I tell you that such a wagon and such a noise you would not believe until I threw sand in your face."

"This wagon," I said, when I knew he was finished, "is what we call a motor car—an automobile. I have already seen one myself, in Gallup.

It is not made to go on sand, but on roads, as you see in towns." On the reservation, at that time, we had no roads. An excited discussion of this phenomenon followed and then my Navajo customers flowed out of the store, gathering again in a knot around the prophet, Roan Horse.

"With four, maybe six horses, with strong harnesses, we can pull this wagon out of the sand and make it run again on its wheels," he was saying. His friends were eager for the idea and broke away to mount their ponies.

Two hours later, with my Navajos as escort, the automobile arrived under its own power, trembling and roaring at the store. It had high, wood-spoke wheels, no fenders, two high seats, no top, and was propelled by chain drive. The men who brought it this far said they had been three days coming the seventy miles from the San Juan, and in one day more hoped to reach Gallup. I told them that while the Indians were here with their ponies, it would be a good idea to have the automobile hauled across the arroyo. It was a hundred yards across and all sand. The men readily agreed. The Indian ponies tugged the monster through to hard ground and the white men stayed with us all night, planning to leave early in the morning. They invited me to go with them and, as I had never ridden in an automobile, like a fool I consented.

At two of the worst arroyos, near Tohatchi, we were lucky enough to find horses to pull us out. But at the other washes, we simply had to dig sand until we hit solid earth. Breaking trail up the rocky slope approaching Sloppy Jack's trading post at Chinaman's Springs was a back-breaking job but we finally made it and reached town about sunset. My friends wanted me to wait over a couple of days and ride back with them. I had had enough digging and pushing, though, and hired a fellow to drive me back to Naschitti in a buckboard. I didn't know it, but this was just a happy prelude to my experience with automobiles.

As chapter 7 attests, it was not just automobiles that introduced rapid change on the reservation. Economic, political, social, and cultural transformation was in the air. Charles Newcomb had just witnessed the tip of an iceberg that heralded a new way of life that changed the people of the Chuska Valley forever.

CHAPTER SEVEN

Oil, Governance, and Livestock Reduction
Changes in Economy, Challenges in Control, 1920–1940

Change was in the air. John and Louisa Wetherill, traders in Kayenta, knew nothing about it until various groups of people, driving their livestock before them, passed by the post at the end of June 1920. Everyone was heading toward Black Mountain (Mesa) to avoid the impending flood that would bring the waters from the Atlantic Ocean over the land to drown those who did not flee to higher ground. This fear, found primarily in the northern part of the Navajo Reservation, prompted those leaving to abandon their crops, with plant stalks now well above ground, to reach safety before it was too late. Even when Louisa, who spoke the Navajo language as well as any Navajo, reasoned that the Rocky Mountains to the east would hold the water back, the anguish was still too much, so only a few returned home as many others sought refuge. She inquired as to the source of this rumor and learned of two. The first was a Navajo man who had been struck by lightning and left for dead but eventually "came back to life," prophesying to many people of the impending doom he had seen in the spirit world. The second source was a missionary who had taught about the sinful nature of man, including those in his congregation, and warned that they could suffer the same fate as Noah in the Bible. Wetherill tried to explain that the minister spoke of things past, not future, just as there were stories of floods in the Navajo creation myths. There were those who had faith in what she said, but could not put their fear behind them. That would take another week or so. When they did return to their homes, they found their crops seared by the sun and life just as hard as when they had left.[1]

Not everyone was as poetic as the trader in describing the events. Agent Evan W. Estep, sitting at the Shiprock Agency, had a different perspective. When he noticed groups of people with their livestock and "most of their earthly possessions" crossing on the bridge over the San Juan, he began inquiring about the exodus. No one was forthcoming as to who started the rumor, but some of the motivation behind it quickly became apparent. The flood was coming to the lowlands and would "destroy practically all of the white people and what few were left after it could easily be killed by the Indians. The medicine man had advised the [Navajos] that their safety lay in going to the top of the mountains; the Chuska, Carrizo, and Lukachukai Mountains were literally covered with Indians, sheep, and horses, the medicine man having denied the Indians a right to bring their cattle with them."[2] The appointed time for the disaster kept shifting from a specific Friday to Saturday to Sunday then Monday. According to doubting Estep: "A medicine man never commits himself so that he is liable to lose. On Monday morning, they began praying that the calamity might be averted, and as it did not come by Monday noon, the prayers of the medicine men brought the result, and the Indians still believe it was only through the prayers of the medicine men that this flood was averted, and feel rather peeved that the white people do not appreciate the efforts of the medicine men to save them from this dire calamity."[3]

There were also some very concrete consequences. Estep believed that the Navajos lost thousands of dollars' worth of livestock by driving their sheep so fast that the lambs could not stay up with the flocks and became dinner for coyotes or died by the side of the road. Some of the sheep broke away from the main stampede and trampled crops along the way. Once the herds reached the mountains, many animals became lost and mixed in to other flocks, thus creating friction among families as they sorted livestock. The anger and frustration did not end there. The Navajos were "decidedly worked up and wild and any effort by force to prevent them from going to the mountains would probably have started trouble. . . . A good many of the Indians have been sullen and rather hard to handle for some considerable time." These Indians would not bring in their horses for testing or their sheep for dipping. Government employees, who had always been on good terms with their neighbors, now received verbal abuse and some were threatened that they might be shot. Navajos complained that dipping sheep was a farce that robbed the owners, while some even drove horses out of a corral where testing was to take place. Eventually, through dialogue and patience, life returned to normal.

Why this aberration? White investigators at the time found no definitive reason. One could suppose that World War I created a sense of anxiety, although the Navajo people had little direct involvement in the conflict and learned about it mostly through pictures in newspapers read on the counters of trading posts. Much closer to home was the 1918–19 influenza epidemic that rampaged through the United States, increasing in its death-dealing potency once it reached the boundaries of the reservation. A recent study estimates that 12 percent (3,377) of the population died during the pandemic, although given the characteristically diffused nature of Navajo society working in the livestock economy, the true number may never be known.[4] Perhaps it was the fluctuations in the economy, where wool, hides, and blankets were at the mercy of faraway forces inscrutable to Navajos living in the desert herding sheep.

Whatever one may see as the cause for this temporary outbreak of anxiety and hostility, there was even more change and reason for concern on the way. Some good, some bad, but all of it pushed the Navajos into a foreign twentieth-century lifestyle with trading posts being part of the mix. This chapter examines a roughly twenty-year period from 1920 to 1940 and some of the events that changed the reservation forever. Some of these occurrences have been covered in full-fledged books that go through detailed analysis. Here, an overview is provided of five different aspects of change—all of which were interrelated—and how they altered the posts and people of the Chuska Valley.

Counting Heads—Reaching Consensus on the Census

1923 was an important time in the governing of the Navajo people. That was when Albert H. Kneale, a highly experienced agent in the Indian Service, assumed control of the Shiprock Agency, where he remained for six years. This was also when Herbert J. Hagerman, former governor of New Mexico, accepted an invitation from Secretary of the Interior Albert B. Fall to become "Special Commissioner to Negotiate with Indians" and to organize political and economic opportunities. It was also the year when the Navajo tribal government and chapter system started. And it was the time that white entrepreneurs received access and began drilling for oil on the Navajo Reservation at Rattlesnake near Shiprock, Beautiful Mountain, Hogback, Table Mesa, and Tocito Dome, all in the Northern Agency. By 1927 there were twenty-nine oil-producing wells on the Navajo Reservation while congressional legislation, officially titled the Indian Oil Leasing Act, outlined procedures for obtaining oil in all of Indian Country throughout the United States.[5] The pace of life had suddenly escalated.

So had the population increase, but how much was anybody's guess. Imposing some type of organization on a mobile society with changing names, locations, and circumstances was a feat in itself. As early as 1908, William T. Shelton tried to explain to Washington why its card system recording family relations and census data would not work and why no one had ever attempted a census on the Navajo Reservation. He discussed the geographical size of his stewardship, how it went against Navajo culture to share one's name, how most family members just used kinship terms, and how names shifted. Although there were some cultural misunderstandings in his explanation, he defined the issues accurately when he wrote: "The children are seldom ever named, they are referred to as Begay which means boy, or Bah which means girl; as a boy grows older if he is the son of Hosteen Nez he is referred to as Hosteen Nez Begay, which means Tall Man's Son; if he should marry Clah's daughter, he would afterwards be called Clah Bar Donny, which means The Left Handed Man's Son-in-law. If he should in time acquire a large flock of goats, he is liable to be called Cli-ze-slon, meaning Many Goats, or he is liable to be known as Be Leen nes ka ha, meaning Fat Horse."[6] Shelton's three-page explanation continued, citing reason after reason why he could not achieve the desired outcome. He closed his missive by saying that many people walked away from receiving goods at the agency because they did not want to give their name, and that even if the agent could obtain it, the information was useless because of the shifting interpretation of what a person should be called. Names could also denote a person's complexion, height or weight, kin relationship, color of hair, color or number of livestock, ancestral clan, or event in a person's life. Seven years later, the Office of Indian Affairs was still requesting an initial census.

Shelton's experience set the stage for a host of agents who followed. In 1917, after estimating there were 6,354 Navajos in his jurisdiction, Evan Estep in his annual report again explained the difficulty and was even more specific about registering Navajos for health care at the clinic, saying it would require "a special force" to accomplish what was requested. "If we attempt to use this [dispensary] card in everyday work, it will result in driving about all the Indians away from the doctor and back to the 'medicine man.' It is very difficult and sometimes impossible to learn the name of a Navajo woman, the mother of a child brought in to school. When you go asking a Navajo man his name, his age, his domestic relation, and a few other questions of that kind and go writing his answers down (if he gives them), he is going to quit you and hike for the mountains or some out of the way place on the reservation where you are not likely to see him again for two or three years. . . . We were only able to register about fifty or sixty of the Indians on this reservation out of hundreds within the draft age, and I doubt if a dozen of those who registered could be found today with a whole regiment of soldiers to look for them."[7] Seven years later, Albert H. Kneale, after admitting there had never been an official census on his part of the reservation, wrote, "They have no title by which they are known or designated, in other words a Navajo Indian has no *name* [agent's emphasis]."[8]

Finally, in November 1929, the government received the first official census for the Northern Navajo Agency. This accomplishment became possible, since by this point, the reservation had been divided not only into agencies but also chapters. In addition, there were more trading posts, better roads, greater awareness about the outside world and how the census worked, more Navajos educated in the boarding schools, and greater restrictions on movement, which helped form communities. One of the most effective ways to solve the name problem was with numbers. In preparation for and as part of the census, the government issued metal identification discs, similar to those used by soldiers in World War I. Inscribed on it were an identification number, indicating jurisdiction and district, and the insignia of the Interior Department. The normal questions found on a census were covered on the enumeration schedule with name, age, sex, degree of blood, marital condition, relationship to head of family, and identification number. Individuals recorded fingerprints on their data card.

The system was far from perfect—people lost their tags, loaned them to others, forgot their number, denied having them—the list goes on, but it was a start. Many Navajos saw the value in the number, with traders and missionaries encouraging them to keep their record current with births and deaths. Some of the people in the Western Navajo Agency tattooed their ID numbers on their body, while others had their name and address stamped on their disc. Each agency had its own set of problems when conducting the census due to weather, terrain, access by roads, size of jurisdiction, vagueness of boundary lines, number of people contacted, and the skill and language ability of government participants. An average time to complete the census in each agency was two-and-a-half to three months. The cover letter accompanying the reservation-wide finished product was quick to note that some agencies did better and were more complete in accomplishing their mission than others. The three most accurate were the Leupp, Eastern, and Northern Navajo Agencies.

There were a number of reasons that the Northern Navajo/Shiprock Agency was among the most successful. The agent had divided the area into twenty-six districts; the manageable size assisted in accuracy. The census taker, Herbert Redshaw, had served as a government farmer in Aneth before working directly at the agency. His eighteen years of service and ability to speak the language fluently, coupled with his extensive knowledge of the communities, ensured that he knew where to go and who to see. Redshaw also selected a reliable interpreter and did the work himself instead of farming it out to surrogates. Accuracy, however, came at a cost in time—five months to complete the project—but when he wrote that there were 8,219 people in the Northern Agency, it corrected all the ballpark estimates of the past.[9] The total number of Navajos living on the reservation came in at 39,806.

Herbert Hagerman and the Formation of Tribal Government

Not only was the demographic information getting organized, but so were the political divisions of the land. The five Navajo agencies (Eastern, Leupp, Northern, Southern, and Western; Hopi, the sixth, was also included) covering an area larger than the state of West Virginia needed to become more geographically manageable. With the appointment of Herbert J. Hagerman as "Special Commissioner to Negotiate with Indians" (within four months the title shifted to "Commissioner to the Navajo Tribe"), a new system that entailed a Tribal Council composed of two elected officials from each of the Navajo agencies and a chairman and vice chairman—twelve delegates total—arose. The organization soon started evolving in size, but the important point here is to recognize it as a representative form of government that was still under the control of Hagerman and the Department of the Interior, who held final say on decisions. Four years later, the chapter system began, dividing each agency into subdivisions of smaller units with an elected president, vice president, and secretary who met with their constituents monthly to discuss local conditions.[10] Gradually, Navajo lands became increasingly recognized, explored, controlled, and exploited for a variety of resources and reasons.

Following his appointment on January 3, 1923, Hagerman soon went to Shiprock to evaluate the task before him. He had barely stepped out of his car when a group of Navajos met him and immediately asked for a meeting. His visit would be short, and so he did not think people would have enough time to gather in from the far reaches of the agency, but once he agreed to a conference, the head men soon arrived. He was amazed. "Some came in from over 100 miles and at that time there was no automobile communication possible to the remote parts of the jurisdiction. They had some means of communication which we still know little or nothing about."[11] After the meeting, he spent three months just traveling around the reservation getting to know the agents, people, and land before convening the Tribal Council for the first time.

Hagerman discovered many things to worry about, but there were three that really stood out. He was appalled at how disconnected or misinformed the Washington bureaucracy was to actual conditions on the reservation. Decisions that impacted thousands of lives were being decided in a dark closet of ignorance. He was not talking about the agents who were underpaid and overworked, but the powerhouses in the capitol that demanded actions that were unreasonable. He lumped his evaluation of the agency and school facilities into one word—"dismal." Recording his impression, he left little doubt as to why. "They were nearly built on the same lines; rectangular, red brick buildings, most unattractive in design, ill-smelling halls, deep steps, narrow corridors, dark reception rooms, stuffy toilets, unattractive furniture. One gets to know this old-fashioned institutional type of Indian office building so well that they could be spotted on a bet from an airplane. They are about as uncomfortable, uncongenial looking structures as you can well imagine. Throughout the Southwest, with the exception of some of the newer schools, the type is everywhere alike; enough to give you the shivers from the moment you sight or smell one."[12]

Hagerman spent six weeks in the Shiprock area, visiting oil structures and every trading post throughout the desert landscape. With his assistant, Mark W. Radcliffe, they battled the road conditions and got "hopelessly stalled in fine sifting sand. . . . We would spin, stall, and push, put blankets under the wheels, all in vain."[13] Then Radcliffe would wander out in the wilderness and return with a dozen smiling Navajos who joked about the situation, received some Camel cigarettes, and then "worked like beavers" to get the car out and on its way. Still, this was not lost time, as he literally rubbed shoulders with the people. He became intimately aware of the third problem—in his estimation the main one for the Navajos—the deterioration of the rangelands, which he also linked to health needs—trachoma, in particular.

The issue of trachoma will be dealt with here in summary fashion, but Hagerman made it a major concern for the Indian Office and was in the forefront of combatting this infectious eye disease that could result in permanent blindness. This was a white man's illness that began infecting the Navajos fifty years prior and had now afflicted an estimated 30 percent of the population.[14] Some of the primary breeding grounds were boarding schools, where the disease was spread, only to have children sent home as unwitting vectors. The special commissioner opined: "How futile to send Navajo boys and girls back to the hogans with a smattering of American history, home economics, some skill in the use of washing machines and a little knowledge of Old Testament myths if they were to take with them eyes oozing with the dreadful virus of trachoma."[15] The nine boarding schools, seven day schools, and two mission schools on the reservation became breeding grounds that spread the infection throughout the population. To Hagerman's credit, he did all he could during his eight-plus years as commissioner; even after he retired from his position, he continued to wage the battle against this cursed disease until his death in 1935.

Returning to 1923, the first meeting of the Tribal Council took place at Toadlena on July 7. Hagerman addressed the council in a morning session, using Jacob C. Morgan and Frank Walker as interpreters. He pointed out that oil and coal were two resources that held the potential of ameliorating the poverty found on the reservation, but that a process had to be followed to open it. The secretary of the interior, the council, and Hagerman—the link between the two—had to agree. At this point the tribe would be in an exploratory phase to determine where and how much oil might be available. A few small leases would be granted, and then as resources developed, additional leases would be bid for in auction. What would the Navajos get? Money from sales would come to the tribe on a ratio—for every eight barrels produced, one would go to the Indians. In the case of the leases sold, Navajos received one out of five. "It is the very best plan which these high officials in Washington could, under the law, arrive at."[16] The council passed the agreement and elected Chee Dodge, a wealthy Navajo businessman, to a four-year term as chairman and Hastiin Begoiden Begay as vice chairman.

Hagerman was the linchpin. To him fell the duties of leasing, regulating production to reduce waste, and maximizing profits while avoiding any perception of impropriety for those involved. In addition to his intense desire to improve health conditions, he sought to restore rangelands, to add two million acres of land to the reservation, to put in place a plan to eliminate a huge population of feral and useless horses, and to present to Washington a more realistic picture of who the Navajo people were and what they needed.[17] As he assumed these tasks, he grew to appreciate those he served. For instance, he mentions that he held the meeting at Toadlena "to get it as far away as possible so as to keep out the white oil men, but many of them were there."[18] He also had "one of the most amusing experiences in my whole experience with the Navajos," right after the three-day meeting concluded. He was tired and so went for a "tramp," with an Indian boy as guide, on the mountain nearby. By chance they encountered a summer hogan around which there were women of all ages, spinning, carding, and weaving wool. "They were having a gloriously good time, gossiping, gesticulating, laughing. I whispered to my Indian guide, asking him what it was all about. He flushed and was very shy about responding, but upon my urging, said they were describing the clothes and manners and speeches of the white men and

Herbert J. Hagerman, a highly efficient and talented person, at one time served as the secretary of the interior and governor of New Mexico territory. He had a huge, though often unrecognized, influence on the tribe, serving as special commissioner to the Navajos. Hagerman helped establish the first Navajo Tribal Council, oversaw the first oil exploration and development, and improved healthcare—especially in battling trachoma. Courtesy of Palace of the Governors Photo Archives, NMHM/DCA, no. 047786.

women at the council. Then I fully saw the meaning and significance of this mimicry. It was highly entertaining and most significant!"[19]

Getting Down to Business—Oil and Roads

Hagerman chose Toadlena to play an important role in the development in the oil fields. In addition to all the resources that had made the trading post and school possible, it was centrally located to all the newly drilled wells. He elected not to have his main office at an agency, where he feared any of the business dealings would get confused with agency business or that there might be a perception of favoritism. By developing its own distinct identity, the commissioner hoped to maintain the friendship and support of the people. The site choice also made monitoring of the active oilfield more practical, there was the Bloomfield Brothers sawmill nearby that could provide lumber from the mountains, George Bloomfield assisted with much of the external and internal construction, relationships and support from the school were helpful, and there were sewer and electrical lines that could be tapped into with a minimum of expense. By December 1924, the workers had completed the house and it was ready for service.[20]

A number of different companies received leases in the oilfield— Midwest at Hogback, Gypsy at Tocito, P&R/Continental on Table Mesa, and Mutual Oil on Boundary Butte. Some wells proved of value immediately, while others yielded oil mixed with water, or just water. Hogback, for instance, produced 1,500 barrels of oil a day; Rattlesnake No. 3 turned out 80 barrels a day, while Table Mesa drilled down 2,065 feet and was an "8000 barrel water well."[21] Exploration continued, and when the market was good, it put cash in the tribal coffers—which incidentally meant that the money went to the entire tribe and not just those living in the Northern Navajo portion of the reservation. For example, in October 1923, the tribe leased at auction 21,500 acres for possible development and received $87,600 in lease bonuses. By 1926, Hogback, Rattlesnake, and Table Mesa were producing 12,173 barrels a day; between 1923 and 1929, the tribe received over $700,000 in bonuses and royalties.[22] While this was nowhere near the boom in oil production that arose in the 1950s in southeastern Utah and other parts of the Northern Navajo, the people of Farmington applauded the prosperity it brought to them. The oil was processed there, which gave a monetary lift to that city and the surrounding communities. Although off-reservation wells competed and a national depression greatly slowed the economy, by 1937, the tribe had received $1,227,705 in royalties.[23]

The impact of these oilfields had both a direct and indirect effect on the Navajos in the area. Oil companies hired some men as laborers and supported local events to maintain goodwill. More money, instead of barter, began to color financial transactions, especially when the traders became aware that men were earning a salary. But two of the biggest boons to accompany the oil industry were transportation and communication, common phenomena where mineral extraction and movement of materials to a shipping point were necessary. Mark Radcliffe, assistant to Hagerman, noted, "Made a trip to Shiprock and Farmington this week. Found the roads in bad shape; it has been snowing again here, and with that and the snow already on the ground, thawing, makes the road almost impossible."[24] In the same breath he wrote, "Mr. Kneale is strong for the construction of a telephone line and informs me that they have enough wire on hand to do the job. The traders will help on the construction, and if we could get a little money for poles and brackets, could have the line up in short time."

That was in December 1923. Kneale notified the commissioner of Indian affairs on January 11, 1926, that the only remaining part of grading the Gallup-Shiprock highway was the last nineteen miles outside the agency.[25] Trader Franc Newcomb described what happened. "The oil company furnished the basic material and the government blacktopped a narrow strip of road from Gallup to Shiprock which looked like a black ribbon running on and on forever with never a crossing. It was a great improvement to have a road that did not blow away during the season of sandstorms. The oil company also ran a telephone line beside the road and permitted us to attach a phone."[26] A year later, Deshna Clah Chischillige, "an educated Navajo of this jurisdiction and a man of excellent character," applied to Kneale for a permit to establish the first filling station and campground next to the Shiprock-Gallup Highway on the east bank of the San Juan River not far from the agency. The manager of the Continental Oil Company (Conoco) had agreed to lend him the gasoline pump, tank, and lubricating tanks for this endeavor. Kneale enthusiastically endorsed both the man and the project.[27] Chischillige was in business.

Traders, Regulations, and Increased Scrutiny

Accompanying all of these many changes was closer scrutiny of daily life on the Navajo Reservation. Dissipating isolation allowed more eyes to examine everything from diet and lifestyle to healthcare and economic practices. So when Hubert Work, secretary of the interior (1923–28), approved a revised "Regulations of the Indian Service Licensed Indian Traders" on June 28, 1927, there was renewed interest followed by a desire for closer compliance. Many of the regulations' tenets were well-established and adhered to—application to be a trader, a $10,000 bond for the applicant, alcohol and gambling forbidden, closed stores on Sunday, and supervision of pricing by the superintendent. Other rules, although not necessarily new, were more problematic: traders were not to deal in objects of antiquity from either prehistoric or historic sites on federal land. There were two other points, however, that struck at the core of Navajo life and were totally ignored. The law stated: "Credit given Indians will be at the trader's own risk, as no assistance will be given by government officials in the collection of debts against Indians. Traders shall not accept pawns or pledges of personal property by Indians to obtain credit or loans." The following rule read: "Traders must not pay Indians in tokens, tickets, store orders, or anything else of that character. Payment must be made in money or in credit if the Indian is indebted to the trader."[28]

A brief discussion of how this system operated will clarify what store owners faced in trading on Indian land. The heart of most economic transactions at Two Grey Hills, Toadlena, and every other post on the reservation lay in the system of pawn that allowed Navajo customers and traders to work together the entire year, not just when wool (spring) and lambs and cattle (fall) were sold.[29] The system was simple and flexible enough to meet needs on both sides of the counter, but underlying it all was the customer-trader relationship that made it work. When Navajo customers could not pay directly for the goods they needed, there were choices. One possibility was to borrow money from a relative or neighbor, putting up some type of collateral that would be given back once he or she paid the loan. While there was liberal sharing among Navajos, especially with family members, as a business proposition, there were problems with an internal pawning of an item. Father Berard Haile felt this was rarely done simply because "tribesmen will pocket the security as sure as the sun goes down," whereas the traders were more flexible and open to argument, in their attempt to keep customers.[30] If an individual did not redeem his or her pawn when the period of grace was over, the object became "dead pawn" and technically could be sold.

However, most traders carried dead pawn for years after, depending on the object, for a number of reasons.

There were many different types of items that customers pawned; indeed, anything that a trader could sell on an open market might be accepted. Objects like silver jewelry, rugs, and other crafts were more likely to be sold to tourists or curio shop owners than things like a medicine bundle or something else that had intense cultural value but little extrinsic worth. Ideally, the trader had to ensure the debt would be paid and the object redeemed, or otherwise, he would be stuck with an item that held little sale value for outsiders. Many objects used as security were heirlooms important to a family who had every intention of eventually repossessing them—and the trader knew it. To sell an item as soon as it came due, was legal and agreed upon by both parties at the time that it became pawn, but to do so was unethical from the trader's standpoint because of his relationship with the individual. Indeed, some people turned over prized possessions to a store owner just for safekeeping. They knew if the trader lost it through theft, fire, or accident, that the owner would receive full value without having to worry about its security.

Along those same lines, when a person pawned an object but then needed it temporarily, some traders loaned it for the occasion and then took it back. For instance, if there was an important social event that a woman wanted to wear her jewelry to, she could approach the owner and ask if she could borrow it until it was over. Often the trader would oblige. The same was true for a medicine man who needed his medicine bundle or a certain object for a ceremony, or for a man who wanted his rifle back for deer hunting. Other traders used the same situations to turn up the heat on their customers to pay off their tickets and remove the items from pawn. Trust and relationship were important principles; if a person betrayed that trust, future dealings were jeopardized. All the posts discussed here had a pawn room, a secure area where the trader tagged items and hung them in such a way that they were easily accessed and visible for the Navajo owner who wanted to come in with the trader and check on its status. A visitor to a post could quickly determine how the economy of the Navajos in an area was doing by the amount of pawn—the more there was, the harder the times. Some items might be worth more than the credit extended on them, creating a temptation, if there was a default, to immediately sell it for a higher value. Most traders avoided doing this to maintain good customer relations. Six months (later changed to a year), by law, was the soonest that an item could be sold, but given the two-season economic pattern of the Navajo economy, this time period came around very quickly. Thus, "How [the trader] administered his pawn was as close as one could get to a bottom-line appraisal of whether the trader had the welfare of his Indian customers at heart or not."[31]

What if customer or trader chose to take advantage of the other? On the Navajo side, he or she accepted the loan on good faith and was expected to pay down the debt—either gradually or all at once—whichever was most practical given their financial situation. Sometimes, when they sold large amounts of wool, lambs, cattle, and the like, the entire pawn ticket—often a tag written for each item as well as a list in a notebook or a tally on a paper bag—was redeemed. More often, the Navajos paid a little at a time on a number of pawned objects. The customer was also free to shop at any other store, but there was an expectation that if there were objects at a place that needed to be reclaimed, the owner should be working toward it. Just as Navajos knew what the prices were at various posts and what goods were available, traders understood where their customers were shopping and what they were buying. Store owners could do little about any breach of faith against them. If a Navajo failed to redeem the pawned object, the trader could sell it, hoping to get at least equal value for the goods initially given, or he could refuse future credit and deny assistance, but in a monetary sense he was hamstrung.

Some posts introduced tokens or tin money that had their own unique design and value assigned—often in denominations of one dollar, a half-dollar, quarter, dime, and nickel—redeemable at that store. This *seco* (dry money) or *béésh tʼáʼí* (thin metal), as the Navajos referred to it, was meant to be used at a specific place, but many traders accepted it from Navajo customers who had traded elsewhere, with the understanding that the trader could go to its point of origin and be reimbursed in money or material. The idea behind this form of scrip was to have the customer trade at the same business. The federal government first discouraged its use, then banned it entirely, but in a cash-poor economy, tokens filled a void and fit in the setting because many

Navajo people were raised on hard currency instead of paper money, which they did not trust. Tin money also made sense because it looked like the currency they were accustomed to. Wool, sheep, lambs, hides, and piñon nuts were usually cash sales, while rugs, jewelry, and other slower moving merchandise were tokens.

Store owners had to be careful as to how much credit they extended. They watched the prosperity and spending habits of their customers, gauging how much each could really afford, given their specific amount of income. The trader had to ensure that he did not lend out more than he could collect; if it was worth it to the customer to not pay off his bill, then he would stop coming.[32] How close the margin of profit could be in trading over some of the most seemingly insignificant transactions is illustrated by Roswell Nelson when Albert Kneale questioned what he charged for sugar. After apologizing for making a general statement, the trader explained "that a price of 15 cents per lb. was being charged for sugar, as this price applies on sales in small quantities where it is necessary to carry the Indian for a period of six months to a year. Where sugar is sold by us for cash, a charge of 12 cents per lb. is made for it, or in lots of 100 lbs. or more, on a cash basis, a charge of 10 cents per lb. is made."[33] To think that this issue over pennies technically went from a trader at Two Grey Hills to the commissioner of Indian affairs in Washington, D.C., shows that there were few places the tentacles of government bureaucracy could not reach.

The revised regulations reached the Navajo Reservation in the summer of 1929. Superintendent C. (Chester) L. Walker of the Western Agency headquartered in Tuba City read them with interest, then raised the question that no one else had seen fit to make an issue. Even though he knew Navajo customers were totally dependent on the system of pawn, he wrote to each of the traders in his jurisdiction to see how they felt about discontinuing the practice. Other agents joined in, giving a more complete picture of conditions on the entire reservation. What follows from posts on the Northern Navajo, who sent their written responses to Hagerman, reflect generally the attitude of most of the traders. Their answers were not surprising but revealed the conditions faced in this sometimes fickle business. The overall reaction was that many would like to see the practice abolished for the welfare of the traders, but realized that to do so would cause great harm and inconvenience to their customers.

George Bloomfield, as a businessman, did not revel in extending credit and would have liked to stop doing so, or at least modify the practice throughout the annual cycle. Calling on his seventeen years of experience as a trader, he felt that both the Indian and the store owner would be thousands of dollars ahead if business were done on a strictly cash basis. The trader could sell closer to the margin, which would save the customer money. He complained that the present system of loaning made "crooks and deadbeats of our Indians," because they went from post to post, swearing that they owed no one else, so received far more credit than they would ever be able to pay back.[34] Bloomfield believed this slackening in personal responsibility was a fairly new and growing phenomenon, unlike the trading practices of the past, when during wool and lamb times, pawn was quickly redeemed. For proof, he shared his current situation. "I will give you the exact figure on my last year's business ending today [October 23, 1929]. Beginning lamb season 1928, my pawns and accounts were $7862.57; end of lamb season 1928, the balance not paid was $3789.00, a carryover of 50 percent. Accounts and pawns on hand beginning lamb season 1929, was $8979.75; amount of accounts still unpaid $3969.27 with pawn $912.75, a total carryover this year of $4872.02. I am sure if the other traders would tell you the truth, you would find almost all of them in the same boat that I am now in."[35]

To correct the situation, he suggested that all accounts be paid within three or four months of their start and that at least by the end of wool and lamb seasons, everyone was on a zero balance. Superintendents should also share in the responsibility by counseling Navajos to pay their bills instead of, as Bloomfield had heard, telling them that the trader could not collect, and so the customer did not have to pay. With pawn and accounts representing half of the trader's investments and profits, if these problems could be cleared up, the customer could expect lower prices at the post. A final problem was the sale of young ewes—a herder's breeding stock—to buyers off the reservation. This was being done mostly along the highway and the eastern border of the reservation. "For the last year, there has been hardly a day that there has been less than from one to a half dozen truckloads of sheep taken off the reservation and sold to traders who are not under license of the department." This had an adverse effect on the growth of flocks and the business of the on-reservation traders.

J. M. Drolet at Naschitti reflected almost identical sentiments as Bloomfield, while Arthur Newcomb added some new twists. He recognized
that his customers, especially in the winter, were generally destitute and
had no choice but to pawn property. The concern was that if the system
of loans were discontinued, it would drive Navajos off the reservation
into the arms of traders who did not know and did not care about the
people they were dealing with. Dead pawn would quickly be sold, alcohol in the border towns consumed, loyalty or obligation to customers
would disappear, and the Navajos would become impoverished and suffer more. On the other hand, Newcomb had extended credit in times
of real hardship, but after the emergency, the borrower did not feel any
urgency to repay. Ill will sometimes followed. Newcomb agreed that the
superintendents needed to encourage their charges to meet their debts.[36]

Superintendent B. P. Six, who replaced Kneale in 1929, generally
favored the current system of pawn, saying that jewelry and other property were the Indians' bank account. Pawning had just recently saved
many Navajos from having to sell their herds. The agent pointed out that
six weeks earlier, a drought had depressed the livestock market, affecting sales negatively. A month and a half later, the range had restored and
the market was doing well. Those Indians who were forced to sell before
the dry spell lost money, while those able to wait a little longer were able
to receive good prices. "It is in situations of this kind that the pawns
show their worth."[37] C. N. Cotton, who owned the wholesale company
called Indian Trader Supplies in Gallup, took an even higher road by
saying that the Navajos were American citizens, that the Constitution
protected their right to own and use property, and that besides, "they
probably owe the many traders on the reservation some four hundred
thousand dollars and the traders will be lucky to get 25 percent of it!
That shows they are perfectly able to take care of themselves."[38] Enough.
C. L. Walker sent his answer to the commissioner of Indian affairs, noting that although the system was not perfect and that the government
still had the responsibility to ensure fairness for the Indian, pawning
goods seemed to be a beneficial practice and should continue.[39] Hagerman, compiling the results from all the different agencies, concurred,
allowing the commissioner of Indian affairs, C. J. Rhoads, in 1930 to
waive the restriction for traders on the Navajo Reservation with the
understanding that they could not sell any dead pawn before twelve

months had elapsed and before proper notification to do so had been made to the owner.[40]

The same year that the issue of pawn arose, Franc Newcomb wrote a lengthy letter to the American Indian Defense Association, whose president was Haven Emerson and whose executive secretary was John Collier. Titling her piece "The Navaho Situation from a Trader's Viewpoint," Franc called upon her seventeen years at Newcomb and shared what she believed to be the best course to follow for the people she lived among.[41] Many of her thoughts and hopes became reality, but not before there was a tremendous faltering in the status quo. She started by pointing out that with sufficient water, the Navajos remained in one place to maintain gardens and a winter home, not departing their residence until the hot weather of June pushed them into the mountains with cooler temperatures. By promoting irrigation where possible and drilling wells where surface water was scarce, communities with gardens and fruit trees would make settlement more permanent. The oil companies had proved that water could be obtained in the desert.

Franc recognized the importance of maintaining Navajo husbandry practices, citing 1,100,000 sheep and goats on the reservation, 65,000 cattle, and 40,000 horses—which supported a number of related industries.[42] While timber and oil were under development, there were also vast, untouched beds of coal and low grade ore. She hastened to add that any industries on the reservation should be on a small scale, should be culturally suitable, should utilize the resources available, and should be FOR and BY (her emphasis) the Indians, who should be suitably trained for new tasks. Rather than force them into an urban lifestyle, "they are better adapted for outdoor work, and small one-man industries." In terms of education, there should be day schools in every community where they would learn reading, writing, and speaking English before they ever left their parents upon completion of the third grade. Then they could attend an on-reservation boarding school near their home until fourteen; for those who wanted to continue with their education, they could move on, while most of the girls would return home at the age of fourteen to learn weaving (estimated four years to master the craft) and other tasks that allowed them to be self-sufficient. Families would "teach her the strict precepts of the older generation, and she would be very strictly chaperoned by her mother or an aunt," rather than becoming like the "graduates of the higher schools [who have] learned to dress and eat like whites, refuse to return to the hard work on the reservation . . . [and] have no home to guard them and no moral restraint whatever. The streets of these Southwestern towns are full of young men and women at night."[43]

For those who would continue further education, they should be trained in industrial work to become nurses, matrons, seamstresses, and other dominant society trades. Back at home, Franc envisioned "community centers with day schools, community bathhouses, community laundries, blacksmith shops, carpenter shops, a corn-grinding mill, and a machine for cleaning beans. And I would like to see an absolute suppression of the liquor traffic on the reservation." Considering the conditions then prevalent in Indian Country and what is now available, this was one trader, who, although enthralled by and immersed in traditional Navajo culture and its preservation, could look into the future and see the potential of the land and its people. But it was decades in coming. First the Navajo people passed through what they consider the second greatest trial and trauma since the Long Walk period.

Cataclysm—Livestock Reduction

Even in the first Tribal Council meeting, that July day in 1923, Hagerman addressed what he termed the Navajos' "whole problem." He pointed out that since their return from Fort Sumner, they had five times the number of people and four times the land than in 1868, and still their population was increasing, as was their stock. Ask the old men, they could tell you that the rich grass available in the land had disappeared and what was now on the ranges was "nowhere near as good. . . . This is your whole problem. You cannot continue to make a fair living on this reservation with your people growing in numbers and with your range growing down in its capacity to carry your sheep, unless you improve your range; unless you improve your sheep; unless you get more land, or lastly, unless you do something else to improve your condition and increase your wealth."[44] The commissioner reminded them that the government was then advancing the quality of livestock through better breeds of animals. As for more land, there had been additions in the past, and perhaps there would be some in the future, but there would never be sufficient land to offset the growing numbers of people and livestock.

Unproductive animals were consuming valuable resources and needed to be eliminated. According to Hagerman, never before had the Navajo people thought of themselves as a collective group that could combine and coordinate efforts to solve problems. Even with the beginning of the agencies, there had not been a unified attempt. Now, with the advent of the Tribal Council, they shared common action and planning. The commissioner directed the first step—rid the reservation of thousands of feral and useless horses. The people resisted, feeling they were losing their wealth unnecessarily, but eventually, they realized that horse reduction was for their benefit. Thousands of horses afflicted with dourine (a venereal disease that causes paralysis and a host of other debilitating symptoms before death) were the first to go, followed by thousands more condemned as useless. This part of livestock reduction was a precursor to even more traumatic events associated with decreasing sheep and goats—the bedrock of most Navajo families' livelihoods. Even as Hagerman entered the turbulent waters of livestock reduction that reached full tide in the early to mid-1930s, tapering off in the mid-1940s, he concluded that "the period I spent with the Navajos between 1923 and 1932 was the most interesting of my whole life."[45]

By 1930 the Great Depression was well underway. It directly impacted the Navajos in sales of wool, lambs, and woven products. In Shiprock, Superintendent B. P. Six scrambled to find ways to break into the sluggish, and sometimes nonexistent, wool market so that the Navajos would have a means to obtain what they needed. At this point, the price of wool was at fifteen cents a pound at the posts. Hagerman looked into the possibility of direct government financial assistance, but funds were not available; another option was to have the traders purchase the wool as agents for the National Wool Marketing Corporation, under the jurisdiction of the Federal Farm Board. By consolidating the small "clips" from individual Indians, combining the administrative efforts into a manageable system, and with the assistance of the superintendents, there might be a way to get money through the chain and into the pocket of the livestock owners. That year's wool clip for the entire reservation was three million pounds; if government officials assumed the responsibility for consolidating their agency's produce and purchasing all this wool, they feared

The Chuska Valley was well known for its large herds of feral horses. When livestock reduction of the 1930s began measuring the carrying capacity of the land and matching it to the numbers of horses, sheep, goats, and cattle grazing upon it, it became obvious that many animals had to be destroyed. For the Navajos who depended on animal husbandry for their economic welfare, the results of the government's efforts were nothing but a tragedy. Courtesy of Milton Snow Collection, Navajo Nation Museum, Window Rock, Arizona.

they would be accused of interfering with Indian sales and profiteering. How could they avoid the look of evil and at the same time sell wool and promote Navajo blankets and rugs?[46] By June, both the commissioner of Indian affairs, C. J. Rhoads, and Hagerman agreed that the Navajos would struggle to understand the complicated procedures entailed in membership in a cooperative association and marketing their products through them. The men felt that the government and its agents should be very careful about either encouraging the Indians to join such organizations or having non-Indian officials represent them.[47] The move toward a cooperative solution was over; back to business as usual.

The era of livestock reduction is multifaceted, complex, and has been discussed extensively.[48] Beginning in the late 1920s, the federal government determined, as a result of the economic and environmental disasters of the Great Depression, that there were too many animals on the

Navajo Reservation, and that the excess needed to be eliminated to save the grass, topsoil, and surrounding areas from the effects of erosion and overgrazing. The Bureau of Indian Affairs attempted to have the Navajos voluntarily reduce their herds, but when this did not happen, the Soil Conservation Service, precursor to today's Bureau of Land Management (BLM), enforced the eradication of large numbers of sheep, goats, cattle, and horses.

In 1931 Sophus Jensen, the farmer at the Shiprock Agency testified to a congressional committee about the conditions in the jurisdiction that he supervised. The committee was interested in facts and figures that indicated how to help the Navajo people raise productive livestock, while factoring in the drought conditions and overgrazing as a part of any solution. Jensen's informed view, based on eighteen years' experience, provides some of the most accurate information concerning what the Navajo people and their trading partners faced as the program reduced the herds and changed the economy. The Northern Navajo had approximately 3,080,000 acres of rangeland with an estimated 6,000 wild horses and Indian ponies, although this was probably a low estimate at the time. Every year there were roundups in which large numbers of horses were either killed or castrated; the farmer pointed out that there were approximately 1,400 Navajo families, each one of which would need about three horses. Committee members asked if the Navajos would get rid of some of the excess horses and reduce the number they needed, to which Jensen replied that it would be good for the range, but "they think an awful lot of their horses."[49] General range estimates used the figure of one horse eating the same amount of grass as five sheep. Now add to this 59,510 goats, half of which Jensen considered worthless, and another 137,000 sheep, and one can see why the committee pushed for getting rid of useless and feral livestock.[50]

What had been a gentle push for Navajos to self-regulate the size of the herds turned into a hard shove that, in some instances, resulted in physical confrontation. Quotas to eliminate sheep and goats and horses at first brought a small remittance to livestock owners, but eventually Navajos received nothing and were given no choice, except to watch their animals get slaughtered in corrals, in canyons, and on the ranges. The Soil Conservation Service hired "range riders" to count livestock, find where Navajo families were hiding them, and oversee a systematic reduction. Imagine this scene, repeated hundreds of times, as witnessed by Martin Johnson, a Navajo living at Sanostee. He and his wife were at home tending their sheep and goats when a range rider, through an interpreter, presented a letter: "This paper says that you will let loose 75 head of goats today. If you don't obey the order, as it is stated, tomorrow the police will come again, and, if you don't let go of the 75 head of goats, you and your wife will both go to jail until you agree to do so."[51] The couple drove the required number to the Hot Springs Trading Post, where they received $75, then watched men working for the government slaughter every animal in a pen. "There was blood running everywhere in the corral as we just stood there and watched. My wife was the one who raised the sheep and goats in her younger years. She cried about her goats as they were killed. Then we just left to go back home."

Emotionally devastated to see their livestock brutally murdered and their livelihood wrenched from their hands, Navajos resisted by hiding animals, falsifying numbers, splitting flocks among other families, and moving to distant ranges.[52] In some instances, feelings erupted into fights. Capiton Benally in Teec Nos Pos acted on his anger with four other men by going to the district supervisor's home and confronting him about the circumstances. They verbally assaulted the agent and knocked him out with a club before tying him and his interpreter with bailing wire, tossing them in the agent's truck, and driving away, all the time listening to the cries and shouts of the superintendent's wife. The men drove the government official's truck or rode horses a couple of miles away to a canyon but were soon pursued by six policemen in a car. As the vehicle approached, the protesters fled on horseback, only to be followed by a posse of men on horses and in trucks. Some of the pursuers got too close and were captured by a handful of men-on-the-run. The groups exchanged shots before the kidnappers fled, but the next day, law enforcement from the Shiprock Agency caught up to Capiton Benally's wife and brought her to jail before sending her to Window Rock, then Phoenix, where she remained for three months. The police eventually apprehended Benally and six other culprits and sent them to jail in Prescott, Arizona. The courts sentenced him to eighteen months incarceration, where he performed labor in the mountains near Tucson before returning home.[53] While it was not necessarily typical for an incident to escalate into armed conflict, by 1934 there was little resemblance of peaceful cooperation when it came to surrendering livestock.

Certainly Agent Kneale, who watched the entire process unfold, did not shrink from criticizing the government's role, and like the Navajos, blamed many of the problems on John Collier, commissioner of Indian affairs (1933–45; note, the title of "Office of Indian Affairs" or "Indian Service" changed in 1947 to "Bureau of Indian Affairs"). With his sociology background and activist approach to changing the Indians' circumstances through self-determination, Collier's time in office was welcomed by many tribes. Not so for the Navajos, who blamed the entire livestock reduction program and its attendant issues on him. Kneale followed suit, arguing that the process of reduction was carelessly conceived: "For the possessor of a few thousand head or even of a few hundred to lose twenty-five percent of her holdings entailed no particular hardship, but for the possessor of fifty head, the loss of twenty-five percent meant the difference between a most carefully eked out, but nonetheless happy and contented, existence, and destitution."[54] Small flocks of sheep were becoming a thing of the past, as the government divided the land into grazing units that specified how many animals of a certain type could be ranged on a specific piece of tribally owned property.

Kneale also pointed out that there was a big difference in making a livelihood from a flock that one can manage and control compared to government-provided work such as the Civilian Conservation Corps and other programs dependent on wages and external sources. Navajo people looked at these federal remedies during the depression as an exchange—jobs for livestock—but that was not the intent of the government. The agent knew better but had to sit by and watch the culture shift within the economy. "There is a vast difference between being dependent upon a little flock of carefully nurtured sheep which furnishes a sure crop every spring and another every fall and between times provides the material for an occasional blanket that may be exchanged for the necessities of life, as well as an animal that occasionally may be converted into mutton . . . and being dependent on a day's labor. The daily wage must necessarily be expended for food at an exorbitantly high price the same day it is received, leaving the laborer poorer at the end of the day than he was at its beginning."[55]

Aftermath

The following previously published statistical information provided in *Both Sides of the Bullpen* draws a quantitative picture of what livestock reduction meant in the Northern and Western Navajo Agencies.[56] By the end of 1938 the mass slaughter of livestock drew to a close, with smaller numbers being removed into the 1940s. The trauma for the Navajo people created through this action was intense, compared by some to the Long Walk period of the 1860s. A few facts and figures from southeastern Utah in the Northern Agency illustrate what happened. During 1930 in the Montezuma Creek and Aneth area, 19,514 sheep and goats passed through dip vats filled with medicine to prevent scabies. The Oljato and Shonto areas produced 43,623 more animals, while some Utah Navajos undoubtedly went to vats at Kayenta, Shiprock, Dennehotso, and Teec Nos Pos. Still others probably skipped the process entirely, but if the totals from Aneth and Oljato areas are combined, at least 63,137 sheep and goats ranged over reservation lands of southeastern Utah.[57]

By 1934 the entire Northern Navajo Agency reported that government officials had killed or sold 70,000 animals and that the Utah Navajos' herds were down to an estimated 36,000.[58] Because the nation was experiencing the depths of the Great Depression, the agent could price a sheep at only $2 and a goat at $1. The annual report went on to say, "An excessive number of goats and sheep were slaughtered for food. There is every reason to believe that the next dipping record will show even a greater reduction than indicated by the number sold."[59] Horses and cattle suffered a similar fate. Garrick and Roberta Bailey note in their economic history of the Navajos that "by the late 1930s, Collier had been successful in implementing most of his policies. . . . Along with the inability of Navajos to secure off-reservation employment, livestock reduction had considerably mined Navajo economic self-sufficiency."[60]

What this meant in actual loss of animals, monetary sums, and sense of well-being will never be fully understood. Tribal figures indicate that dependence on agriculture and livestock had decreased to 57 percent in a little more than a decade, although this figure varied by region, by outfit, and by individual, depending on the extent of the losses.[61] In New Mexico, one study noted that between 1930 and 1935, 61 percent of the goats—the poor Navajos' food staple—were eliminated.[62] Thus a round estimate of 50 percent seems conservative concerning stock loss. To maintain this number of animals grazing on reservation lands, the government in 1936 introduced the Taylor Grazing Act to the Navajos, which divided the land into grazing sections evaluated by how well each one could support a cow, a horse, or five sheep as a unit of measure. The tribal government then allotted a family a permit to graze a certain number of animals on a specific piece of land. This limited Navajo herders to such an extent that very few remained economically self-sufficient. Men left home to earn money; women herded the sheep and goats that were left, wove rugs, and hoped their husbands would return to help keep the family intact. The end result—dependence on the wage economy and a new way of life.

What, then, was the traders' and Navajos' reaction to this sudden, dynamic shift that affected every facet of the trading business? Grace (Bloomfield) Herring put it plainly: "He [John Collier] just wrecked it as far as the livestock is concerned. They aren't like they used to be. There used to be herds and herds and herds out there—they're not there anymore. He really put a damper on that—no good."[63] Most traders sympathized with their Navajo friends but had to be careful, realizing that their relationship with the federal bureaucracy as well as their customers could be jeopardized. Fundamental to the entire system of commerce was the credit extended to families dependent on a yearly cycle. By 1940, traders were offering a third less credit in pawn. Dead pawn went to pay for debts much more quickly. Family heirlooms that had previously remained on the racks of trading posts for extended periods of time were now purchased by tourists or sold to off-reservation buyers who paid cash and made good profits by selling to the general public. As one trader (anonymous) said, "Formerly the head of a family could pawn $250–$300 with the trader. The trader could afford to wait six months between wool clip and lamb sale. He knew exactly what economic conditions the Indians were in. . . . Now there is no economic certainty."[64] Other traders complained of what they saw. From Aneth: "40 percent of families not worth more than $30 a year credit on sheep and wool." From Shiprock: "Pawn being sold off as quick as dead." From Rock Point: "Out of 100 families last season receiving credit—only 20 will get it next season." From Toadlena: "Allowing 50 percent to 75 percent less credit now [1940]. Indians requiring 30 percent more store food. One third of community is allowed no credit at all." To most traders, "The government never considers us on matters of policy. It's just, 'Where's the road to this place?'"[65] They felt that the government had placed too much emphasis on removing the stock without making constructive efforts to improve the herds still in operation.

For those living on the reservation—traders and Navajos alike—the flood, discussed at the beginning of this chapter, had arrived in the form of modern change. In just a twenty-year period, the benefits and drawbacks of contemporary society had invaded Navajo lands, and altered a lifestyle that had been slowly evolving over more than a hundred years. Some of these modifications were desirable and sought after: the automobile and truck, paved roads, expansion of trading posts, unified tribal organization, economic growth and diversity, livestock improvement, and population increase. Other aspects were less desirable—overgrazing and loss of topsoil, livestock reduction, expansion of infectious diseases, dependence on a fickle wage economy and job market, a national depression, and the advent of World War II. The end result of both the positive and negative impacts was that the Navajos were catapulted into the twentieth century and were no longer insular. When markets changed in New York, it affected an Indian in Shiprock. A centralized tribal government approved when and where oil wells would be drilled. It also controlled how many and what type of livestock could graze on a specific parcel of land and what family held the permit to use it. The people elected representatives, creating a campaign and voting system based as much on promises and popularity as it did on long-standing knowledge about who could best lead a community. Money and checks began replacing wool and blankets pushed across the counter, while men and women left the reservation to help in the war effort and returned with an enlarged view of what the world offered that could be integrated into their life. Like the rest of America, the Navajo people became increasingly interested in U.S. consumerism on an ever-broadening scale. While many of the old ways persisted, there were growing expectations that pulled people far away from the more traditional life.

CHAPTER EIGHT

Weaving a Two Grey Hills Rug

Fashioning Excellence through Tradition,
1920 to Present

The events that led to the loss of many traditional Navajo practices also had an impact on weaving in general, and on the production of Two Grey Hills blankets in particular. This chapter discusses the entire procedure—from sheep to loom to sale—of this art form and how weavers think about the process and product they create. Two Grey Hills weaving is considered to be the best of all regional styles found on the reservation in terms of craftsmanship and complexity of design. That is saying a lot, considering that there were at one point over a dozen competing regional styles—Shiprock, Crystal, Lukachukai, Teec Nos Pos, Ganado—to name a few. Here, Two Grey Hills provides the example of what it took to excel, how individual traders and weavers made a difference, and why their products became synonymous with matchless quality.

All of the magnificent art that came from the loom had humble beginnings. Navajo sheep and goats grazing in the Chuska Valley or residing in corrals on a homestead provided the materials and the birthplace for this distinctive accomplishment. Historically, it has been an evolutionary process that was a long time in coming. The Navajos have been involved with livestock for over three centuries, the first substantial number of animals—sheep, goats, cattle, and horses—being appropriated either directly from the Spanish or indirectly through Puebloan groups between 1650 and 1700. The people shifted from their lifestyle as hunters and gatherers to a growing reliance on agriculture and animal husbandry to the point of almost total dependence on these economic resources. From this relationship with livestock came wool production and weaving. The life of a shepherd and the formation of crafts took on a distinctive Navajo flavor, imbued with cultural practices and beliefs.

Humble Beginnings—Caring for Sheep

In Navajo teachings, Changing Woman, that beneficent deity that nurtures and cares for the people, created sheep. In one version of Blessingway lore, the holy people, as they planned for future Five-Fingered Beings, decided to form the animals so that there would be more for humans to live on. After prayers and physical preparation, Changing Woman formed the first sheep, selected a small portion of plant material nearby, added a pinch of fabric and precious stones then rolled the mixture into small balls, inserting it in the animals' cleft hoofs and corners of their eyelids. Speaking to the soon-to-be-Navajos and the holy people, she said, "By means of these, you will be able to live on. Time and again it will transform into fabrics of all kinds and into jewels of all kinds. It represents your pets from the tip of which fabrics and jewels of every description will begin to sprout, thus making life possible for you. And you must plead for them, pray to their feet, their head, pray to their bones." This relationship between man and animal continues today.[1]

Daily life and herding practices assumed the rhythms of the Navajo calendar as seasons, religious ceremonies, and traditional teachings defined what and when things should be done. Careful consideration of animal cycles and physical needs delineated those patterns. The month of October, in Navajo ceremonial thought, was a time of change when summer ceremonies, such as the Enemyway and other warm weather traditions, gave way to those performed when the frost was in the ground such as the Yé'ii Bicheii dance and telling winter stories. Movement from summer camps to winter ranges by this time had also been accomplished, depending on weather conditions. Breeding sheep can only take place during the fall or very early winter, which perfectly matched the Navajos' annual movements, since to have sexual intercourse too early could mean cold weather births and the loss of that year's lamb crop. Shearing sheep and goats was best in March and April before the weather became too hot. This calendar of events gave rise to the two prime times for payment of bills at the trading posts.

Even today, herding is a daily process that consumes a lot of time and energy for a few caretakers. Sheep are gregarious animals that prefer staying bunched in a flock as opposed to goats, who are more adventurous, harder to control, and less finicky as to what they eat. One or two individuals can control a herd of sheep as they gently graze over the land, and so children might assume this task as early as the age of eight, while an elderly grandmother astride a horse with a few dogs to keep predators away and the animals moving, is also able to control several hundred sheep.[2] As the animals eat and move toward water and better range, the herders guide that movement so that the flock is able to return to home base without the need to be driven for long distances. This is an important point. Navajo beliefs prefer that the animals, if at all possible, be corralled by night, since evil influences as well as predators like coyotes lurk in the dark. Thus the sheep are often moved out of the pen at sunrise, allowed to graze, and then put back into their corral by midmorning, then taken out in mid-to-late afternoon for a second feeding.

If water and fresh grass is the goal, it is not uncommon to let them drift all day with a round trip of ten miles. In other instances such as driving the herd to a trading post for sale or distant dipping vats, a canyon or some other holding area would be used at night. In the days before easy wagon access, and later pickup trucks and windmills, water was a driving influence, one sheep requiring roughly four gallons a day in the summer.[3] Terrain dictated techniques and the number of people involved; when caring for sheep in the woods on the Chuska-Tunicha range, more people and tighter control of the flock was important. Navajo youth soon began learning from older people and from experience how to manage their flocks. Winter and early lamb births in the spring presented their own set of problems.

Navajo people identify closely with their flocks on both a collective and individual-animal basis. As with so many things in their universe, the owners establish a relationship with the sheep, know their personalities, and know when they are missing. A Navajo cultural belief posits that as long as the owner takes good care of the animal and shows respect, a sheep will provide the wool and meat required of them. The status of a family, individual pride, and a sense of belonging is reflected in the number and condition of the animals in the herd. Mutton is the meat of choice, eaten at a four-to-one ratio of sheep over goat. "Mutton hunger is a recognized condition of Navajos who must live away from the family herds. 'I want some fresh mutton,' means that the speaker, in fact, does want some mutton to eat, but it also carries the connotation of homesickness."[4] This bond helps explain the emotional trauma associated with the Livestock Reduction period, as well as the older practice of singing a protection song, on a daily basis, that starts with the first animal out of the corral in the morning and ends with the last one to exit. The relationship continues at shearing time, when each owner takes care of his or her own sheep.

Wool as a Way to Wealth

Enough has been provided here to give a sense of the bonds created within a family for its flock and its personal nature derived from this lifestyle. A well-known phrase, "sheep is life," became a subtitle for a program that started in the 1990s to restore high grades of wool to Navajo weavers on the reservation and the name of an annual meeting to discuss its progress. To the Navajos, however, it has meaning beyond the economic sense by encapsulating a worldview centered on a relationship that started four hundred years ago. The history of sheep and the wool they produce provides a parallel image to much of the story of the Navajo people. What follows is a condensed chronology of what has happened to Navajo wool and how it has had an effect on weaving as it parallels events already discussed.

Four hundred years ago, as the Spanish entered and settled the Southwest, they brought with them the distinctive breed of churro sheep that thrived in a desert environment of grass and rough terrain. Navajos quickly realized the benefit in obtaining these animals for food and wool, and so trade and raid became the practical means to obtain them. Spanish rancheros, pueblo Indian communities, and eventually Mexican and Anglo livestock owners were prime sources for animals that disappeared with Navajo raiders interested in expanding their herds by hundreds of thousands. Churro sheep composed the bulk of this stock. Then came the Long Walk period. Like the Navajos who were pursued by every neighboring tribe and Anglo-Hispanic forces, these animals also became the target for reduction or control. Large numbers of livestock were killed, captured and sold, or otherwise removed from

Navajo ownership so that by the time the Navajos returned from Fort Sumner, their herds had to be greatly replenished. The government decided to give the returning Indians 14,000 sheep to join the flocks of churros never captured.

Beginning as early as 1859, however, a program of cross-breeding with merino, and later Rambouillet sheep, had begun, and it would greatly affect the amount and type of wool available for Navajo use. Flocks increased rapidly, and as the government continued to monitor the situation, it introduced more merinos and Rambouillet sheep, all with an eye to help the Navajo economy, which was primarily centered on sending the wool clip to eastern markets. Lyle McNeal, a contemporary advocate for churro sheep, suggested that Navajo agents viewed the scrubby "Navajo sheep" as not providing the best type of wool for weaving and as not being great meat producers. The fewer the better, so introducing more productive breeds became the plan to assist the Indians on their path into the twentieth century. Livestock Reduction of the 1930s was a culmination of this attitude, where "Navajo sheep" were targeted for elimination, since they were viewed as being among the least desirable in an inflated livestock economy.[5]

What this change meant to traditional Navajo weavers would not start to be realized until the U.S. Department of Agriculture, Bureau of Animal Industry conducted a study completed in January 1942. For years, people had noticed a decline in the quality of textiles produced by the Navajos. Fully aware that wool and weaving were still of great importance even after stock reduction, the bureau set out to determine the reason for the deterioration. The resulting thirty-six-page study, written in detailed scientific terms, quantified the information that Navajo weavers had been aware of for decades.[6] The manuscript noted that approximately 750,000 pounds of wool or one-fourth of the total use of this material was turned into blankets or rugs that brought to the weavers $385,000 annually.[7] Central to the decline was the quality of wool available for production. James O. Grandstaff, chief investigator, studied Navajo textiles, which he categorized into four major time periods of weaving, starting around 1800 and ending in 1915. To these eras, he applied six physical criteria for the quality of wool found in rugs and blankets—fineness of fiber, length, shrinkage, crimp (waviness), oil/lanolin, and kemp (inner short, coarse, nonelastic fiber located under the longer, outer wool). The ideal for a weaver was to have long, straight fibers, with a minimum of lanolin, and a porosity in the fiber that absorbed dyes.

Grandstaff's conclusions were important, given the general direction that the government, although well-intentioned, had pushed the Navajos. The best period of weaving, defined as producing the highest quality blankets and rugs, had been between 1850 and 1890. One of the reasons for this superiority depended on the quality of wool being used. The design, dyes and colors, quality of workmanship, and intended use of product were other considerations in the evaluation—but the wool was what made it possible. The answer, spelled out in clear terms, that it was the "Navajo sheep," the ones the agents tried to replace or breed out with merino and Rambouillet, that had given the era its winning success. The churro had "small fleeces of open, light-shrinking wool containing a mixture of short, fine undercoat fibers and long, coarse outercoat fibers and kemp fibers. The wool also has less crimp than most improved wools. . . . Navajo wool of medium fineness had the most desirable length and proportion of undercoat and outercoat fibers for satisfactory carding and spinning and produced the best textured rug. . . . The openness of fleece and the low percentage of grease [lanolin] and crimp in the fibers in Navajo wool greatly facilitated its manufacture by hand methods."[8] This was directly opposite the wool of the Rambouillet that since the 1920s had introduced "short-stapled, heavy-shrinking wool with a well-defined crimp" and a good deal of grease that was very difficult to remove by boiling. Given the simple hand tools used by the Navajo weaver to create a blanket, these inherent drawbacks in the "improved" wool led only to inferior products made out of uneven and lumpy yarn that was also weaker when compared to earlier wool and weavings.

The number of Navajo sheep was also in decline—by 1952 only 36 percent of sheep remained, compared to the amount owned in 1930. Even more telling was that by the late 1970s, there were only 450 churro sheep of the original stock still found on the reservation.[9] Enter Lyle McNeal, a Utah State University professor in Animal, Dairy, and Veterinary Sciences, who noted the need and began the Navajo Sheep Project (NSP) in 1978. The first animals that he identified as original stock churro were in the Shiprock area, although he scoured other parts of the reservation for additional breeding stock. This is important to

Churro sheep have a four-horn configuration that gives them a distinctive appearance. Well adapted to a desert environment, their wool is particularly important for weavers creating rugs and blankets in the regional style of Two Grey Hills, which uses naturally colored—white, gray, brown, and black— wool. Here, Ed Davies has found an alternative use. Courtesy of Two Grey Hills Trading Post Archive Collection.

note because Two Grey Hills weaving is very dependent on naturally colored, undyed wool coming directly from the sheep. As Jan Dohner, wool enthusiast and admirer of Two Grey Hills weaving, pointed out, "Churro wool comes in a wide range of natural colors. The sheep grow fleeces in solid and spotted shades of black, apricot, cream, gray and a rare and treasured brown. These natural shades—reflecting the colors of the desert—form the basis of the palette of the Navajo weaver." Dohner also indicated how important the availability of this wool was to Two Grey Hills weavers.[10]

McNeal's project began with six churro ewes and two rams, but by 1994, could boast more than 800 registered churros found throughout the United States, a large concentration of which was on the Navajo Reservation.[11] The organization continued to give training to Navajos in animal breeding, nutrition, sheep and range management, shearing, preparation, packaging and marketing of wool and lamb, and other educational programs. The ultimate goal was to create more self-sufficiency for the Navajos and to develop a twenty-first-century economy from a historic heritage. The NPS also gave rise to a second Navajo organization—Diné bi Iina—or Navajo Way of Life, that instructs and encourages the use of traditional teachings and practices. Central to this group are the care of churro sheep and the processing of their wool.

Dyeing to Be an Artist

While many weavers in the Two Grey Hills area do as much as they can with wool coming directly from the sheep, there are others who use dyes to color the yarn or buy already dyed wool. The introduction of synthetic dyes from the trading post has already been discussed, but a brief look at natural, vegetal dyes will add another dimension to the artistry of the weaver. The Navajos use over thirty different plants to obtain the colors desired in weaving, each plant having its own process and additives to successfully dye the wool. Certain minerals and clays are also used. Here, a brief overview of general activities and a few specific examples provide a glimpse at this traditional practice and what it takes to be successful. Applicable in all instances is the relationship that the weaver has with the plant as she sets about to obtain what is needed. Generally, as when plants are picked for religious, medicinal, or food purposes, a healthy specimen of that species is given an offering of special ground stones and shells (*ntł'iz*) and a prayer is rendered that identifies the person requesting the assistance, how the plant will be used, and the desired outcome—in this case, success in creating beautiful colors. This plant becomes the representative to witness that proper respect has been shown so that the request may be granted. The woman then leaves that plant and harvests others nearby for the intended purpose. Any remains that are not used are buried.[12]

With materials in hand, the weaver is ready to begin the lengthy process of preparing the wool. Each individual may have their own secrets or different ways of working with wool, just as each dyed batch may have its own shades and tones, but the general process is fairly standard.[13] After shearing the wool from a sheep, the fleece must be cleaned. This includes removing all sticks, dirt, and droppings. Depending on the qualities and condition of the product, the weaver next has a choice as to how to do a more detailed and technical cleaning. Dry-clean wool is obtained by immersing the newly-clipped fleece in white clay or crushed gypsum dissolved in water, then hanging on bushes or rocks the thoroughly soaked material to dry in small batches in the sun. The wool turns from a creamy yellow to a brighter white and is smoother than that which is washed, the second technique.

Washing wool, which requires a thorough cleaning because of more dirt and lanolin, meant using either narrow leaf (*Yucca gluaca*) or broad leaf (*Yucca bacata*) yucca. The root of these plants can be either used fresh or stored, but must be crushed and swished in water to have it lather. The solution removes the dirt and grease, but the wool is not pressed or twisted hard, just floated loosely in the water and not wrung dry, otherwise it forms lumps. Once removed, the wool is thoroughly rinsed and dried, then carded using two carding combs (*bee ha'nilchaadí*) and spun into yarn. The tighter the spin on the hand spindle (*bee'adizí*), the tighter the yarn. Some weavers spin their wool two or three times to get a product that is strong and compacted for a tighter weave. Two Grey Hills rugs are famous for their tightness and their natural wools that have been highly worked.

Gathering the dyes for weaving is an art all by itself. Nonabah Bryan, as recorded by Stella Young in 1940, gives a memorable description of some of the work she did in collecting the dyes for a year of weaving. Time, season, distance, and knowledge came together in a complex understanding of what to do. Young recounted how Bryan selected the materials she had gathered one by one at the proper season over the past year. From the higher elevations came mountain mahogany root dug in the early fall, which gave the strongest color after digging, pounding, and drying the bark. Toward the end of September she traveled to the nearest mesa, where she picked the red fruit of the prickly pear, rubbed it in the sand to remove the stickers, and brought it home to dry. Ocher came from a coal mine twenty-five miles distant, while piñon pitch came from the foothills of the mountains nearby, where she gathered cans full of it one day on her way home from a squaw dance. Several rolls of dried sumac had come during the summer from the arroyo at the back of the Wingate school. Sagebrush was no problem because it grew all around her home and remained green all winter. Her whitener, gypsum, she found in some shale near a coal deposit.[14] Weavers needed to read the land and its resources.

Dyeing wool is not an exact science. For instance, the same species of plants grown in two separate areas may render different shades of the same color. If a mordant is used to fix a color, it may deepen or change it; the amount and type used can also create a difference. Longer boiling may deepen the color as does longer submersion in the dye; the season in which a root or plant is obtained could provide a different color; and if it became necessary to use another type of plant or mineral to cast the same color, there was no guarantee of a match. Bryan put it succinctly: "The old Navajo had no exact measurements and even today [1940] on the reservation only approximate measures are used. Cactus fruit, plants and the barks of various trees are measured in pans, sumac and Navajo tea are made into rolls, rugs are so many hand-lengths in size. Sufficient supplies of either wool or dye materials were seldom on hand so they used what they had. If in the early spring, the supply of wool was depleted, a strip a few inches wide was sheared along either side of the backbone of the sheep. More could not be taken lest the animal die of cold. For these reasons, every rug was an experiment."[15] Given these conditions, the wonder is how the Two Grey Hills weavers and others produced such technically perfect work.

Relationships—Loom, Yarn, and Weaver

Once the weaver has dyed her yarn and then dried it, it is rolled into a ball and brought to her loom. In Charles Amsden's *Navaho Weaving*, an accepted classic on the topic since first published in 1934, one finds a chapter devoted to the construction and use of the Navajo loom.[16] Archaeologists believe that this rectangular upright loom (*dah'iistp'ǫ*), made of juniper or preferably piñon, and capable of being used either inside or outside, originated with the prehistoric Puebloan cultures—the ancestors of the Hopi, Zuni, and other tribes—of the Southwest.[17] Inside this frame are the moveable parts of the loom including a tension bar that allows the weaver to loosen or tighten the vertical warp strings so that as she sits at the loom, she can move the rug downward as she weaves upward. Various other pieces of wood, serving as a shed rod, heddle, and batten separate the warp strings so that the yarn (weft) can be woven into it, moving from left to right across the loom. A weaving fork or comb (*bee'adzooí*) tamps the yarn as different colors are interspersed to form a design.[18]

The Navajos have a different explanation of how the loom and weaving originated as gifts from Spider Man and Spider Woman. There are a number of different versions of how the process started, with one telling how before the Navajos emerged into this world, Spider Man and his wife obtained the seeds of a fine fibrous plant they called cotton. The couple instructed the Navajos that they were to grow this plant, and that from it they would make clothes and not have to use the skins of animals. Once they obtained the fiber, they made a spindle with a round disk on it to spin it into a strong thread for weaving. "Then the chief medicine woman said: 'You must spin towards your person, as you wish to have the beautiful goods come to you; do not spin away from you.' For it was in their minds to make cloth which they could trade for shell and turquoise beads and she knew their thoughts. She said: 'You must spin towards you, or the beautiful goods will depart from you.'"[19]

Spider Man assumed the task of making the loom, just as this is the responsibility of men to do today. The upper cross pole was made from the sky, the lower one from earth. He fashioned the warp sticks from sunrays, the upper strings holding the warp to the pole from lightning, the lower strings from sun halo, the heald from rock crystal and sheet lightning, which he secured to the warp strands with rain ray cords. A comb of white shell; spindles of cannel coal, turquoise, abalone, and white bead; spindle sticks of various forms of lightning; black, blue, yellow, and white winds powered the spindles, which allowed them to "travel all around the world."[20] Little wonder that with an object so powerful, weavers were cautioned to weave in moderation. Other customs arose: when a girl baby was born, her hands and arms were rubbed with a spider's web found over a hole in the ground so that she will not tire from weaving; a woman should not hit a person with her weaving tools, the receiver will become paralyzed; spanking a child with weaving tools will make him or her sick; and the loom should not stand too long—it will tire and hurt the weaver.[21] A sense of relationship between loom and weaver pervades the act of creation.

Thus, a traditional Navajo woman will settle down to her loom, sitting on the calves of her legs, soles of her feet pointed up, and weave for hours. But it is not merely a matter of making a rug or blanket to sell for those who follow the old ways—it is a continuation of relationships. Navajo weavers at Two Grey Hills and elsewhere stress that they are thinking, singing, and praying the world into existence. One woman said, "All weavers talk about the great amount of thinking they do for each rug. When you set up your loom, it is like giving birth; weaving the rug is like raising the child and then you want to put it in a good home for a good life;" another woman added, "When a rug is sold, the weaver is selling part of herself."[22] Yet another person felt, "The rug has songs and prayers too. It's got some good songs in it. So you don't mess around with a rug; it's very sacred. I should learn how to sing the weaving songs, but I haven't yet. When you finish your rug, you always say a prayer that will help you again. I do that."[23] Most Navajo weavers agree that there is a special bond between them and what they create that transcends the physical world.

A good example of the relationship that a weaver has with a rug, and which very much supports the previous quotes, is found in the weaving of a "spirit trail," or "pathway." Noël Bennett, an avid scholar and practitioner of weaving, studied this phenomena found in Navajo textiles and explains why so many weavers introduce it into their work. The spirit trail is a line of contrasting color found in rugs with borders. This line of yarn, often concealed, goes from the background through the selvage, or outer edge, of the fabric and is frequently located in the upper right corner of the piece. Since typical Two Grey Hills rugs and blankets, as well as baskets, have a border, this topic is particularly relevant.

Early traders noted the frequency of incorporating this practice. In 1930 Dane and Mary Coolidge estimated that seven out of eight rugs they examined at trading posts contained a break or "trail" hidden in the border. Forty years later, a sampling of holdings at nine different posts suggested a sizable decrease in the practice—of 175 bordered rugs, only 20 (less than 12 percent) had a "pathway."[24] The Coolidges suggested the reason for the decline was that fewer weavers were following traditional teachings. What was the pathway's initial purpose? The words used in English and Navajo to describe it offer an interesting contrast in explaining how it is viewed. The white man used such words as "Spirit Trail" and "Devil's Road or Highway," exemplifying the belief that evil spirits would remain in the rug upon completion and could not escape unless there was a pathway. Certainly in Navajo religious beliefs, openings are left in ceremonial practices, physical movements, and art creations to allow a flow of spirit in and out of the object or event.

Navajo weavers, however, use four different words—path, door or way out, woven out, and my mind's road—to describe what they have created. There is no sense of evil in any of these terms, because the pathway is to allow the thoughts of the weaver to leave. This brings peace of mind after weaving so much of one's thought into the rug; it prevents blindness, sickness, weakness, and an inability to weave successfully in the future from taking place. Excessive weaving, becoming obsessed in thought, loss of creativity, or weaving oneself into the rug can all be avoided by putting the pathway in so that one can remain free from these problems. Otherwise, a Blessingway (Hózhǫ́jí) ceremony is needed to remove the bad influence. Bennett summarized nicely the reason for this "mind's road" in weaving: "And so a complex concept emerges from a seemingly simple line—a concept involving the weaver's fear that in channeling all her energies and mental resources into a rug with an enclosing border, she may encircle and thereby entrap her spirit, mind, energies, and design. In jeopardy are future loom experiences: the continued use of design, the well-being of weaving muscles, and of paramount concern, her vision and sanity. The moment of Pathway is a moment of liberation, of peace, of security—and a wish for the future: may the next weaving be even better."[25]

There are other beliefs that illustrate the very personal nature of weaving. Some artisans tell of how designs appear to them in dreams, how they see designs and patterns in the world around them, and how they become mentally saturated with the process. One weaver said, "My rugs are like my children, with individual personalities and needs" and later compared the pathway as "an umbilicus whose break gives independent life to the newly emerged rug."[26] Shirley Brown, a contemporary Two Grey Hills weaver who does not follow many of the more traditional practices, still has an intimate experience at the loom. At first she explained the mechanical nature of what she did—evaluating how much yarn she had, the colors, size of the loom, and possible designs and layout. But once the process started, she described the emerging rug as a part of her that gets woven in. "Sometimes I feel like doing it and sometimes I don't. I guess it just depends on how I'm feeling or I'll just keep all of my feelings a secret and weave in a spirit line. . . . Then I feel free and just let go of all my problems or whatever I'm feeling that I wove into the rug, and you know that things are okay."[27]

Shirley wove in not only her feelings, but also some design elements that reminded her of a cherished granddaughter, who then became part of the rug. Other people and events became connected to elements and patterns she created, serving as a mnemonic device of that part of her life as the yarn played across the loom. Problems with a husband, the joys of family life, the time the sheep strayed away, when her son struggled with cancer—her life was just as embedded in the rug as the various colors and tightness of weave. To her, the rug had a spirit, and to intentionally damage it was both an emotional and physical attack on her well-being. Shirley also told of taking a picture of her work, sometimes wishing she had not sold it. Then, "No matter, because I needed the money so it is done, and it's over with. Just cherish the picture. So I go back to the pictures and I sometimes think, 'This is what I was feeling. This is what was going on in my life, you know, I made it through and I'm okay and it's okay and things like that.'"[28]

Identifying and Evaluating a Two Grey Hills Rug

The remainder of this chapter turns to the woven products of Two Grey Hills—what these icons in weaving look like, the influence of traders on this distinctive regional style, and what the weavers gain from their creative process. Expert weavers, accomplished traders, and knowledgeable art critics have provided many detailed descriptions of what, generally, are the identifying characteristics of a Two Grey Hills rug. Anthropologist and weaver Gladys Reichard mentions the near absence of the color red; a border composition of either black, gray, white, or brown—all natural colors that come from wool; and the symmetrical balance—either bilateral or quadrilateral—of many small elements woven into the rug, leaving little space unfilled. The tight yarn and weaving provides some of the best work on the reservation.[29] While each weaver determines the compactness of the weave, an average weft count for many rugs is less than 80 strands per inch, but some Two Grey Hills rugs have been counted up to 110 per inch.[30] The spun materials are so thin and tight that they are more like a wall hanging (tapestry) or blanket than a rug. Weaving expert Gilbert S. Maxwell adds to Reichard's observation by saying, "The blacks, whites, grays, and browns [are] woven into sophisticated patterns—small geometric groupings balanced in the final symmetrical whole. The Two Grey Hills rug is also characterized by a black border. It can be said of this rug that the 4x6 foot size is pretty much the standard."[31]

Anthropologist Ann Hedlund sees the designs on a Two Grey Hills rug and the border spaces being placed evenly according to scale, creating "an easy rhythm that allows the eye to move equally from the rug's corners to center and back. Frequently there is a play between positive and negative spaces. Background and foreground become interchangeable. Often a playfulness shows up with geometric illusions of three dimensions and with designs running beyond the edges."[32] A variety of elements found in an ever-increasing repertoire of design include steps, diamonds, plain and complex crosses, reversed swastikas, plain and recurved frets, stars, rhomboids, hooks, triangles, squares, and rectangles. Pictorial rugs also woven in the area draw upon forms of the everyday world. The overall design of a rug has a central image often made with a single or double diamond. "It is formed of larger or smaller steps, or is a smooth-edged band, or is outlined by some geometric form, as solid triangles or other outline figure. There may be projections from the great diamond, in the form of hooks or stepped triangles. Within the dominant figure there is simpler or more elaborate patterning, as another diamond with hooks, triangles, or frets emanating from it. . . . Corner designs in the Two Grey Hills rugs are usually made up of more or less triangular figures with straight sides paralleling the two edges of the blanket and a stepped interior side. Variety in this seemingly simple motif is endless."[33]

While the tremendous creative talent of Navajo weavers is abundantly apparent in their products of the loom, traders and the Anglo market also played a role that cannot be ignored. Returning to the posts of the early 1900s and some, by now, familiar names—Moore, Davies, Bloomfield, Herring, Newcomb—one can trace the influence these men had in shaping designs and quality. J. B. Moore, trading at Crystal, gives a prime example of providing guidance to Navajo weavers to improve their product and boost their sales. Rather than sit idly behind the counter waiting to see what slid across the wooden boards, he actively worked with weavers to introduce design elements and technically improve the $13,000 worth of rugs he dealt with each year.[34] As noted previously, 25 percent of the wool used in these rugs he collected, sent back east for cleaning and carding, had shipped back to him, and then distributed to his best weavers. The reason for this expensive and inefficient endeavor is now obvious—the women making rugs could not thoroughly clean the wool because of the oil introduced by the new merino and Rambouillet strains, which meant that dyes would either not adhere or were uneven in color. Also, the tight curl found in this clip was very difficult to remove when hand carded, requiring an industrial machine to straighten the crimp.

Moore explained how difficult it was for Navajo people to gather dyes to color the wool and why the old process of dyeing had given way to the store-bought consistency of aniline dyes. In 1911 he wrote "Practically no [native dyes] are used now. . . . At the cost of a great deal of pain and labor, for a brief season of each year they can get, and used to do so, a bright yellow color from the flower of a certain weed, but very rarely is this done now. And, early with the coming of the Spaniards, they got the indigo for their blue dye, and by combining this with their native yellow would get a peculiar shade of green. But always the yellow and the green were used very sparingly on account of the difficulty in getting them. They never had a red vegetable dye, but do now, and at times then, no doubt will use a dull and dingy red procured from some mineral kind of clay paint rock occasionally found on the reservation. But for their red color at all times they have depended upon the white man; First, the old time bayeta or flannel introduced by the Spaniards, unraveled, recarded and spun furnished them the color and later, the red dyes sold by the traders to them. Practically all of the blanket work of the present is done in the trade dyes now on the market and has been for years."[35] By having wool that was uniformly dyed in soft water, not generally found on the reservation, and under more controlled conditions found in a factory environment, 25 percent of the weavers selling to Moore could obtain a more refined product. Still, the real problem for the trader was marketing. Moore saw no issue in getting the blankets or rugs made, but moving them in sales was the key to any profit. As previously mentioned, he estimated that traders and wholesalers had at least $200,000 to $250,000 worth of woven products waiting to be bought at the cost paid to the weavers. No trader could function under these conditions without a strong buying market.[36]

Fast forward fifty years (1960) to trader Don Jensen, who had been working at Crystal since 1944. He painted a far different picture as to the weavers and sales in this same area. He estimated that in his region there were fifty women who considered themselves weavers, twelve to fifteen of whom were really good.[37] By this time, the quantity of rugs that he traded had decreased by 25 to 30 percent; when he first arrived, perhaps one in five rugs was vegetal dyed—now they were almost all that way. Jensen, over six feet tall, said that when he first entered the post's back room, blankets "used to be piled as high as my head. Now they are taken as fast as I can get them." Black was the only aniline dye he sold because it was hard to have a consistent color if depending solely on the natural shades of black found in sheep's wool. Seventy-three-year-old weaver Desba Nez believed she was the first woman in the area to use vegetal dyes, beginning around 1940.[38] She experimented with coloring starting with the dyes used on Navajo moccasins and then expanded her palette. What she received at this time for an eight-by-ten-foot rug of excellent quality was $400 to $500.[39]

Before moving next to the Ed Davies and George Bloomfield era, when the fabrics from Two Grey Hills developed into a distinctive regional style, one cannot totally leave behind the strong influence of what was taking place at Crystal. It set the stage for these next two men, working in harmony together, to introduce many of their own ideas, taking their art form to an unprecedented height. Although a rug of Two Grey Hills origin has been documented as one of the first of its kind and was purchased in 1910, this regional style did not really get started until around 1915.[40] Davies's grandchildren remember it hanging in the store as an example of what the trader pointed to for encouraging other weavers. Bloomfield and Davies, as with Moore in his area, picked out the best craftswomen trading at their posts and consciously worked with them through gentle criticism and rigorous evaluation to improve quality, technique, and design. Rather than buy a rug in the store, the trader would take a weaver into his house, away from the other customers, to discuss in detail what was good and what could be improved. They also took sherds from Puebloan pottery that had new designs such as the fret and step motif, now so typical of the Two Grey Hills style. Bloomfield

Marketing products from the reservation has always been a concern of both traders and weavers. The Shiprock Fair was one of the first unified attempts to display Navajo artistry to tourists and the general public for home decoration as well as practical use items. This 1912 photo (above) shows a developing Two Grey Hills weaving style. Courtesy of Susan E. Woods Family Photo Collection. Pictured below are the booths sponsored by various posts and the products developed by the residents from their region. Northern Arizona University, Cline Library Staplin Collection, NAU.PH.2000.48.3

wrote, "They soon caught on and then we took pictures of the best rugs and got the weavers to put the best patterns in their next rug. We paid more for the good ones and that surely appealed to them. In a few years we had what was called 'Two Grey Hills' rugs and commenced to get prizes on them at fairs in Shiprock. We encouraged the weavers to use only black, white, and native brown wool, [and] also never to use cotton warp. We first bought the rugs by the pound, but soon bought them by size, weave, and pattern. . . . We saw their rugs grow from a dollar a pound to $500 to a thousand dollars for a rug."[41]

Bloomfield credits Mrs. Tauga-Clitso (Dághá Clitso—Yellow Mustache) as being the first in his area to weave a Two Grey Hills rug and win first prize at Shiprock. A common size for rugs of this style is four by six feet, with the largest one that Bloomfield knew of being nine by twelve feet.[42] He and Davies, early on, also instituted the use of the characteristic black border, feeling that by framing the internal designs, the rug looked better. Promoter Fred Harvey agreed, leaving a standing order for all that Davies and Bloomfield could provide. These men's concerns for their Navajo neighbors—in Bloomfield's words—"They are my people and I am all out for their advancement"—gave reason for them to "work so hard on them [the rugs]."[43]

The Weavers

The tradition of counseling and working with the weavers continued when George sold the Toadlena store to his son-in-law Charles Herring in 1942, and he held on to the business until 1956. One day, Gilbert S. Maxwell approached Herring about a rug woven by a skilled weaver named Daisy Tauglechee (Dághá Łichíí—Red Mustache), forty-five years old at that time, who lived a mile from the store. Maxwell was often visiting the area to buy large quantities of rugs for his company, Maxwell and Sons, located in Farmington. He bought Daisy's rug, took it on tour to Albuquerque and Santa Fe, and returned enthused with its reception. During the trip, interested people calculated a 16-warp-per-inch and 80-weft-per-inch thread count. This was a high-quality weave, but Herring was not satisfied, wondering what could be done to improve it. The answer: maybe moving the warp to 20 and keeping the weft at 80. After thinking about it for a while, the trader waited for Daisy to appear at the store, then asked if she was interested in improving her already excellent weaving. She agreed. Herring remembers, "I took a pad, ruler, and pencil and marked off a section on the piece of paper indicating the size of the loom that would be set up to weave the rug on. I told her I would show her how she could improve, marked off the inches, and put pencil marks indicating the warp and weft. Then I told her that when she strung up the next loom, to put at least 20 warp per inch, or more, on it. Then I told her to spin the yarn for her weft just as fine as she possibly could and still get her string to hold together. Well, that is what she did. As a result, she obtained the quality of a rug to have as high as 24 or 26 warp per inch, and from 80 to as high as 130 weft per inch. This type of rug is classed as a tapestry. It is as fine of quality as yard goods."[44] The fact that she had previously created some of the best and most technically proficient rugs to date, did not prevent her from obtaining an even higher achievement. Herring boasted that he became the only one that she would sell to, and Daisy received excellent compensation for her efforts in comparison to the price of other rugs at the time. This was around 1950 when a Two Grey Hills rug thirty-three by forty-four inches might retail at $2,000. Maxwell observed that ten years later, the price had increased 100 percent. When asked if there were now rugs superior to those of Two Grey Hills, he responded that there were extremely high quality weavings made with vegetal dyed wool coming from Wide Ruins, Chinle, Sawmill, and Nazlini using red, black, white, and gray; if a person liked rainbow colors, Teec Nos Pos had fine examples, but "there are no rugs to compare with Daisy's," and none commanded a better price.[45]

Success could also breed contention and mistrust. Herring tells of an incident when a Navajo woman entered the store with a small rug she wanted to use as payment for a previous debt and to get some groceries. The two haggled over the price, but eventually reached a settlement, which zeroed her account and gave her some remaining cash. The trader continued with his business, then noticed that she had gone behind the counter, taken the rug, and moved to the front of the store. Herring inquired what was wrong, she claimed that he had not paid a fair price, and that she was taking her weaving back. He hopped over the counter, retrieved the rug, and said that he would hold it until she paid her debt and returned his money. One reason for the conflict was that a group of people milling around the store goaded her on by saying the trader had cheated her. There can be a lot of social pressure brought on to community members by their peers, and this woman had succumbed to it. After thinking about it for some time and waiting for those people to leave the store, the woman let the transaction stand. Herring understood the type of jealousy mixed with pride she was feeling, stating that the Navajo people could be very effective in that way.[46]

An excellent example of rising above all such pressures and performing far beyond established norms is seen in the weaving and recording of ceremonial sandpaintings by Navajo women at the turn of the century and by Hosteen Klah (Hastiin Tłah) somewhat later. It is interesting to note that the Northern Navajo Reservation—from Shiprock to Chaco Canyon and the Chuska Valley—was the earliest location for this tradition-bending practice, and traders provided the catalyst. According to Navajo religious beliefs, a sandpainting image that depicts the holy people and other sacred symbols should not last longer than the period that the picture is in use for healing—generally characterized from sunrise to sundown or sundown to sunrise. To ignore this cardinal rule is to invite sickness and possible death brought on by offended holy people. However, if a medicine man performs a propitiating ceremony, the taboo is lifted and the weaver will not be punished. Many of the first Yé'ii rugs were woven by the wives of medicine men who controlled such power.

Shiprock trader Will Evans tells of Fat One's Son (Neesk'áhí Biye'), a powerful healer, whose wife and daughters were expert weavers who specialized in reproducing various sandpaintings in rugs. To other Navajos, copying these sacred images carried serious risks including the weaver becoming blind and suffering an early and painful death. These women were taking terrible chances, and so it was not surprising when Fat One's Son came to Evans and said, "During the period of many sleeps my women have made the Yé'ii Bicheii and sandpainting blankets and sold them to you. My wife's health is not good. She is failing. I fear the effects of the sacred designs and I will hold a sing for her benefit. Will you help me?"[47]

The trader said he would and gave a liberal supply of coffee, sugar, flour, and baking powder to the old man, an allowance that aided him materially in entertaining the company that was present at the "sing." Fat

One's Son then sent for a noted medicine man from across the range, and during a period of three days they sang, used their sacred objects, and made sandpaintings. There was a continuous feast for visitors arriving from time to time. A stout horse, several goats, and two or three muttons were consumed, together with the donated flour, coffee, sugar, and other food brought by friends and relatives.

At the end of three days, Fat One's Son said, "It is finished. The medicine has worked. My women will be protected." The sing proved beneficial to his wife, who continued to weave sandpainting blankets. She and her daughters and daughters-in-law were preserved from evil due to the ceremony, but when he died, there were no more medicine blankets from the looms of his women; their protection and shield was gone. Evans closed his thoughts on what he had observed by honoring the good work done by these women.

There were others who found themselves in similar circumstances. As traders adjusted to market pressures driven by tourism, they approached weavers to put pictures of holy people as depicted in sandpaintings into their rugs and blankets. In those early days, some weavers traveled long distances to avoid the ostracism and keep their identity secret.[48] Rebecca M. Valette, Navajo textile expert, traces the first known such blanket back to Win Wetherill, while he worked as a trader at Two Grey Hills in 1902. Since his brother, Richard, and wife, Marietta, were in deep financial trouble, he gave this first-of-a-kind blanket to Marietta as a birthday present, hoping that she could sell it for a handsome profit. The name of the weaver, the wife of a medicine man, was not given, but the fact that she and her husband were now, "by the vengeance of the gods as the Navajos think" because of her work, added selling value to the five-by-eight-foot blanket—since "no Navajo woman will make another."[49] As a favor, Win brought the blanket to the Saint Louis Fair in 1904 and sold it for $1,000, a very high price for the time, since most blankets then were bringing in between $30 and $60. Other early figure blankets came from Gallegos Canyon, Hogback, Ojo Alamo, and Newcomb trading posts. Franc Newcomb knew of a rug purchased by John Wetherill sometime before 1906, stating, "The first ceremonial blanket of which we have any record was a copy of a painting from the Shooting Chant, called 'The House of Winds.' It was made by a woman living at Raton Springs, and the feeling against it was so great in her own locality that she was obliged to carry it 60 miles to the trading post at Ojo Alamo where she sold it to Mr. John Wetherill. The Indians to whom this rug was shown at the Wetherill trading post were very much upset, and predicted that some calamity would visit this section of the country."[50]

In 1919, Franc Newcomb moved center stage in normalizing the use of sandpainting figures in weaving. As mentioned in other chapters, Hosteen Klah was an extremely powerful medicine man who befriended Arthur and Franc and not only helped them with trading post activities, but provided Franc with over five hundred pictures of sandpaintings and associated figures. He was also a hermaphrodite and so shared both the male world of powerful ceremonies and the female world of weaving, the two coming together in his portrayal of figures usually left alone. Born in 1867, Klah learned to weave while quite young and copied a design from an Ancestral Puebloan mountain sheep blanket found by archaeologists in a cave on Cabezon Mountain in 1893. In 1910 he copied a fragment from another blanket found in Chaco Canyon; in 1915 a museum curator asked him to weave an entire rug using the design elements from the fragment. It took an entire summer, but Klah, his sister, and grandmother each contributed their expertise in making the nine-by-eleven-foot rug.[51]

Klah was an iconoclast, because he could afford to be—he knew the songs and prayers that kept him safe. From a traditional Navajo perspective, handling, copying, and re-creating materials from Ancient Puebloan culture fostered some very real problems that connected the dead, evil thoughts, witchcraft, and other antisocial values to these products. One of the central teachings about why these earlier people were destroyed revolves around their taking designs given to them by the holy beings and turning the sacred into the profane. The miscreants painted or chipped these sacred images on pottery, in rock art, and on their clothing, angering the gods, negating the images' power, and giving cause for the people's destruction. No doubt Klah, having been raised in the midst of extensive ruins, was well aware of what he was doing. The same is true with his reproducing the sacred symbols of sandpaintings—whether on paper or in weaving.

In 1919 he wove a rug depicting two Yé'ii Bicheii dancers, which he sold to Ed Davies for a number of sheep. This was no ordinary undertaking. Knowledgeable traditionalists demanded the rug be destroyed and that an Evilway ceremony be held to ameliorate the harmful influences of breaking with tradition. Arthur told the excited clientele that the rug was going to Washington, D.C., where it would serve as a wall hanging and not be walked on, and he reassured them that any evil influence engendered by its existence would be off the reservation. Only then did things quiet down.[52]

But not for long. Klah, with Franc's urging, decided to weave a "Whirling Log Painting," depicting the first large sandpainting in a Yé'ii Bicheii ceremony. To do this, he had large logs brought down from the Tunicha Mountains for a frame capable of holding a twelve-foot square rug. The Newcombs became heavily involved. "Klah insisted that the rug have a background of native tan wool that was not dyed. A rug of this size would require twenty pounds of raw wool, and as this tan color was found only on the underside of the brown sheep, it did not seem possible to collect this much. Arthur and Klah motored to every trading post on our side of the reservation, buying a few pounds of tan wool at each until they had the right amount."[53] Again, his family became involved gathering dyes, carding and spinning wool, and giving general support. The Newcombs provided a canvas to cover the loom when not in use, and Arthur paid for a guard to watch it at night in case someone tried to destroy the work. This was not without reason.

Community reaction was immediate. People were angry that these forms would be captured for permanent display. Klah was unperturbed. He chanted his prayers, vowing nothing would happen, and nothing did. His reputation spread, and soon he had so many orders for similar compositions that he could not fill them all, while Arthur beamed with happiness at the blue ribbons his friend was accruing at weaving competitions and the high prices being paid for his work. The medicine man decided to increase his family's output. He had more big looms made for accomplished relatives who wove, and performed a nine-day Yé'ii Bicheii ceremony for his two nieces. This secured the blessings of the holy people so that there would be no offense. He carefully watched his weavers, ensuring that they made no mistakes, and he sang Blessingway songs to prevent harm. Still, older Navajos protested, anticipating the girls would be struck with blindness or paralysis in their arms for weaving these sacred symbols.

As time passed, however, and the dire predictions never happened, other weavers noticed the high prices these rugs or tapestries were commanding and decided to have their own ceremonial protection so they too could dive into the business. They intentionally wove into the image some inaccuracy so as not to offend the holy people with a perfect reproduction, unlike Klah, who strove for total accuracy.[54] Valette writes, "In 1923 thousands of Navajos were in attendance in Gallup, New Mexico when medicine men conducted a Blessingway ceremony for the new El Navajo Hotel, with its large public sandpainting murals. By then stylized Yé'ii, Yé'ii Bicheii, and sandpainting blankets were being exhibited at Indian fairs in Santa Fe, Gallup, and Shiprock. The religious restrictions that had worried the early sandpainting weavers no longer wielded the same power."[55] Much of this change was rooted in the Two Grey Hills and Newcomb Posts.

Preserving Navajo Culture through Art and Business

In addition to the monetary side of running a trading post, Franc Newcomb, like Louisa Wetherill in Kayenta, had a passion for studying and preserving aspects of Navajo culture. Both women were skilled in working with medicine men, who were the keepers of the history and cultural knowledge of their people. Both reported that as the elders were passing away, there was a good deal of information that was disappearing, and both spent countless unpaid hours studying, recording, and publishing information that would otherwise have been lost. Louisa was the more linguistically fluent of the two, but Franc had a gift for art and sketching that preserved the visual record of sandpaintings. Both had their own renowned specialists (Louisa—Wolfkiller, and Franc—Hosteen Klah) who were anxious to share their knowledge and expertise.

At one point in 1934, Franc approached the commissioner of Indian affairs, John Collier, to see if his bureau would support her efforts to travel across the Navajo Reservation visiting medicine men to record whatever ceremonial knowledge they were willing to share. She asked for no money for herself, only enough for two young Navajo women who would assist her with some of the translation and other work required on a three-month camping trip. Part of this request included the use of a government car (estimated at $75 per month), $100 pay per month for the assistance of the medicine men, $90 for food, and some other incidental expenses that would total to $355 per month and $1065 for the entire project.[56] Permission was denied due to other pressing needs of the Indian Office and its agencies. There is, however, no missing the sense of dedication that Franc felt and her desire to preserve that which she saw fading before her eyes.

While Hosteen Klah's work was dramatic, on the edge, and expensive, one cannot lose sight of the more average daily trade in rugs that filled most of the post store rooms. At Newcomb, Franc explained the contrast. A sandpainting rug six by six feet sold for $250; the trader purchased a saddle blanket by the pound, paying about a dollar; a floor rug was perhaps $2.50 and up; deviations in price depended on the weave and pattern.[57] The Newcombs also bought wool from off the reservation, which they shared with other trading posts—Two Grey Hills, Toadlena, Sheep Springs, and Tocito. This was necessary when there was not enough wool produced during the year to support the weavers in the area. At times the Newcombs might order an entire railroad carload that could be divided with others, sometimes just a half car. Black wool, which was popular with the weavers in the area but not in demand with large wool purchasing organizations, was cheaper. If a pound of wool cost ten cents, the Newcombs sold it for twelve cents to cover freighting, then waited for the markup on a finished product. That might come when men like Julius Ganz from Santa Fe or Herman Schweitzer would make their annual trip to the various posts to purchase woven products that they would then sell to larger markets. In the East, sales could be brisk, and as word spread among the elite, there were frequent requests for "samples," but this was not a popular order to fill. The traders were more focused on their Navajo clientele than they were with individual sales with people who were not standing in front of them. Too much could go wrong.

Schweitzer also bought a lot of the silverwork done by a local Navajo named Peshlakai (Béésh Łigaii). The Newcombs obtained rolls of Mexican silver dollars or bars of silver from government mints, then sold them to the smith with the understanding he would let them purchase his work. "For a long time we made a good bit with silverwork. Dudes wanted our silver. We would buy up all of the dead pawn from Lukachukai, Red Rock, and posts back on the reservation; we also bought their rugs to sell."[58] The real key behind all these transactions was to have the customer continuously return to the post, as volume in sales provided more opportunity for profit as opposed to the one big "killing" with the sale of an extraordinary rug.

A final point to be made in the promotion of Indian arts and crafts is about the role that organizations back east played in advertising and preserving these cultural treasures. In 1931 the United Indian Traders Association formed to promote better practices among traders and dealers, to ensure that purchased arts and crafts were authentically made by Indian people, and to assist in the welfare of traders primarily working in the Southwest. Protecting the public and Indians from imitation crafts required the support of the government to verify that materials and artisans were what and who they claimed to be. Traders would define what was genuine, but the government was the one who placed a certifying tag on each item to assure the customer. Navajo rugs became a particular target, as many aficionados deplored what they considered the degradation of the craft, as new dyes, patterns, and low-grade weaving sent woven products into a decline.[59]

Three years later, Charles Amsden reported in an article, "Reviving the Navaho Blanket," the organization's successes and failures. The ultimate goal was to bring back the old designs, colors, and craftsmanship found in earlier Navajo weavings. He noted that by this time, Navajo weaving had degenerated to the point that it was impossible to believe it was the same people who had made the earlier blankets and rugs a few decades previously. To let the weavers and traders know what had been lost, the Eastern Association of Indian Affairs took photos of old rugs from museums and private collections to illustrate the color and tightness of weave and design that was now lacking. Problems with matching dyes, showing an entire design on a large piece, and educating weavers in the field offered some setbacks. By 1934 Amsden wrote, "The revival today is an accomplished fact, whatever its future destiny," pointing out that 60 percent of the rugs taken in by some traders met the revived standards, although he was quick to say that this was a small number.[60]

There were three beliefs supporting this revivalist movement to return to the weaving of the old days. First, vegetal dyes were rarely bright and garish, whereas the aniline dyes that were now in common use contrasted sharply and had become the expected. Good, although subdued taste, would prevail. Second, there was a cadre of knowledgeable enthusiasts helping traders and weavers to revisit the old standard. And finally, Navajo women were highly intelligent, respected the craft of former weavers, and viewed their work with reverence. Plus, vegetal dyes, from a trader's perspective, held their color longer than those that were aniline. The big problem was reversing what the purchasing public perceived as a "Navajo blanket," having been conditioned to expect bright colors and less freedom of style. Amsden quipped, "Long relegated to the sun-porch and the den, the Navajo rug must be made worthy of the living room and the bedroom; it must harmonize with the French wallpaper, the Colonial furniture, the figured curtains. A certain degree of boldness may be allowed it at times, that it may attune itself to the sharper note of aluminum and red leather in modernistic interiors; but whatever the situation, it must chime in with the prevailing harmony."[61]

The author was not trying to dictate what passed over the counter of a trading post or to bend the will of the weaver to a set of qualities that a group of easterners and traders devised. Indeed, just the opposite. The revival was geared to return to past standards, when weavers had more liberty to choose color and design. "Nature created the colors in the Navajo country and the patterns in which they were displayed bore the authentic tribal stamp. There is the true Navajo expression, not in the later rug which got its colors from Philadelphia and its pattern from Chicago. Far from wanting to change the Navajo, we would make him more Navajo, less white man; far from dictating his weaving, we would protect it from the dictation which has brought it in both technic and artistry, already so low. Thus the revivalists, and so the issue is joined."[62]

This statement raises the question of what has been the motivation and direction in weaving from the outset. Did J. B. Moore help or hinder the Navajo weaver by marketing through catalogs a new and exciting form of blankets and rugs that caught the white public's imagination and increased the demand tenfold? Were Ed Davies and George Bloomfield coercive characters bending Navajo will to create a Two Grey Hills regional style that has consistently been accepted as some of the best craft on the reservation? Were the Newcombs only interested in pirating sacred Navajo symbolism for profit and fame, and what was Hosteen Klah's motivation? Amsden would probably see these traders and others moving the Navajos toward an "industrialized craft of weaving" that now needs to "throw off its shackles and emerge untrammeled as a joyous art! . . . The best weavers will practice it, for the benefit of an exacting clientele. Better remuneration, greater pride in work, fuller independence of individual, tribal, and racial expression—all will result, and Navajo weaving will have taken a new lease of life. This the sponsors of the revival confidently believe."[63]

The discussion of Navajo weaving has moved a long way from the corral and herding practices mentioned at the beginning to the boudoir of the elite living in the East, fighting a crusade that affected the traders in their posts thousands of miles away. Cultural pride and independence for the Navajo people had to be balanced with the very pragmatic side of life played out in a desert environment, being responsive to a distant economy that dictated important life-changing decisions, as well as practical necessity. What can be said with certainty is that through it all, there emerged the regional style of Two Grey Hills weaving that is looked upon with pride by those who weave and sell the rugs and those who buy the product. Their lives, on both sides of the counter, have been changed forever.

CHAPTER NINE

To Post-posts

The End of an Era, 1940 to Present

By the 1940s, with livestock reduction and commensurate land use reforms; with World War II and all of its social, economic, and political changes; and with a dissolution of insular barriers opening more challenges to Navajo values by the dominant society—the road to more rapid change became inevitable. For the last eighty years this process has continued to shift life at Shiprock, Two Grey Hills, and the Chuska Valley on many levels—too numerous to examine in depth in one chapter. Following a brief overview of these culture-changing elements, the story of the trading post will serve as a prime example of how this played out in one of the most important institutions on the Navajo Reservation in terms of both cultural preservation and cultural change. As agents, traders, and Navajo people attest, there is no more concrete example that links the past to the present with more clarity, no better illustration of what has happened to this frontier institution, than the story of these posts, spanning over a century of development and decline. The reasons for these changes lie at the heart of the Navajo people's history.

The Challenge of Change

Change arrived in many forms. Livestock reduction opened the door, while trooping in behind it came the wage economy with the Civilian Conservation Corps, civilian and military employment during World War II, extractive mineral industries, and contract labor. Trading posts played major roles in getting Navajo workers off the reservation to be employed in railroad crews, as seasonal harvesters, as Anglo livestock

240

herders, and as general itinerant employees. Those offering and those seeking jobs looked to the stores as a central meeting place for a geographically dispersed community. There, opportunities for work became available and often served as the pickup and drop-off point for laborers in projects that might last for six months or longer. Ideally, when the men or families returned, they would have money in their pockets and a good reputation as employees that could be called on for future hire. For those women and family members who did not accompany their husbands or fathers, they endured an uncomfortable dependence on a wage earner who was to return and assist with needs at home. Many women still speak of the 1940s and 1950s—before educational opportunities opened new doors for them—as difficult years when they had to wait for money to appear. They no longer had enough livestock to independently sustain themselves and were unable to earn a livelihood solely by weaving.

Uranium and coal mining, as well as gas and oil exploration, were significant industries that not only permitted Navajos to remain on the reservation, but provided sufficient money, especially when added to government assistance. They allowed people to purchase goods at the local post. By the 1950s, as more extractive industries opened new doors, they also helped close the old one of barter; more and more people turned to a cash-and-carry financial practice. Individual checks arrived at the post, where the trader held them for signature and then payment for goods obtained on credit, before releasing the remainder to the owner. Unlike the old days, where the exchange of each object was physically monitored, the use of checks, the ability to read, and higher math calculations left some Navajo customers uncertain about the fairness of the transaction and the honesty of the trader. A growing sophistication in business created a less personal environment and an increasing distrust.

Transportation also underwent revolutionary change. The days of horse and wagon shifted to the automobile and an ever-expanding road system that included bridges, well-maintained dirt roads, and eventually macadam highways. Industry, dependent upon shipping by truck, encouraged tribal, state, and federal government investment in key arteries that fed the growing wealth pouring off Navajo lands. During the 1950s and 1960s, paved roads on the reservation increased from 205 to 517 miles; by 1972, that number had mushroomed to 1,370 miles.[1]

Families adopted trucks and cars as the daily workhorse that took them with greater ease to their destination. While different parts of the reservation more quickly adopted the car and pickup truck between 1950 and 1975, by the end of this time, the dependable horse and wagon were relegated to history and had "virtually disappeared from even the remotest part of Navajo country."[2] Paying for a vehicle represented a major expense in a family's economy. People still hauled firewood and water, traveled long distances to ceremonies and family events, participated in the Shiprock Fair every October, and went to work and school every day—but now those activities depended on a gasoline-fired steed.

At the same time, expanding educational opportunities on and off the reservation challenged, as never before, Navajo language and cultural knowledge. Indeed, the dominant society's practices, in general, proved far too alluring. The tribe had its hands full in trying to teach speed reading and writing and arithmetic skills, on one hand, while trying to slow both the loss of cultural identity and the increase of linguistic poverty on the other. That struggle continues. The repository for past practices and beliefs became more and more the domain of the grandparents who had lived during the livestock economy and the medicine men familiar with traditional teachings.

Many of these changes had a profound impact on community life. Take for instance Shiprock. From its humble beginnings under Shelton in 1903, the town had grown to 6,103 in 1980, 7,850 in 1990, and 9,126 in 2010—tied with Tuba City (9,265) for being the two largest chapters in the Navajo Nation.[3] Shiprock is now abuzz with tribal, state, and federal offices, a regional hospital, fast food restaurants, gas stations, and a host of supportive service industries—a far cry from when Deshna Clah Chischillige opened the first gas station and restaurant to travelers in 1927. The dramatic growth of this town contrasts sharply with what has happened with Two Grey Hills, exemplifying many of the smaller communities on the reservation. Using the same years as baseline, this Navajo chapter had a population of 977 in 1980, 831 in 1990, and 500 in 2010.[4] The trend is unmistakable for both Shiprock and Two Grey Hills—the draw of an urban lifestyle with all of its amenities has replaced the old way of life. One who looks at the dry, barren land surrounding the post and then suggests that the people living there now are all that the environment can support need to consider that the twenty-five inches of rain that the Chuskas receives annually represent half of the surface water that falls on the reservation. Although estimates vary widely—from 2,000 to 10,000 to 17,000—there were Ancestral Puebloans living in the Chuska Mountains and Valley in support of the Chaco civilization; even the lowest figure is four times that found today in the same places. Only a few Navajo families make the summer pilgrimage to their ancestral camps to tend sheep in the cool forests of the Chuskas.

Social concerns of the 1960s and 1970s fostered protest with assaults on established practices, a torch that a number of Navajo groups brandished. Black, Red, and Brown Power movements along with women's rights, environmental concerns, and a growing drug culture became de rigueur as former ways of life sustained attack. Trading posts, a long-standing institution on the reservation, became a target purported to be a leech on the ever-increasingly popular Indian culture. They were ripe for criticism. To some antagonists, the trader and his way of life was a dinosaur that needed to be confined if not destroyed. Much of this task fell to DNA (Dinébeiina Nahiilna Be Agaditahe Incorporated—literally, "Lawyers Moving the People's Lives"), a Navajo legal counsel, founded in 1967. By 1972–73, the Federal Trade Commission, closely allied with DNA, held a series of hearings that gave rise to increasingly restrictive regulations that governed the posts. While traders continued to operate after these hearings, the pursuing DNA fostered a climate of lawsuits and "victimization" among the Navajos. Pawn, credit, and control of checks became prime sources of contention to the point that few traders wished to continue following new government rules. What had been an institution built on relationships had deteriorated into a source of impersonal transaction.

Certifying the System

With this contextual background, a closer look at the collapse and end of the trading post will be more clearly understood. In 1941, general superintendent of the Navajo Reservation (1935–42), E. Reeseman Fryer, submitted a report to the Department of the Interior outlining general conditions on the entire reservation. Many of his facts and fig ures came from reports written in the late 1930s, after stock reduction had taken its toll on the Navajo economy. Fryer provided insight into the current state of traders and posts as well as what the Navajos were buying. Of the 175 posts on or near the reservation, he drew information from a wide variety that ranged across different areas. His interest in aspects of trading was apparent: "During the past fifty years, the trader has been the most important factor in shaping and controlling Navajo economy, government agencies not excepted." After recognizing aspects of the wage economy, introduction of the car, and so on, he continued. "Despite these changes, the trading institution still channels and regulates most of the Navajo commercial economy and if it is desired to plug leaks into that income, examination of the trading institution should be made."[5]

Navajos sold over $500,000 worth of rugs in 1939.[6] What they were buying at the posts was food—an estimated 60 percent of their income to supplement their crops (primarily corn) and livestock that they consumed. Sheep outnumbered goats in a seven-to-one ratio, but Fryer believed that many Navajos preferred goat meat over mutton since the traders handled lots of goat skins but not much meat. Yet change loomed on the horizon. "There are a great many so called civilized conveniences for which the Navajo does not now feel a need. . . . As [they] become increasingly aware of the many things in white life, these desires will increase." Ten years later, this point would be underscored.

Fryer next reported that the traders were generally helpful and a very necessary link in the Navajo economy. In 1936 the purchases at the posts amounted to $2.5 million dollars, with $1.5 million (62 percent) for food, $675,000 (26 percent) for clothing, and $280,000 (12 percent) for "household and other productive equipment." Post customers obviously depended heavily on traders for the necessities of life. The report also noted that there was very little difference in what a poor Navajo would eat when compared to a wealthy one. The rich man just sold more jewelry and ate more, but not necessarily better. "The present tendency is a growing dependence on trader-supplied food. The quantities of goods bought by the Navajo are increasing and the quality changing." This, no doubt, was due to the tremendous impact of livestock reduction and the shift from independence to dependence on things coming in from the outside yet purchased in the old traditional pattern. Some of the tried and true objects of the past like Arbuckle coffee had given way to canned coffee;

and canned milk, peanut butter, and baked bread had been added to store shelves. Clothing accounted for the second most important Navajo expenditure. While modern attire became more available, the materials to make Navajo women's traditional dresses and blouses, all of which Navajos purchased at the post, became increasingly expensive.

Jumping ahead, roughly ten years, change was apparent. On March 20, 1948, the Navajo Tribal Council passed a resolution to regulate trading. Among its stipulations, the tribe wanted to establish prices, tax sales, and increase the cost of renting the land (which the tribe owned) upon which the post (which the trader leased) was built. Trader reaction was immediate. They feared being forced out of business by unrealistic demands and so sought redress from Congress, claiming that it was the responsibility of the commissioner of Indian affairs, who had historically been the person to regulate trade, not the Indians. The Tribal Council countered that there were unfair markups on prices, that traders had too much control of Navajo lives, and that the system needed to be effectively monitored. The solicitor of the Department of the Interior upheld the right of the commissioner of Indian affairs to control the trade; he quickly nullified the Tribal Council's resolution, but initiated a study to examine the issues.

During November and December 1948 and January 1949, a team of investigators, led by Dr. Bonney Youngblood from the Department of Agriculture, surveyed 26 of the 102 on-reservation posts, selecting from them every type of store ownership—individual, partnership, absentee, wholesaler, Navajo community, and corporation. All of the eighteen districts found on the reservation had at least one of their posts examined; names of specific stores were not given because of the personal nature of the financial information and records, but Two Grey Hills or a post nearby certainly would have been included. Members of the Tribal Council and the United Indian Traders Association were involved in the planning and review of the findings, but the main source of information came from community members and their neighbors, the traders. Evaluation of the post and its business included everything from location and isolation (closest to a city—21 miles, farthest—185 miles) to services (paid and unpaid) and the prices of ninety-one items on the shelves. The investigators considered the size of the sampling of posts (between 25 and 30 percent) to be large and more than a fair representation. Equally important, "An overwhelming majority of the traders were most cooperative, and showed no reluctance to give the information requested from them. . . . Apparently the traders welcomed an opportunity to show that their business was legitimate and that they were needed by the Navajos."[7]

The findings of the survey were instructive and painted a picture of increasing change. It also provided a mid-mark between trade in the old days and the death knell of the posts twenty-five years later. One of the first issues addressed was that of profit and markup. During 1947, the target year, the highest markup of any of the posts was 56.5 percent and the lowest 11.1 percent, with an average net profit for 23 posts of $9,262 per store.[8] For some traders, this last figure included what they considered their salary, while others did not itemize one. The range of profit indicated that there were five posts barely squeaking by with less than $5,000 a year for the owner's efforts after subtracting a $5,000 salary. Youngblood established in a previous study that profits should not exceed 33 percent of the entire costs of running the store. Only five posts surpassed that amount, with the average for 21 posts being 24.9 percent. Conclusion: "Most trading posts are operating at a reasonable profit, and many of them well below an acceptable maximum." This is an important point to remember, since it is one of the major issues raised about the continuation of trading posts in the future.

The investigators recognized that prices on the reservation were high, not because of freighting charges but rather due to credit risks, that if not handled properly, could leave the trader destitute. Some traders charged 10–25 percent interest, while others charged none but raised the cost of the basics—flour, sugar, coffee, canned milk, and shortening—to cover unpaid bills. By reducing credit losses, the owner could reduce his prices. Some traders did not take any security or pawn for a loan if the Navajo family was truly impoverished, but no loan was to go unpaid after twelve months. To remedy this problem, Youngblood recommended that only one retail price should be offered for an item, regardless if it was paid for in cash or given on credit, and there needed to be some type of security— pawn, chattel mortgage, or crop lien—held for the promised payment.

Traders also received permission to have a ten-year, rather than three-year, lease on their facility so that they could invest in improvements such as refrigeration and lighting, secure vaults to protect pawn, and other modern conveniences. Enlarging the stores for more and better merchandise allowed for greater volume, which lowered prices. Some stores remained small with limited sales, and so in order to have a sliding scale between them and high volume posts, a rental charge of $100 for businesses doing up to $25,000 became the suggested payment for the smaller posts, and $100 plus one-half of 1 percent on businesses over $25,000 for the larger posts. No new leases were to be granted unless the applying trader could show that his business would not harm an already established store. The report also recognized the traders' services—paid and unpaid—to the community. Noncommercial services included handling mail, transporting customers, assisting with family burials, providing water for Indian livestock, recruiting for work opportunities (primarily railroad and seasonal harvesting), and counseling in domestic and financial matters. All of this strengthened communities and led to more positive relations between the two cultures.

Other suggestions came from this report. Changes to the Code of Federal Regulations implemented these findings, such as having the United Indian Traders Association and the Bureau of Indian Affairs develop a code of fair trade practices to encourage store owners to unify their operations into a consistent pattern. Among those changes were displaying retail prices on shelves, limiting markup on goods, standardizing and following bookkeeping procedures, implementing sanitation in handling merchandise, and recording pawn and money deposits in a specific way. With the exception of a few minor differences and suggestions, the report was well received by the Tribal Council, the United Indian Traders Association, the traders themselves, and the federal government. Everyone involved in the process recognized that there would be changes in the future as the dominant culture became more accessible and created new demands, but few could have guessed that the next twenty-five years would be so different from the previous fifty.

Attack on the Posts Begins

Social, political, and legal movements characterized the 1960s and 1970s. As previously noted, one of those strident forces on the Navajo Reservation was DNA, a group of lawyers bent on defending every Navajo client in any perceived wrong. One of the most effective spokesmen and executive director of this nonprofit organization was Peterson Zah from Low Mountain, Arizona. For fourteen years he served on this front, fighting legal battles that at times went all the way to the Supreme Court. Zah later became the first elected Navajo Nation president (1991–95). So it is not surprising that on August 28, 1972, as deputy director of DNA, he signed the scathing indictment titled "The Trading Post System on the Navajo Reservation, Staff Report to the Federal Trade Commission."

Compared to all previous reports and investigations on trade, this one far surpassed, in scope and tone, the angry desire to bring about dramatic change. Written in the days of the American Indian Movement (AIM) and other Red Power organizations fomenting discord, there was nothing subtle about the anger and hate underlying these findings. Zah's prologue sets the stage: "We have seen hearings and investigations of this type dealing with the so called 'Indian problems,' but in every case, the results amount to too little, too late. . . . First, I wondered what can be the meaning of another investigation when the abuses are so flagrant and have been carried on so long that people would have to be blind to be unaware of them. Second, I have never understood why those who complain of the traders' exploitation must always bear the burden of proof. The traders are guests of the Navajo people on this reservation. They are given the privilege of doing business here by the Navajo Tribe, and they are given a legal monopoly by the BIA."[9] Zah later complained that the Navajo people were the "last to receive protection from those who push the little guy around."

The next seventy pages outline the reasons for these feelings, which are summarized by three major issues: (1) withholding welfare and government checks, (2) post price fixing, and (3) violations of the Truth and Lending Act, particularly in pawn transactions. To get to the root of this perceived evil, the Los Angeles Regional Office of the Federal Trade Commission surveyed 142 (95 percent) posts on and off the reservation, interviewed 162 Navajo consumers, held investigative meetings in seven reservation communities, and interrogated a handful of traders and lawyers from United Indian Traders Association, as well as expert witnesses. A lot was at stake, the report stated: "Reservation trading posts annually gross in excess of $20 million. Individual posts range in annual sales volume from $100,000 to more than $500,000."[10] These figures seem somewhat high given that the report mentioned that in

1940, livestock and agriculture accounted for 58 percent of reservation income, but by 1970 this figure had fallen to 7 percent.[11] Transportation and commuter lifestyle accounted for much of this decline. Still, for those without transportation and who were dependent on the posts, 90 percent of the gross sales in a typical store were still based on credit.

There were a number of factors that facilitated the abuse of the trading post system. Authors of the report were quick to point out that customers were illiterate and unfamiliar with commercial transactions as found in the dominant society and in handling larger sums of cash. Add to this geographic isolation of posts and communities, lack of competition, "credit saturation" where a trader extended a customer's purchasing power up to the limit of a known income so as to keep the individual tied to one store with no funds to shop elsewhere, and ambiguous agreements about the value and redemption of a pawned object, and one can see potential problems. Prices appeared too high, in some cases exceeding the national average by 27 percent and off-reservation posts by 17 percent, but these figures were misleading, since a pound of coffee that averages $1.25 might be bought at one store for $1.00 and at another for $2.25. The reason: "The monopoly enjoyed by most trading facilities also accounts for the great variance in price among all posts."[12]

Since government checks and wage labor had replaced the livestock economy, the system had moved from an "every-six months' pay day" to a monthly predictable amount. Stores often served as post offices with the trader and his wife as mail handlers. They could withhold checks until signed over to them to pay bills and control expenditures with less chance of loss. If a check were sent elsewhere, the trader did not extend credit. Any funds remaining could be made into a "due bill" stating that so much money was available to purchase more goods at the same store. Shifty techniques such as hiding the amount of a check from a recipient, laying it face down on the counter, and even physically assaulting the customer were other complaints. Additional accusations leveled at the system included offering a lesser value for a pawned item, losing pawn tickets or filling them out incorrectly, charging unfair interest rates, and "pawn hostaging" where the Navajo had to pay all of his other bills before he could redeem his pawn.

Following this litany of complaints, the answer to fix everything was simple—put the tribe in charge of correcting circumstances and enforcing the law. The threatening sword to enforce this change was to withhold licenses from traders, preventing them from conducting business on the reservation. To ensure compliance with shifting conditions, there were to be regulations that prohibited traders from opening their customer's mail, post owners that were no longer allowed to handle mail, regularized bookkeeping, annual tribal audits of these books, a $25,000 bond required for each post as opposed to a $10,000 one, periodic review of licenses by the tribe, written notification to the owner of pawn thirty days prior to its becoming "dead" and up for sale, and the return to the previous owner of any extra value gained through the sale of a pawned item. Traders were to send each month copies of pawn records to the tribe as well as periodic billing statements to clients. Posts were to have enough money to cash all checks, prices needed to be lowered, and interest was to be capped at 24 percent, all of which demanded tribal control. "We recommend that primary enforcement responsibilities be granted to the Navajo Tribe. To be effectual, the Tribe must have sole authority over trader licensing."[13] Tribal courts would handle any sort of adjudication.

Introducing tyrannical control and administrative demands onto an already challenged system of trade and a group of overworked owners proved to be too much. No doubt there were those who abused their positions, and every example given in the report had its point of genesis, but to broad-brush the entire system as intentionally corrupt pushed beyond the limits of fairness. Adding these responsibilities to the Navajo Nation, who had its own economic and political struggles, only brought in a heavy-handed cop to add another contentious layer of bureaucracy. Willow Roberts Powers examines this crucial plight in *Navajo Trading: The End of an Era* and provides an excellent analysis of its complexity. One point that became painfully apparent was how the old traders, whose family business went back three or four generations, were not only financially but also emotionally hurt by the charges leveled against them. Much of what they did was based as much on caring relationships as it was on real-world finance. Certainly the extra work now required was daunting, the financial burden heavier, and the environment far more complex for both trader and customer. When the business became an institution filled with distrust, anger, and legal action, many decided to leave.

There were those traders who stayed, but the new regulations dragged them into a different corner and brought their customers along with them. This was particularly true of posts located in isolated parts of the reservation. Many store owners felt that they had no choice but to go to the same cash-and-carry system found in the dominant society. Even though the 1972 study pointed out that 90 percent of Navajo customers still preferred the credit system and pawning items, the traders, in order to protect themselves, had to insist on money on the counter. Any mistake in lending money or pawning goods could turn into an expensive lawsuit and expulsion from the reservation. The personalized interaction of trade began to be replaced by new stores—first in the border towns and then on the reservation. In the mid-1970s, Thriftways and Circle Ks started to appear in "high traffic communities," with Fedmart and Bashas' appearing in the early to mid-1980s.[14] One thing that quickly became apparent was that the loose, friendly atmosphere of exchange that had characterized the business of the trading post was now lost to the impersonalized hard currency exchange of the dominant society. Chain stores and markets could not handle that soft rug slid across the counter to purchase flour and sugar.

Powers summarized her findings that provided the subtitle of her book "the end of an era." There is no missing the feelings engendered by the controversy. "The DNA lawyers went to work with their own values and principles, their own philosophy of legal assistance for those whose rights appeared to be trampled on. Being well trained, they used manipulation, media events, and impressions to bring change. They succeeded, though many of them claim that it was Peter MacDonald [Navajo Nation president] and, later, the arrival of chain supermarkets onto the reservation that really made the difference. If so, the irony was that in the end it was a bigger business that appears to have accomplished what the regulations and the law did not. By this logic, traders should have been allowed to become larger concerns rather than restricted to small ones. . . . Despite the fact that trading, at least in the view of many traders, had no future and would under any circumstances have slid into its current small niche, the events of 1972 did affect it. Treated as greedy monopolists by the FTC, as minor potentates by the DNA, and as patronizing outsiders by the younger generation of Navajos, traders were everybody's villains. Many felt hurt, and a few were bitter. Some retired, some moved off the reservation; others stayed where they were and continued trading, especially those in the most distant reaches of the reservation."[15]

Two Grey Hills—Surviving the Onslaught

Fortunately, Two Grey Hills was one that remained steadfast. Returning to the years prior to the turmoil, this post had a string of owners
who managed to adjust to shifting circumstances. Tracing the store's
genealogy of the men and women who became owners, part owners,
and managers during a fifteen-year period (1932–47) is dealt with here
in summary fashion. Following Roswell Nelson and his brother Pratt's
tenure at Two Grey Hills, Maurice G. Kirkpatrick and his wife, Essie,
assumed control, followed by a series of partners who ran the business
until 1946. This included Victor Walker, who had his father, Olin C.
Walker, operate it until May 1946, when three men—Willard Leighton,
Derald Stock, and Nelson Jack bought the business. Soon the paper trail
on Jack ends. In 1958 Willard Leighton died, and in 1980 Derald Stock's
sudden death gave Marie Leighton, Willard's wife, an opportunity to
purchase the remaining interests and gain full ownership. Les Wilson
clerked for Marie starting in 1983 until February 1987, when he bought
all interests, becoming sole owner of the store, where he continues to
make his livelihood today.[16]

Often these traders hired help that provided consistency at the post.
For instance, during the Leighton-Stock years, Samuel Kent Teller
(1918–2000), handled the daily business of Two Grey Hills. Whether
buying sheep, evaluating rugs, selling food, stocking shelves, or freighting, for thirty-two years (1946–78) he did much of the work as a trusted
employee.[17] What makes his experience notable was that as a Navajo
man in the absence of the owner, he interacted with many of his peers
in what could often be an uncomfortable situation. Whether living
either at Two Grey Hills or later Newcomb, he had to follow the rules
in extending credit and making payments, which was often difficult for
a Navajo employee when faced with friends and relatives. They would
often expect exchanges to be more in keeping with traditional practices
of "helping through giving," not in keeping with the hard-edge purchasing procedures of Anglo America. Teller avoided this problem and
served faithfully during his employment.

Many of the owners left no substantive record of their experience at
Two Grey Hills, the Leightons being the exception. Interviews between
Frank McNitt and Willard fill in the gaps of life at the store over a

Les Wilson (*left*) and his wife Irma Henderson (*right*) stand with Betty Yazzie (*center*), weaver of the Two Grey Hills rug (*background*). As the latest and longest owner of the post, Les continues to have a steady stream of weavers selling various types of products—from rugs and blankets to sash belts and clothing. Betty is a faithful provider of high quality rugs and tapestries, all of which have a spirit line, as do over half of the woven rugs received today. Photo by author.

thirty-seven year period (1946–83). Many of the changes discussed previously in the 1948 and 1972 reports on trading happened during the Leighton's time. This included physical additions to the store that gradually developed over the years. By 1950 Willard reported at the height of this expansion that what had been a simple trading post with a few outbuildings had morphed into a business that handled "general merchandising, buying and selling of Indian livestock and other Indian made or grown products, sale of gas and oil, lunch room or café, soda fountain, automotive repairs, hotel or other accommodations."[18] To support these and other activities, he had acquired the trading post with nine store and ware rooms, a gasoline pump, hay barn, a corn and grain storage building, lumber shed, ice plant and storage room, two-car garage, circular hogan (for house guests), camp house (hogan for visiting Navajos), root cellar for food storage, a six-room house, rental house and spare storage, and three lesser structures. Diversity in sales—from rugs to gas to ice—represented the key to survival in an increasingly complex and demanding world.

The financial picture tells a somewhat different story. In a 1950 report, the store's merchandise stood at $20,416, rugs valued at $1,132, with hides, wool, silver, and piñon nuts in inconsequential amounts.[19] Yet between accounts receivable and pawn, there was $15,000 waiting to be collected. This is what was on hand at the time. Sales for all of 1949 totaled $92,000 including cash sales ($44,626), cattle ($6,000), wool ($3,640), lambs ($9,770), piñon nuts ($1,900), and rugs ($24,230). Leighton's profit for the year was slightly under $16,000. He estimated that in a normal year, he obtained 80 sacks of wool, each weighing 200 to 250 pounds, with a total of 16,000 to 20,000 pounds annually. Individual rugs varied in price from $15 to $1,500, with most being woven within a twenty-mile radius. A normal inventory might be valued at $18,000 to $20,000, plus $11,000 in pawn.[20]

Willard was proud of the weaving that came from his area, modestly crediting Ed Davies as the one who had done the most to perfect the Two Grey Hills style. Frank McNitt, on the other hand, felt like Leighton had played a huge role in fostering improvement through counseling with weavers. He, like so many others before him, believed it most profitable to work with three or four of the best ones to improve upon their designs and technical skills, while still buying and encouraging the less skilled weavers' products to keep the art flourishing. Willard said, "Every trader who has been at Two Grey Hills has been conscientious in working with weavers to improve their rugs. Now the weavers have a sort of pride in the fact that their area produced the best rugs on the reservation. Charlie Herring worked with them all the time; there wouldn't have been a Daisy Tauglechee without a Charlie Herring. I never spent less than an hour buying a good rug."[21] He estimated that 90 percent of the rugs he sold went to distributors who came to the store. Leighton also noted that the tourist industry was becoming increasingly important in the sale of woven products. Other outlets included the Fred Harvey Company, the annual Shiprock Fair, Window Rock Tribal Fair, Gallup Ceremonial, and seasonal shoppers—fall to Christmas being the best time of the year.

During his time at Two Grey Hills, Leighton saw a significant decline in the number of weavers as well as the quality of their efforts. A year after Willard died in 1958, Don Watson, an expert in Navajo weaving and owner of the Museum of Navajo Rugs in Cortez, Colorado, spoke to the issue. Believing Navajo rugs were decreasing in number, he reported that some traders saw production dropping off as much as 20 percent each year. While Watson felt this figure may be an exaggeration, he was concerned about both the quantity and quality of what he saw being woven. At the heart of the issue was the rising generation, who went to school and decided that the tedious labor called for in weaving a rug was too much. Time invested did not produce enough profit, while the labor could be daunting for someone used to sitting in school all day and not having to perform manual tasks. Watson wrote, "Most of the weavers earn about six cents an hour. Some earn as much as ten cents. Real works of art like the Two Grey Hills [rugs] made by Daisy Tauglechee pay more but are extremely rare." The article continues, "Watson said that last year Daisy Tauglechee, one of the most famous Navajo weavers, made only two tapestries. She received $1,100 for one of these and $1,600 for the other."[22]

Trader Ed Foutz from Shiprock sold large numbers of rugs he purchased at Two Grey Hills, Newcomb, and Sanostee during the 1970s and 1980s, but marketing them in the old way was becoming increasingly difficult. H. Jackson Clark, a jack-of-all-trades businessman who spent decades on the reservation, took a somewhat different approach to the trading business. When growing up, he had become very familiar with Navajo crafts and understood the beauty and utility of these weavings. In May 1957, his new employer, Dave McGraw, owner of the Pepsi-Cola Bottling Company in Durango, asked Clark to go down on the reservation and boost sales against their competitor, Coca-Cola. The young man was thrilled. His first task was to go to a trading post that had a $2,500 bill for goods received but not paid for. Clark did not give the name of the store, but he mentioned it was "south of Shiprock" and a place where he "had purchased a fine Two Grey Hills rug from [the owner] several years before."[23] Although the description and events do not sound like it refers to the Two Grey Hills Post, no doubt it is one of the stores nearby.

The experience is instructive. Clark described a once-flourishing trading post on its last legs. Livestock reduction and a shifting economy had taken its toll. "My optimism vanished when I drove up to the store. The screen door, hanging by one hinge, twisted in the wind. The store was filthy. The cash register drawer was open as if to say, 'there's no money here.' A dozen or more Navajo men sat in the sun outside the door waiting for the railroad retirement man to come by and sign them up. They had all worked on railroad construction during the previous year. A few dusty cans of Spam, beans, and coffee sat on the otherwise bare shelves. To top it off, my old friend was drunk."[24] Each recognized the other person, then the trader invited the young salesman into his living quarters for a drink—at ten o'clock in the morning. On the way through a storage room, Clark spied a tall stack of beautiful blankets and hit upon an idea. Realizing that there was no money to pay a large bill, he offered to exchange the owed amount for blankets and suggested an advance to the trader of $1,000 worth of Pepsi-Cola to jump-start sales. The owner was eager for the deal and took a nap as Clark selected high-quality blankets that would sell. Clark closed the agreement with $3,500 worth of weavings in his vehicle and a promise that cases of cola would be on their way from Durango the next day.

Dave McGraw was not enthused. In fact he was downright angry, ordering Clark to return the blankets immediately and to somehow get the nonexistent money from the impoverished storekeeper. Dejected and rejected, Clark went home that evening in his truck full of blankets, scarcely ready to endure a scheduled dinner party. He and his wife, Mary Jane, were entertaining some fairly prominent people from Durango—two doctors, a lawyer, and a banker. Gradually, he formulated a plan that included food, a number of different opportunities to imbibe alcohol, and a displaying of the blankets. By the end of the evening, Clark had sold everything he had for $3,600 cash, which he handed to McGraw the next morning. Not only did this pay the bill and sell an additional $1,000 of Pepsi to the trader, but also provided Dave with a $100 bonus. Clark ended his narrative by saying, "I continued trading Navajo rugs for Pepsi until the 1970s, when we began to buy almost everything directly from the weavers. In the meantime, Pepsi became the leading soft drink on the northern Navajo reservation."[25] Although this rags-to-riches story is almost too good to be true, it does illustrate the plight of many trading posts at "the end of an era," how rugs and blankets still carried high value, and how the eating habits and store needs of the

Navajos had shifted from Arbuckle coffee and flour to a more modern "Pepsi generation."

While Leighton was at Two Grey Hills, he met and married Marie Carson, one of trader Stokes Carson's four daughters, who continued to run the post with her helper and co-owner Derald Stocks even after her husband's death. Stokes, in his biographical account, credits his son-in-law with increasing the price of rugs so that more money returned to the weavers, but he still felt it was an eerie place. The Chuskas loomed large in the background, the desert stretched for miles, and witches seemed to pervade the dark evenings that settled over the deserted Puebloan ruins. Late one night as Willard drove home, his car's headlights picked up a man standing on the side of the road, his back turned to the oncoming vehicle. As he drew closer and things became clearer, the trader realized that this individual "stood there with wolf skins half off his body, the wolf's head over his shoulder. Startled and scared, Willard did not stop until he reached the trading post."[26] To some readers, this type of experience seems fanciful or impossible, and yet trader and Navajo eyewitness accounts often tell of supernatural powers or events that challenge the thinking of the dominant society. For Willard and Stokes, it was real and a part of life in the Two Grey Hills region.

Last of the Breed—Les Wilson and Irma Henderson

When Marie Leighton sold the post in 1987 to Les Wilson, she handed it over to a person who remained there longer than any other trader. Les had arrived four years earlier to serve as manager, but when the opportunity arose, he bought the store in its entirety and became an enthusiastic promoter of Two Grey Hills weaving. He brought with him a solid background in trading post experience, having clerked in Shonto in 1972, where he learned from an "off the deep end method" how to operate a post with 75 percent of his customers purchasing on credit. Four years later he began working at the Many Farms Trading Company, where he stayed for six years before going to Two Grey Hills. Red Mustache (Dághá Łichíí) has since earned the title of the longest resident trader to work there since its beginning in 1897. As a repository of the post's most contemporary history, he has been interviewed on two different occasions and can best explain how trading is now conducted. The roughly twenty-year space between these interviews (the first in 1999, the second in 2017), when added to the previous evaluation of posts, provides a constructive picture of how this institution has declined. Unless otherwise noted, the following discussion of the current Two Grey Hills comes from these interviews.[27]

By 1999, Les had been there for sixteen years. He estimated that there were one hundred weavers who traded at the post, but this figure included young and old, skilled and novice, dedicated and dabbler. He purchased almost any rug, within reason, that came through the door for two reasons. First, there was little doubt that the number of good weavers was in decline, and so he wanted to encourage anyone who had an interest in practicing the craft to continue. Second, the tourist traffic was a big part of the business, and so less expensive works also sold. Les was not abandoning the idea of maintaining the excellence of his weavers, but he knew that everyone had to start somewhere, and that achieving the best required all different levels of work to get there. "You need to support all the weavers, not just the best, or there eventually won't be any best. There has to be the whole supporting cast of people with different levels of skill in order to produce the finest. Part of our mission here is to keep the weaving alive."

Growing negative influences challenged maintaining the skill and interest. Among the culprits at that time were dropping wool prices, removal of a federal wool subsidy, high hourly wages that far surpassed the money received from weaving at an hourly rate, welfare assistance, and a lack of interest by the younger generation accustomed to television and a different way of life. Weaver Sarah Natani, advocate and teacher of the craft, complained about her two teenage granddaughters: "They should be interested in sheep, in weaving. Instead, they sit and watch TV and we have to hire a sheepherder."[28] The trading post itself had become marginalized so that the rug accounts that had been so prominent in the past were vanishing. Navajos spent most of their money in off-reservation border town stores where groceries—the mainstay for posts in the past—were now in larger variety and cheaper; Les estimated that the big accounts in his store had dropped from two-thirds of his customer base to 25 percent of that number. As elderly Navajos raised with the old system of exchange died, so too did the stable, larger accounts that had been the lifeblood of the business. Gasoline had now become one of the post's best-paying commodities. Gas, groceries, and weaving for tourists, all cash and carry, were now the prime money-makers.

When Les first arrived at Two Grey Hills, he estimated that there were about two hundred accounts held at the store for credit; by 1999 those had dropped to around twenty-four, and there had never been any pawn since he began. The Federal Trade Commission rules had ensured that anything of this nature was off reservation. Now it was cars, trucks, trailers, and horse trailers that secured a loan at pawn shops, which underwent little scrutiny. Gallup had become an important center for pawn, with stores holding a large clientele booming in business. Take for instance Russell Griswold's store in April 1993 that averaged 300 items a day taken in as collateral. While the owner accepted everything from laptop computers to musical instruments, much of the traditional wealth of the Navajo people was also secured in Griswold's steel vault. There were 4,557 bracelets, 1,831 turquoise or coral necklaces, 1,053 silver watchbands, 950 wedding baskets, 460 ceremonial buckskins, and 2,644 Pendleton shawls.[29] Bill Richardson, another trader of long standing and Gallup's largest pawnbroker, estimated that he had close to two million dollars out on pawn loans at the same time. New Mexico law allowed a 10 percent fee for the first thirty days and a 4 percent charge for the next four months, after which it became "dead" and could be sold. One wonders if Peterson Zah, DNA, and the Federal Trade Commission had anticipated what their rulings would do to drive the credit business into these off-reservation and lightly monitored stores.

Another important facet of the business that Les saw slipping away by 1999 was the availability of wool and sheep. Navajo family flocks had shrunken dramatically. Trader Russell Foutz, living in Gallup in 1985, noted the decline. "Twenty years ago, he was able to round up 50,000 lambs in one season for Armour Packing. Fifteen years ago, he shipped about 5,000 lambs from Teec Nos Pos alone. Last year [1984], there were only 400."[30] There was no livestock industry at the Two Grey Hills Trading Post by 1999. Les bemoaned the fact that "most families don't have a flock of sheep anymore—even the weaving families. Sheep raising, as you probably know, has gone way down on the reservation in twenty years, and it has been replaced by cows and horses, or people just don't lead that lifestyle anymore. . . . So we're trying to fill the demand there for good wool that goes into Two Grey Hills." To keep weaving production active, the trader now sold wool from churro sheep to maintain the basis for the industry, but even these efforts, tied in to the already discussed Navajo Sheep Project, were being challenged.

Part of the problem for the Two Grey Hills weavers was that not just any type of wool would do. Lyle McNeal was sensitive to the need and had spent the last twenty years expanding the herds of churro sheep across the nation. From 1977 when his Navajo Sheep Project started, he had tripled the numbers from 435 to 1,500 found in twenty-three states, Canada, and Mexico, but not many of these animals made it to the Two Grey Hills area because each one cost $250—far more than most Navajos could pay.[31] While weavers praised this wool for the length of its strands, durability, and lack of oil, it was the undyed colors that had become the hallmark of this regional style. McNeal wrote, "It is easier to breed a white or black, but when you start dealing with the grey colors or chocolate brown colors—like they need for Two Grey Hills—it's very difficult to breed. There are a lot of sets of genes involved. It's like playing one-armed bandits."[32] Even at the centennial celebration of the post's establishment at the end of June 1997, the three hundred people in attendance were acutely aware of not only the challenges of the past, but also those lying ahead in the future.[33] Les and his wife, Irma Henderson, did not disguise their concern for the effects Shiprock, Gallup, and the burgeoning Thriftway Stores were having on their struggling enterprise.

At this same time, McNeal faced his own challenges. In August he delivered 120 yearlings and two-year old rams to qualifying families on the Navajo Reservation but at the same time announced that the NSP Project would no longer be supported by Utah State University. In an open letter to members of the organization, he rebuked the university's administration for its lack of interest and aggressive grabbing of the organization's physical assets housed on the campus. Facilities established in 1986 at a cost of $200,000, and now appraised at $1.3 million to $1.6 million, were declared surplus property and to be sold. Part of the school's thinking was that the entire project should be moved closer to the Navajo Reservation and that supplying sheep was not in line with the university's mission. The administration would sign no future leases for NSP; fortunately, Dan McCarthy from Illinois granted free use of his property in Bloomfield, New Mexico, for a year. There was even talk about eliminating the herd through a "sale for slaughter" approach, which luckily did not happen.[34] McNeal left little doubt about his feelings for those who opposed the project. "USU won't reimburse us for any of the NSP facilities. We must raise funds all over again to prepare the new site. Since May 31, 1997, USU has frozen our account, restricted access to grants set aside in a holding account, and reduced my salary at 25 percent, which amount had been illegally paid by the NSP since 1989. Because the NSP is no longer a part of USU, administrators directed that I must take on additional extension responsibilities to justify maintaining 100 percent salary or else take a salary cut."[35]

There are, of course, two sides to every issue, and only one is presented here, but there is no missing the effect it had on the replenishing of churro sheep on the reservation. In spite of his closing this letter on a positive note of being "excited and very stimulated by the upcoming challenges"; in spite of the letter's title, "20th Anniversary—The Dream Survives"; and in spite of the subtitle on the letterhead, "Serving People, Preserving Cultures," this marked the beginning decline of the Navajo Sheep Project. In less than a year, McNeal had passed the reins of leadership to another and greatly decreased his involvement. From this point onward, the organization slowly dwindled due to financial and political issues.

McNeal's legacy, however, lives on at Two Grey Hills. At the same time that the role of the NSP began to diminish, Irma Henderson inherited her mother's herd of churro sheep. She, like so many other Navajo women her age, did not have a strong interest in herding or weaving for a livelihood, but as the years went by, she realized the importance of these activities in preserving traditional culture. She decided to take up weaving, care for the twenty-one sheep she now owned, and pass these skills—and the wool—along to others interested in the craft. She put on shearing demonstrations, explained how to clean, card, and spin the wool, and used weaving as her own emotional therapy and connection to heritage. She did not begrudge the two hours it took to shear a sheep with manual steel clippers that do the job all at once rather than requiring a second cutting when using electric clippers. It was hard, dirty work, what she called "mind over mutton," but at the end of the day it brought a sense of satisfaction that overcame the backache from bending over struggling animals.[36] To Irma and her husband, this was their way of keeping the legacy alive. Les believed, "There needs to be people like ourselves working with weavers and doing all we can to promote weaving. . . . Weaving probably would have died sixty or seventy years ago without traders promoting it."[37]

Closing an Era

Move ahead twenty years to a second interview with Les and Irma in 2017. Shifts in the business had become even more dramatic. Two Grey Hills was one of the last old community posts to still sell groceries (the gas pump was long gone) and to cater to local weavers. All the other stores, with an exception or two—such as the Hubbell Trading Post, now preserved as a historic museum—had been bulldozed, converted to a convenience store, or sat deteriorating as a faint reminder of yesteryear. The couple could see the past shrinking before their eyes. Les also watched the shrinking bank statements. He used to have forty to fifty credit customers, which had now shrunk to four. These had been the steady flow of trade, not the cash sales, where groceries and monthly checks met the needs of both store and patrons. People still came in asking for credit, but unless they were a weaver or customer in good standing, the chances of getting a loan were not good. Still, the whole transaction had to balance somewhat between business and friendship. Over his thirty-four years at Two Grey Hills, he estimated that he had lost up to 25 percent of the credit extended. One customer wittingly wrote bad checks and then walked away from any responsibility to meet her obligation; another just refused to pay and never returned. Part of the problem was that many of the Navajo people thought that because Les was a white man, he was rich, even though there was no money in the cash register. The trader refused to fold to discouragement; it was the weaving that kept him going—"I've only kept it open because of the rugs and given up on everything else. Just the weaving."

Irma has a somewhat different perspective. Born and raised at Sanostee, herding a flock of forty sheep with her siblings in the Chuska Mountains when a young girl, attending school at Shiprock, and helping her mother prepare wool and weave, she learned her role as a Navajo woman through traditional upbringing. Later in life, she met Les as a chance customer at Two Grey Hills and they began their life together.

Two Grey Hills Trading Post remains an avid supporter of weaving and local crafts. On January 27, 2019, weavers attended a "Spin Off," where a potluck luncheon and "show and tell" was followed by carding and spinning wool. The attendees shared techniques and talked about contemporary projects. *From left to right*: Mary Charles, Gilbert Begay, Irma Henderson, Sarah Natani, Victoria Manygoats, Rose Chico, and Betty Yazzie. Photo by author.

Her entire view of being the wife of a trader and her interaction with the customers was colored by Navajo teachings about relationships (*ké*). Her Navajo name became Woman of Two Grey Hills, while her husband's had changed from Red Mustache (it was now white) to The One You Walk Under because his six-foot-four-inch stature was not common among the Navajos.

Even though Irma was not raised very far away, when she moved to this new community, there were a lot of people who would not talk to her because she was an outsider and wife of a trader. She always introduced herself by clan affiliation—Mexican and Many Hogans Clans—but people were still reticent. Even her mother commented on her changed status. One day Irma was cooking some food that had come from the store and received sharp counsel: "Now that is not your store. You just don't take things out of the store unless you pay for it." Irma told her husband what her mother had warned, but he did not say much. "So it was really a lot of pressure, and it was hard for me to relate to people. I didn't know quite what to say or how to act or anything like that. I was afraid of the people in the area." Even to this day, she avoids going into the store, entering it only when she has to. "It always upsets me because I know which person owes us money and there are those who knowingly buy things but have no intention of paying." With little leverage to encourage fiscal responsibility, Les and Irma find themselves in the same dilemma traders faced for over a hundred years.

The Two Grey Hills Trading Post still sits amid the Puebloan ruins on the baked landscape of the Chuska Valley. The economic reason for which it was established and for which it still exists, hangs by two slim threads that have been inextricably bound since its beginning—weaving and supplies to maintain the weavers. No more cans of tomatoes or free tobacco, no more wagon parts or horse's bridles, no more gas and groceries. On December 31, 2017, the store closed its doors to all of that with a renewed commitment to sell the rugs and other woven products for which it is famous and to provide the tools, wool, and other supplies necessary to keep the weavers in business. Les still stocks a hundred rugs produced locally, just as he did twenty years ago. Their production has not slackened but has maintained a steady flow, despite dire predictions from the past that within a short time there would be no weavers. The ebb and flow of money coming to the trader during spring wool and fall lamb sales has shifted to the seasonal travel of tourists seeking a quality product from a historic post that for almost one hundred years has held the undisputed title for premier weaving. Born from humble circumstance, Two Grey Hills rugs and tapestries continue to compete with other regional styles on the reservation.

Parting Thoughts

Today as travelers glide over the smooth surface of Highway 491 (formerly Route 666), the main artery that connects Shiprock to Gallup, they travel in twenty-first-century comfort, a far cry from what Frank Noel, Joe Wilkins, N. C. Wyeth and others encountered well over a hundred years ago. Viewing the Shiprock community in the rearview mirror beyond the flurry of road signs, one sees a large complex urban center with all the amenities—schools, hospitals and clinics, social service and police facilities, shopping complexes, and air-conditioned homes sporting satellite dishes with SUVs parked in driveways. It takes a few miles before the trappings of civilization diminish into stark desert country with its towering rock formations set in undulating plains of sage-brush—things that William T. Shelton would have been more familiar with than the town he established. To say that times have changed is an understatement. To understand what and how it happened is the role of history, as discussed here.

Returning to the time of the Ancestral Puebloans to after the Long Walk of the Navajos, some of the greatest challenges came from survival on the land and the hostilities of neighbors—man against nature and man against man. Following an unsettled period of Spanish, Mexican, Ute, and Navajo aggression and struggle for possession of resources, large-scale armed conflict ended. The path to ownership opened to the Navajos through the reservation system, which grew in prominence. Unlike many American Indian groups who watched landholdings diminish and a meaningful two-way economic relationship remain out of reach, the Navajos expanded their traditional livelihood based in agriculture, livestock, wool, and weaving, marketing their products to mainstream America. A class of middlemen or traders was there to bridge the cultural gap and exchange what both sides desired. While some people today may interpret this time as an opportunity for the white man to take advantage of the Navajos, for the most part, the two groups benefited, receiving what each desired. Both peoples understood the value of what the other had to offer and accepted the terms. To frame this in the words of historian and poet Edward Everett Hale (1822–1909), "Coming together is a beginning, keeping together is progress, working together is success."[38] Both groups succeeded, the Two Grey Hills Trading Post serving as an example of this relationship. Neither side of the counters became rich, but each got what was wanted.

Growth in population, economic development, and the necessity of control pushed the federal government to take two major steps—expand the size of the reservation through executive orders and establish agencies to oversee internal affairs and provide services on various levels. Shelton, as the first agent, might be criticized for his heavy-handed rule of his charges, but he also must be credited with turning an open environment into a productive landscape and assisting the Navajos to meet challenges brought on by the dominant society. There is no missing his and subsequent agents' belief that white, Anglo-Saxon, Protestant (WASP) values were the pathway to a successful future. There were those like Black Horse, Ba'álílee, Bizhóshí, Little Singer, and others—who opposed this intent and fought to maintain old practices. Strong personalities jockeyed for control on both sides, neither one embracing compromise until required. Force and Anglo law prevailed.

As the land became more settled, the economy also grew with oil development, transportation networks, health and education systems, and tribal control. Starting with lonely women missionaries like Mary Eldridge and Henrietta Cole, to the boarding schools at Shiprock and Toadlena, to the public schools of today, the Navajo people have embraced education as a ladder to the future. Establishment of the first Tribal Council at Toadlena under the supervision of Herbert Hagerman to the Navajo Nation's present government, there has been steady growth in sovereignty by which the people have elected their own leaders and formulated their own decisions. Economic development currently sits within their purview as oil continues to be pumped, coal extracted, and agricultural projects operate along the San Juan River. The nascent healthcare of yesteryear has now grown to the point where medical doctors work beside medicine men to heal. Finally, in terms of weaving, some of the finest work is still being created, as beautiful Navajo rugs continue to bring high prices. Some Two Grey Hills rugs go for many thousands of dollars.

What is pictured here is an optimistic summary of what has been accomplished through past efforts. There were certainly issues along the bumpy road to progress: the long hours spent by weavers, which, when calculated monetarily, resulted in wages far below what seems fair; boarding schools that created trauma through family separation and unyielding discipline; low prices paid for oil, gas, and coal; the horrors of livestock reduction; a loss of financial independence; a growing dependence on a wage economy that coaxed people from the reservation; the BIA's manipulation of tribal government and its wards; and the environmental issues of today. There is no intent to deny these and other problems of the past. Still a great deal of good has been accomplished. Very few Navajos today wish to go back to life in the past—traveling by horse and wagon on muddy, icy roads instead of in cars on paved highways; herding sheep and hauling wood rather than learning in air-conditioned classrooms; or eating a limited diet derived from the land, animals, and limited trading post shelves versus shopping in supermarkets and enjoying meals in restaurants. This is not to denigrate the past, but to recognize that progress comes at a price, change has been constant, and for the most part it has been positive. Of course today's society has its own brand of problems and issues—drugs, alcohol, diabetes, pollution, language and culture loss, technological captivity, and so much more.

Were the problems of yesteryear any more trying than those faced today, and were the people back then any different than those now? More important, how well prepared are Navajos to face the future? The story of Shiprock, Two Grey Hills, and the Chuska Valley is about cultural adaptation and suggests a bright future. Whether facing natural or man-made challenges, the people adapted, adopted, and survived. Change was constant, tradition its anchor. No doubt what the next hundred years holds for the Northern Navajos will be as interesting and different as its past. Perhaps the words of John F. Kennedy, in speaking of the past and future in a different context, summarized it best when he said, "Geography has made us neighbors. History has made us friends. Economics has made us partners, and necessity has made us allies. Those whom God has so joined together, let no man put asunder."[39]

Notes

Introduction

1. N. C. Wyeth, "A Sheepherder of the Southwest," *Scribner's Magazine* 45 (January 1909): 17.

2. Ibid.

3. Frank McNitt, *The Indian Traders* (Norman: University of Oklahoma Press, 1962).

4. For example see Hilda Faunce (Wetherill), *Desert Wife* (Lincoln: University of Nebraska, 1928, 1981); Frances Gillmor and Louisa Wetherill, *Traders to the Navajos: The Story of the Wetherills of Kayenta* (Albuquerque: University of New Mexico Press, 1934, 1979); Franc Johnson Newcomb, *Navaho Neighbors* (Norman: University of Oklahoma Press, 1966); Gladwell Richardson, *Navajo Trader* (Tucson: University of Arizona Press, 1986); Willow Roberts (Powers), *Stokes Carson: Twentieth Century Trading on the Navajo Reservation* (Albuquerque: University of New Mexico Press, 1992).

5. Richard White, *"It's Your Misfortune and None of My Own": A New History of the American West* (Norman: University of Oklahoma Press, 1991).

6. Colleen O'Neill, *Working the Navajo Way: Labor and Culture in the Twentieth Century* (Lawrence: University Press of Kansas, 2005).

7. Louise Lamphere, *To Run after Them: Cultural and Social Bases of Cooperation in a Navajo Community* (Tucson: University of Arizona Press, 1977).

8. Klara Kelley and Harris Francis, *Navajoland Trading Post Encyclopedia* (Window Rock, Ariz.: Navajo Nation Heritage and Historic Preservation Department, 2018).

9. Martha Blue, *Indian Trader: The Life and Times of J. L. Hubbell* (Walnut, Calif.: Kiva, 2000); Erica Cottam, *Hubbell Trading Post: Trade, Tourism, and the Navajo Southwest* (Norman: University of Oklahoma Press, 2015).

10. Teresa J. Wilkins, *Patterns of Exchange: Navajo Weavers and Traders* (Norman: University of Oklahoma Press, 2008).

11. Kathy M'Closkey, *Swept under the Rug: A Hidden History of Navajo Weaving* (Albuquerque: University of New Mexico Press, 2002).

12. Robert S. McPherson, *Both Sides of the Bullpen: Navajo Trade and Posts* (Norman: University of Oklahoma Press, 2017).

13. Note of clarification: blankets are generally thinner and vary in size from a saddle blanket to a large wall covering, whereas a rug also varies in size but is heavier, thicker, and woven to withstand greater wear and tear.

14. McNitt, *The Indian Traders*.

15. Marley Shebala, "Navajos Preserve Traditions through Sheep," *The Independent* (Gallup, N.Mex.), June 30, 1993, p. 2.

16. "Obituary," *Ann Arbor News*, October 11, 2015, p. 25.

1. Setting the Stage

1. See "Physiography of Chaco Canyon," in *The Geology of Chaco Canyon, New Mexico*, Smithsonian Miscellaneous Collections, vol. 122, no. 7, https://www.nps.gov/parkhistory/online_books/chcu/smc-122-7/sec2.htm.

2. Herbert E. Gregory, *The Navajo Country: Topographic and Hydrographic Reconnaissance of Parts of Arizona, New Mexico, and Utah*, Water Supply Paper 380 (Washington, D.C.: Government Printing Office, 1916), 25.

3. Ibid.

4. Ibid., 27.

5. R. Gwinn Vivian, *The Chacoan Prehistory of the San Juan Basin* (New York: Academic Press, 1990), 28.

6. Ibid., 83–90.

7. For a somewhat dated yet standard work see Vivian, *Chacoan Prehistory*; Stephen H. Lekson, *The Archaeology of Chaco Canyon: An Eleventh Century Pueblo Regional Center* (Santa Fe: School of American Research, 2006); and Monica L. Murrell and Bradley J. Vierra, *Bridging the Basin: Land Use and Social History in the Southern Chuska Valley*, vol. 4, NMDOT Cultural Resource Technical Series 2014-2 (Santa Fe: New Mexico Department of Transportation, 2014) for good general overviews of the archaeological work of the San Juan Basin and Chaco Canyon.

8. See Robert S. McPherson, *Viewing the Ancestors: Perceptions of the Anaasází, Mokwič, and Hisatsinom* (Norman: University of Oklahoma Press, 2014), for the Navajo account of the departure of the Anasazi from the San Juan Basin.

9. As mentioned previously, the literature about Chaco is immense. A good, brief overview is found in Arthur H. Rohn and William M. Ferguson, *Puebloan Ruins of the Southwest* (Albuquerque: University of New Mexico Press, 2006).

10. James W. Judge, "Chaco Canyon—San Juan Basin," in *Dynamics of Southwest Prehistory*, edited by Linda S. Cordell and George J. Gumerman (Washington, D.C.: Smithsonian Institution Press, 1989), 241.

11. Ibid., 225; Robert P. Powers, "Outliers and Roads in the Chaco System," in *New Light on Chaco Canyon*, ed. David Grant Noble (Santa Fe, N.Mex.: School of American Research, 1984), 48.

12. Ibid.; Deanna Grimstead, Sharon M. Buck, Bradley J. Vierra, and Larry V. Benson, "Another Possible Source of Archaeological Maize Found in Chaco Canyon, NM: The Tohatchi Flats Area, NM, USA," *Journal of Archaeological Science: Report 3* (2015): 183.

13. Michael P. Marshall et al., *Anasazi Communities of the San Juan Basin* (Albuquerque: Public Service Company of New Mexico, 1981), 113.

14. Ibid., 332–33.

15. Larry Benson, "The Chuska Slope as an Agricultural Alternative to Chaco Canyon: A Rebuttal of Tankersley et al. (2016)," *Journal of Archaeological Science: Reports (2016)*, http://dx.doi.org/10.1016/j.jasrep.2016.10.017.

16. Richard A. Friedman, John R. Stein, and Taft Blackhorse Jr., "A Study of a Pre-Columbian Irrigation System at Newcomb, New Mexico," *Journal of GIS Archaeology* 1 (April 2003): 9.

17. Ibid., 13.

18. Maxwell McCrae Forton, "Corridors of Interaction: Tracing Chuskan Ceramics and Lithics to Assess Regional Interaction of Chaco Canyon" (master's thesis, Binghamton University, State University of New York, 2017), 27.

19. Ibid., 29; H. Wolcott Toll, "Trends in Ceramic Import and Distribution in Chaco Canyon," in *Recent Research on Chaco Prehistory*, edited by James W. Judge and James D. Schelberg, Division of Cultural Research, U.S. Department of the Interior (Albuquerque, N.Mex.: National Park Service, 1984), 115.

20. Judge, "Chaco Canyon," 231.

21. Powers, "Outliers and Roads," 52–54.

22. See Kathryn Gabriel, *Roads to Center Place: A Cultural Atlas of Chaco Canyon and the Anasazi* (Boulder, Colo.: Johnson Books, 1991); Mark D. Varien and Richard H. Wilshusen, eds., *Seeking the Center Place: Archaeology and Ancient Communities in the Mesa Verde Region* (Salt Lake City: University of Utah, 2002).

23. Christopher H. Guiterman, Thomas W. Swetnam, and Jeffrey S. Dean, "Eleventh-Century Shift in Timber Procurement Areas of the Great Houses of Chaco Canyon," *Proceedings of National Academy of Science* 113, no. 5 (February 2016): 1186.

24. Amanda C. Reynolds, Julio Betancourt, Jay Quade, Jonathan Patchett, Jeffrey S. Dean, and John Stein, "87SR/86SR Sourcing of Ponderosa Pine Used in Anasazi Great House Construction at Chaco Canyon, New Mexico," *Journal of Archaeological Science* 32 (2005): 1064, 1071.

25. Forton, "Corridors of Interaction," 38.

26. Judge, "Chaco Canyon," 232.

27. Ibid., 248.

28. Powers, "Outliers and Roads," 57–58; H. Wolcott Toll, "Material Distributions and Exchanges in the Chaco System," in *Chaco and Hohokam: Prehistoric Regional Systems in the American Southwest*, edited by Patricia L. Crown and James W. Judge (Santa Fe, N.Mex.: School of American Research Press, 1991), 105–6; Vivian, *Chacoan Prehistory*, 486–90.

29. Edward Sapir, "Internal Linguistic Evidence Suggestive of the Northern Origin of the Navaho," *American Anthropologist* 38, no. 2 (April–June 1936): 224–35.

30. Harry Hoijier, "The Chronology of the Athapaskan Languages," *International Journal of American Linguistics* 22 (October 1956): 219–32.

31. Clyde Kluckhohn and Dorothea Leighton, *The Navaho*, rev. ed., (Cambridge: Harvard University Press, 1974), 33; Alfred V. Kidder cited in Gladys A. Reichard, *Social Life of the Navajo Indians* (New York: Columbia University Press, 1928), 155; David M. Brugge, "Navajo Prehistory and History to 1850," in *Handbook of North American Indians*, vol. 10 (Washington, D.C.: Smithsonian Institution, 1983), 490.

32. Alan D. Reed and Jonathan C. Horn, "Early Navajo Occupation of the American Southwest: Reexamination of the Dinétah Phase," *Kiva* 55, no. 4 (Fall 1990): 297.

33. McPherson, *Viewing the Ancestors*, see endnote 8.

34. Deni J. Seymour, *From the Land of Ever Winter to the American Southwest: Athapaskan Migrations, Mobility, and Ethnogenesis* (Salt Lake City: University of Utah Press, 2012).

35. For an extensive discussion of this highly complex principle, see John R. Farella's *The Main Stalk: A Synthesis of Navajo Philosophy* (Tucson: University of Arizona Press, 1984).

36. Navajo sacred geography is a vast topic that will be discussed here only as it relates to the specific area of study. A brief overview of the Navajos' Four Sacred Mountains and a host of other sites can be found in Robert S. McPherson, *Sacred Land, Sacred View: Navajo Perceptions of the Four Corners Region* (Logan: Utah State University, 1992, 2001).

37. Richard F. Van Valkenburgh and Scotty Begay, "Sacred Places and Shrines of the Navajo: Part I, The Sacred Mountains," *Museum Notes of Museum of Northern Arizona* 11, no. 3 (September 1938): 32.

38. Frank Mitchell, "Blessingway—Version II," in *Blessingway: With Three Versions of the Myth Recorded and Translated from the Navajo by Father Berard Haile, O.F.M.*, ed. Leland C. Wyman (Tucson: University of Arizona Press, 1970), 396–97.

39. Martha Nez, interview by Robert S. McPherson, August 10, 1988; Charlie Blueyes, interview by Robert S. McPherson, June 7, 1988; Editha Watson, "Talk by Editha Watson," March 17, 1968, Doris Duke #796, Doris Duke Oral History Collection, Special Collections, Marriott Library, University of Utah, Salt Lake City, 9–10; Richard F. Van Valkenburgh, *Diné Bikéyah* (Window

Rock: Office of Navajo Service, 1941), 27; Van Valkenburgh, "Sacred Places," 31, 33; Slim Curly, "Blessingway—Version I," in Wyman, *Blessingway*, 158, 306; and Laurance D. Linford, *Navajo Places: History, Legend, Landscape* (Salt Lake City: University of Utah Press, 2000), 193–94.

40. Wyman, *Blessingway*, 20, 309.

41. Paleowest Archaeology, "Navajo-Gallup Water Supply Project Ethnographic Overview of Native American Cultural Association with the San Juan Basin, New Mexico," Technical Report 13–30 (Phoenix: U.S. Department of the Interior Bureau of Reclamation, 2013), 38.

42. Ibid., 57.

43. Irma Wilson, interview by Robert S. McPherson, September 12, 2017.

44. Linford, *Navajo Places*, 194, 174–76, and 181.

45. An excellent study of the importance of bears and how they fit into this nine night ceremony is found in Leland C. Wyman, *The Mountainway of the Navajo* (Tucson: University of Arizona Press, 1975).

46. Washington Matthews, *Navajo Legends* (Salt Lake: University of Utah Press, 1897, 1994), 155.

47. Mitchell, "Blessingway," 430; Don Mose Jr., *The Legend of the Navajo Hero Twins* (Blanding, Utah: San Juan School District, 2005), 68–70.

48. Washington Matthews, *The Mountain Chant: A Navaho Ceremony*, Fifth Annual Report of the Bureau of Ethnology (Washington, D.C.: Government Printing Office, 1887), 407.

49. Matthews, *Navajo Legends*, 39.

50. Charlotte Frisbie, *Tall Woman: The Life Story of Rose Mitchell, A Navajo Woman, c. 1874–1977* (Albuquerque: University of New Mexico Press, 2001), 454.

51. Shirley Brown, interview by Robert S. McPherson, September 12, 2017.

52. River Junction Curly, "Blessingway—Version III," in Wyman, *Blessingway*, 556–61.

53. This phrase is still used today in praying that the evil of witchcraft will not harm an individual. It can turn away the power and/or object being used to destroy an individual.

54. Watson, "Talk by Editha Watson," 14–15; Linda Hadley, *Hózhóójí Hane' (Blessingway)* (Rough Rock, Ariz.: Rough Rock Demonstration School, 1986), 29–30; Matthews, *Navajo Legends*, 119–21; Stephen H. Jett, "Notes—'Shiprock Pinnacle' and 'Shiprock Wash'" given to author with permission granted for use—in author's possession.

55. There is a vast literature concerning the history of the Southwest and its peoples. For the reader who desires a broad framework in which to place events discussed in this chapter, a number of general histories are recommended. For those interested in the role of the Pueblo Indians alone and with the Spanish, see William B. Carter, *Indian Alliances and the Spanish in the Southwest, 750–1750* (Norman: University of Oklahoma Press, 2009). For Ute relations with different

tribes and with Euro-American groups in the Southwest, see Virginia McConnell Simmons, *The Ute Indians of Utah, Colorado, and New Mexico* (Boulder: University Press of Colorado, 2000) and Ned Blackhawk, *Violence over the Land: Indians and Empires in the Early American West* (Cambridge, Mass.: Harvard University Press, 2006); Herbert E. Bolton's path-breaking work on the Spanish Southwest is excellent, but for an up-to-date version of Spain's organization and history during its two hundred years of occupation, see David J. Weber, *The Spanish Frontier in North America* (New Haven, Conn.: Yale University Press, 1992); and for the Mexican period, see Weber, *The Mexican Frontier, 1821–1846: The American Southwest under Mexico* (Albuquerque: University of New Mexico Press, 1982); for the roughly fifty years of initial American occupation covered in this period, more specific works will be cited later.

56. Unless otherwise specified, the following information is taken from a six-volume set of original historical documents collected and edited by J. Lee Correll. This material spans the Spanish, Mexican, and American interaction with the Navajos through June 1868 and provides English translations of Hispanic correspondence as well as American accounts. J. Lee Correll, *Through White Men's Eyes: A Contribution to Navajo History—A Chronological Record of the Navajo People from Earliest Times to the Treaty of June 1, 1868*, vol. 1 (Window Rock, Ariz.: Navajo Heritage Center, 1979), 82. For ease of reference, subsequent citations will be abbreviated as *TWME* followed by volume and page numbers.

57. Ibid., 92.

58. Ibid., 95.

59. Ibid., 114.

60. Ibid., 133, 155.

61. Ibid., 159.

62. Ibid., 230.

63. Virginia Hoffman, *Navajo Biographies*, vol. 1 (Tsaile, Ariz.: Navajo Curriculum Center, 1974), 9; Franc Johnson Newcomb, *Hosteen Klah: Navaho Medicine Man and Sand Painter* (Norman: University of Oklahoma Press, 1964), 4–5.

64. Hoffman, *Navajo Biographies*, 9–14; Newcomb, *Hosteen Klah*, 5–9.

65. Hoffman, *Navajo Biographies*, 17–20; Newcomb, *Hosteen Klah*, 14–18.

66. Newcomb, *Hosteen Klah*, 32–33.

67. Frank McNitt, ed., *Navaho Expedition: Journal of a Military Reconnaissance from Santa Fe, New Mexico, to the Navaho Country, Made in 1849 by Lieutenant James H. Simpson* (Norman: University of Oklahoma Press, 1964), 63.

68. Ibid., 64.

69. Ibid., 68.

70. Ibid., 187, 193.

71. *TWME*, vol. 1, p. 374.

72. Ibid., 376–77.

73. Ibid., 389, 392, 394.

74. *TWME*, vol. 2, pp. 22, 26.

75. Ibid., 25.

76. Ibid., 59, 60, 62; Clifford E. Trafzer, *The Kit Carson Campaign: The Last Great Navajo War* (Norman: University of Oklahoma Press, 1982), 27.

77. See L. R. Bailey, *The Long Walk: A History of the Navajo Wars, 1846–68* (Pasadena, Calif.: Westernlore Publications, 1978); Peter Iverson, *Diné: A History of the Navajos* (Albuquerque: University of New Mexico Press, 2002); Broderick H. Johnson, ed., *Navajo Stories of the Long Walk Period* (Tsaile, Ariz.: Navajo Community College Press, 1973); Lawrence C. Kelly, *Navajo Roundup: Selected Correspondence of Kit Carson's Expedition Against the Navajo, 1863–1865* (Boulder, Colo.: Pruett, 1970); Gerald Thompson, *The Army and the Navajo: The Bosque Redondo Reservation Experiment, 1863–1868* (Tucson: University of Arizona Press, 1982).

78. *TWME*, vol. 2, pp. 136, 164.

79. Ibid., 174.

80. Ibid., 186.

81. Francis Toledo in Johnson, *Navajo Stories of the Long Walk Period*, 144.

82. Newcomb, *Hosteen Klah*, xvii–xix, 49.

83. L. R. Bailey, ed., *A Military Exploration of the Navajo Country in 1859 by Captain J. G. Walker and Major O. L. Shepherd* (Los Angeles: Westernlore Press, 1964), 54.

84. *TWME*, vol. 2, pp. 320–21.

85. *TWME*, vol. 3, pp. 36, 80.

86. Ibid., 365.

2. From Pre-posts to Posts

1. For a general overview of events between 1868 and 1900, see Iverson, *Diné*; Bill P. Acrey, *Navajo History: The Land and the People* (Shiprock, N.Mex.: Central Consolidated School District No. 22, 1988); and Ruth M. Underhill, *The Navajos* (Norman: University of Oklahoma Press, 1956). For a more detailed accounting of this period, see William Haas Moore, *Chiefs, Agents, and Soldiers: Conflict on the Navajo Frontier, 1868–1882* (Albuquerque: University of New Mexico Press, 1994); and Robert S. McPherson, *The Northern Navajo Frontier, 1860–1900: Expansion through Adversity* (Logan: Utah State University, 2001).

2. Galen Eastman, cited in David M. Brugge, *A History of the Chaco Navajo* (Albuquerque: National Park Service, 1980), 75.

3. Garrick Bailey and Roberta Glenn Bailey, *A History of the Navajos: The Reservation Years* (Santa Fe, N.Mex.: School of American Research Press, 1986), 28.

4. Newcomb, *Hosteen Klah*, 62–67.

5. Henry C. Adams, as cited in Brugge, *A History of the Chaco Navajo*, 146–47.

6. Theodore Dodd, *Annual Report of the Commissioner of Indian Affairs*, Navajo Agency, U.S. Department of the Interior (Washington, D.C.: Government Printing Office, 1867): 200–201. (Hereafter *Report of the Commissioner of Indian Affairs* will be cited as *RCIA*.)

7. Bailey and Bailey, *A History of the Navajos*, 38.

8. Ibid., 41–43.

9. Ibid., 50.

10. McNitt, *The Indian Traders*, 51.

11. Ibid., 60.

12. John H. Bowman to CIA, February 22, 1886, *RCIA*, 5–6.

13. Ibid., 7.

14. Ibid. It is not clear why Bowman failed to mention Juan Lorenzo Hubbell's trading post at Ganado, which opened in 1878.

15. *RCIA*, Navajo Agency, August 9, 1889, p. 260; U.S. Congress, House, *Report of the Secretary of War*, "Report of Colonel Grierson," H. Ex. Doc. 1, part 2, vol. 1, September 1, 1889, pp. 179–81.

16. W. A. Smith to Governor E. S. Stover, October 21, 1890, Record Group 75, Letters Received—New Mexico, by the Office of Indian Affairs 1881–1907, National Archives, Washington, D.C. (hereafter cited as Letters Received—New Mexico).

17. *RCIA*, Navajo Agency, August 22, 1890, p. 166.

18. *Albuquerque Citizen*, January 17, 1891.

19. *Durango Herald*, January 17, 1891.

20. *RCIA*, "Commissions and Negotiations for Reduction of Reservations," 1892, p. 75.

21. Walter Dyk, *A Navaho Autobiography* (New York: Johnson Reprint Company, 1947), 50.

22. Application of Wilkin and Noel, License Book, vol. 15, entry 942, November 3, 1897, Letters Received—New Mexico.

23. Linford, *Navajo Places*, 277.

24. Frank Leland Noel and Mary Eliza Roberts Noel, *Eighty Years in America* (Salt Lake City: self-published, 1962).

25. Ibid., 21.

26. Ibid.

27. Hambleton Bridger (H. B.) Noel, interview by Frank McNitt, January 11 and 18, 1958, Frank McNitt Collection, box 10, State Records Center and Archives, Santa Fe, New Mexico.

28. McNitt, *The Indian Traders*, 78.

29. Win Wetherill is best known for his life at Covered Water Trading Post depicted by his wife, Hilda Faunce, who called him "Ken." This book about their life is *Desert Wife* (Lincoln: University of Nebraska Press, 1928, 1981).

30. Samuel E. Shoemaker to George W. Hayzlett, June 18, 1901, Letters Received—New Mexico.

31. B. S. Rody to Commissioner of Indian Affairs, September 4, 1901, Letters Received—New Mexico.

32. Shoemaker to Hayzlett, July 7, 1901; Charles S. Lusk to W. A. Jones, Commissioner of Indian Affairs, July 8, 1901, Letters Received—New Mexico.

33. Hayzlett to CIA, July 27, 1901; Rody to CIA, January 24, 1902; Winslow Wetherill to CIA, March 1, 1902, Letters Received—New Mexico.

34. Wetherill to CIA Jones, May 8, 1903, Letters Received—New Mexico.

35. Hayzlett to CIA, July 10, 1903, Letters Received—New Mexico.

36. Rody to CIA, January 11, 1904; William T. Shelton to CIA, April 29, 1904; Shelton to CIA, May 18, 1904, Letters Received—New Mexico.

37. Shelton to CIA, May 18, 1904, Letters Received—New Mexico.

38. Ibid.

39. Shelton to CIA, May 18, 1904, (different letter than above), Letters Received—New Mexico.

40. Linford, *Navajo Places*, 258.

41. The following account of the opening of the Sanostee post comes from Will Evans, *Along Navajo Trails: Recollections of a Trader, 1898–1948*, edited by Susan E. Woods and Robert S. McPherson (Logan: Utah State University Press, 2005), 39–45.

42. Ibid., 42–43.

43. Ibid., 45.

44. Ibid., 128.

45. H. B. Noel, interview.

46. Noel and Noel, *Eighty Years in America*, 23.

47. Ibid., 24.

48. H. B. Noel, interview.

3. Of Bibles, Books, and Regulations

1. Bernard James Byrne, *A Frontier Army Surgeon: Life in Colorado in the Eighties* (New York: Exposition Press, 1935), 153–54; Galen Eastman, "Reports of Agents in New Mexico," September 1, 1882, *Report of the Commissioner of Indian Affairs* (Washington, D.C.: Government Printing Office, 1883), 129. (Hereafter *Report of the Commissioner of Indian Affairs* will be cited as *RCIA*.)

2. For examples of this lawlessness, see Eleanor D. MacDonald and John B. Arrington, *The San Juan Basin: My Kingdom Was a County* (Denver: Mido Printing, 1970); Jon M. and Donna McDaniel Skovlin, *In Pursuit of the McCartys* (Cove, Ore.: Reflections, 2001); Robert S. McPherson, *As If the Land Owned Us: An Ethnohistory of the White Mesa Utes* (Salt Lake City: University of Utah Press, 2011); and McPherson, *Northern Navajo Frontier*.

3. Willard L. Steinsiek, "Mary Louise Eldridge," *New Mexico Conference United Methodist Historical Journal* 2 (November 2015): 4.

4. Pauline G. Malehorn, *The Tender Plant: The History of the Navajo Methodist Mission Farmington, New Mexico, 1891–1948* (Farmington, N.Mex.: self-published, 1948), 20.

5. Ibid.; Robert A. Trennert, *White Man's Medicine: Government Doctors and the Navajo, 1863–1955* (Albuquerque: University of New Mexico Press, 1998), 85.

6. *RCIA*, "Navajo Agency," U.S. Department of the Interior (Washington, D.C.: Government Printing Office, 1893), 113.

7. *RCIA*, "Proceedings of the Board of Indian Commissioners at the 14th Mohonk Conference—Address of Mrs. Eldridge," October 14, 1896, p. 46.

8. Steinsiek, "Mary Louise Eldridge," 7.

9. Article from *The Index* (1899) cited in Agnes Miller Furman, *Tohta: An Early Day History of the Settlement of Farmington and San Juan County, New Mexico* (Wichita Falls, Tex.: Nortex Press, 1977), 139.

10. MacDonald and Arrington, *San Juan Basin*, 99.

11. Malehorn, *Tender Plant*, 21–22; *San Juan Times* (newspaper), August 3, 1893, p. 1.

12. George W. Hayzlett to Commissioner of Indian Affairs, April 25, 1899 and March 24, 1900, Record Group 75, Letters Received—New Mexico, by the Office of Indian Affairs 1881–1907, National Archives, Washington, D.C. (hereafter cited as Letters Received—New Mexico).

13. *Annual Report of the Women's National Indian Association* (Philadelphia: December 1898), 26–27.

14. Ibid., 27.

15. Evans, *Along Navajo Trails*, 77.

16. Ibid., 78.

17. Mary G. Burdette, "A Visit to Our Missions," *The Indian's Friend: A Publication of the Women's National Indian Association* (Philadelphia) 14, no. 3 (November 1901): 2, 8–10.

18. Lewis A. Myers, *A History of New Mexico Baptists* (Albuquerque: Baptist Convention of New Mexico, 1965), 99.

19. Ibid., 316.

20. Ibid., 204.

21. "The Navajo Indian and Civilization," *Fruitland Tribune*, September 14, 1906, p. 3; "Indian Mission—Two Grey Hills," Baptist Church Calendar, New Mexico State Archives, Santa Fe, New Mexico.

22. Lemuel Call Barnes, "Missionaries to the Heathen," *Baptist Home Mission Monthly* 31, no. 6 (June 1909): 297.

23. Ibid., 295.

24. Ibid., 300.

25. For a more detailed account of the Miller incident and events surrounding it, see McNitt, *The Indian Traders*, 131–40.

26. Thomas V. Keam, "Navajo Agency," *RCIA* (Washington, D.C.: Government Printing Press, 1873), 304.

27. Ibid.

28. *Navajo Nation Population Profile, 2010 U.S. Census* (Window Rock, Ariz.: Navajo Nation, 2013), 45.

29. William T. Shelton to Commissioner of Indian Affairs (hereafter CIA), May 21, 1904; and John Charles (Supervisor of Construction) to CIA, January 20, 1906, Letters Received—New Mexico.

30. Charles to CIA, January 20, 1906, Letters Received—New Mexico.

31. R. M. Pringle to CIA, April 16, 1904; Shelton to CIA, August 20, 1904; Shelton to CIA, June 6, 1905, Letters Received—New Mexico.

32. Shelton to CIA, June 6, 1905, Letters Received—New Mexico.

33. Shelton to CIA, November 23, 1904, Letters Received—New Mexico.

34. Charles to CIA, January 20, 1906; Shelton to CIA, November 2, 1906, Letters Received—New Mexico.

35. Shelton to CIA, May 2 and July 30, 1904, Letters Received—New Mexico.

36. Shelton to CIA, May 18 and August, 1908; May 26, 1909, Letters Received—New Mexico.

37. Shelton to CIA, November 24, 1903; Ruben Perry to Shelton, December 7, 1904, Letters Received—New Mexico.

38. Charles H. Dickson to CIA, January 6, 1905, Letters Received—New Mexico.

39. Mary L. Eldridge, sworn deposition before Charles H. Dickson, January 2, 1905; Samuel E. Shoemaker, sworn deposition before Dickson, January 2, 1905, Letters Received—New Mexico.

40. Shelton to Dickson, December 30, 1904; Dickson to CIA, April 8, 1905, Letters Received—New Mexico.

41. Dickson to CIA, April 8, 1905, Letters Received—New Mexico.

42. George Butler to CIA, December 5, 1896, Letters Received—New Mexico.

43. Shelton to CIA, December 28, 1903; February 27, 1904; May 17, 1904; July 21, 1904; and July 22, 1904, Letters Received—New Mexico.

44. Shelton to CIA, February 24, 1905 (two separate letters), Letters Received—New Mexico.

45. Shelton to CIA, March 6, 1905, Letters Received—New Mexico.

46. Ibid.

47. "The Shiprock Agency," *Farmington Enterprise*, September 21, 1906, p. 3.

48. Ibid.

49. Shelton, "Report of Superintendent of San Juan Schools," July 23, 1907, Letters Received—New Mexico.

50. For a history of the Aneth school during Shelton's time see Robert S. McPherson, "Howard R. Antes and the Navajo Faith Mission: Evangelist of Southeastern Utah," *Utah Historical Quarterly* 65, no. 1 (Winter 1997): 4–24.

51. Shelton to CIA, July 23, 1907, Letters Received—New Mexico.

52. John L. Conway, "San Juan School," *Farmington Enterprise*, April 15, 1908, p. 3.

53. Ibid.

54. Shelton to CIA, January 21, 1909, Letters Received—New Mexico.

55. "Shiprock, An Object Lesson in Industrial Democracy," *Farmington Times-Hustler*, September 19, 1912, p. 1.

56. Shelton to CIA, March 31, 1904, Letters Received—New Mexico.

57. Maurice Kildare, "Girl on a Strange Frontier," *True West* (June 1971), 44.

58. Report to the Office of Indian Affairs, August 17, 1910, Letters Received—New Mexico.

59. Shelton to CIA, June 28, 1906, Letters Received—New Mexico.

60. Ibid.

61. Shelton to CIA, August 30, 1906, Letters Received—New Mexico.

62. Shelton to CIA, December 30, 1906, Letters Received—New Mexico.

63. Ibid.

64. Shelton to CIA, December 11, 1906, Letters Received—New Mexico.

65. Ibid.

66. Shelton to CIA, January 5, 1907, Letters Received—New Mexico.

67. "Shiprock Has First Navajo Indian Fair," *Farmington Enterprise*, October 29, 1909, p. 1.

68. Ibid.; Walter Dyk, *A Navaho Autobiography* (New York: Johnson Reprint Company, 1947), 143; *RCIA*, "Navajo Blankets," vol. 2, 1914, p. 36.

69. Newcomb, *Navaho Neighbors*, 27–28.

70. "Shiprock Has First Navajo Indian Fair," 1.

71. Newcomb, *Navaho Neighbors*, 31.

72. "Shiprock Has First Navajo Indian Fair," 1.

4. Troublous Times and Temperaments

1. See Acrey, *Navajo History*, 108–10.

2. Fr. Murray Bodo, O.F.M., *Tales of an Endishodi: Father Berard Haile and the Navajos, 1900–1961* (Albuquerque: University of New Mexico Press, 1998), 179–89.

3. Ibid., 188.

4. William T. Shelton to Commissioner of Indian Affairs, December 15, 1913, Major James McLaughlin Papers, Assumption Abbey Archives, microfilm no. 5, on file in the Denver Public Library, Denver, Colorado.

5. Shelton to Commissioner of Indian Affairs, February 15 and March 2, 1905 Record Group 75, Letters Received—New Mexico, Office of Indian Affairs 1881–1907, National Archives, Washington, D.C. (hereafter cited as Letters Received—New Mexico).

6. *Mancos Times*, September 1, 1905, p. 4.

7. Shelton to Charles E. Dagenett, March 13 and October 25, 1905, Letters Received—New Mexico.

8. Shelton to CIA, December 5, 1913, McLaughlin Papers, Denver Public Library.

9. For a detailed study of the kinaaldá teachings, ceremony, and purpose, see Charlotte Johnson Frisbie, *Kinaaldá: A Study of the Navaho Girl's Puberty Ceremony* (Salt Lake City: University of Utah Press, 1993); and Ruth Roessel, *Women in Navajo Society* (Rough Rock, Ariz.: Rough Rock Demonstration School, 1981).

10. Shelton to CIA, December 5, 1913, McLaughlin Papers, Denver Public Library.

11. Shelton to CIA, February 25, 1909, Letters Received—New Mexico.

12. Shelton to Alfred Hardy, Additional Farmer, November 11, 1907, Letters Received—New Mexico.

13. Shelton to CIA, February 8, 1905, Letters Received—New Mexico.

14. Shelton to CIA, May 15, 1905, Letters Received—New Mexico.

15. Shelton to Cook and Jensen, July 10, 1911; Shelton to H. B. Noel, August 1, 1911, Letters Received—New Mexico; R. Clayton Brough, Dale L. Jones, and Dale J. Stevens, *Utah's Comprehensive Weather Almanac* (Salt Lake City: Publisher's Press, 1987), 290; Harold and Fay Muhlestein, *Monticello Journal: A History of Monticello until 1937* (Monticello, Utah: self-published, 1988), 105, 108.

16. Wilhelmina Bero, "Account of the Flood of 1911," *New Mexico Conference United Methodist Historical Journal* 2 (November 2015): 16.

17. Shelton to Peter Paquette, October 9, 1911; Shelton to W. M. Peterson, October 28, 1911, Letters Received—New Mexico; quotation from "Disastrous Flood," *Montezuma Journal*, October 12, 1911, p. 1.

18. Bero, "Account of the Flood," 19.

19. Shelton to Lewis C. Day, October 24, 1911; Shelton to C. J. Crandall, October 28, 1911; Shelton to L. M. Peterson, October 28, 1911, Letters Received—New Mexico.

20. McNitt, *The Indian Traders*, 345–46.

21. Arthur Chapman, "Right Man in Right Place," *Farmington Enterprise*, October 13, 1911, p. 1.

22. Bero, "Account of the Flood," 16–22.

23. "Pushed Back the Floods," *Mancos Times-Tribune*, October 20, 1911, p. 1.

24. Shelton to CIA, November 6 and 9, 1911, Letters Received—New Mexico.

25. For a detailed account of this individual's actions, see Robert S. McPherson, "'Too Much Noise in that Bunch across the River': Ba'álílee and the 1907 Aneth Brawl," *Utah Historical Quarterly* 77, no. 1 (Winter 2009): 26–51. The following information comes from this article.

26. The following information on this individual comes from Robert S. McPherson, "Howard R. Antes and the Navajo Faith Mission: Evangelist of Southeastern Utah," *Utah Historical Quarterly* 65, no. 1 (Winter 1997): 4–24.

27. The most complete study and source of information used here, unless otherwise noted, is found in Frank McNitt, *Richard Wetherill: Anasazi, Pioneer Explorer of Southwestern Ruins* (Albuquerque: University of New Mexico Press, 1957, 1966).

28. Ibid., 219.

29. Shelton to CIA, July 18, 1908, Letters Received—New Mexico.

30. See Evans, *Along Navajo Trails*, 91–104.

31. McNitt, *The Indian Traders*, 347–58.

32. There is yet another view of this event, that of Bizhóshí. On November 1, 1913, reservation superintendent Peter Paquette and Father Anselm Weber interviewed Bizhóshí concerning the incident at the Shiprock Agency. Part of the transcript from that meeting follows. Bizhóshí began by telling of his return to his home after a twelve-day absence only to find his family gone. Then, with a group of relatives and friends, he started out to retrieve his missing family members.

> We did not intend when we started to have war or have a fight. We camped on this side of the San Juan. I said we would go to the Superintendent and beg four times for the children and women before we would take any steps. Early in the morning we rode up to the San Juan School. All the young fellows were ahead. When I overtook the young men they were all in front of the police quarters but he [a policeman] did not answer me where they were. I asked the policeman why he had taken them to the Agency. . . .
>
> The Clerk would not let us take the women. I begged him to let us [have] the women. I told him we would camp before the store. We would take the women over there and get them something to eat. The Clerk said no. I asked him eight times. I told him we would go over by the store and wait for Mr. Shelton to come back but the Clerk would not listen to us. We got the women out. One of the women ran toward where we went to go. We put one of the women on a horse. We went out the same way we came in. It was the road toward the store. When we went out that way there were some white people and some school children blocking the way so we could not get out. Then I rode up and I asked them to let us pass on and stay in front of the store until Mr. Shelton got back but they would [not] open the way for us. They blocked the way so I rode among the crowd and one of the white men (a farmer) got hold of my bridle rein. Another called 'Yellow Man' (Jensen) got hold of the rein on the other side and would not let us go. We found there were only two policemen there. All at once one of the policemen jumped one of our men. I got hold of this fellow. I got hold of the policeman's wrist and held the policeman's hand. I then began whipping my horse. One of the white men, a farmer, tried to stop me. He is just about as ugly as I am. I ran my horse through the crowd. Some of the young fellows whipped the policeman. The white people did not do anything at all. . . .

I do not think we have done anything wrong. They came and stole the women and we stole them back.

Cited in Peter Iverson, ed., *"For Our Navajo People": Diné Letters, Speeches & Petitions, 1900–1960* (Albuquerque: University of New Mexico Press, 2002), 124, 127.

33. Shelton to CIA, December 5, 1913, Letters Received—New Mexico.

34. Chee Dodge began his political career at a young age as a translator. He eventually became the first chairman (now called president) of the Navajo Nation from 1922 to 1928 and later 1942 to 1946. A sharp businessman, Dodge combined wealth with a lifestyle that rivaled that of some of the most affluent whites living in New Mexico of his day. He died in 1946.

35. Iverson, *"For Our Navajo People,"* 127–28.

36. Newcomb, *Navaho Neighbors*, 34.

37. "Shiprock Indian Trouble," *Farmington Times-Hustler*, November 13, 1913, p. 1. For additional information about the role that newspapers played during this incident as well as a complete reporting of government activities, see Davidson B. McKibbin, "Revolt of the Navajo," *New Mexico Historical Review* 29, no. 4 (Fall 1954): 259–89.

38. Bizhóshí Biyé, as cited in Howard M. Bahr, ed., *The Navajo as Seen by the Franciscans, 1898–1921: A Sourcebook* (Lanham, Md.: Scarecrow Press, 2004), 376.

39. McLaughlin to Secretary of the Interior, telegram, November 17, 1913, McLaughlin Papers, Denver Public Library.

40. Hugh L. Scott, *Sign Talker: Hugh Lenox Scott Remembers Indian Country*, ed. R. Eli Paul (Norman: University of Oklahoma Press, 2016), 217.

41. Bahr, *The Navajo as Seen by the Franciscans*, 378.

42. Evans, *Along Navajo Trails*, 101.

43. Bahr, *The Navajo as Seen by the Franciscans*, 383.

44. Scott, *Sign Talker*, 220.

45. Ibid., 385.

46. Shelton to CIA, December 5, 1913, McLaughlin Papers, Denver Public Library.

47. Fintan Zumbahlen to Anselm Weber, January 20, 1914, in Weber Letters, box DEC 242, folder BII 8, Franciscan Archives, Cincinnati, Ohio.

48. Zumbahlen to Weber, July 1, 1914, ibid.

49. *The Thirty-First Annual Report of the Executive Committee of the Indian Rights Association, for the Year Ending December 10, 1913* (Philadelphia: Office of the Indian Rights Association, 1914), 15.

50. Shelton to CIA, September 26, 1914, Letters Received—New Mexico.

51. "Is Shelton Forced to Resign?" special edition of *Farmington Enterprise*, January 21, 1916, p. 1.

52. Shelton to Will Evans, January 24, 1916, Letters Received—New Mexico.

53. "Shelton Asked to Resign," *Farmington Enterprise*, March 3, 1916, p. 1.

54. "Mr. Shelton," *Farmington Enterprise*, March 3, 1916, p. 3.

55. McNitt, *Richard Wetherill*, 313.

56. "The Shelton Reception," *Farmington Times-Hustler*, May 4, 1916, p. 1.

57. "Sheltons Celebrate 50th Wedding at Their North Carolina Home," *Farmington Times-Hustler*, February 25, 1941, p. 5.

5. Earning a Good Reputation

1. "Indian Trader License" file, May 18, 1897, Record Group 75, Letters Received—New Mexico, Office of Indian Affairs 1881–1907, National Archives, Washington, D.C. (hereafter cited as Letters Received—New Mexico).

2. John B. Arrington, interview by Frank McNitt, August 27, 1958, Frank McNitt Collection, John Arrington folder, State Records Center and Archives, Santa Fe, New Mexico.

3. Ibid.

4. Ibid.

5. "Indian Trader License" file, November 8, 1909; Shelton to Commissioner of Indian Affairs, August 24, 1912, Letters Received—New Mexico, 1908–1949, Office of Indian Affairs, National Archives, Washington, D.C. (hereafter cited as Letters Received—New Mexico, 1908 to 1949).

6. William H. Harrison to CIA, June 16, 1908; Harrison to CIA, August 29, 1908; Superintendent, Western Navajo Agency to CIA, October 15, 1908, Letters Received—Western Navajo Agency.

7. Navajo Agency (Fort Defiance) to Indian Traders, January 30, 1905, Letters Received—New Mexico.

8. Ibid.

9. For a detailed study of trade dynamics and cultural insight, see Robert S. McPherson, *Both Sides of the Bullpen*.

10. Will Evans, "General Notes on the Navajo," November 15, 1907, *Farmington Enterprise*, 1.

11. Ibid.

12. Ibid.

13. Trader responses are located in General Services File—Education-Industries, Record Group 75, Letters Received—New Mexico, 1908–1949. The dates of the responses used here are: Reitz/Davies, September 11, 1911; Oliver, August 27, 1911; Noel, August 5, 1911; Arnold, August 14, 1911; Moore, September 2, 1911; Walker, August 5, 1911.

14. Olin C. Walker to CIA, September 1, 1911, "Genuine Navajo Blankets" (pamphlet attached to letter), Letters Received—New Mexico, 1908 to 1949.

15. Ibid.

16. Charles Avery Amsden, *Navaho Weaving: Its Technic and History* (Glorieta, N.Mex.: Rio Grande Press, 1934, 1982), 195.

17. McNitt, *The Indian Traders*, 254.

18. Ibid., 257.

19. J. B. Moore to CIA, September 2, 1911, Letters Received—New Mexico, 1908 to 1949.

20. Arrington, interview by McNitt.

21. CIA to J. S. Lockwood, August 25, 1913; Lockwood to CIA, January 2, 1914; Assistant CIA to Lockwood, April 4, 1914, Letters Received—New Mexico, 1908 to 1949.

22. Shelton to CIA, April 24, 1914, Letters Received—New Mexico, 1908 to 1949.

23. Ibid.

24. Pearl Davies, interview by Frank McNitt, August 4, 1958, Frank McNitt Collection, Two Grey Hills folder, State Records Center and Archives, Santa Fe, New Mexico.

25. Shelton to CIA, August 11, 1914, Letters Received—New Mexico, 1908 to 1949.

26. Ibid.

27. Ibid.

28. Shelton to O. M. McPherson, November 6, 1915, Letters Received—New Mexico, 1908 to 1949.

29. McPherson to CIA, November 15, 1915, Letters Received—New Mexico, 1907 to 1949.

30. H. S. Traylor to CIA, "Report on San Juan," June 19, 1916, Letters Received—New Mexico, 1908 to 1949.

31. Ibid.

32. Evan W. Estep to CIA, July 1, 1918, Letters Received—New Mexico, 1908 to 1949. Subsequent citations concerning traders as viewed by Estep come from this same source.

33. Traylor to CIA, June 19, 1916, Letters Received—New Mexico, 1908 to 1949.

34. McNitt, *The Indian Traders*, 259–60.

35. Ibid., 261.

36. Estep telegram to Indian Office, May 4, 1919, Letters Received—New Mexico, 1908 to 1949.

37. Estep to CIA, May 11, 1919, Letters Received—New Mexico, 1908 to 1949.

38. Ibid.

39. Estep to CIA, August 2, 1919, Letters Received—New Mexico, 1908 to 1949.

40. Edward H. Davies to CIA, September 25, 1919, Letters Received—New Mexico, 1908 to 1949.

41. CIA To Estep, July 24, 1920; Arthur J. Newcomb to Estep, August 5, 1920, Letters Received—New Mexico, 1908 to 1949.

42. Estep to CIA, August 19, 1920, Letters Received—New Mexico, 1908 to 1949.

43. CIA to Estep, July 24, 1920; Davies to Estep, August 18, 1920, Letters Received—New Mexico, 1908 to 1949.

44. Toadlena Trading Company Application for Renewal of License, December 1, 1920, Letters Received—New Mexico, 1908 to 1949.

45. Two Grey Hills Application for Renewal of License, July 3, 1922, Letters Received—New Mexico, 1908 to 1949.

46. Davies to CIA, September 1, 1921, Letters Received—New Mexico, 1908 to 1949.

47. Estep to CIA, September 26, 1921, Letters Received—New Mexico, 1908 to 1949.

48. CIA to Davies, August 5, 1921, Letters Received—New Mexico, 1908 to 1949.

49. Estep to CIA, May 3, 1920, Letters Received—New Mexico, 1908 to 1949.

50. Estep to Licensed Indian Traders, November 18, 1922, Letters Received—New Mexico, 1908 to 1949.

51. Walter Runke to Commissioner of Indian Affairs, May 5, 1919, Western Agency, Record Group 75, National Archives, Washington, D.C.

52. Stewart Hatch, interview by Robert S. McPherson, May 7, 2010, in possession of author.

53. Amasa Jay Redd, interview by Charles S. Peterson, July 27, 1973, CRC-C7, p. 45, Charles Redd Center for Western Studies, Brigham Young University, Provo, Utah.

54. Tom Kirk, *The Kirk Clan: Traders with the Navajo*, Brand Book no. 6, in Peoples of the Far West series (San Diego: Corral of the Westerners, 1979), 149; also cited in McPherson, *Both Sides of the Bullpen*, 119.

55. Runke to Cato Sells, June 7, 1919; F. E. Brandon, "Industrial Survey," October 25, 1922, Western Navajo Agency, Record Group 75, National Archives, Washington, D.C.

56. Ibid., 152.

57. "Industrial Survey," report.

6. Living around a Post

1. "Indian Trader License" File, June 1, 1925 and August 20, 1930, Record Group 75, Letters Received—New Mexico, 1908–1949, Office of Indian Affairs, National Archives, Washington, D.C. (hereafter cited as Letters Received—New Mexico, 1908 to 1949).

2. Roswell T. Nelson, interview by Frank McNitt, October 31, 1957, Frank McNitt Collection, Two Grey Hills folder, State Records Center and Archives, Santa Fe, New Mexico.

3. Selawasane's Story, Exhibit A, December 19, 1929, Special Report by H. H. Fiske to Commissioner of Indian Affairs, January 2, 1930, Letters Received— New Mexico, 1908 to 1949.

4. Statement of Jim Curley, Exhibit D, December 18, 1929, Special Report by H. H. Fiske to Commissioner of Indian Affairs, January 2, 1930, Letters Received—New Mexico, 1908 to 1949.

5. Fiske to CIA, Final Report, January 2, 1930, Letters Received—New Mexico, 1908 to 1949.

6. Pearl Davies, interview by Frank McNitt, August 4, 1958, Frank McNitt Collection, Two Grey Hills folder, State Records Center and Archives, Santa Fe, New Mexico.

7. Nelson, interview by McNitt; "Indian Strikes Down Wife of Trader in Attempted Robbery," *Farmington Times-Hustler*, September 30, 1927, p. 1; "Navajo Who Committed Assault is Captured," *Farmington Times-Hustler*, October 7, 1927, p. 1; Albert H. Kneale, *Indian Agent* (Caldwell, Idaho: Caxton Printers, 1950), 365–68.

8. The correct spelling of this name, which means "Left" or "Left-handed," is Tł'ah. Anglo pronunciation of the Tł sounds like Kl, and so for consistency with Franc Newcomb's spelling, I have not changed the name.

9. "Indian Strikes Down Wife," 1.

10. Kneale, *Indian Agent*, 367.

11. For a more complete explanation of how divination works, see Robert S. McPherson, *Dinéjí Na'nitin: Navajo Traditional Teachings and History* (Boulder: University Press of Colorado, 2012), 13–43.

12. Anglo spelling of this medicine man's name varies: Bí-al, Biyal, Beal, Beyal, and Bijal, among others. Born near the Bears Ears in southeastern Utah in the 1830s, he and his family went to Fort Sumner in the 1860s, and then moved to the Chaco area. He later became close friends with the Newcombs, assisting them in their interaction with the Navajos.

13. Franc Johnson Newcomb, *Navaho Neighbors*, 186.

14. Ibid., 188.

15. Marietta Wetherill with Kathryn Gabriel, ed., *Marietta Wetherill: Reflections on Life with the Navajos in Chaco Canyon* (Boulder: Johnson Books, 1997), 133.

16. Ibid., 133–34.

17. George R. Bloomfield, "Biography," compiled by Lucy G. Bloomfield, 1965, Frank McNitt Collection, Two Grey Hills folder, State Records Center and Archives, Santa Fe, New Mexico.

18. William T. Shelton to CIA, September 7, 1914, Letters Received—New Mexico, 1908 to 1949.

19. Shelton to CIA, June 22, 1915; O. M. McPherson report to CIA, November 15, 1915, Letters Received—New Mexico, 1908 to 1949.

20. *Farmington Times-Hustler*, April 22, 1927, p. 3; G. E. E. Lindquist to Board of Indian Commissioners, December 4, 1931; R. M. Daly to CIA, December 16, 1933; Daly to CIA, March 11, 1934, Letters Received—New Mexico, 1908 to 1949.

21. Bloomfield, "Biography."

22. In the original, Lucy Bloomfield spelled the name as "Natana," although the correct spelling is Naat'áanii. I have maintained her original spelling.

23. Lucy G. Bloomfield, "Natana (Navajo Chief)," n.d., Frank McNitt Collection, Two Grey Hills folder, State Records Center and Archives, Santa Fe, New Mexico.

24. Ibid.

25. "Toadlena Notes of Interest," *Farmington Times-Hustler*, October 14, 1927, p. 3.

26. Lucy G. Bloomfield, "A Navajo Indian Fire Dance," *Improvement Era* 27, no. 8 (June 1924): 905–11.

27. Ibid., 906.

28. Grace Bloomfield Herring, "Life Story of Grace Jacqueline Bloomfield Herring," n.d., Frank McNitt Collection, Two Grey Hills folder, State Records Center and Archives, Santa Fe, New Mexico, 8.

29. Ibid., 9.

30. Grace Herring, interview by Karen Underhill, February 11, 1998, NAU. OH.75.5, Special Collections, Cline Library, University of Arizona, Flagstaff, Arizona.

31. Ibid., 16–17.

32. Charles Edward Herring, "Life Story of Charles Edward Herring," n.d., Frank McNitt Collection, Two Grey Hills folder, State Records Center and Archives, Santa Fe, New Mexico. 18.

33. Ibid., 22.

34. Ibid., 23.

35. Ibid., 25.

36. Ibid., 26.

37. Herring, interview by Underhill.

38. Newcomb, *Navaho Neighbors*, 21–22.

39. Franc Johnson Newcomb, interview by Frank McNitt, July 25, 1958, Mrs. Franc Newcomb File, 1973-024 Frank McNitt Papers, State Archives of New Mexico, Santa Fe.

40. Newcomb, *Navaho Neighbors*, 39.

41. Ibid.

42. Ibid., 138.

43. Ibid., 139–40.

44. Ibid., 168–69.

45. Newcomb, *Hosteen Klah*, 101–2.

46. Ibid.

47. Albert H. Kneale to CIA, December 20, 1926, Letters Received—New Mexico, 1908 to 1949.

48. Newcomb, *Navaho Neighbors*, 84.

49. Ibid., 86.

50. Charles George Newcomb, unpublished transcript of Newcomb's life recorded by Frank McNitt in "Traders" File, n.d., 1973-024 Frank McNitt Papers, State Archives of New Mexico, Santa Fe.

7. Oil, Governance, and Livestock Reduction

1. Gillmor and Wetherill, *Traders to the Navajos*, 234–35. Frances Gillmor created from this experience the novel *Windsinger* (Albuquerque: University of New Mexico, 1930, 1958), a story about a young Navajo man and his quest to be with the holy people during this time of chaos.

2. Evan W. Estep to Commissioner of Indian Affairs, August 28, 1920, Record Group 75, Letters Received—New Mexico, 1908–1949, Office of Indian Affairs, National Archives, Washington, D.C. (hereafter cited as Letters Received—New Mexico, 1908 to 1949).

3. Ibid.

4. Benjamin R. Brady and Howard M. Bahr, "The Influenza Epidemic of 1918–1920 among the Navajos," *American Indian Quarterly* 38, no. 4 (Fall 2014): 459–91.

5. Acrey, *Navajo History*, 200.

6. William T. Shelton to CIA, June 5, 1908, Letters Received—New Mexico, 1908 to 1949.

7. Estep to CIA, December 14, 1917, Letters Received—New Mexico, 1908 to 1949.

8. Albert H. Kneale to CIA, April 9, 1924, Letters Received—New Mexico, 1908 to 1949.

9. Ibid.

10. For a more detailed examination of the Tribal Council and chapter system during the early years, see David E. Wilkins, *The Navajo Political Experience* (Tsaile, Ariz.: Diné College Press, 1999), 81–88.

11. Herbert J. Hagerman, unpublished "Memoirs," n.d., Record Group 200, Gift Collection, Private Papers of Herbert J. Hagerman, Box 2, National Archives, Washington, D.C., 8 (hereafter cited as Hagerman Papers).

12. Ibid., 10.

13. Ibid., 12.

14. Ibid., 18.

15. Ibid., 19.

16. Hagerman, "Record of the Proceedings of the Opening of the Tribal Council of Navajo Indians Held at Toadlena, New Mexico, Saturday, July 7, 1923," Hagerman Papers.

17. Francis C. Wilson, New Mexico Association on Indian Affairs, "Honorable Herbert J. Hagerman: A Tribute," n.d., Hagerman Papers.

18. Hagerman, "The Indians of the Southwest: A Memorandum," July 1, 1931, Hagerman Papers, 41.

19. Ibid., 42.

20. Hagerman to CIA, November 6, 1923; Mark W. Radcliffe to Hagerman, December 10, 1924, Hagerman Papers.

21. Radcliffe to Hagerman, June 3, 1924, Hagerman Papers.

22. Bailey and Bailey, *A History of the Navajos*, 121–22.

23. Acrey, *Navajo History*, 200.

24. Radcliffe to Hagerman, December 23, 1923, Hagerman Papers.

25. Kneale to CIA, January 11, 1926, Letters Received—New Mexico, 1908 to 1949.

26. Newcomb, *Hosteen Klah*, 163.

27. Kneale to CIA, March 3, 1927; Deshna Clah Chischillige to Kneale March 8, 1927, Letters Received—New Mexico, 1908 to 1949.

28. "Regulations of the Indian Service Licensed Indian Traders," June 29, 1927 (Washington, D.C.: Government Printing Office, 1929), 3.

29. For a detailed summary of pawn and how it worked in both traditional and contemporary Navajo culture, see William S. Kiser, "Navajo Pawn: A Misunderstood Traditional Trading Practice," *American Indian Quarterly* 36, no. 2 (Spring 2012): 150–81.

30. Bahr, *The Navajo as Seen by the Franciscans*, 541.

31. Edward T. Hall, *West of the Thirties: Discoveries among the Navajo and Hopi* (New York: Doubleday, 1994), 152.

32. Stewart Hatch, interview by Robert S. McPherson, November 13, 2010.

33. Roswell T. Nelson to CIA through Superintendent of the Northern Navajo Agency, December 17, 1927, Letters Received—New Mexico, 1908 to 1949.

34. George R. Bloomfield to Hagerman, October 23, 1929, Letters Received—New Mexico, 1908 to 1949.

35. Ibid.

36. J. M. Drolet to Hagerman, September 16, 1929; Arthur J. Newcomb to Hagerman, October 9, 1929, Letters Received—New Mexico, 1908 to 1949.

37. B. P. Six to Hagerman, September 25, 1929, Letters Received—New Mexico, 1908 to 1949.

38. C. N. Cotton to Hagerman, September 10, 1929, Letters Received—New Mexico, 1908 to 1949.

39. C. L. Walker to CIA, August 12, 1929, Letters Received—New Mexico, 1908 to 1949.

40. C. J. Rhoads to Walker, March 1, 1930, Letters Received—New Mexico, 1908 to 1949.

41. Frances L. Newcomb to John Collier, "The Navajo Situation from a Trader's Viewpoint," December 11, 1929, Letters Received—New Mexico, 1908 to 1949.

42. Ibid.

43. Ibid.

44. Hagerman, "Record of the Proceedings of the Opening of the Tribal Council of Navajo Indians Held at Toadlena, New Mexico, Saturday, July 7, 1923," Hagerman Papers.

45. Hagerman, "Memoirs," 30.

46. B. P. Six to Hagerman, April 1, 1930; Rhoads to Hagerman, April 10, 1930; Hagerman to Rhoads, April 25, 1930, Hagerman Papers.

47. Rhoads to Hagerman, June 2, 1930, Hagerman Papers.

48. For more on the Navajo livestock reduction of the late 1920s and 1930s see Kenneth R. Philp, *John Collier's Crusade for Indian Reform, 1920-1954* (Tucson: University of Arizona Press, 1977); Richard White, *The Roots of Dependency: Subsistence, Environment, and Social Change among the Choctaw, Pawnees, and Navajo* (Lincoln: University of Nebraska Press, 1983); Ruth Roessel and Broderick Johnson, eds., *Navajo Livestock Reduction: A National Disgrace* (Tsaile, Ariz.: Navajo Community College Press, 1974); Donald L. Parman, *The Navajos and the New Deal* (New Haven: Yale University Press, 1976); Lawrence C. Kelly, *The Navajo Indians and Federal Indian Policy* (Tucson: University of Arizona Press, 1968); and L. Schuyler Fonaroff, "Conservation and Stock Reduction on the Navajo Tribal Range," *Geographical Review* 53, no. 2 (April 1963): 200–223.

49. "Survey of Indian Conditions throughout the United States," May 15, 1931, Hearings before a Subcommittee of Indian Affairs, U.S. Senate, 71st Cong., S. Res. 79 and 308 and S. Res. 263 and 416, Part 18 (Washington, D.C.: Government Printing Office, 1932): 9737.

50. Ibid.

51. Roessel and Johnson, *Navajo Livestock Reduction*, 94.

52. For the Navajo perspective filtered through the eyes of traditional teachings and the emotional aspect of livestock reduction, see Robert S. McPherson, "History Repeats Itself: Navajo Livestock Reduction in Southeastern Utah, 1933–1946," *American Indian Quarterly* 22, nos. 1–2 (Spring 1998): 1–18.

53. Roessel and Johnson, *Navajo Livestock Reduction*, 33–38.

54. Albert H. Kneale, *Indian Agent* (Caldwell, Idaho: Caxton Printers, 1950), 378.

55. Ibid., 378–79.

56. McPherson, *Both Sides of the Bullpen*, 282–83.

57. Annual Report, 1930, Bureau of Indian Affairs, Navajo Archives, Edge of the Cedars Museum, Blanding, Utah, n.p. (hereafter Navajo Archives).

58. Annual Report, 1934, Navajo Archives.

59. Ibid.

60. Bailey and Bailey, *A History of the Navajos*, 197.

61. White, *Roots of Dependency*, 312.

62. Maria Chabot, "Some Aspects of the Navajo Problem," New Mexico Association of Indian Affairs Report, 1941, in Museum of New Mexico, Laboratory of Anthropology, Santa Fe, 6.

63. Grace Herring, interview by Karen Underhill, February 11, 1998, NAU. OH.75.5, Special Collections, Cline Library, University of Arizona, Flagstaff, Arizona.

64. Chabot, "Some Aspects of the Navajo Problem," 16.

65. Ibid., 19–20.

8. Weaving a Two Grey Hills Rug

1. Slim Curly, "Blessingway—Version I," in Wyman, *Blessingway*, 245–46.

2. This and the preceding information about traditional and contemporary herding practices is from James F. Downs, *Animal Husbandry in Navajo Society and Culture* (Los Angeles: University of California, 1964), 31.

3. Ibid., 34.

4. Ibid., 37–38.

5. Lyle G. McNeal, "A Struggling Survivor," *Native Peoples* (Winter 1991): 39–44.

6. James O. Grandstaff, "Wool Characteristics in Relation to Navajo Weaving," Technical Bulletin no. 790 (January 1942), United States Department of Agriculture, Washington, D.C., 1–36.

7. Ibid., 3.

8. Ibid., 34–35.

9. McNeal, "Struggling Survivor," 43; Emily Blair Chewning, "Weaving a Legacy," *Arts and Antiques* (Summer 1994), 93.

10. Jan Dohner, "Tales from a Woven History—Traditional Weaving with Churro Wool," *Fiberarts* (September–October 1995): 24.

11. Chewning, "Weaving a Legacy," 94; McNeal, "Struggling Survivor," 43.

12. Vernon O. Mayes and Barbara Bayles Lacy, *Nanise', A Navajo Herbal: One Hundred Plants from the Navajo Reservation* (Tsaile, Ariz.: Navajo Community College Press, 1989), 2–3.

13. Unless otherwise noted, the information about dyeing wool is taken from Nonabah G. Bryan and Stella Young, *Navajo Native Dyes: Their Preparation and Use* (Lawrence, Kans.: Branch of Education, U.S. Department of Interior, 1940).

14. Ibid., 8.

15. Ibid., 6.

16. Amsden, *Navaho Weaving*, 31–47.

17. Ibid., 32.

18. For more detailed information about the construction and operation of a Navajo loom in addition to Amsden's work, see Gladys A. Reichard, *Weaving a Navajo Blanket* (New York: Dover Publications, 1936, 1974); Reichard,

Navajo Shepherd and Weaver (Glorieta, N.Mex.: Rio Grande Press, 1936, 1984); and George Wharton James, *Indian Blankets and Their Makers* (New York: Dover Publications, 1914, 1974).

19. Aileen O'Bryan, *Navaho Indian Myths* (New York: Dover Publications, 1956, 1993), 37.

20. Franciscan Fathers, *An Ethnologic Dictionary of the Navajo Language* (St. Michaels, Ariz.: St. Michaels Press, 1910, 1968), 222.

21. O'Bryan, *Navaho Indian Myths*, 38; Ernest L. Bulow, *Navajo Taboos* (Gallup, N.Mex.: Southwesterner Books, 1982), 58.

22. Quotes from notes by Charlotte Anderson attending the Navajo Weaving Conference, Heard Museum, Phoenix, Arizona, March 19–20, 1994.

23. Ann Lane Hedlund, "Contemporary Navajo Weaving: Thoughts that Count," *Plateau Magazine of the Museum of Northern Arizona* 65, no. 1 (Winter 1994): 5.

24. Noël Bennett, *The Weaver's Pathway: A Clarification of the "Spirit Trail" on Navajo Weaving* (Flagstaff, Ariz.: Northland Press, 1974), 9–10.

25. Ibid., 35.

26. Hedlund, "Contemporary Navajo Weaving," 14.

27. Shirley Brown, interview by Robert S. McPherson, September 12, 2017.

28. Ibid.

29. Reichard, *Navajo Shepherd and Weaver*, 150–51.

30. Clara Lee Tanner, "Modern Navajo Weaving," *Arizona Highways* 40, no. 9 (September 1964): 9.

31. Gilbert S. Maxwell, *Navajo Rugs—Past, Present, and Future* (Palm Desert, Calif.: Desert-Southwest, 1963, 1984), 28.

32. Hedlund, "Contemporary Navajo Weaving," 19.

33. Tanner, "Modern Navajo Weaving," 9.

34. J. B. Moore to Assistant Commissioner of Indian Affairs, September 2, 1911, Record Group 75, Letters Received—New Mexico, 1908–1949, Office of Indian Affairs, National Archives, Washington, D.C. (hereafter cited as Letters Received—New Mexico, 1908 to 1949).

35. Ibid.

36. Ibid.

37. Don Jensen, interview by Frank McNitt, July 2, 1960, 1973-024 Frank McNitt Papers, State Archives of New Mexico, Santa Fe.

38. Desba Nez, interview by Frank McNitt, July 2, 1960, 1973-024 Frank McNitt Papers, State Archives of New Mexico, Santa Fe.

39. Jensen, interview by McNitt.

40. Diana Heil, "Two Grey Hills Unravels its Mystery Weave," *New Mexico Magazine* 76, no. 8 (August 1998): 78.

41. George Bloomfield to McNitt, July n.d, 1958, Frank McNitt Collection, Trading Post File Box 10, State Records Center and Archives, Santa Fe, New Mexico.

42. Bloomfield, interviews by McNitt, August 1 and 15, 1958, ibid.

43. Ibid.

44. Charles Edward Herring, "Life Story of Charles Edward Herring," n.d., 21–22, Frank McNitt Collection, Two Grey Hills folder, State Records Center and Archives, Santa Fe, New Mexico.

45. Gilbert S. Maxwell, interview by Frank McNitt, July 31, 1958, Frank McNitt Collection, Toadlena Trading Post folder, State Records Center and Archives, Santa Fe, New Mexico.

46. Herring, "Life Story," 22.

47. Evans, *Along Navajo Trails*, 138–39.

48. Rebecca M. Valette, "Early Navajo Sandpainting Blankets: A Reassessment," *American Indian Art Magazine* 37, no. 2 (Spring 2012): 55.

49. Ibid., 57–58.

50. Franc Newcomb, as cited in Valette, "Early Navajo Sandpainting Blankets," 63.

51. Newcomb, *Hosteen Klah*, 114–15.

52. Ibid., 115.

53. Ibid., 157.

54. Ibid., 161–62.

55. Valette, "Early Navajo Sandpainting Blankets," 79–80.

56. Franc Newcomb to John Collier, March 25, 1934, Letters Received—New Mexico, 1908 to 1949.

57. Franc Newcomb, interview by Frank McNitt, September 3, 1957, Frank McNitt Collection, Newcomb Trading Post folder, State Records Center and Archives, Santa Fe, New Mexico.

58. Ibid.

59. "President's Report," Annual Report of the Eastern Association on Indian Affairs (Washington, D.C.: Government Printing Office, 1932), 3.

60. Charles Amsden, "Reviving the Navajo Blanket," *Masterkey* 8, no. 2 (March 1934): 141.

61. Ibid., 145–46.

62. Ibid., 146.

63. Ibid., 148–49.

9. To Post-posts

1. Bailey and Bailey, *A History of the Navajos*, 266.

2. Ibid.

3. Larry Rodgers, *Chapter Images: 1992 Edition* (Window Rock, Ariz.: Navajo Nation—Division of Community Development, 1993), 168; Navajo Division of Health, *Navajo Population Profile: 2010 U.S. Census* (Window Rock, Ariz.: Navajo Nation, 2013), 35–36.

4. Rodgers, *Chapter Images*, 171; Navajo Division of Health, *Navajo Population Profile*, 36.

5. E. R. Fryer, "General Statement of Conditions in the Navajo Area Including Hopi," Record Group 75, Letters Received—New Mexico, 1941, Office of Indian Affairs, National Archives, Washington, D.C.

6. Ibid.

7. Bonney Youngblood, "Report to Commissioner of Indian Affairs on Navajo Trading," April 1949, Bureau of Indian Affairs, Navajo Agency Correspondence, National Archives, Washington, D.C.

8. Ibid. The following information unless noted otherwise is derived from this report.

9. Federal Trade Commission, "The Trading Post System on the Navajo Reservation, Staff Report to the Federal Trade Commission," (Washington, D.C.: Government Printing Office, 1972), vii.

10. Ibid., 3.

11. Ibid., 8.

12. Ibid., 17.

13. Ibid., 53.

14. Willow Roberts Powers, *Navajo Trading: The End of an Era* (Albuquerque: University of New Mexico Press, 2001), 213.

15. Ibid., 246–47.

16. This is a general accounting for the ownership of the Two Grey Hills Trading Post during this period. Some dates are approximations and a number of hired employees were left unmentioned, due to breaks in the record and the flurry of hires. All information is derived from Trader License Applications—New Mexico, Bureau of Indian Affairs, National Archives, Washington, D.C.

17. Kathy M'Closkey, "Trading Accounts: Sam Teller of Two Grey Hills," *New Mexico Historical Review* 78, no. 2 (Spring 2003): 131–32.

18. Willard M. Leighton to Navajo Tribe, January 5, 1950, Application for License File—Navajo, National Archives, Washington, D.C.

19. Ibid.

20. Willard Leighton, interview by Frank McNitt, August 12, 1958, Frank McNitt Collection, Two Grey Hills folder, State Records Center and Archives, Santa Fe, New Mexico.

21. Ibid.

22. Bill Bryan, "Quality Navajo Rugs Scarce on Reservation, Says Trader," January 18, 1959, *Farmington Daily Times*, B-8.

23. H. Jackson Clark, *The Owl in Monument Canyon and Other Stories from Indian Country* (Salt Lake City: University of Utah, 1993), 83.

24. Ibid., 84.

25. Ibid., 88.

26. Roberts (Powers), *Stokes Carson*, 119.

27. Les Wilson, interview by Brad Cole, March 31, 1999, NAU.OH.75.36, Special Collections, Cline Library, Northern Arizona University, Flagstaff, Arizona; Les Wilson and Irma Henderson, interview by Robert S. McPherson, September 11, 2017, in possession of author.

28. Nancy Plevin, "Changing Times May Doom Weaving Tradition," *Farmington Daily Times*, August 4, 1995, p. A-8.

29. Jerry Kammer, "Pawn Drives a Thriving Economy," *Indian Trader*, October 1993, pp. 17–18.

30. N.A., "Trading with the Navajos, Part II," *Maazo Magazine: A Magazine for the Navajo Nation*, Spring 1985, 11.

31. Plevin, "Changing Times," A-8.

32. Ibid.

33. Alex Dorgan-Ross, "Traditional Trading Post Celebrates Centennial," *Durango Herald*, June 24, 1997, p. 1.

34. Lyle G. McNeal, "Director's Closing Remarks," *Navajo Sheep Project Newsletter*, Fall/Winter 1997, in possession of author, 3.

35. Lyle G. McNeal to Members of the Navajo Sheep Project, August 16, 1997, in possession of author.

36. Malcolm Brenner, "Just a Matter of Shear Pleasure," *The Independent*, April 12, 1999, p. 1.

37. Wilson, interview by Cole.

38. Edward Everett Hale, https://wn.com/edward_everett_hale/biography, accessed December 24, 2018.

39. John F. Kennedy, address to Canadian Parliament, May 17, 1961, https://www.brainyquote.com/quotes/john_f_kennedy_114923

Bibliography

Government Archives, Documents, and Collections

Annual Report, 1930. Bureau of Indian Affairs. Navajo Archives, Edge of the Cedars Museum, Blanding, Utah.

Annual Report of the Commissioner of Indian Affairs. Navajo Agency. U.S. Department of the Interior. Washington, D.C.: Government Printing Office, 1867–1896.

Annual Report of the Women's National Indian Association. Philadelphia: Association Executive Board, December 1898, pp. 26–27.

Bloomfield, George R. "Biography." Compiled by Lucy G. Bloomfield, 1965. Two Grey Hills folder, 1973-024 Frank McNitt Papers, State Archives of New Mexico, Santa Fe.

Bloomfield, Lucy G. "Natana (Navajo Chief)," n.d. Frank McNitt Collection, Two Grey Hills folder, 1973-024 Frank McNitt Papers, State Archives of New Mexico, Santa Fe.

Bryan, Nonabah G., and Stella Young. *Navajo Native Dyes: Their Preparation and Use.* Lawrence, Kans.: Branch of Education, U.S. Department of Interior, 1940.

Chabot, Maria. "Some Aspects of the Navajo Problem." New Mexico Association of Indian Affairs Report, 1941. Museum of New Mexico, Laboratory of Anthropology, Santa Fe.

Federal Trade Commission. "The Trading Post System on the Navajo Reservation, Staff Report to the Federal Trade Commission." Washington, D.C.: Government Printing Office, 1972.

Grandstaff, James O. "Wool Characteristics in Relation to Navajo Weaving." Technical Bulletin no. 790 (January 1942). United States Department of Agriculture, Washington, D.C., 1–36.

Gregory, Herbert E. *The Navajo Country: Topographic and Hydrographic Reconnaissance of Parts of Arizona, New Mexico, and Utah.* Water Supply Paper 380. Washington, D.C.: Government Printing Office, 1916.

Hagerman, Herbert J. Private Papers of Herbert J. Hagerman. Record Group 200, Gift Collection. National Archives, Washington, D.C.

Herring, Charles Edward. "Life Story of Charles Edward Herring," n.d. Frank McNitt Collection, Two Grey Hills folder, 1973-024 Frank McNitt Papers, State Archives of New Mexico, Santa Fe.

Herring, Grace Bloomfield. "Life Story of Grace Jacqueline Bloomfield Herring," n.d. Frank McNitt Collection, Two Grey Hills folder, 1973-024 Frank McNitt Papers, State Archives of New Mexico, Santa Fe.

Indian Rights Association. *The Thirty-First Annual Report of the Executive Committee of the Indian Rights Association, for the Year Ending December 10, 1913.* Philadelphia: Office of the Indian Rights Association, 1914.

Matthews, Washington. *The Mountain Chant: A Navaho Ceremony.* Fifth Annual Report of the Bureau of Ethnology. Washington, D.C.: Government Printing Office, 1887.

McLaughlin, James. James McLaughlin Papers. Assumption Abbey Archives, Microfilm no. 5. Denver Public Library, Denver, Colorado.

McNeal, Lyle G. *Navajo Sheep Project Newsletter.* Fall/Winter 1997 and Summer 1997. In possession of author.

Murrell, Monica L., and Bradley J. Vierra. *Bridging the Basin: Land Use and Social History in the Southern Chuska Valley.* Vol. 4 of NMDOT Cultural Resource Technical Series 2014-2. Santa Fe: New Mexico Department of Transportation, 2014.

Navajo Division of Health. *Navajo Nation Population Profile, 2010 U.S. Census.* Window Rock, Ariz.: Navajo Nation, 2013.

Newcomb, Charles George. Unpublished transcript recorded by Frank McNitt. "Traders" file, n.d. 1973-024 Frank McNitt Papers, State Archives of New Mexico, Santa Fe.

Paleowest Archaeology. "Navajo-Gallup Water Supply Project Ethnographic Overview of Native American Cultural Association with the San Juan Basin, New Mexico." Technical Report 13-30. Phoenix: U.S. Department of the Interior Bureau of Reclamation, 2013.

"Physiography of Chaco Canyon," in *The Geology of Chaco Canyon, New Mexico.* Smithsonian Miscellaneous Collections, vol. 122, no. 7. https://www.nps.gov/parkhistory/online_books/chcu/smc-122-7/sec2.htm

"President's Report." Annual Report of the Eastern Association on Indian Affairs. Washington, D.C.: Government Printing Office, 1932.

Record Group 75. Letters Received—New Mexico, by the Office of Indian Affairs, 1881–1907. National Archives, Washington, D.C.

Record Group 75. Letters Received—New Mexico, by the Office of Indian Affairs, 1908–1949. National Archives, Washington, D.C.

"Regulations of the Indian Service Licensed Indian Traders," June 29, 1927. Washington, D.C.: Government Printing Office, 1929.

Rodgers, Larry. *Chapter Images: 1992 Edition*. Window Rock, Ariz.: Navajo Nation—Division of Community Development, 1993.

"Survey of Indian Conditions throughout the United States," May 15, 1931. Hearings, Subcommittee of Indian Affairs, U.S. Senate, 71st Cong., S. Res. 79 and 308 and S. Res. 263 and 416, Part 18. Washington, D.C.: Government Printing Office, 1932.

Toll, H. Wolcott. "Trends in Ceramic Import and Distribution in Chaco Canyon," in *Recent Research on Chaco Prehistory*, edited by James W. Judge and James D. Schelberg. Division of Cultural Research, U.S. Department of the Interior. Albuquerque: National Park Service, 1984.

Trader License Applications—New Mexico. Bureau of Indian Affairs, National Archives, Washington, D.C.

U.S. Congress, House. *Report of the Secretary of War*. H. Ex. Doc. 1, Part 2, Vol. 1, 1889.

Weber, Anselm. Weber Letters. Franciscan Archives, Cincinnati, Ohio.

Books and Articles

Acrey, Bill P. *Navajo History: The Land and the People*. Shiprock, N.Mex.: Central Consolidated School District No. 22, 1988.

Amsden, Charles Avery. *Navaho Weaving: Its Technic and History*. Glorieta, N.Mex.: Rio Grande Press, 1934, 1982.

———. "Reviving the Navajo Blanket." *Masterkey* 8, no. 2 (March 1934): 133–49.

Bahr, Howard M., ed. *The Navajo as Seen by the Franciscans, 1898–1921: A Sourcebook*. Lanham, Md.: Scarecrow Press, 2004.

Bailey, Garrick, and Roberta Glenn Bailey. *A History of the Navajos: The Reservation Years*. Santa Fe, N.Mex.: School of American Research Press, 1986.

Bailey, L. R. *The Long Walk: A History of the Navajo Wars, 1846–68*. Pasadena, Calif.: Westernlore, 1978.

———, ed. *A Military Exploration of the Navajo Country in 1859 by Captain J. G. Walker and Major O. L. Shepherd*. Los Angeles, Calif.: Westernlore, 1964.

Barnes, Lemuel Call. "Missionaries to the Heathen." *Baptist Home Mission Monthly* 31, no. 6 (June 1909): 290–301.

Bennett, Noël. *The Weaver's Pathway: A Clarification of the "Spirit Trail" on Navajo Weaving*. Flagstaff, Ariz.: Northland Press, 1974.

Benson, Larry. "The Chuska Slope as an Agricultural Alternative to Chaco Canyon: A Rebuttal of Tankersley et al. (2016)." *Journal of Archaeological Science: Reports (2016)*. http://dx.doi.org/10.1016/j.jasrep.2016.10.017.

Bero, Wilhelmina. "Account of the Flood of 1911." *New Mexico Conference United Methodist Historical Journal* 2 (November 2015): 16–23.

Blackhawk, Ned. *Violence over the Land: Indians and Empires in the Early American West*. Cambridge, Mass.: Harvard University Press, 2006.

Bloomfield, Lucy. "A Navajo Indian Fire Dance." *Improvement Era* 27, no. 8 (June 1924): 905–11.

Blue, Martha. *Indian Trader: The Life and Times of J. L. Hubbell*. Walnut, Calif.: Kiva Publishing, 2000.

Bodo, Fr. Murray, O.F.M. *Tales of an Endishodi: Father Berard Haile and the Navajos, 1900–1961*. Albuquerque: University of New Mexico Press, 1998.

Brady, Benjamin R., and Howard M. Bahr. "The Influenza Epidemic of 1918–1920 among the Navajos." *American Indian Quarterly* 38, no. 4 (Fall 2014): 459–91.

Brough, R. Clayton, Dale L. Jones, and Dale J. Stevens. *Utah's Comprehensive Weather Almanac*. Salt Lake City: Publisher's Press, 1987.

Brugge, David M. *A History of the Chaco Navajo*. Albuquerque: National Park Service, 1980.

———. "Navajo Prehistory and History to 1850." In *Handbook of North American Indians*, vol. 10, ed. Alfonso Ortiz. Washington, D.C.: Smithsonian Institution, 1983.

Bulow, Ernest L. *Navajo Taboos*. Gallup, N.Mex.: Southwesterner Books, 1982.

Burdette, Mary G. "A Visit to Our Missions." *The Indian's Friend: A Publication of the Women's National Indian Association* (Philadelphia), 14, no. 3 (November 1901): 2, 8–10.

Byrne, Bernard James. *A Frontier Army Surgeon: Life in Colorado in the Eighties*. New York: Exposition Press, 1935.

Carter, William B. *Indian Alliances and the Spanish in the Southwest, 750–1750*. Norman: University of Oklahoma Press, 2009.

Chewning, Emily Blair. "Weaving a Legacy." *Arts and Antiques*, Summer 1994, pp. 93–98.

Clark, H. Jackson. *The Owl in Monument Canyon and Other Stories from Indian Country*. Salt Lake City: University of Utah, 1993.

Correll, J. Lee. *Through White Men's Eyes: A Contribution to Navajo History—A Chronological Record of the Navajo People from Earliest Times to the Treaty of June 1, 1868*. Vols. 1–6. Window Rock, Ariz.: Navajo Heritage Center, 1979.

Cottam, Erica. *Hubbell Trading Post: Trade, Tourism, and the Navajo Southwest*. Norman: University of Oklahoma Press, 2015.

Curly, Slim. "Blessingway—Version I." In *Blessingway: With Three Versions of the Myth Recorded and Translated from the Navajo by Father Berard Haile, O.F.M.*, edited by Leland C. Wyman. Tucson: University of Arizona Press, 1970.

Dohner, Jan. "Tales from a Woven History—Traditional Weaving with Churro Wool." *Fiberarts*, September/October 1995, p. 24.

Downs, James F. *Animal Husbandry in Navajo Society and Culture*. Los Angeles: University of California, 1964.

Dyk, Walter. *A Navaho Autobiography*. New York: Johnson Reprint Company, 1947.

Ellis, Florence H. *An Anthropological Study of the Navajo Indians*. New York: Garland Publishing, 1974.

Evans, Will. *Along Navajo Trails: Recollections of a Trader, 1898–1948*. Edited by Susan E. Woods and Robert S. McPherson. Logan: Utah State University Press, 2005.

Farella, John R. *The Main Stalk: A Synthesis of Navajo Philosophy*. Tucson: University of Arizona Press, 1984.

Faunce, Hilda. *Desert Wife*. Lincoln: University of Nebraska Press, 1928, 1981.

Fonaroff, L. Schuyler. "Conservation and Stock Reduction on the Navajo Tribal Range." *Geographical Review* 53, no. 2 (April 1963): 200–223.

Forton, Maxwell McCrae. "Corridors of Interaction: Tracing Chuskan Ceramics and Lithics to Assess Regional Interaction of Chaco Canyon." Master's thesis, Binghamton University, State University of New York, 2017.

Franciscan Fathers. *An Ethnologic Dictionary of the Navajo Language*. St. Michaels, Ariz.: St. Michaels Press, 1910, 1968.

Friedman, Richard A., John R. Stein, and Taft Blackhorse Jr. "A Study of a Pre-Columbian Irrigation System at Newcomb, New Mexico." *Journal of GIS Archaeology* 1 (April 2003): 4–10.

Frisbie, Charlotte Johnson. *Food Sovereignty the Navajo Way: Cooking with Tall Woman*. Albuquerque: University of New Mexico Press, 2018.

———. *Kinaaldá: A Study of the Navaho Girl's Puberty Ceremony*. Salt Lake City: University of Utah Press, 1993.

———. *Tall Woman: The Life Story of Rose Mitchell, A Navajo Woman, c.1874–1977*. Albuquerque: University of New Mexico Press, 2001.

Furman, Agnes Miller. *Tohta: An Early Day History of the Settlement of Farmington and San Juan County, New Mexico*. Wichita Falls, Tex.: Nortex Press, 1977.

Gabriel, Kathryn. *Roads to Center Place: A Cultural Atlas of Chaco Canyon and the Anasazi*. Boulder, Colo.: Johnson Books, 1991.

Gillmor, Frances, and Louisa Wetherill. *Traders to the Navajos: The Story of the Wetherills of Kayenta*. Albuquerque: University of New Mexico Press, 1934, 1979.

———. *Windsinger*. Albuquerque: University of New Mexico Press, 1930, 1958.

Grimstead, Deanna, Sharon M. Buck, Bradley J. Vierra, and Larry V. Benson. "Another Possible Source of Archaeological Maize Found in Chaco Canyon, NM: The Tohatchi Flats Area, NM, USA." *Journal of Archaeological Science: Reports* 3 (2015): 181–87.

Guiterman, Christopher H., Thomas W. Swetnam, and Jeffrey S. Dean. "Eleventh-Century Shift in Timber Procurement Areas of the Great

Houses of Chaco Canyon." *Proceedings of National Academy of Science* 113, no. 5 (February 2016): 1186–90.

Hadley, Linda. *Hózhóójí Hane' (Blessingway)*. Rough Rock, Ariz.: Rough Rock Demonstration School, 1986.

Hall, Edward T. *West of the Thirties: Discoveries among the Navajo and Hopi*. New York: Doubleday, 1994.

Hedlund, Ann Lane. "Contemporary Navajo Weaving: Thoughts that Count." *Plateau Magazine of the Museum of Northern Arizona* 65, no. 1 (Winter 1994).

Heil, Diana. "Two Grey Hills Unravels its Mystery Weave." *New Mexico Magazine* 76, no. 8 (August 1998): 78–82.

Hoffman, Virginia. *Navajo Biographies*. Vol. 1. Tsaile, Ariz.: Navajo Curriculum Center, 1974.

Hoijier, Harry. "The Chronology of the Athapaskan Languages." *International Journal of American Linguistics* 22 (October 1956): 219–32.

Hyde, George E. *Indians of the High Plains*. Norman: University of Oklahoma Press, 1959.

"Indian Mission—Two Grey Hills." Baptist Church Calendar, n.d. New Mexico State Archives, Santa Fe, New Mexico.

Iverson, Peter. *Diné: A History of the Navajos*. Albuquerque: University of New Mexico Press, 2002.

———, ed. *"For Our Navajo People": Diné Letters, Speeches & Petitions, 1900–1960*. Albuquerque: University of New Mexico Press, 2002.

James, George Wharton. *Indian Blankets and Their Makers*. New York: Dover Publications, 1914, 1974.

Johnson, Broderick H., ed. *Navajo Stories of the Long Walk Period*. Tsaile, Ariz.: Navajo Community College Press, 1973.

Judge, James W. "Chaco Canyon—San Juan Basin." In *Dynamics of Southwest Prehistory*, edited by Linda S. Cordell and George J. Gumerman. Washington, D.C.: Smithsonian Institution Press, 1989.

Kelley, Klara, and Harris Francis. *Navajoland Trading Post Encyclopedia*. Window Rock, Ariz.: Navajo Nation Heritage and Historic Preservation Department, 2018.

Kelly, Lawrence C. *The Navajo Indians and Federal Indian Policy*. Tucson: University of Arizona Press, 1968.

———. *Navajo Roundup: Selected Correspondence of Kit Carson's Expedition Against the Navajo, 1863–1865*. Boulder, Colo.: Pruett Publishing, 1970.

Kildare, Maurice. "Girl on a Strange Frontier." *True West*, June 1971, 40–48.

Kirk, Tom. *The Kirk Clan: Traders with the Navajo*. Brand Book no. 6, in Peoples of the Far West series. San Diego, Calif.: Corral of the Westerners, 1979.

Kiser, William S. "Navajo Pawn: A Misunderstood Traditional Trading Practice." *American Indian Quarterly* 36 no. 2 (Spring 2012): 150–81.

Kluckhohn, Clyde, and Dorothea Leighton. *The Navaho*. Rev. ed. Cambridge: Harvard University Press, 1974.

Kneale, Albert H. *Indian Agent*. Caldwell, Idaho: Caxton Printers, 1950.

Lamphere, Louise. *To Run after Them: Cultural and Social Bases of Cooperation in a Navajo Community*. Tucson: University of Arizona Press, 1977.

Lekson, Stephen H. *The Archaeology of Chaco Canyon: An Eleventh Century Pueblo Regional Center*. Santa Fe: School of American Research, 2006.

Linford, Laurance D. *Navajo Places: History, Legend, Landscape*. Salt Lake City: University of Utah Press, 2000.

Lipe, William D. "The Mesa Verde Region: Chaco's Northern Neighbor." In *In Search of Chaco: New Approaches to an Archaeological Enigma*, edited by David Grant Noble. Santa Fe, N.Mex.: School of American Research Press, 2004.

MacDonald, Eleanor D., and John B. Arrington. *The San Juan Basin: My Kingdom Was a County*. Denver: Mido Printing Company, 1970.

M'Closkey, Kathy. *Swept under the Rug: A Hidden History of Navajo Weaving*. Albuquerque: University of New Mexico Press, 2002.

———. "Trading Accounts: Sam Teller of Two Grey Hills." *New Mexico Historical Review* 78, no. 2 (Spring 2003): 123–46.

Malehorn, Pauline G. *The Tender Plant: The History of the Navajo Methodist Mission Farmington, New Mexico, 1891–1948*. Farmington, N.Mex.: self-published, 1948.

Marshall, Michael P., John R. Stein, Richard W. Loose, and Judith E. Novotny. *Anasazi Communities of the San Juan Basin*. Albuquerque: Public Service Company of New Mexico, 1981.

Matthews, Washington. *Navajo Legends*. Salt Lake: University of Utah Press, 1897, 1994.

Mayes, Vernon O., and Barbara Bayles Lacy. *Nanise', A Navajo Herbal: One Hundred Plants from the Navajo Reservation*. Tsaile, Ariz.: Navajo Community College Press, 1989.

Maxwell, Gilbert S. *Navajo Rugs—Past, Present, and Future*. Palm Desert, Calif.: Desert-Southwest, 1963, 1984.

McKibbin, Davidson B. "Revolt of the Navajo." *New Mexico Historical Review* 29, no. 4 (Fall 1954): 259–89.

McNeal, Lyle G. "A Struggling Survivor." *Native Peoples* (Winter 1991): 39–44.

McNitt, Frank. *The Indian Traders*. Norman: University of Oklahoma Press, 1962.

———, ed. *Navaho Expedition: Journal of a Military Reconnaissance from Santa Fe, New Mexico, to the Navaho Country, Made in 1849 by Lieutenant James H. Simpson*. Norman: University of Oklahoma Press, 1964.

———. *Richard Wetherill: Anasazi, Pioneer Explorer of Southwestern Ruins*. Albuquerque: University of New Mexico Press, 1957, 1966.

McPherson, Robert S. *As If the Land Owned Us: An Ethnohistory of the White Mesa Utes*. Salt Lake City: University of Utah Press, 2011.

———. *Both Sides of the Bullpen: Navajo Trade and Posts.* Norman: University of Oklahoma Press, 2017.

———. *Dinéjí Naʼnitin: Navajo Traditional Teachings and History.* Boulder: University Press of Colorado, 2012.

———. "History Repeats Itself: Navajo Livestock Reduction in Southeastern Utah, 1933–1946." *American Indian Quarterly* 22, nos. 1–2 (Spring 1998): 1–18.

———. "Howard R. Antes and the Navajo Faith Mission: Evangelist of Southeastern Utah." *Utah Historical Quarterly* 65, no. 1 (Winter 1997): 4–24.

———. *The Northern Navajo Frontier, 1860–1900: Expansion through Adversity.* Logan: Utah State University, 2001.

———. *Sacred Land, Sacred View: Navajo Perceptions of the Four Corners Region.* Logan: Utah State University, 1992, 2001.

———. "'Too Much Noise in that Bunch across the River': Baʼálílee and the 1907 Aneth Brawl." *Utah Historical Quarterly* 77, no. 1 (Winter 2009): 26–51.

———. *Viewing the Ancestors: Perceptions of the Anaasází, Mokwič, and Hisatsinom.* Norman: University of Oklahoma Press, 2014.

Mitchell, Frank. "Blessingway—Version II." In *Blessingway: With Three Versions of the Myth Recorded and Translated from the Navajo by Father Berard Haile, O.F.M.*, edited by Leland C. Wyman. Tucson: University of Arizona Press, 1970.

Moore, William Haas. *Chiefs, Agents, and Soldiers: Conflict on the Navajo Frontier, 1868–1882.* Albuquerque: University of New Mexico Press, 1994.

Mose, Don, Jr. *The Legend of the Navajo Hero Twins.* Blanding, Utah: San Juan School District, 2005.

Muhlestein, Harold, and Fay Muhlestein. *Monticello Journal: A History of Monticello until 1937.* Monticello, Utah: self-published, 1988.

Myers, Lewis A. *A History of New Mexico Baptists.* Albuquerque: Baptist Convention of New Mexico, 1965.

Newcomb, Franc Johnson. *Hosteen Klah: Navaho Medicine Man and Sand Painter.* Norman: University of Oklahoma Press, 1964.

———. *Navaho Neighbors.* Norman: University of Oklahoma Press, 1966.

Noel, Frank Leland, and Mary Eliza Roberts Noel. *Eighty Years in America.* Salt Lake City: self-published, 1962.

O'Bryan, Aileen. *Navaho Indian Myths.* New York: Dover Publications, 1956, 1993.

O'Neill, Colleen. *Working the Navajo Way: Labor and Culture in the Twentieth Century.* Lawrence: University Press of Kansas, 2005.

Opler, Morris E. "The Apachean Culture Pattern and Its Origins." In *Handbook of North American Indians*, vol. 10, edited by Alfonso Ortiz. Washington, D.C.: Smithsonian Institution, 1983.

Parman, Donald L. *The Navajos and the New Deal.* New Haven: Yale University Press, 1976.

Philp, Kenneth R. *John Collier's Crusade for Indian Reform, 1920–1954.* Tucson: University of Arizona Press, 1977.

Powers, Robert P. "Outliers and Roads in the Chaco System." In *New Light on Chaco Canyon,* edited by David Grant Noble. Santa Fe, N.Mex.: School of American Research, 1984.

Powers, Willow Roberts. *Navajo Trading: The End of an Era.* Albuquerque: University of New Mexico Press, 2001.

———. *Stokes Carson: Twentieth Century Trading on the Navajo Reservation.* Albuquerque: University of New Mexico Press, 1987.

Reed, Alan D., and Jonathan C. Horn. "Early Navajo Occupation of the American Southwest: Reexamination of the Dinétah Phase." *Kiva* 55, no. 4 (Fall 1990): 283–300.

Reichard, Gladys A. *Navajo Shepherd and Weaver.* Glorieta, N.Mex.: Rio Grande Press, 1936, 1984.

———. *Social Life of the Navajo Indians.* New York: Columbia University Press, 1928.

———. *Weaving a Navajo Blanket.* New York: Dover Publications, 1936, 1974.

Reynolds, Amanda C., Julio Betancourt, Jay Quade, Jonathan Patchett, Jeffrey S. Dean, and John Stein. "87SR/86SR Sourcing of Ponderosa Pine Used in Anasazi Great House Construction at Chaco Canyon, New Mexico." *Journal of Archaeological Science* 32 (2005): 1061–75.

Richardson, Gladwell. *Navajo Trader.* Tucson: University of Arizona Press, 1986.

River Junction Curly. "Blessingway—Version III," in *Blessingway: With Three Versions of the Myth Recorded and Translated from the Navajo by Father Berard Haile, O.F.M.,* edited by Leland C. Wyman. Tucson: University of Arizona Press, 1970.

Roessel, Ruth. *Women in Navajo Society.* Rough Rock, Ariz.: Rough Rock Demonstration School, 1981.

Roessel, Ruth, and Broderick Johnson, eds. *Navajo Livestock Reduction: A National Disgrace.* Tsaile, Ariz.: Navajo Community College Press, 1974.

Rohn, Arthur H., and William M. Ferguson. *Puebloan Ruins of the Southwest.* Albuquerque: University of New Mexico Press, 2006.

Sapir, Edward. "Internal Linguistic Evidence Suggestive of the Northern Origin of the Navaho." *American Anthropologist* 38, no. 2 (April–June 1936): 224–35.

Scott, Hugh L. *Sign Talker: Hugh Lenox Scott Remembers Indian Country.* Edited by R. Eli Paul. Norman: University of Oklahoma Press, 2016.

Seymour, Deni J. *From the Land of Ever Winter to the American Southwest: Athapaskan Migrations, Mobility, and Ethnogenesis.* Salt Lake City: University of Utah Press, 2012.

Simmons, Virginia McConnell. *The Ute Indians of Utah, Colorado, and New Mexico*. Boulder: University Press of Colorado, 2000.

Skovlin, Jon M., and Donna McDaniel Skovlin. *In Pursuit of the McCartys*. Cove, Ore.: Reflections Publishing, 2001.

Steinsiek, Willard L. "Mary Louise Eldridge." *New Mexico Conference United Methodist Historical Journal* 2 (November 2015): 3–15.

Tanner, Clara Lee. "Modern Navajo Weaving." *Arizona Highways* 40, no. 9 (September 1964): 6–13.

Thompson, Gerald. *The Army and the Navajo: The Bosque Redondo Reservation Experiment, 1863–1868*. Tucson: University of Arizona Press, 1982.

Toll, H. Wolcott. "Material Distributions and Exchanges in the Chaco System." In *Chaco and Hohokam: Prehistoric Regional Systems in the American Southwest*, edited by Patricia L. Crown and James W. Judge. Santa Fe, N.Mex.: School of American Research Press, 1991.

Towner, Ronald H. *Defending the Dinétah: Pueblitos in the Ancestral Navajo Heartland*. Salt Lake City: University of Utah Press, 2003.

"Trading with the Navajos, Part II." *Maazo Magazine: A Magazine for the Navajo Nation*, Spring 1985, pp. 8–11, 41–42.

Trafzer, Clifford E. *The Kit Carson Campaign: The Last Great Navajo War*. Norman: University of Oklahoma Press, 1982.

Trennert, Robert A. *White Man's Medicine: Government Doctors and the Navajo, 1863–1955*. Albuquerque: University of New Mexico Press, 1998.

Underhill, Ruth M. *The Navajos*. Norman: University of Oklahoma Press, 1956.

Valette, Rebecca M. "Early Navajo Sandpainting Blankets: A Reassessment." *American Indian Art Magazine* 37, no. 2 (Spring 2012): 54–65.

Van Valkenburgh, Richard F. *Diné Bikéyah*. Window Rock, Ariz.: Office of Navajo Service, 1941.

Van Valkenburgh, Richard F., and Scotty Begay. "Sacred Places and Shrines of the Navajo: Part I, The Sacred Mountains." *Museum Notes of Museum of Northern Arizona* 11, no. 3 (September 1938): 29–34.

Varien, Mark D., and Richard H. Wilshusen, eds. *Seeking the Center Place: Archaeology and Ancient Communities in the Mesa Verde Region*. Salt Lake City: University of Utah, 2002.

Vivian, R. Gwinn. *The Chacoan Prehistory of the San Juan Basin*. New York: Academic Press, 1990.

Weber, David J. *The Mexican Frontier, 1821–1846: The American Southwest under Mexico*. Albuquerque: University of New Mexico Press, 1982.

———. *The Spanish Frontier in North America*. New Haven, Conn.: Yale University Press, 1992.

Wetherill, Marietta, with Kathryn Gabriel, ed. *Marietta Wetherill: Reflections on Life with the Navajos in Chaco Canyon*. Boulder: Johnson Books, 1997.

White, Richard. *The Roots of Dependency: Subsistence, Environment, and Social Change among the Choctaw, Pawnees, and Navajo.* Lincoln: University of Nebraska Press, 1983.

———. *"It's Your Misfortune and None of My Own": A New History of the American West.* Norman: University of Oklahoma Press, 1991.

Wilkins, David E. *The Navajo Political Experience.* Tsaile, Ariz.: Diné College Press, 1999.

Wilkins, Teresa J. *Patterns of Exchange: Navajo Weavers and Traders.* Norman: University of Oklahoma Press, 2008.

Wyeth, N. C. "A Sheepherder of the Southwest." *Scribner's Magazine* 45 (January 1909): 17–21.

Wyman, Leland C., ed. *Blessingway: With Three Versions of the Myth as Recorded by Father Berard Haile.* Tucson, Ariz.: University of Arizona Press, 1975.

———. *The Mountainway of the Navajo.* Tucson: University of Arizona Press, 1975.

Interviews

Arrington, John B. Interview by Frank McNitt, August 27, 1958. John Arrington folder, 1973-024 Frank McNitt Papers, State Archives of New Mexico, Santa Fe.

Bloomfield, George. Interviews by Frank McNitt, August 1 and 15, 1958. George Bloomfield folder, 1973-024 Frank McNitt Papers, State Archives of New Mexico, Santa Fe.

Blueyes, Charlie. Interview by Robert S. McPherson, June 7, 1988.

Brown, Shirley. Interview by Robert S. McPherson, September 12, 2017.

Davies, Pearl. Interview by Frank McNitt, August 4, 1958. Two Grey Hills folder, 1973-024 Frank McNitt Papers, State Archives of New Mexico, Santa Fe.

Hatch, Stewart. Interview by Robert S. McPherson, May 7, 2010.

Henderson (Wilson), Irma. Interview by Robert S. McPherson, September 12, 2017.

Herring, Grace. Interview by Karen Underhill, February 11, 1998. NAU. OH.75.5. Special Collections, Cline Library, University of Arizona, Flagstaff.

Jensen, Don. Interview by Frank McNitt, July 2, 1960. 1973-024 Frank McNitt Papers, State Archives of New Mexico, Santa Fe.

Jett, Stephen H. "Notes—'Shiprock Pinnacle' and 'Shiprock Wash.'" n.d. In possession of author.

Leighton, Willard. Interview by Frank McNitt, August 12, 1958. Two Grey Hills folder, 1973-024 Frank McNitt Papers, State Archives of New Mexico, Santa Fe.

Maxwell, Gilbert S. Interview by Frank McNitt, July 31, 1958. Toadlena Trading Post folder, 1973-024 Frank McNitt Papers, State Archives of New Mexico, Santa Fe.

Nelson, Roswell T. Interview by Frank McNitt, October 31, 1957. Two Grey Hills folder, 1973-024 Frank McNitt Papers, State Archives of New Mexico, Santa Fe.

Newcomb, Franc Johnson. Interview by Frank McNitt, July 25, 1958. Mrs. Franc Newcomb File, 1973-024 Frank McNitt Papers, State Archives of New Mexico, Santa Fe.

Nez, Desba. Interview by Frank McNitt, July 2, 1960. 1973-024 Frank McNitt Papers, State Archives of New Mexico, Santa Fe.

Nez, Martha. Interview by Robert S. McPherson, August 10, 1988.

Noel, Hambleton Bridger (H. B.). Interviews by Frank McNitt, January 11 and 18, 1958. Box 10, 1973-024 Frank McNitt Papers, State Archives of New Mexico, Santa Fe.

Redd, Amasa Jay. Interview by Charles S. Peterson, July 27, 1973. CRC-C7, Charles Redd Center for Western Studies, Brigham Young University, Provo, Utah.

Watson, Editha. "Talk by Editha Watson," March 17, 1968. Doris Duke no. 796, Doris Duke Oral History Collection. Special Collections, Marriott Library, University of Utah, Salt Lake City.

Wilson, Les. Interview by Brad Cole, March 31, 1999. NAU.OH.75.36, Special Collections, Cline Library, Northern Arizona University, Flagstaff.

Wilson, Les, and Irma Henderson. Interview by Robert S. McPherson, September 11, 2017.

Newspapers

Albuquerque Citizen (N.Mex.), 1891

Ann Arbor News (Mich.), 2015

Durango Herald (Colo.), 1894–1997

Farmington Enterprise (N.Mex.), 1906–1916

Farmington Daily Times (N.Mex.), 1959–1995

Farmington Times-Hustler (N.Mex.), 1912–1941

Fruitland Tribune (N.Mex.), 1906

The Independent (N.Mex.), 1993–1999.

Indian Trader (N.Mex.), 1993

Mancos Times (Colo.), 1905

Mancos Times-Tribune (Colo.), 1911

Montezuma Journal (Colo.), 1911

San Juan Times (N.Mex.), 1893

Index

References to illustrations appear in italic type.

Abiquiu, N.Mex., 27–28, 36
Acoma village, 9
Adams, Henry C., 42
Aghaałá Peak (El Capitan/Much
 Wool), 20–21
Ahsonchee (Asdzaan Ch'ii), 176
Albuquerque, N.Mex., 27, 43, 45, 90,
 149, 229
alcohol, 46, 100–102, 129, 154–55,
 162–63, 202
Algert, C. H., 63–64, 134
Algert Company, 134–35, 137
American Indian Defense
 Association, 201
American Indian Movement (AIM),
 248
American Museum of Natural
 History, 172
Amsden, Charles, 133, 220, 237–38
Anasazi, 7
Ancestral Puebloans, 7–11, 12, 15,
 17–18, 22, 26, 31, 84, 111, 171,
 172, 233, 243, 265
Anea, Juan, 33
Aneth, Utah, 43, 86, 106, 108–10,
 188, 208–9
Antes, Evelyn, 109

Antes, Howard Ray, 109–11, 120, 124
Antiquities Act, 172
Apaches, 17, 30, 37, 160
Arbuckle coffee, 74, 177, 244, 257
Archuleta, 31
Armijo, Julian, 28, 33–34
Armour Packing, 259
Arny, William F. M., 46
Arrington, John B., 70, 126–27, 134,
 303
Arviso, Jésus, 77
Asdzaan Nez Tso (Tall Heavy
 Woman), 71
Athabascans, 17
Atlantic and Pacific Railroad, 43, 46
automobiles, 130, 145, 181–82, 189,
 210, 241–42, 259, 266
Ayres, John, 77
Aztec, N.Mex., 17, 43, 113

Baʼálílee, 104, 108–10, 124, 266
Babbitt Brothers, 149
Badger Spring, 176
Bailey, Garrick, 150, 208
Bailey, Roberta, 150, 208
Baldwin, Harry C., 72–73, 92
Balukai Mesa, 20

309

CPSIA information can be obtained
at www.ICGtesting.com
Printed in the USA
LVHW101154250522
719519LV00017B/215

9 780806 190082